HOW YOU TOO CAN MAKE AT LEAST $1 MILLION
(but probably much more)
IN THE MAIL-ORDER BUSINESS

HOW YOU TOO CAN MAKE AT LEAST $1 MILLION (but probably much more) IN THE MAIL-ORDER BUSINESS

by Gerardo Joffe

Advance Books, Box 7584, San Francisco, CA 94120

Books by Gerardo Joffe:

- HOW YOU TOO CAN MAKE AT LEAST $1 MILLION (but probably much more) IN THE MAIL-ORDER BUSINESS
- ANAGRAPHICS 1

1st Printing, January 1978

Library of Congress No. 77-92067
ISBN 0-930992-02-4

Publisher:

ADVANCE BOOKS
Box 7584
San Francisco, California 94120

To Priscilla,
the "secret ingredient" for success, and

To Michael, Rachel and Joseph
the best cheering section anybody ever had.

Contents

A Brief Foreword

A SHORT AUTOBIOGRAPHY AND WHY I THINK I CAN BE OF HELP TO YOU

Dear Reader:

I am writing this book after a good deal of hesitation and foot dragging. First, this is in some measure an " autobiographical" book, and there is some reluctance to let others peek into one's own personal life. Second, and perhaps more important, it's a "get rich" book. There are so many of those on the market just now. Most of them are essentially wealth fantasy books, written by people who never started or ran a business and whose principal, if not only, thought in writing such a book was to enrich themselves. There have been one or two notable successes in this line of publishing. Some of them pretend to teach how you can get rich by being lazy; others try to show you how you can get rich by being dumb; still others advocate "legal larceny" in order to amass that illusive $1,000,000. Many of them are based on some "secret formula, which I wish to share with my fellow man." Naturally, I would hate to have this book lumped with them.

You will find this book very down to earth, rather short on "general philosophy," and long on specifics. I have had a great deal of success in the mail-order business and I believe that I can assist you in achieving as much success or more than I have had.

But since this book is indeed to some degree about myself, perhaps I should fill you in with at least a few personal points. In the pages that follow, I shall give you a great deal of advice. Naturally, you have a right to know just who I am and what entitles me to dispense, with such authority, so many pearls of wisdom.

I am Jewish and was born in Berlin, Germany. I fled Germany in 1938, as a young boy, just before the outbreak of the war, and went to Bolivia. I went to work in the tin mines and spent the next eight years working underground, living and working at elevations of 15,000 feet or more. Being barely over twenty years old, I reached some sort of an early climax in my business career by becoming the chief engineer of the Colquiri Mines, the world's second largest tin mines. If you think that was an unusual accomplishment for someone so young, who did not even have the benefit of a college education, you are only partly right. Those were the years in which twenty-one year old boys were full colonels in the United States Air Force.

With the war over, I left for the United States and enrolled at the Missouri School of Mines in Rolla, Mo. Since I didn't speak too much English, my attending college wasn't all that much of a snap, but I did manage to graduate with a B.S. in Mining Engineering. I financed college by working as an underground miner during all vacations and between semesters.

With work in metal mining being scarce at the time, I took a job in petroleum engineering, working the oil fields of Arkansas-Texas-Louisiana for the next seven years or so. That was awfully hard work, and rather unrewarding in every sense of the word. By that time I had also acquired a wife and the beginnings of a family. I was in my middle thirties and had spent all of my working life either underground or sloshing through oilfield mud. It occurred to me that there must be more to life and that I might have some talents that I had not yet fully exploited. I also thought how satisfying it would be to be really successful — including making a whole lot of money — possibly even that proverbial "million dollars." I was not entirely uninterested in the good life, but frankly the challenge of it all, finding out whether I could do it, whether I could be successful in something entirely different appealed to me even more.

I mention my age at the time I made my big change and the fact that I had family responsibility only so that you, who may possibly be about that age now, won't think that to start all over is "impossible." What I shall tell you to do in the pages that follow will not call for as much change as I imposed upon myself. But if you want to attain the success that you think you deserve and are capable of, you will have to make a few changes and accommodations.

In a complete break with the past, I left mining, the oil fields and my entire past life behind me, went to the Harvard Business

School and got my M.B.A. degree. I went to work in New York for a very large company, but after about two years of that, I realized that I wasn't really cut out for the big corporate life — the jockeying for position, the game playing and everything that went with it. Like so many others, I drifted to California and tried my hand at a number of different things, without being too successful at any of them

I got into the mail-order business almost by accident. I had invented a "gadget," which I was unable to sell by "conventional" means. Somebody told me that it could be sold by mail. So I went ahead — virtually without money, without any kind of guidance or previous experience and, armed only with gall and ignorance, started a mail-order business. I called it Haverhill's. The friendly soul who had advised me that my gadget would sell by mail was wrong. It didn't. But I had to keep the pot boiling, and I added some other products that did sell.

I must have done a few things right — by trial and error, by good instincts and perhaps even by a little luck. Sometimes, in looking back at those very early days, I wonder how I survived in business. But I did. From a standing start, I developed a business in five years that was recognized as one of the most unusual and most innovative ones in the mail-order field. I made a decent living and good profits. Five years out of the starting gate, I sold Haverhill's to Time Inc., the country's foremost publisher, for just over one million dollars.

I had accomplished what I had set out to do.

I stayed with Haverhill's, as a subsidiary of Time Inc., for a few years. Then after a brief pause, and with the permission of Time Inc., I started a second business, Henniker's, patterned almost exactly along the same lines as Haverhill's. That was about three years ago. Using the same principles that I had developed at Haverhill's and that I had so successfully applied, I am now positioning Henniker's for the eventual sale to another large company. I am a little ahead of schedule and, perhaps in two years or so, I shall sell Henniker's for at least one million dollars. I might hold on a little longer this time and try to do a little better. After all, there has been inflation and all that. *Two* million dollars really sounds like a better figure.

Nobody can exactly duplicate what someone else has done. There are matters of personality, opportunity, timing and perhaps even a little "luck" (although I am convinced that it plays a relatively small role). You may not do as well as I did, or you may do a whole lot better. But I shall tell you, without holding back anything at all, how I built two very successful mail-order businesses. I shall tell you exactly how I went about it, and I shall teach you in much detail what to do and what snares and pitfalls to avoid so as to get your very best crack at success.

It is my hope and almost my expectation that this book will help you to your first million dollars. There is no reason why you shouldn't do as well as or better than I did. But even if you don't make it that big right away, there is no question that I shall get you off to a very good start and that I can be a big help toward your making it all the way.

I have written the book. I am giving you the "tools." The rest is really up to you.

Good Luck and God Speed towards the success of your mail-order business and toward your first million dollars.

Gerardo Joffe
San Francisco, January 1978

Chapter 1

HOW TO START A MAIL-ORDER BUSINESS

There are certain "fundamentals" about how to start a new business. It doesn't make all that much difference, whether you wish to open a filling station, a stationery store, a TV repair service shop — or a mail-order business. But right after those "fundamentals," things get to be a little different as far as the start-up of a mail-order busines is concerned.

And they become especially different if, from the very beginning, you wish to position yourself for substantial success. The purpose of this book is to show you how to build a *national mail-order business that you will eventually be able to sell for at least one million dollars.* Sure, you will start from scratch, from square one. You will do a lot of crawling, before you walk and run. But I wish to assist you in building something that, from its inception, has the germ to develop into a business of real consequence. In this chapter we shall talk about how to get started and how to lay the groundwork for such a business.

SORRY, I THINK YOU'LL NEED SOME MONEY

First off, I might have to shatter an illusion that you may have held and that may have been promoted to you by others. It is that you can start a successful mail-order business without capital or with perhaps just $100 or some such insignificant amount. It may be possible in theory — I suppose you can place a $50 ad that takes off like a rocket and puts you into financial orbit. But I have never heard of a verified case. I asked a number of old hands in this business and they haven't either.

To start without money sounds good in theory. It might be possible to develop some small specialty that you can regularly advertise in classified space and that, with a good deal of work, will yield you a small income of a few hundred dollars a month. Surely, this would be nothing to sneeze at, but very few people are successful even in that. Because there are very few products that can consistently sell in this manner, develop any kind of volume, cover advertising expense and overhead, let alone make a profit. And even if there were a reasonable chance of accomplishing this, it is simply not what this book is about. This book is about building a real business and about getting rich. And it is hard to get rich if you have no money at all to begin with.

Another and more obvious reason for having at least a reasonable amount of money is that everything you need to start a business costs money. If you have no established credit and if you have no financial statement that shows at least a reasonable capital structure, people will deal with you only on a cash in advance or c.o.d. basis. If you have no money, you will have a hard time complying with that. Even if you have a reasonable amount of cash and a fairly decent looking financial statement, you will find that most people you will deal with will be very cautious — they have been burned too often and therefore will, at least at first, extend credit sparingly.

My good advice to you is to bend absolutely every effort, from the very beginning, to pay your bills on time or ahead of time. Try to establish, first on a moderate scale and then on a larger scale, your credit worthiness. Your credit is as important to you as a girl's "reputation" used to be to her in the old days (now, I suppose, this concept no longer really exists). There can be few things more destructive to a new business than bad credit experiences by suppliers (you would be surprised how quickly word spreads along the grapevine). And few things are more helpful than people's having good credit experience with you and your being able to refer new suppliers to them for information.

If I were asked to name a figure, I would say that you should have not less than $5,000 and, if at all possible, $10,000 available to go into this business. You need not have it available in actual savings, but you should be able to lay your hands on this kind of money, perhaps by getting a personal loan from your bank for part of it or perhaps even for the whole amount. You should be able to afford the "prudent gamble" of this investment. This means that if worse came to worst (remember there is no guarantee for success in this or any other business), you could afford to lose this stake without being totally wiped out.

HOW TO GET OFF ON THE RIGHT FOOT WITH YOUR BANKER

When I started Haverhill's, I really had no money at all and no ready savings. I made the rounds of San Francisco banks and told my story to a number of flint-eyed and stone-hearted loan officers, who listened to me, but were reluctant to make a commitment. I finally went to a small local bank which had just recently opened, the San Francisco National Bank, the creation and practically the personal fiefdom of one Don Silverthorne. Mr. Silverthorne was a man of enormous physical proportions, a bon-vivant, a pillar of the San Francisco social scene and the virtual monarch of the San Francisco National Bank.

I told my story and made formal application to the loan officer of the San Francisco National Bank. He looked over the information of what I wanted to do, what income I had from my job, what insurance, what assets, what liabilities, etc. He told me that there would be no question that this loan (I had requested $10,000) would be approved and that it was simply a matter of "formalities" to be completed. "Please come back tomorrow," he said. "Your loan will be approved by then."

I was pleased that I had solved my financial problem and counted quite firmly on these funds. When I returned the next day, the loan officer, somewhat sheepishly, handed my application back to me. It had been defaced by the word DISAPPROVED in enormous block letters stamped diagonally across it. I was angry and surprised and asked the loan officer why, after having just yesterday approved this application, he was now rejecting it. He looked around furtively, lowered his voice to a whisper and said: "Look, Mr. Joffe, in this bank only Mr. Silverthorne makes the decisions. He didn't like this application, he didn't explain why, told me to reject it, and I am not about to ask him for his reasons." I was really outraged and wrote a scathing and indignant letter to Mr. Silverthorne, complaining about the high-handed way in which he ran his bank and treated would-be customers. This was the good-bye kiss to the San Francisco National Bank, as far as I was concerned. I was simply letting off some steam.

Imagine my surprise when, two days later, Mr. Silverthorne's secretary called me, told me that there must have been some misunderstanding and invited me for the following day to an interview with the great man himself. I went and found Mr. Silverthorne in a palatial office, surrounded by walnut, leather and jade, an environment befitting the last of the Borgias, rather than the president of a small bank. I must confess that I was impressed and somewhat awed. He was a magnificent figure and he talked to me in a kind but rather condescending manner for about two or thee minutes. My loan application was in front of him. He didn't look at it once. Suddenly he said, "My boy, I like the cut of your jib." (I was forty years old, but, honestly, those were the words. I had read them once in Captain Hornblower, but I had never actually heard anybody utter them.)

"How much money do you want?" he asked. I hesitated for one second and said, "$10,000." He immediately made a 180° swivel turn in his chair, opened a drawer, took out a standard form and wrote out an order to his cashier to open a credit for $10,000 for me. I opened and closed my mouth three times and cursed myself for not having said $20,000, instead of $10,000, because I had a feeling that he might have approved that also. I debated for a few seconds whether I should reopen the subject, but then prudence won out and I decided to leave well enough alone.

Just about one month later, Mr. Silverthorne's bank went into bankruptcy. He was indicted and convicted of all kinds of dreadful crimes against the banking laws, for self-dealing and whatnot. Deposits in the bank were, of course, protected by FDIC — up to $10,000 at the time — so I did not lose any money. I transferred Haverhill's account to another bank and came out unscathed of the whole affair. But I always remembered Mr. Silverthorne fondly for recognizing quickly that I was a good credit risk, that my business plans made sense and had potential and that I was going to turn into a good customer for the bank. I understand that I was the only person who wrote Mr. Silverthorne while he was in detention, and told him how grateful I was to him, how I appreciated that he had extended credit to me when I needed it, and that my thoughts were with him in his present misfortune.

Your experiences with your bank should be much less dramatic. Let's assume that you decided that $10,000 would be the right amount with which to start your business. And let's assume that you have $5,000 in savings and, therefore, want to borrow $5,000 from your bank. You may have borrowed money from the bank before — for an automobile loan, home improvement loan or for any other purpose. And I hope that you handled this loan very punctually, because if you did not, you may now have a little trouble.

But even if you have never borrowed money from the bank, if you have kept your checking account with them in good order and with at least reasonable balances, you should have no real problem getting your loan.

Your banker will ask you for a personal financial statement. Since your affairs are probably not very complicated this will be easy to do, especially since he will give you a standard form to fill out.

He will, in all likelihood, ask you to prepare a business plan. You are miles ahead to establish yourself as a person that knows what he is doing if you prepare such a plan beforehand and have it available, together with your own financial statement, when you request your loan.

Just hand it to him — he will be impressed. Your business plan should generally consist of the following parts:

- a descriptive cover letter
- the "plan" itself
- a financial statement (balance sheet) at the beginning of your business, and
- a projected statement (called a "pro-forma") after one year's operation, and a pro-forma operating statement for that year.

I am showing you examples of what these might look like for a new mail-order business.

This presentation is similar in format to what I prepared for Haverhill's when I got started. You should be able to handle the financial projections yourself. If you have any problem with it, give your raw data — your assumptions and plans — to your accountant (we shall talk about him a little later) and he will do it for you. But if you possibly can, do it all yourself. You should really try to understand your business even before you get started.

John Lambert
43 Elm Street
San Francisco, CA 94121

Mr. Frank Lloyd
Assistant Vice President
and Loan Officer
Second National Bank of San Francisco
18 Montgomery Street
San Francisco, CA 94104

Dear Mr. Lloyd:

I have been a depositor with your bank for several years. I maintain my checking account at your bank and have taken out several loans.

About three years ago, I borrowed $850 for a home improvement loan. This loan has been repaid in full.

Last year I borrowed $500, which I needed to meet unexpected medical expenses and for payment of taxes. This was a short-term (six months) non-installment loan, also promptly repaid. At present, I carry my automobile loan with your bank. This is a 24-installment loan of which, at this writing, 9 installments have been paid.

I give you the foregoing information as background for the loan request I wish to make herewith.

I plan to start a mail-order business in fine foods, especially cheeses. I plan to run this business initially on a part-time basis, i.e. I shall keep my present job as assistant sales manager for the Fern and Trimble Company. I expect that I can handle this business initially by working at it evenings and week-ends only. My wife, who has a good deal of clerical and bookkeeping experience, will assist me.

I attach hereto the outline of my business plan and financial schedules. I wish to capitalize this business initially with $10,000. We plan to contribute $5,000 from savings and we wish to apply for a $5,000 loan from your bank. In addition, we wish to request a $3,000 line of credit on a "when needed" basis, for peak working capital requirements and for financing domestic letters of credit.

As to the $5,000 loan, I propose to pay interest only for the first six months and then repay the loan, with interest, in 30 equal installments, beginning with the seventh month.

In order to give an example of the documentation that you should hand to your bank when you apply for a business loan, we have invented the couple of John and Mary Lambert of San Francisco. They plan to start a mail-order business, specializing in cheese. They will call their business ''The French-California Gourmet.''

Naturally, my wife and I plan to guarantee these loans and their punctual repayment. If required, we would be willing to collateralize the loans with a general lien against our assets.

In addition to my business plan, I also submit pro-forma financial statements of this business, at the outset and after the first year, and a pro-forma profit-and-loss statement for the first year.

Further, I submit my personal financial statement as of today, prior to the planned investment in this business.

I propose to operate this business as a Subchapter S corporation initially, to be transformed into a regular corporation when the condition of the business seems to warrant it. The proposed name of the business is "The French-California Gourmet."

Thank you for your consideration of my loan request. Please call me for an interview after you have reviewed the included material.

Sincerely yours,

John Lambert

John Lambert

This is John Lambert's descriptive cover letter that he hands to his bank, together with his formal business plan and financial statement. It summarizes what he wants to do and why and for what purpose he wants to borrow money from the bank.

BUSINESS PLAN for
THE FRENCH-CALIFORNIA GOURMET
A Subchapter S Corporation

Business Purpose: To engage in the sale by mail order of fine foods, especially cheeses.

Principals and Background:

John Lambert: 39 years old, U.S. citizen, resident of San Francisco for the last 10 years,.presently employed by the Fern and Trimble Company as Assistant Sales Manager, current salary (exclusive of bonuses, etc.) $21,500. Education: High school, two years of college.

Mary Lambert: 37 years old, U.S. citizen (native of France), housewife, two children, previously employed as secretary/bookkeeper. Has background in the fine food business and cheesemaking. Education: In France, equivalent of high school, one year of secretarial/business school, and two years of college.

During the first year of business, John Lambert proposes to keep his job, since the expected demands of this new business do not warrant his full-time attention. This is also desirable in order to prevent excessive drain on working capital. Mary Lambert will perform all clerical and bookkeeping functions and will assist in wrapping and mailing merchandise.

Legal, Accounting, Insurance, Banking

Law firm of Hacker and Wirtz will organize a Subchapter S corporation and will handle all legal requirements of the corporation. They will also handle any other legal matters that may arise from time to time in the course of business.

Snow and Warren, CPA's, will be the firm's accountants. They will set up books, table of accounts, and will monitor punctual payment of taxes and contributions. We shall keep our own books, which they will close (without audit) every quarter, at which time they will prepare quarterly financial statements.

Our insurance brokers will be Sorenson and Tidwell. We shall carry standard business insurance with special emphasis on product liability.

Our bank of deposit is the Second National Bank of San Francisco. We are applying for a $5,000 capital loan and a $3,000 "peak need" working capital line of credit.

Specific Business Plan

Mary Lambert has a "secret recipe" for a fine soft cheese (please refer to and taste attached sample).

On this and the following two pages we have John Lambert's formal business plan. Its primary purpose is for presentation to the bank. It is also of good value to John Lambert himself, because putting his plans on paper will help him to clarify his own thinking about his new business.

This is a family recipe and can be prepared from domestic and (partly) inported ingredients, in the kitchen of our home, at least for the immediate future. Under refrigeration, this cheese will maintain its freshness almost indefinitely. Shelf life under ordinary home or store conditions is about three months.

We have an inventory of about 1,000 pounds of this cheese in a rented freezer. This will be our beginning inventory. The production cycle of the cheese, from special preparation to full maturity, is about two months. The raw material ingredients per pound of the cheese cost approximately $1.22. We plan to sell this product at $3.50 per pound plus $2.00 postage per shipment. This is in line with what similar premium cheeses sell for. We plan to offer the cheese in 3-pound and 5-pound packages.

We have over the years sold small quantities of the cheese on an informal basis and had very good acceptance. We have also, during the last year, supplied two retail stores with this cheese on an on-going basis.

Repeat orders from these sources are steady. All of this leads us to believe that, if properly promoted, this cheese has mail order potential. Until now, sales have been quite small, about 100 to 200 pounds a month. We sell the cheese at $2.25 to the two retail accounts. In turn, they sell it at the suggested retail price of $3.50 per pound.

I realize that we cannot sustain a mail order business on the basis of one product alone. Therefore, we have entered into a preliminary agreement with the Iowa Cheese Company of Dubuque, Iowa. They are a manufacturer/wholesaler of cheeses, meats and other gourmet products. They will allow us to use their catalog (over-printed with our name) for distribution to our customers. Our original print order will be for 10,000 catalogs, which will cost us $2,000. We shall receive a "commission" of 35% on all sales made through this catalog.

We plan to promote sales of our cheeses by advertising in gourmet magazines and up-scale consumer publications. This space advertising will offer a choice of 3 pounds and 5 pounds of cheese. We shall also conduct a "teaser/promotional" space advertising campaign, offering a "free" sample (by charging $1.00 for postage), with an offer to apply this dollar to the first purchase of cheese. We don't have any immediate plans to conduct direct mail promotions on this product because we do not think it lends itself to it. We do, however, plan to include the catalog of the Iowa Cheese Company with each package.

Business Plan 3.

We expect to invest approximately $140,000 in "promotional input" (advertising) during the first year, which we expect to produce sales of 90,000 pounds of cheese, approximately $315,000. In addition, we expect to sell about $55,000 of merchandise through the bounceback catalog of the Iowa Cheese Company. This is just over $1 per catalog, which is standard for the industry. We have not considered any additional revenue from our proposed retail store (see below).

Since all sales will be prepaid (cash with order) and since we expect that, after an initial period, media will extend standard credit terms, our cash requirements will be modest in relation to the projected volume of the business. Our initial capital, plus the stand-by working capital requested for "peak needs" shall suffice.

We expect to have a customer list of approximately 60,000 names by the end of the first year. We plan to promote vigorously the rental of this list to other firms engaged in the gourmet food business and for other purposes. We have entered into a preliminary agreement with an agent/broker in New York (Advance List Service) who will promote rental of this list. We expect to derive net revenue from such rentals of approximately $10,000 during the first year. Our list (master file) will be maintained by San Francisco Computer Service. They will also produce our shipping labels and weekly sales analyses and reports.

Assuming that things proceed according to plan, we propose to combine our mail order business with a gourmet retail outlet after approximately six months operation. We plan on a location on the edge of the downtown area (not in the prime shopping district), where we shall also have offices, storage and manufacturing space available. We believe it is important for a mail order business to have a retail outlet. Also, we expect the retail store to become a profit center of its own. Leasehold improvements for this store, mostly for store fixtures and refrigeration equipment, are protected to be on the order of $10,000. We expect to be able to finance most of this under a lease/rental plan.

Pro-forma financial statements are attached.

John Lambert

JOHN LAMBERT

Mary Lambert

MARY LAMBERT

THE FRENCH-CALIFORNIA GOURMET
A Subchapter S Corporation

PRO-FORMA BEGINNING BALANCE SHEET

Assets		
Cash		$10,000
Inventory (1000 lbs. of cheese at cost)		1,220
Equipment Cheesemaking equipment, typewriter, other office equipment (cost)		3,650
	TOTAL ASSETS	$14,870

Liabilities & Capital		
Note Payable, 2nd National Bank, current portion		$ 1,000
Note Payable, 2nd National Bank, non-current portion		4,000
Note Payable, Stockholder		6,870
	TOTAL LIABILITIES	$11,870
Paid in Capital		3,000
	TOTAL LIABILITIES & CAPITAL	$14,870

This is John Lambert's pro-forma beginning balance sheet for his new company, The French California Gourmet. It reflects John's cash contribution of $5,000 and inventory and equipment contribution of $4,870. We shall see later why $6,870 of this total $9,870 contribution is "note payable to stockholder."

THE FRENCH-CALIFORNIA GOURMET
A Subchapter S Corporation

PRO-FORMA BALANCE SHEET AFTER FIRST YEAR'S OPERATION

Cash		$17,070
Inventory		
Finished cheese: 5000 lbs.	$ 6,100	
Cheese in process: 10,000 lbs.	12,200	
		18,300
Equipment (exclusive of equipment required under lease/rental plan), after depreciation		4,500
Leasehold Improvements		5,000
Prepaid Catalogs		2,000
Other Prepayments		1,000
TOTAL ASSETS		$ 47,870

Liabilities & Capital	
Accounts payable (supplies & media)	$15,000
Current portion of bank note	2,000
Taxes payable and other current liabilities	2,000
TOTAL CURRENT LIABILITIES	19,000
Non-current portion of bank note	2,000
Note payable to stockholder	6,870
TOTAL LIABILITIES	$27,870
Paid in Capital	3,000
Retained Earnings	17,000
TOTAL LIABILITIES & CAPITAL	$47,870

This is how John Lambert projects the financial statement of the French California Gourmet after the first year of operation. He has retained $17,000 in earnings and has reduced his debt to the bank from $5,000 to $4,000.

THE FRENCH-CALIFORNIA GOURMET
A Subchapter S Corporation

PRO-FORMA PROFIT AND LOSS STATEMENT FOR FIRST YEAR OF OPERATION

($000)

Gross Sales	$370
Less: Returns and Allowances	(20)
Net Sales	350
Less: Cost of Goods Sold	(146)
Gross Margin	204
Less: Selling Expenses	(20)
Gross Profit	182
Less: Promotional Input	(140)
Trading Profit	42
List Rental Income	10
Income before General and Admin. Expenses	52
Less: General and Administrative Expenses	(35)
Profit before Taxes	$ 17

John Lambert's P & L statement for his first year of operation shows pre-tax earnings of $17,000. It seems to be a reasonable projection of sales and profit.

THE FRENCH-CALIFORNIA GOURMET
A Subchapter S Corporation

NOTES TO PRO-FORMA P & L STATEMENT
($000)

Sales

90,000 pounds of cheese @$3.50	$315,000
Catalog merchandise	55,000
	$370,000

Cost of Goods

90,000 pounds of cheese @$1.22	$110,000
Catalog merchandise (65%)	36,000
	$146,000

NOTE: Credit for returned merchandise is not considered, since in all likelihood any returns will have to be discarded.

Selling Expense

Consists of data processing, packing materials, bank card discounts and other variable expenses that are directly attributable to sales. Postage expenses (and UPS) are not considered, since it is expected that postage income ($2.00 per package) will equal, if not exceed, postage expense.

Promotional Input

Space advertising, mostly in gourmet and "up-scale" consumer magazines. Costs projected are net of agency commission, since we plan to establish

a house advertising agency.	$110,000
50,000 purchased catalogs*	10,000
Advertising production expense	20,000
	$140,000

*NOTE: We expect to sell just over $1 of product for each catalog distributed. This is in line with industry experience.

List Rental

List is expected to build to 60,000 names in one year. Average size of list during year is expected to be 30,000. Our list manager/broker assures us that the list will be rentable after it reaches size of 15,000 names. He expects to turn over the list 12 times per year, i.e. to rent 360,000 names @$30.00 net profit to us per thousand, i.e. for a net profit of approximately $10,000.

Notes to Pro-Forma P & L Statement 2.

General and Administrative Expense

We believe that this is a conservative projection of these expenses. We expect to draw a minimal salary of $100 per week each, mostly in order to establish our bonafides as employees of this business and, in the case of Mrs. Lambert, to assure her coverage under insurance, workman's compensation and social security.

We do not expect to have additional salary expenses during the first six months operation, and salaries (including associated payroll expenses) of not more than $2,000 per month during the second six months. The balance of the $35,000 earmarked for general and administrative expenses is primarily for office supplies, rent (in second half of year), telephone, legal, insurance, accounting and interest on loan.

John Lambert

JOHN LAMBERT

Mary Lambert

MARY LAMBERT

These notes to John Lambert's pro-forma P & L for the first year of The French California Gourmet's operation are as important as the P & L statement itself. It details and explains every item in the summary P & L. John Lambert's plans seem to be solidly based — everything is soundly conceived and well thought through.

FINANCIAL STATEMENT: JOHN and MARY LAMBERT

Assets	
Cash in bank, savings account and on hand	$12,500
Savings bonds	2,500
Listed securities, at current market (see list)	6,250
Home: 43 Elm Str., San Francisco -- current appraisel	55,000
Furniture and fixtures (nominal)	1,000
Automobile (1975 Chevrolet)	3,000
Cheese Inventory & Cheesemaking equipment	4,870
TOTAL ASSETS	$85,120

Liabilities & Net Worth	
Owed to stores, bank cards, etc.	$ 1,250
Owed on installment contracts	850
Owed to 2nd National Bank on auto loan	1,600
Owed to S. F. County Savings (1st mortgage on home)	28,250
TOTAL LIABILITIES	$31,950
Net Worth	53,170
TOTAL LIABILITIES AND NET WORTH	$85,120

Notes to financial statement:

1. This statement is prior to investment in THE FRENCH-CALIFORNIA GOURMET COMPANY.
2. I (John Lambert) am presently employed by the Fern & Trimble Company as Assistant Sales Manager. My current salary is $21,500 per year, plus various bonuses and benefits.
3. Life insurance in force:
   $50,000 in term insurance on John Lambert (including $10,000 company insurance), $10,000 full life insurance on Mary Lambert.
4. We have never declared bankruptcy, nor compromised a debt.
5. We are not co-guarantors of any loan.

John and Mary Lambert's financial statement shows a net worth of over $50,000, very respectable for a young couple. Since John and Mary will personally have to guarantee any loan that will be granted by the Second National Bank of San Francisco, it is necessary for them to present their personal financial statements to the bank.

John Lambert

JOHN LAMBERT

Mary Lambert

MARY LAMBERT

Later in this chapter we shall talk about the "legal organization" of your new business. You will find that I shall advise you to incorporate. You know that one of the advantages of incorporation is that you are not personally liable for the corporation's debts. So it might come as somewhat of a surprise to you that your banker will ask you (and your wife, if you are married) to sign a personal note for the loan he plans to give you and probably to provide collateral. Don't be surprised, and don't try to argue about it. There is no way that you could get a loan without it. And, of course, the bank is justified in requesting it. Because, although you are technically a "separate person" from your corporation, you are in absolute control. The bank, naturally, looks to you personally for repayment of their loan.

In dealing with your bank, it is always well to remember the obvious: they are not in the risk-taking business — *you* are. They are in the money lending business. And they want to be very sure that they will get their money back.

But there is also another point, a test for yourself really, and it's this: you should be willing and be spiritually prepared to put your own money on the line for what you believe in. Why should the bank have more confidence in your project than you have yourself? And if you come to the conclusion that you would rather not sign that note, that you would rather not risk your money in your venture, it might be the tip-off that you are not yet quite ready to be in business for yourself, that you should perhaps wait a little while, work out your plans in more detail, and then try again when you are really ready. Putting your name on that note is, in a way, "the moment of truth."

Even if you do not need an immediate bank loan, you should, from the very beginning, let your banker know what you are doing and where you expect to be heading. You still should submit a business plan to him, because it is quite certain that you will need banking services and working capital loans as you go along. Everything will go more smoothly if you keep your banker informed. Although he may not request it from you, you should hand him quarterly financial statements so he will know how you are doing. And if things go wrong, if you do not come up to your projections, or if you should have any other business reverses, do not be tempted to keep them from him, especially if he has lent you money. Nobody likes surprises — bankers are no exception.

One special point in this connection: it may happen — it does in the best of families and the best of businesses — that you will not be able to repay a loan or an installment on time. If that happens, don't hope that your banker might just forget about it. I assure you he won't — they never do! Be sure to tell him why, offer to make a reasonable part payment and tell him how you are going to take care of the rest. But you must tell him beforehand and you must make that reasonable part payment, or he will be very concerned.

You may get advice to the effect that you should investigate your bank carefully to determine whether they will be able to supply the financial services that you will require. But I don't think that is good advice. Because the best bet for your business bank is the bank that you are already working with personally. At least they have had some experience with you. Also, virtually any bank in the country can provide the services that a small business needs. And as far as a bank's policies are concerned, they are all pretty much the same. Remember, a bank's business is to render services and to make loans. And they love to do both. But they want services rendered to be profitable and they want to make good loans, loans that will be repaid. And most bankers have pretty much the same criteria as to what is and what is not a good loan.

It is, of course, possible that you don't yet have a bank or that the business that you have done with your bank is so insignificant that it wouldn't really cut any ice. In that case, it may pay you to do some "shopping." You may mostly wish to look into such things as to whether there are any charges for depositing checks (this could be a fairly important factor, especially if you have a business that involves a large number of small deposits), other charges, minimum balances expected and so-called "compensating balances" expected if you borrow from the bank. Also, you might be able to get a feel for their general "liberality" and understanding for the small businessman. This you might best find out from other businessmen who work with that bank. If you have not much else to go by, you are usually better off with a small bank than with a large bank. The smaller bank honestly seems to appreciate new business: they are usually flexible and accommodating, more reasonable in their fees and usually have less rigid loan policies.

Now that you have your financing arranged and have selected your bank, let's talk about what kind of organization you should use for your new mail-order business.

BE ON YOUR OWN OR IS THERE COMFORT IN COMPANY?

Probably the first decision you will have to make about organization is whether to "do it yourself" or whether you should have any partners or participants in your new venture.

As far as I am concerned, the answer is clear-cut: be on your own! The main reason, of course, that you want to go into business is to get rich — and chances are you will accomplish that. But there is usually also another reason — sometimes it is expressed and quite clear, and sometimes it may be hidden and not acknowledged. And it is that people who have the spirit of entrepreneurship are dynamic, strong individuals — and since you bought this book, I must assume that you are one of them. Such people are usually more comfortable on their own than in a setting in which they have to take orders or even suggestions from others. They don't really want to consult with others about what should be done, they don't like to be responsible to others for mistakes made, they don't really want to share success and eventual rewards. They even want to nurse the wounds of their own failures. The true entrepreneur is essentially a lone wolf.

The biggest mistake I believe you can make is to sell "a piece of the action" to others, in order to raise capital. It is a mistake you would live to regret! Even if these people are your best friends (or relatives), you will find that you will be defensive and apologetic if there are setbacks and things don't go well. And you might be surprised how nasty some people, even "good friends," can become if there are actual reverses and losses. At best you have fatally damaged your relationship with them.

But let's take the opposite case, the more hopeful and more likely one, namely that you will be very successful. Unless you have made very sophisticated buy-back arrangements with your investors (and, frankly, it would take some brass to impose a lot of conditions on friends who are willing to invest money in your new enterprise) you will be unhappy ever after for having sold a big chunk of yourself for what you will then consider a trifling amount. And these are commitments that are almost impossible and very expensive to get out of. You will feel like a champion prizefighter who does all the work and takes all the licks and then has to split the purse of every fight with any number of hangers-on.

The time to bring in others — either by going public or by selling your company to a large publicly held corporation — is much later. It is after you have created a going and growing business, with a demonstrated record of achievement and earnings.

There are only two possible exceptions to my almost inflexible opinion about this:

1. If your parent, rich uncle or doting maiden aunt have a good deal of money, a portion of which they have set aside especially for you in any case — perhaps by inheritance — you may take your share now in order to help you get started in your business. But do it only if you are convinced (it isn't enough that they tell you — you must be convinced) that there are absolutely no strings and no accountability on your part. You have no partners and if you lose any of the money (you shouldn't if you read this book carefully, but there are no guarantees!) you simply blew it, you will decide to forget it, because it is money you would have gotten later anyway.
2. You know a person who will put up the same amount of money you do, but, much more importantly, who has talents that can be immediately applied to the new business, and whose talents are complementary to yours.

   The key word is *complementary.* You definitely don't want somebody who can do the same things as you. For instance: you are a copywriter and he/she is a copywriter; you are a merchandiser, and he/she is a merchandiser. But if one of you, let's say, is really knowledgeable about mail-order advertising and the other about systems analysis and business organization, if one of you is savvy in merchandising and the other in art direction and catalog preparation, you may have a very powerful combination and an even better chance for success.

   But there is one other very important point, and if you are not completely satisfied on it you should still turn thumbs down on this combination: you must know each other well, preferably have been through a few scrapes together and be sure that you can work well together, under all circumstances and whatever the stress. An incompatible partner is almost worse than an incompatible mate (you spend more time with your partner!) and dissolution of a partnership can be messier and costlier than a divorce.

So, with these two possible exceptions, my advice is to be on your own. And now you will have to decide what form of organization to choose.

HOW TO HAVE YOUR CAKE AND EAT IT: "SUBCHAPTER S"

You know that there are three basic types of business organizations: proprietorship, partnership and corporation. Let's forget about partnership for right now (you will see in a minute why we can do that, even if you should find that "exceptional person" we just talked about). So this leaves you with the choice between proprietorship and corporation.

The nice thing about a proprietorship is that it is very quickly organized, hardly any red tape and legal expenses are involved. Usually just some simple business permits are required, depending on your jurisdiction. But that is about the only good thing about it. There are two grave disadvantages, which in just about all cases outweigh by far the quickness and inexpensiveness:

1. You are personally and totally responsible for debts, obligations and liabilities that you incur in your business, and that is not restricted to "legitimate debts." It includes judgments, liens and whatnot.
2. Profits and losses of your business are "passed through" to you directly. If you lose money (which is possible in the early stages of your business) you can offset it against any other income you might have, and that would, of course, be a tax advantage. But if you make money, as I firmly expect you to, certainly after the start-up period, any business income will be considered as if it were income directly to you, and this may be a serious tax disadvantage.

The annoying thing about a corporation is that certain rather rigid formalities have to be gone through. There is quite a bit of red tape, and inevitable legal expense — we'll see in a minute how to hold that down. By the way, you may have seen books advertised that promise to show you how to form your own corporation for $50. My advice: don't! If you are a do-it-yourself addict, take out your own gall bladder or something, but if you are serious about going into business, by all means, let an attorney help you with the formalities required.

But the red tape, a little extra time, legal expenses, and certain formalities that are required after incorporation (keeping of minutes, directors and stockholders' meetings, etc.) are really the only disadvantages and they are quite minor. Except in very special circumstances, you will not be personally liable for any debts or obligations of the corporation — unless, of course, you specifically assume them (as you will have to with the bank, but with nobody else). Any profits will be taxed at the corporate rate and will not be passed through to you. And within reasonable limits, you can regulate your own salary so that between your corporation and yourself personally you can optimize your tax situation and net income.

"Great," you say. "But what happens if we suffer losses?" We have just decided that this is certainly a possibility to be considered in the start-up period of your mail-order business. "Wouldn't I then be better off if I had a proprietorship? I could then pass these losses through to myself and lose effectively only about $.50 for every dollar lost in the business."

You are quite right, but this is one of the few cases in which you can have the best of all worlds. You form what is called a "Subchapter S" corporation. This is considered a true corporation, in all respects, with all its advantages, except for tax purposes. Because with a "Subchapter S" corporation (the owner, or we should now call him stockholder) is taxed as if it were a proprietorship.

This is a great advantage as long as your business is new, you have expenses and possible losses, and you still haven't climbed up the profit curve. You then work in line with your business plan. As soon as you feel that you are in a solid profit position, you shift your "Subchapter S" corporation into a "regular" corporation. It's a quick thing for your attorney to do, almost as easy as shifting gears in a car. One word of caution, though: you cannot shift from "Subchapter S" corporation to "regular" and then back again. You will have to stay there for a long time. Your attorney will tell you all the details.

One proviso: California does not recognize the "pass through" concept of the "Subchapter S" corporation, and considers it like a "regular" corporation for income tax purposes. I haven't done any research on that, but I suspect that this is probably true for all or most other states. So the tax advantage of the "Subchapter S" corporation applies only to federal income taxes. They are, however, always the major consideration, state income taxes being much less significant.

There are some other wonderful things about corporations — "Subchapter S" or "regular" ones — that are not too readily available to you in a proprietorship or partnership. There are pension plans, deferred compensation plans and other tasty tax goodies. Many of these won't have any practical value to you until you are making a fair amount of money. But you should be aware of them. It is something to keep in mind.

I asked you a while ago to forget about partnerships for the time being, even in the exceptional case that you find that super-person that we have been talking about. And the reason is that partnerships have all the disadvantages of proprietorships — only worse. Each partner is responsible for the entire business. Suppose there is a judgment against a business. If your partner can't pay his share, you are responsible for the whole shooting match. This can't happen if you and your "partner" are stockholders in a "Subchapter S" (or any other) corporation.

Your business organization is, of course, something you will discuss with your attorney. But unless he has very weighty reasons to the contrary or unless you have a most unusual tax situation, my advice is to go the "Subchapter S" route — keeping your eye peeled to changing it into a regular corporation when you know the time is right — when you are solidly in the black.

DON'T GIVE YOUR MONEY TO YOUR BUSINESS — LEND IT!

And while we are talking about the structure of your business (hopefully we are agreed that you should start out as a "Subchapter S" corporation) there is a point of some importance to keep in mind in making your investment — let's assume it's $10,000 — into your business. You might be inclined to pay it all in as "capital," that would seem to be the natural way to do it. But don't! Your interest lies in classifying as much as possible of your investment (all of it if it were possible) as a *loan* to the corporation, and not as "capital" or equity. The IRS won't let you get by with 100%, of course, or anything close to it. They would consider it a sham and they would be right. But while there is no hard and fast rule about it, it is usually pretty safe to work it on as much as a 3 to 1 ratio. This would mean that, of your $10,000 investment, you could put in $7,500 as a loan to the company and $2,500 as equity capital.

You may wonder what the advantage of this somewhat complicated sounding arrangement is. Why should you make a loan to your own company, rather than just put up the "capital" and be done with it? Here is the reason: if things go well, you will want to (and if they go very well, you will have to — the IRS won't let you "hoard" money indefinitely) distribute money to yourself — after all, you went into this to enjoy a few nice things on the way to getting rich. There are three basic ways you can do that:

1. Pay yourself a dividend. This is terrible, because a dividend is not a tax deductible expense to your corporation, and it is certainly income to you. In fact, it's about the worst kind of income you can get, because the IRS does not consider dividends as "earned income" (which has a tax ceiling of 50%) but "unearned income." Being that, the taxes go right through the ceiling.

2. Take it as a salary — give yourself a nice raise. You will usually get by with it, because the numbers you work with will be pretty small at first and the IRS will probably not argue whether your raise was reasonable or not. This is quite a bit better from a tax point of view, because while it is certainly taxable income to you (thank heavens, it is "earned income"), it is also a deductible expense to your company. So it is pretty much a wash-out tax-wise, except that you have to make all these payroll "employees' contributions" in paying your own salary.

   But there is a hidden disadvantage: if you pay out money to yourself as salary it will have to be an expense to the corporation and that reduces your company's income by that amount. As we go along with this story, you will see that one of the names of this game is to produce a record of earnings. You want to do everything you reasonably can so as not to reduce them.

3. You can repay your loan to yourself. Now, this is absolutely beautiful: because repayment of your loan is not an expense to the corporation and therefore does not reduce

its earnings. And, of course, since you are just getting your loan repaid, you personally don't have to pay any taxes on it at all.

A word of caution: you may be tempted to think of lending money to your own corporation as just putting it from one pocket into the other. But do not fall into this error. All dealings between you and the corporation have to be on a rather formal basis. In order to make this loan valid, there will have to be minutes showing that it has been authorized, there has to be a definite repayment schedule arranged, interest has to be fixed (and paid). Your attorney will do all of these things for you.

A GOOD TIME TO TAKE CARE OF YOUR KIDS

One final word about money and corporate organization. You are pretty sure that you are going to be successful, aren't you? So why not make plans right now — when it is inexpensive and has hardly any tax consequences — to do something for your kids (assuming, of course, that you are married and have children — if you don't, you may skip this part). Give them "a piece of your cake" and put it in a trust fund for them. Once you make it big, they make it big too, their money can't be touched, and the best part is that it's all virtually tax free.

A technical point: you cannot do that with the "Subchapter S" corporation, but only after you have transformed it into a regular corporation. But that is no hardship. Because you will wish to make that transformation when you are solidly in the profit column. And, of course, that is when you want to take care of your kids, not before.

I wasn't quite alert enough to make my children stockholders of Haverhill's at the very beginning. In fact, I let a few years go by before I gave each of my three children a 10% interest in Haverhill's. By that time I had a pretty good idea as to where things were headed. When I sold Haverhill's to Time Inc., about five years after I had founded it, for just a little over $1 million, each of my children had over $100,000 of Time Inc. stock in a trust account. We all worry about taking care of our children: in fact, I find that it is one of the causes of greatest anxiety for people. But I have this problem licked: whatever happens to me — even if I don't happen to make that second or third million, if I should lose a piece of the first one, if I should get sick, or even if I should depart for that great mail-order house in the sky, my kids are taken care of, and I don't have to worry about them — at least not financially.

You can lay the groundwork for that too. You may not find it necessary to do it at the very beginning. But you should definitely keep your mind on it and do it well before you go into orbit, because then it might be expensive.

Here, too, your attorney will show you how to set up such trusts and he will advise you about timing.

A LEAN AND HUNGRY ATTORNEY — YOUR SECOND BUSINESS PILLAR

And this brings us to your attorney, who is the second pillar (the bank was the first, and we shall talk about the other two right away) of what you might call your business council.

You will get many contradictory opinions in business advice books about how to pick an attorney. Some may tell you to get a list of attorneys or law firms from the Bar Association in your city, that you should have interviews with several (to see whether or not they are suited to your requirements), etc. But I don't think that is necessarily good advice. If you already have an attorney with whom you get along and if he has a business practice, go with him. If not, keep in mind that, in all likelihood, your legal problems are going to be quite simple and very straightforward. You will not need any kind of high-priced hotshot to do your work. My good advice is to stay away from "prestigious" law firms, because the average mortal simply cannot afford their fees, certainly not if he has just gone into business. You should get acquainted with a young, "hungry" attorney, with whom you feel at ease and with whom you feel you can establish a good working relationship. Chances are that he will go all out to do a good job for you. He will understand that you are on a limited budget, and that you are starting a new business. He knows how it is, because he is starting a new business himself — and he will be reasonable with his fees.

One of the first things to reach an understanding about is the cost of establishing your organization. Be firm and insist on a time-fee basis, with a certain amount as maximum. Large law firms try to hold you up for absolutely incredible "standard fees" (they will mumble that the Bar Association has established these "guidelines") for such simple services. The young lawyer will work for you on a time basis and it will be much, much less expensive.

If you pick the right guy, this young lawyer will grow in experience and professional maturity as your business grows and you will be able to establish a good working relationship with him. I was fortunate to do just that. The young lawyer I worked with when I started business is now a partner in one of San Francisco's important law firms. Things have worked out well for both of us.

By now, you already have two pro's working for you — your banker and your lawyer. And if you don't have a candidate up your sleeve yourself, it is quite likely that they will be able to lead you to the right accountant for you.

PILLAR #3: A TIGER OF AN ACCOUNTANT

What about an accountant? He is the third pillar of your business council. Here I can give you just about the same advice that I gave you about the attorney. An accountant may not be quite as important to you, certainly not in the beginning, as your attorney. What you will need right away is a bookkeeping service, because your business does not warrant a full-time bookkeeper. It is possible that you or your wife can keep your books and if you can, it will be convenient and save you some money. But you will definitely need an accountant in due course, if for no other reason than to keep you out of tax trouble.

A good arrangement for you, just starting a small mail-order business, is to do the bookkeeping and record keeping yourself (if you know how) or have it done by a bookkeeping service. But, once every quarter, let your accountant pull all the numbers together, "close the books" and prepare financial statements. These statements, although they won't be "audited," will be more acceptable to your bank than anything you or your bookkeeping service might prepare. Also, in going over your books and over your business at least once a quarter, your accountant will be able to point out areas where you should change your procedures, he will be able to show you where better or different controls would be in order, and even where you might have to look out for hanky-panky — theft of merchandise or embezzlement (oh, yes, it does happen). But if you are lucky, you can get a young CPA who is starting out or in the process of creating a practice and not too proud to do a little regular bookkeeping (they call it "write up" work) or who has a nonprofessional in his office who does that kind of work and whom he supervises. If you can find that, you're likely to have a winner. You may know such a person or a friend may know one.

Just as with your attorney, you and your accountant might grow together. You won't need too much professional advice in the beginning, but it is good to have a CPA in your corner who can look over your shoulder and who can answer questions when they come up.

One question that will come up is the one that we have already discussed, namely when to transform your "Subchapter S" into a regular corporation. Ask your CPA to keep an eye out for that and he will give you the green light when he decides that you are ready.

There are also a number of pesky and annoying, but absolutely necessary tax matters to handle, which he will get out of your hair and take care of for you. I refer to such regularly recurring things as tax withholding deposits, federal and state employer's tax and employees' withholding, sales taxes, etc. These things are unexciting and dreary, but they have to be done. The tax people are absolutely humorless and if any tax date is missed, you are subject to disproportionate fines. I have missed a few in the course of the years, usually by only a few days. In each case, I wrote impassioned letters to the IRS or to the California Board of Equalization, asking for forgiveness of the fine. I found only stony incomprehension. I wasn't successful one single time.

AND FINALLY: YOUR INSURANCE MAN

There's one last pillar that you will need, and that is a good insurance man. Here is some good advice: do not go to a life insurance man (if you have a friend in the life insurance business, don't even discuss it with him) who does business insurance as a "sideline." You need a sharp guy who is savvy in business insurance. I wouldn't call it an absolute requirement, but if you can get a person with a CPCU behind his name (it stands for Certified Property and Casualty Underwriter) you have at least some reasonable assurance that you are not dealing with a complete dumb-dumb.

I won't tell you again about what kind of person you should be looking for — you know what I want you to get: a young tiger.

Explain your business to him and he'll get you the comprehensive coverage you need.

One thing he will be on the lookout for is adequate liability insurance, especially "product liability" insurance. This is insurance against any defects in the merchandise that you sell and that may harm somebody. Very few legitimate and valid claims should occur with the kind of business I shall advise you to start. But once you are reasonably successful and have a few bucks in the bank, there will be occasional kooks coming out of the woodwork who will insist that your fruitcake poisoned them, your mousetrap pinched their baby's toe or your corkscrew spoiled their vintage wine.*

You can turn such claims over to your insurance broker and he will take care of them for you. And that's a blessing, for some of these folks are quite determined, would be difficult for you to handle, take lots of time and cost quite a bit of money.

MYTH REAFFIRMED: YES, KITCHEN TABLE IS JUST FINE

I feel sort of bad that I had to give you a piece of sobering news a while back and that I may have destroyed a belief which you may have held for a long time. And that is the cherished conviction that you can start a mail-order business with very little or without any capital at all.

As I told you before, I suppose it can be done, but I have never seen it happen or have heard of a confirmed case. So while I hate to throw cold water on that illusion, there is another "myth" connected with mail order. It is that you can start your business right from your home and that you don't have to give up your job to do it.

This "myth" is fortunately correct — you can indeed start your new mail-order business at home and on a part-time basis. You

---

* If you think these claims are far-fetched, let me tell you what happened not long ago here in San Francisco. A young woman (she claimed later to have been of "unblemished virtue") was riding in one of our San Francisco cable cars and was thrown to the floor when, in order to avoid an accident, the car came to an abrupt stop. She got a bump on her head all right, but she claimed that this blow had turned her suddenly into an insatiable and uncontrollable nymphomaniac. This caused her serious damage and she sued the city for, I think it was, $100,000. Believe it or not, the city lost. Thank goodness I didn't sell that cable car to the City of San Francisco, so I didn't have to worry about any kind of liability. But I tell you that story only to alert you to what can happen, the harebrained verdicts juries can come up with and that you should be protected against any liability even from such unlikely, kooky claims.

don't have to, and indeed I urge you not to, give up your job. You have to be prepared to work an extra few hours when you come home in the evening, but that shouldn't be a sacrifice, considering what you stand to gain. If you are lucky enough to have a wife who has some clerical talents and who doesn't mind getting her hands dirty taking checks out of envelopes (take my word for it, she'll learn to love that in no time at all), wrapping packages, running to the post office and keeping some records, you are doubly blessed. Your chances to succeed are that much increased and you'll be able to hang onto your job that much longer. So, fortunately, it's quite true: you can start your mail-order business in relative privacy (nobody really needs to know) and right from that proverbial kitchen table. This last statement, by the way, should not be taken quite literally. You'd better set a small room or a desk aside for your mail-order work. You don't want your kids to get into your paper-work, and customers do not appreciate having gravy stains on their merchandise or getting a half-finished popsicle included in their package.

Seriously, although I advise you to keep your job for the time being and to conduct your mail-order business on a part-time, after hours basis, everything has to be done neatly, promptly and professionally from the very beginning. And this means, among other things, that you want to keep your mail-order business separate from whatever else you are doing. Keep in mind that the customer who sends you his money is not prepared to make allowances for you, just because you are a rookie. Once he pays his money he is entitled to professional service and the best in merchandise.

Remember also that you don't want him to know that you are just learning the business and getting your toes wet. That is another of the beauties of the mail-order business: it is perhaps the only business in which you, as a rank beginner, thinly financed and without any track record, can compete on an almost equal footing with the giants. What you will need is to select merchandise that has a professional "feel," place advertising that looks professional and fulfill orders in a professional manner. I shall teach you how to do all of this as we go along. American consumers are knowledgeable and quite demanding — they have been around merchandise, advertising and service a long time. They demand professional service and they know (and get quite unhappy) when they don't get it.

There is another advantage in being able to start your new mail-order business without giving up your present job. You will be able to run it without burdening it with a salary for yourself. The entire thrust of this book, the recipe to great riches, is that you must create a business that will show an ever-increasing record of earnings. We have said that briefly before when we talked about how to put your investment into your business. A young business is like a very tender plant. It cannot afford too many bruises and a salary for the owner would be such a bruise. If you can create a business that will produce, say, $20,000 of pre-tax profit the first year — without paying yourself any salary at all — you have done a pretty good job. If you can increase that to $30,000 the next year and to $50,000 the year following you have built a business with an established record of earnings and one which at that time should be worth, say $200,000 to $300,000.

But if during the first year you would have drawn $20,000 in salary out of this business and, as things got better and you wanted to savor your new affluence, say $25,000 and $30,000 in the second and third years, respectively, your record of pre-tax earnings would be zero for the first year, $5,000 for the second year and $20,000 for the third year. That certainly won't be a very impressive showing and even less impressive if earnings were measured as a percentage of sales. In contrast to the first example, this business would show meager earnings and little growth in earnings and would, therefore, not be a valuable property. Of course, you are not ready to sell this business at this point in any case, so you might think it is not important. But it is: remember, you are building a record, and earnings are what this game is all about!

The longer you can hold on to your job during the start-up stage of your new mail-order business, the better off you will be. But if things go as well as they should, there will inevitably come a moment when it would be wiser and more profitable to quit your job and give all of your time to your mail-order business. The right moment to do this is when you know that you have passed the "vulnerable" stage of your business (which means you are firmly established and are no longer likely to suffer serious reverses or even to be wiped out) and that you can contribute more by giving full time to your business, rather than holding on to your job. In practice, this point is not always that easy to determine. As a rule of thumb: in case of doubt, hold on to your job a little longer.

And don't forget this important point: unless you have other resources, the minute you quit your job, you will have to draw salary from your new business. Your purpose must be to build the value of your business. And the value of your business will be determined as a multiple of earnings that you can show. Therefore, the "value" of your business will be decreased by some multiple of your draw. And, in addition: if you have to take substantial salaries out of your business, you will put a crimp in your working capital that you might not yet be able to afford.

MOMENT OF TRUTH: SHOULD YOU REALLY BE IN THE MAIL-ORDER BUSINESS?

So far we have talked only about the "mere mechanics" of business — bankers, lawyers, accountants, insurance people, corporations, etc. But before you really get going, before you start in business, let's discuss what personal qualities you have to have so as to have a good chance for success and ultimate great wealth. And then let's find out whether you have these qualities.

The mail-order business is in many respects not too different from most other businesses. You have to be able to bring something to it — some special talent that you can apply. You wouldn't plan to buy a fast food franchise if you didn't like teenagers and didn't like cooking. You wouldn't plan on going into the automobile repair business if you didn't like to work with your hands. The same is true with the mail-order business. There are qualities that are needed and others that are helpful for success. Between yourself and your wife (if she is willing and able to help you in building your business — and if you are married, I urge you to put her in harness: it will help your business and, surprise, it will help your marriage) you should have at least a few of them.

Have a look at the following check list and try to answer as frankly as possible. In every case, your answers should refer to your "team," that is, you and your wife (if she has decided to work with you).

1. Do you have the ability to organize your work and your time? Do you usually do what you set out to do, don't apologize, alibi or explain, but get the job done? Are you truly a "self-starter," which means can you motivate yourself to work, even if nobody is supervising you, watching

you or cracking the whip over you? Do you feel that you can work as well on your own (and truly be your own boss), rather than being part of a team or reporting to someone else?

very much	to a degree	very little	none
☐	☐	☐	☐
3	2	1	0

2. Do you stand up well under pressure and frustrations? Can you, when things go wrong, take it on the chin, and bounce right back again?

very much	to a degree	very little	none
☐	☐	☐	☐
3	2	1	0

3. Do you get along well with people? (Although almost by definition, your contact with your customers will be at a distance mostly, you will have to have understanding and empathy for people's feelings to be successful in the mail-order business.)

very much	to a degree	very little	none
☐	☐	☐	☐
3	2	1	0

4. Do you have at least elementary knowledge of ordinary business procedures: filing, typing, the elements of bookkeeping and are able to keep orderly records?

very much	to a degree	very little	none
☐	☐	☐	☐
3	2	1	0

5. Do you keep abreast of the times through periodicals, television, magazines so that you know what is timely, new and wanted by the American public?

very much	to a degree	very little	none
☐	☐	☐	☐
3	2	1	0

6. Are you the kind of person that generates ideas? Do you look at a procedure and don't just accept it because "we have always done it this way"; a person who looks at a product or a process and thinks of ways to improve it? Are you a person who sees a need for a product or service and wonders "why don't they . . . (or even better yet: why don't *I* . . .) do something about this?

very much	to a degree	very little	none
☐	☐	☐	☐
3	2	1	0

7. Do you have sufficient command of language so that you can conduct business correspondence with suppliers, customers and business associates, or perhaps even write promotional and advertising copy?

very much	to a degree	very little	none
☐	☐	☐	☐
3	2	1	0

8. Do you think that you have a "nose" for merchandise? Does your personal choice in products, clothing, furniture, etc., usually turn out to have been the "right" one? Do your friends compliment you on your taste, and are you usually happy with your purchases some time after you have made them?

Very much	to a degree	very little	none
☐	☐	☐	☐
3	2	1	0

9. Are you inventive? Can you, yourself, conceive or produce anything saleable, any product or service that could be advertised for mail-order sale? It could be anything from a delicious home-made preserve or fruitcake, a new type of clothes hanger, a device to roll your own cigarettes to an exchange service for coin collectors.

very much	to a degree	very little	none
☐	☐	☐	☐
3	2	1	0

10. Do you have any artistic abilities? Do you have any technical training in art or in graphic processes? Can you do paste-up work? Could you prepare your own art work for advertising and catalogs? Can you make illustrations?

very much	to a degree	very little	none
☐	☐	☐	☐
3	2	1	0

11. Do you think that you have the ability for copywriting or at least that you have a slumbering talent in that direction that you could develop?

very much	to a degree	very little	none
☐	☐	☐	☐
3	2	1	0

12. Do you have a way with figures — a bent for analysis of data? (Successful mail-order is very much a numbers game.) Are you able to evaluate results or facts, to project costs and profits, and to make go/no-go decisions on the basis of often only partial results?

very much	to a degree	very little	none
☐	☐	☐	☐
3	2	1	0

13. Do you have knowledge of business management, or any special aspects of it, such as accounting, control, systems analysis or data processing?

very much	to a degree	very little	none
☐	☐	☐	☐
3	2	1	0

14. Can you think of any other qualities or attributes you have that would be helpful in the successful running of a mail-order business: if so, list them here, and score yourself on the same basis, from high to low:

____

____

____

☐	☐	☐	☐
3	2	1	0

Have you filled out this questionnaire? Take it seriously, but don't agonize over the answers. Just put down what you think is the honest, proper response. No use fooling yourself. But then do one more thing: read the questions to your wife (or, if you are not married, to someone who knows you very well, personally and in business) and ask him/her to answer these questions for you. Then compare your answers with his/hers. If you have answered honestly, you will find that most of the "checker's" answers will be the same as yours or not more than one notch apart. If they are one notch apart, think it through once more (don't discuss it with your wife or friend) and make the correction if you think it's appropriate. If you are more than one notch apart (especially on more than one question) you either haven't been truly honest with yourself, your wife or friend doesn't really know you as well as you thought, or either of you didn't understand the questions.

Now this questionnaire/checklist has to be taken with a slight grain of salt. You've seen these things in Sunday supplements — such as "are you a good husband?", for instance. If you get 30 points or more you are every maiden's dream, and if you get fewer than 30 points you are a rat. If you give yourself 3 points for every "very much" answer, all the way down to "0" for any "none" answer you can obviously get a maximum of 42 points, and a minimum of "0" points. You don't need an industrial psychologist, me, or anybody else to tell you that if you get 42 points, you're a natural genius for the mail-order business, you should get started immediately, and please don't waste another precious minute — there's a lot of money out there waiting for you. And if you score "0" (not too likely, because you would not be reading this book) you probably know already that you are not destined to be a success in the mail-order business.

So, that leaves all those in-betweens, scoring from 1 to 41. I believe that, on the basis of this checklist, we can, between the two of us, make a pretty good analysis of your chances for success in starting and running a mail-order business.

Score 1 to 10. Your chances for success aren't really very good right now. If you scored high on at least two out of questions (1), (2), or (3), you may try to take some courses or other instruction to improve yourself in some of the more "technical" aspects. I would advise you against going into any business just yet. It doesn't look as if you are ready.

Score 11 to 20. You are a borderline case. Your chances, of course, are better the closer you are to 20. Again, if you scored pretty well on (1), (2), and (3) — which are in a way the most important questions (and should, therefore, really carry more weight because they express your inherent personality traits) — you should be doing all right. With reasonable effort, you could improve your "score" (which means really your ability to succeed) on points (4), (5) and (7). Do proceed with caution. Get started if you feel confidence and the urge, but make a real effort to acquire some "points" in areas in which you struck out.

Score 21 to 30. Your chances for success in the mail-order business are from quite good to very good. With this kind of score, I shall assume that you did well in (1), (2) and (3) and you probably have at least three or four areas of "technical" strength on which you should try to build. That means that you should exploit your abilities in these fields and get competent outside help for those areas in which you need assistance. My advice is to take stock once more, work out your business plans (you will know how to do that after you are finished with this book), and take the jump. Chances are that you will succeed.

Score 31 to 41. You would seem to be a natural for this business and I can see no reason why you shouldn't go ahead and get started just as soon as possible. You obviously have many areas of strength to build on, many talents that you can immediately bring to bear and exploit. Sit down and work out your business plan — and just be careful not to make any really bad blunders. Because your only possible danger is that you are perhaps too smart and too savvy. You might, therefore, tend to be over-confident and be tempted to jump into a situation with both feet when others, less talented, might tread more carefully. But you are pretty much of a cinch to make a success in the mail-order business.

I hope that your score was in one of the two highest groups, because, unless you stub your toe badly, you should have pretty smooth sailing. If you are in one of the two lower groups, follow the suggestions that I have given you. But above all, please remember two things:

1. A questionnaire is just that. It is meant to bracket you, but it's far from being an accurate tool. You can have a low score and still become a roaring success. And you

can score in the top 10 percentile and still lose your shirt in business. But the fellow that graduated in the top 10% of his medical school class is more likely to become a top surgeon than the one who graduated in the bottom 10%, isn't he?

2. The most important questions, I believe, are the "personal traits" of questions (1), (2) and (3). You should proceed with some caution if you scored low in these, even if your over-all score is high. On the contrary, if your over-all score is on the low side, but you scored staunchly on those questions you have a pretty good bet. You can always hire "technicians" and specialists. The personal qualities, the ability to forge ahead in the face of adversity, to be able to organize yourself, are the essence of your personality. They are indispensable traits for success and cannot be hired or bought.

WHAT TO NAME YOUR NEW MAIL-ORDER COMPANY?

Now let's turn for a moment to an entirely different topic: the naming of your new mail-order company. You may think that this is something on which you should not waste much time — just about any name will do. I must agree that it is perhaps not the most important thing in the world, but it is worthy of your attention and careful thought. Because you are not just trying to start a business that will make you a living: you are going to create a property that you will eventually wish to sell for a million dollars or more. Such a property has to have class and the right kind of image from its very beginning. While there is a whole lot more to creating class and image — and we'll hear much about this as we go along — the name of your business can have positive, neutral or negative connotations. Naturally, you will try for a positive connotation.

Don't deprecate the name: we shall never know, but I have a feeling that Xerox might not be what it is today if it had called itself "Amalgamated Copy Machines Corporation." And could Adolf Hitler have created as much disaster as he did, if he had kept his original name and his fanatical followers had had to scream "Heil Schicklgruber?"

The name of your company should, by all means, be catchy. It should be a name that people can remember, that sounds well, rolls easily off the tongue and that looks well graphically. And it must be a name that you can register and that is not already used by some other company. There can be really very few things more annoying and disheartening than to have established a whole series of ads and promotional material, letterheads, legal registrations, etc., and then to get a registered letter from somebody's attorney, usually from some other state, informing you that you are infringing on his client's name. This problem should not arise in your own jurisdiction or in your own state, because your state's Corporation Commissioner won't give you a charter to operate if the name you selected is already taken. But as a mail-order business you will want to be able to work in all jurisdictions and in all states. You could be in serious difficulties if the name you have chosen is already taken in any state in which your ads appear, especially if there is any possibility of "confusion" in the public's mind. If you have a Chicago mail-order business, specializing in optical goods, you shouldn't have too many problems if there is a bakery in Salem, Oregon, by the same name. But it pays to be careful, and you might want to discuss with your attorney to: 1. make a search to be sure that the name chosen is not being used competitively; and 2. to register the name, because you expect the name to become a valuable property within a few years from now.

I have little question that just the name, Henniker's — nothing else — is worth between $100,000 to $200,000 right now. It is a name that has been associated with quality and service for years, and for which literally hundreds of millions of advertising impressions have been created. So naturally, it is valuable. It is registered and trademarked, and nobody can take it away. Do think of your own company's name in these terms.

After thinking about it for a while and poking around, I determined that geographical names are best because they have no apparent meaning. Just as in a Rorschach test, any connotation is formed in the customer's mind (and you will try to influence that). I had also concluded that place names from the south of England had the most pleasing sound to the American ear. When I started Haverhill's, I did indeed go to the map of south England, but could not find anything that really pleased me. I figured that if I didn't find what I wanted in England, I should look to New England and I concentrated on Massachusetts, a state for which I have some special affection. I came up with three names that I liked, namely

Concord, Barnstable and Haverhill. I found that there was already a somewhat similar business operating under the name of Barnstable. Concord seemed to have too many other connotations, and mostly reminded me of Manischewitz wine. I, therefore, decided on Haverhill.* I added the "s" for no particular reason, only because I thought it looked good, and because such worthy companies as Macy's, Bloomingdale's, Gimbel's and many others had done the same. They seemed to be doing all right, so I figured I should emulate them.

Frankly, I have never been to Haverhill, Mass. But from the inception and creation of my first company, I had always associated it with beautiful merchandise and nice things. I had the most romantic notions about it and somehow imagined Haverhill as a place surpassing in beauty and romance such localities as Cannes, Acapulco or St. Moritz.

Unfortunately, it turned out on later research that Haverhill, far from being in any way exotic, was a somewhat grim mill town whose best days seemed to be long past. More disconcerting was the startling discovery of the existence of a disease called the "Haverhill Plague." It is transmitted by rats and, at least according to my medical friends, "makes the bubonic plague look like the chicken pox."

Well, this association did not seem to do us any harm. When I finally left Haverhill's, we had close to one million loyal and satisfied customers who, in their great majority, did indeed associate Haverhill's with beautiful, romantic, useful and practical things. There are only about 40,000 folks now living in Haverhill, Mass., so you can safely say that there are many more people in this country who connect the name of Haverhill's with the great business that we had created, rather than with the city for which it had been named.

I followed a somewhat similar procedure in the naming of my new company, namely Henniker's. Henniker is a town in New

---

* A little footnote for the geography freaks among you: it wasn't until years later that I told one of my British friends about how I had spotted Haverhill in Massachusetts, after not being able to find anything suitable in south England, as I had hoped. He was amazed, whipped out his atlas and showed me a town in south England by the name of Haverhill, just about 50 miles northeast of London. I just hadn't seen it on my first search.

Hampshire, and if it has any claim to fame (so far), it is that it is the birthplace of Louise Beach, a somewhat obscure, but rather pleasant American composer. Naturally, I hope and fully expect that I shall be able to do for Henniker, New Hampshire, what I did for Haverhill, Massachusetts.

You should also be concerned about the graphic appearance of your firm's name. Certain letters are graphically more "elegant" than others; certain combinations of letters look more pleasing. I find that letters with "ascenders" (b, d, f, h, k, l, t) are in general more pleasing to the eye than letters without them. Also, certain letters take less space than others (i, l, and perhaps t) and you can make your "logo" graphically more pleasing and more compact if you use them. I always thought that "dunhill," the famous international tobacco firm, had one of the most pleasant sounding and graphically most attractive trademarks in the United States, particularly the syllable, "hill." I must confess that I was not quite unaware of the graphic good looks of the "dunhill" name and its pleasing sound when I finally decided on Haverhill's as the name for my first company.

One small point, in conclusion, on this topic. If you possibly can, stay away from letters with "descenders" (g, j, p, q, y). It is not that they are particularly unattractive, but in combination with ascending letters, your logo will take up more space than it should. You may learn very quickly that space is an expensive commodity and you, therefore, do not wish to waste it.

Once you have decided on a name, get together with your "advertising man" (we shall talk about him later) and tell him to give you several (at least six) proposals for the "logo" of your company. That is the special style, the "trademark" if you wish, in which your name will always appear. Listen to his advice, but ultimately make your own decision. You will have to live with the name and with the logo for a long time. To change either is a major undertaking; so the time to be picky and choosy is now!

YOU'LL HAVE TO START THINKING ABOUT WHAT TO SELL

Obviously, in order to start in business you have to have a line of products to sell. This is the "nut" of your business because without products you don't have a business, you don't have anything, however prettily you present it. The selection of merchandise and dunhill

Haverhill's

haverhill's

henniker's

The Dunhill logo is perhaps one of the most elegant. Our first Haverhill's logo was too ornate, too ''gingerbready,'' so we modernized it and made it more in line with what we and our merchandise represented. With Henniker's we hit the right ''image'' on the first try.

the establishment of a line of merchandise is such an important topic that we shall give the whole next chapter to it and come back to it — in other parts of the book. Let's just make a few points right now:

- You should definitely have more than one product — it will be impossible to sustain your business, even over a short period of time, with one product alone, unless you are lucky enough to catch on to a super blockbuster like the Hula Hoop. This, unfortunately, happens very seldom and you should not plan on it.
- You need more than one product, because it is a cardinal rule, never to be broken, that you should make a merchandise offer, an attempt to sell something else to your customer, with every package, every letter, every communication you send out. Just like the first kiss, the first sale is always the most difficult, and in merchandising it is the hardest and most expensive part.
- Once you have gained your customer's confidence by the quality of your merchandise and service it is comparatively inexpensive and much easier to make a follow-up sale. After all, your customer now knows that you can be trusted and that your merchandise lives up to what you promised. By making him a "bounceback" offer you are doing it to a willing and almost captive audience.
- Consider very seriously to start out with an attractive, but inexpensive item that will be a "self-liquidator" — that is one in which you hope to recover your merchandise cost and space cost, but do not expect to make any or much additional profit. The purpose of this is to get as many established customers as quickly as possible to whom, at relatively small cost, you can then send other and more lucrative merchandise offers.

We developed this successful "self-liquidator" concept at Haverhill's and it has since been widely copied. Our first offer of such a self-liquidator was *Mack-the-Knife,* which has become an advertising classic. I am showing you here the original version of this ad. In the large quantities in which we purchased Mack-the-Knife, we had a landed cost of $.35 per knife. Our "fulfillment cost" — processing the order, packing it and mailing it out cost us an

Mack the Knife was the first promotional ad that Haverhill's launched and perhaps the first ad of this kind ever in the United States. The $1 price and the $2 Gift Certificate proved irresistible. It created tens of thousands of fine customers for Haverhill's and did so at a profit. When Mack returned to Henniker's three years later, we had to sell him for $1.99.

additional $.25. Thus, by selling Mack-the-Knife for $1.00 we had a $.40 profit contribution per unit. Now, alas, things have changed and we have to charge $1.99 for the same item. Naturally, that makes it much less attractive. We ran "Mack" for years, in scores of consumer publications and always with success. Take, for instance *The New Yorker.* In the old Haverhill's days, one column (the size of this ad) cost us approximately $1,000. We would never sell fewer than 4,000 knives off such an ad and would gain 4,000 new customers. We would have a net profit of approximately $600, namely 4,000 x $.40, less the $1,000 cost of the ad. While this does not seem like a very large amount of money, please keep in mind that we did have 4,000 new names. I shall show you later that each of these names may be worth as much as $3 to $5 — and we acquired them at a *net profit* to us of about $.15 each. This is quite remarkable if you consider that the average mail-order house is delighted if they can acquire a new customer at a *cost* of $1 each, or perhaps even more.

Have a good look at the "Mack" ad. We shall discuss it some more when we talk about space advertising. But let's bring out some interesting points now:

- You will notice that we offer a $2 Gift Certificate with the purchase of the knife; this credit could be applied to the next (real!) purchase.
- In order to reduce processing costs and avoid problems with our bank, we request that the $1 be sent in cash. We found this to be helpful. It's easier for people to take a dollar out of their wallets and slip it into an envelope than to write a check. We also found, however, that a dollar is pretty much the limit in cash that people will entrust to the mails.

  We tried a similar program on a two-dollar article some time later and found that asking for cash caused many anxieties. It was preferable to ask for a $2 check instead. Since, in the case of Mack-the-Knife and similar promotions, we asked for a flat dollar, we could not charge sales tax and, therefore, had to absorb that for California deliveries. I don't know about your state, but under California law you may not state in any promotion that you are absorbing the tax. You may do it if you wish, but you are not allowed to advertise it.

Later in this book when we talk about space advertising, I shall give you other examples of self-liquidators. Unfortunately, the time of the $1 self-liquidator is over, a victim of inflation. It's practically impossible to get any reasonable kind of merchandise at a cost which, including fulfillment expenses, will pay its way, let alone leave you any kind of reasonable margin if you limit yourself to charging just a dollar.* So we switched to "$1 plus $.50 for postage" items or even to $2 items. They were not quite as wildly successful as the "straight buck" items, but would, almost without exception, make a profit and gain us many new customers. One self-liquidator that many companies have tried successfully (although Haverhill's never did it, it just wasn't our style) was packs of little stick-on labels with the customer's name and address. This seems to have been profitable to quite a few companies, but I believe that they have run their course. There are so many of them around now that I doubt that they can still be successfully used.

FROM THE VERY FIRST, THINK OF CUSTOMER SERVICE!

But we are still in the formative stages of your business. Here is another point that you should keep in mind. Under no circumstances give yourself a P. O. Box address. Be sure to give yourself a regular business address, with street and house number prominently stated. The greatest hurdle to overcome in mail order is to convince the customer that you are on the up-and-up. A post office box number makes the customer hesitant and suspicious, because he doesn't know exactly where you are. You may be a "fly-by-night," and he might not be able to locate you, he can never come and punch you in the nose if you did not fulfill his order properly or if you took off with his money for Brazil or other points south.

It is absolutely essential for success in the mail-order business to remember that behind every check there is a real person who entrusted his money to you. And that person expects (and has a right to expect) the best service and merchandise as advertised. By the time you handle hundreds of orders and hundreds of checks a day, it is easy to forget that and to think of the mechanics, rather

* As you will see in the chapter about space advertising, however, we have developed an extremely successful "FREE" promotion — our ORGANIZER. Unfortunately, as you know, there is no "free lunch" and you will find that the "FREE" ORGANIZER is not really entirely "free."

than the people. But these are very real people out there. It is up to you to gain their confidence. And one of the requirements to gain that confidence is to let them know, right in your advertising, exactly where you are conducting your business.

At Haverhill's we felt so strongly about it that we immediately sent a postcard to every customer acknowledging the order. As postage rates increased, we found to our regret that this became so expensive that we could no longer afford it. But we did have (and still do have) one solid rule: if shipment of any order, for any reason at all, will be delayed for more than one week, we send the customer a postcard acknowledging the order, informing him of the delay, and of the approximate expected shipment date. At the same time we offer refund if desired. I show you examples of such post-cards. You may be pleased to know that the great majority of customers so notified will prefer to wait for the merchandise (provided they can expect it within a reasonable time), rather than have their money back. They want mostly to be reassured that they have contact with a concerned human being and that they are not being neglected, turned over to a computer or intentionally being ripped off.

Every communication with your customer should reflect your seriousness and that of your business. Remember, it is serious business for anybody to send you money. Therefore, in order to reassure your customer of your concern and professionalism, every package, every communication, every letter that goes out should reflect this spirit and this attitude. While you don't need anything super-fancy — after all, you are a business, not a society dowager — the quality of your letters and printed matter should reflect the stamp of quality that you wish to impart on your business. This is one area in which you should not be stingy and in which you should be prepared to spend some money. Do things properly and with quality, right from the beginning!

These are just a few quick thoughts. This area of customer service is so important, so vital to the success of your mail-order business, that we shall take a whole chapter, later in this book, to deal with just this topic.

SOME FIRST THOUGHTS ABOUT ADVERTISING

What makes the mail-order business "go" is, of course, the advertising of the merchandise that you have selected. You have

WE SHALL GET YOU ORGANIZED
BEFORE THE END OF MAY!

Dear Customer:

After running just one test ad of our nifty ORGANIZER in The National Observer and in one regional edition of The Wall Street Journal we are up to our armpits in orders and digging out methodically and sucessfully.

We are proud of you and all of our other fine customers: they know a good deal and a fine item when they see one.

Your dollar has been received. Shipping procedures on these "mass promotions" are somewhat different than on regular merchandise and things take a little longer. Your ORGANIZER will be shipped, not later than May 20, and you should have it within ten days or so thereafter.

We thought you would be glad to have this word of assurance that all is well. You will be very pleased with your ORGANIZER. We, of course, are delighted to have you as a customer (if you are not yet one) and hope to have many future occasions to serve you.

Thanks and best regards,

Chris Simpson
Chris Simpson
Customer Service

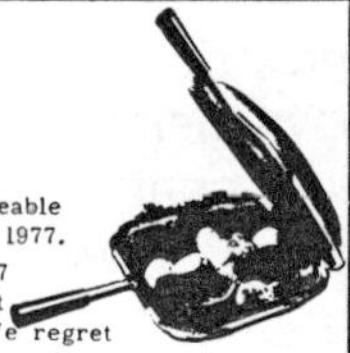

henniker's 779 Bush St., Box 7584, San Francisco, CA 94120

We are in trouble -- we are out of LA BISQUERA '77.

We are being overwhelmed and snowed under for what knowledgeable gourmets consider to be the most valuable cooking discovery of 1977.

We shall not be able to fulfill your order for LA BISQUERA '77 until the third week of April. This means that you will have it by the end of April or, at the latest, the first week of May. We regret that deeply because our business and our relationship with our customers is based on filling orders within 48 hours of receipt.

But wait, please -- don't say "I knew it, same old story, here we go again, etc."

1. We are not cashing your check -- we are not debiting your BA or MC account until we actually ship LA BISQUERA '77 to you.
2. You are entitled to immediate service and prompt shipment. If you feel that you don't wish to wait for your LA BISQUERA '77, return this card to us with your notation "REFUND" (give your BA/MC number if it applies) and we shall fulfill your wish. Naturally, we hope you you won't do that, because we really think that LA BISQUERA '77 will add a new dimension to your cooking and eating experience. But if that is what you prefer, that is what we'll do.

One piece of 'good news': The price of LA BISQUERA '77 had to be increased to $16.95 because of unrelenting cost pressure on the manufacturing end. Naturally, your order, even if a charge, will be honored at the old price.

Again, we regret the delay and we thank you for your courtesy!

Chris Simpson Chris Simpson, Customer Services C.S 73-2

Postcards that tell the customer that there will be a delay with his order. We send these out for all orders that will be delayed for more than one week. Since non-receipt of merchandise is the most frequent customer service complaint in the mail-order business, it behooves you to keep all such delays to the absolute minimum and, in the rare case that they do occur, to notify your customers promptly.

now organized and started your business. You now have to give some thought to the creation of this advertising. In the course of this book we shall talk about space advertising, direct mail advertising and catalog advertising. And I hope that by the time we get through, even if you do not have any previous experience in this field, you and your staff will be able to create such advertising—the lifeblood of your mail-order business — right on your own premises. At least, even if you don't create it yourself, you will be able to judge intelligently the work that outside agencies create for you. You will be able to accept or reject it and make valuable suggestions for improvement.

But in the beginning stage, unless you have considerable experience yourself or unless you are associated with somebody who has such experience, my advice to you is not to attempt either to write or to design your own mail-order ads. It is definitely not a field for the do-it-yourself enthusiast, but a highly professional task. Keep in mind that any ad you put into a publication has to compete in attractiveness, in attention and "pull" with every other ad in that publication. A so-so, humdrum ad will simply not do the job, regardless of how good the product is.

Since you will need advertising help immediately, even for the creation of your logo, I thought it would be to your advantage if I gave it some mention in this "start-up" chapter.

There are reputable and successful mail-order agencies in many parts of the country (most are concentrated in the New York area, in Chicago or on the West Coast). You may wish to write to the Direct Marketing Magazine, 224 7th Street, Garden City, New York 11530. They will be glad to give you a list of suitable agencies or free lance agents in your area. When you write to these agents, be sure to ask them for samples of their work and quite frankly discuss their fees with them. Be sure that you also understand that, in addition to the fee, production expenses will apply.

A somewhat "sticky" point may be the matter of advertising commissions. This (except in special cases) is 15% of the cost of advertising placed. Of course, these commissions should go to the agency, and not to you. For large accounts, that is all the agency would get — just the commission. They could not afford and would not do that with you. Your account is too small. But it would be proper, and generally acceptable that you work with your agency on a fixed fee minimum basis, against which earned commissions would be counted. It is also possible that you may deal with an agency or an agent that is only interested in creating advertising against a fixed fee without wishing to place advertising for you. In such a case, it behooves you to form a "house agency" as quickly as possible, so that the commissions won't be "lost" and you can earn them yourself.

A "house agency" would, for legal and accounting purposes, be identical with your corporation, but it would be doing business under a "fictitious name." You may think that this "fictitious name" business sounds somewhat shady, but it is quite on the up-and-up and perfectly legal. Your attorney friend will tell you how to go about it. Having a house agency has the great advantage that you will be entitled to the agency discount of 15%, plus another 2% if you pay on the 10th of the month following the advertising schedule. As soon as your advertising budget reaches even a moderate level, say, $3,000 to $5,000 per month, you will come close to paying your creative expenses out of that commission. The, as your advertising expenditures become more substantial, $6,000 to $20,000 per month, advertising commissions that you earn will not just pay your creative expense but will become an actual source of profit for you.

Most publications will good-naturedly and without any fuss accept your hosue agency and allow your discount. They appreciate your business, they don't want any hassle. The payment they expect is really the stated rate ("rate card" rate) less 15%, and they realize that somebody has to pay the cost of creating the advertising — either you or an outside agency. If you have not yet established your credit, they may ask you for pre-payment, but that is a different story. Some very few publications refuse to recognize house agencies and decline to grant the 15% discount, except to "recognized agencies." It is my personal opinion — supported by a few of my attorney friends — that they are on very shaky legal ground and possibly liable to restraint of trade in doing that. But if given a reasonable chance to accept the fiction of an "independent and bonafide agency" most all publications will not quarrel with the house agency concept.

YOU CAN'T WORK WITHOUT CREDIT CARDS

One other thing you should do right away is to set up a relationship with MasterCharge and BankAmericard, now in the process of being combined into one, namely "VISA." Depending on your volume, they will charge you a commission from 2% to 3% of sales for their service. It is a good investment. Except for your promotional items, namely the self-liquidators that you sell for $1 or $2, you should encourage your customers to use MC or BA. It is practically impossible to conduct a mail-order business without it. If you do not offer credit card service you will deprive yourself of such a large proportion of sales that you will be unable to operate profitably. You do not need the customer's credit card. Your customer simply puts his account number and expiration date on the coupon and that is all there is to it. If you have any reason to question a number or if the amount of the order exceeds the "floor limit" that MC or BA have granted you, you can call a toll-free number, verify the card and get authorization to charge in just a matter of seconds.

You may ask what about the other cards — American Express, Diner's Club, Carte Blanche. The answer is simple: forget it! There are four principal reasons:

1. Their discount rates are much higher than those of BA or MC — around 6% or more. That does take a bite out of your profits.
2. You can treat a BA or MC draft just like a check. This means that your checking account is credited the minute you deposit the draft, just as if you deposited a check. But with American Express, Diner's Club or Carte Blanche, you may have to wait weeks before you get credit.
3. If there is ever any problem, a misunderstanding, an improper debit, you can, by using BA or MC, usually straighten it out with somebody in your bank, right on the telephone. With the "prestige cards" it is usually a long hassle and often a lost cause.
4. About everybody who has credit cards — regardless of what other cards he carries — has either BA or MC (or both). Don't worry about the few that don't. Most of those probably don't "believe in" credit cards anyway and will send you a check if they like your offer.

There is another "must" in this business: it is a *toll-free telephone order line.* You need immediate access to credit cards, from the first day you open your business. The toll-free line, though eventually indispensable, can wait until later, let's say until you process something like fifty orders per day. The reason that you don't want this service right away is that it would burden you with a monthly fixed overhead that you can't really afford at this point and that wouldn't be warranted by your volume. But we'll talk about this in some detail later in this book.

TWO OTHER WAYS TO GET INTO THE MAIL-ORDER BUSINESS

This chapter would not be complete without telling you about two other ways of getting into the mail-order business:

1. You can get into one of these "Mail-Order Courses" — "Buy Wholesale — We Do Everything for You — Profits Assured" deals that you will see advertised regularly, especially in mass publications.
2. You can buy an existing, going mail-order business.

As to the first, my heartfelt and urgent advice is to stay away altogether. The standard proposition is that you "join the organization" (it usually costs about $100) and that you buy a certain number of catalogs — there is usually a minimum, and the price per catalog goes down slightly the more catalogs you buy. This is supposed to be an incentive for you to place a hefty order. The firm you are dealing with — your "coach, sponsor and benefactor" — will kindly imprint your name and address on the catalogs "without charge."

The merchandise featured in the catalog is usually humdrum and commonplace, the kind of stuff that is easily available in any dime store or hardware store, usually at lower cost. The deal, after you have purchased the catalogs, is to procure mailing lists (if you don't yet know what these are, we shall talk about them later on), send the catalogs out and wait for the money and the orders to roll in. (The ads touting those deals often show a beaming couple holding fistfuls of bills of large denominations). Then, all you have to do is to take your cut, send the balance to your sponsor, who will then (hopefully) forward the merchandise to your customer. Everything is drop-shipped — "No Investment Necessary."

This is the essence of the proposition. There is also usually some mumbo-jumbo about teaching you the mail-order business, but it is window dressing and quite incidental. The promoter's whole idea is to get your membership fee, sell you the catalogs at a profit and also to get his cut of the profits of whatever merchandise you may be able to sell.

Everything is wrong with this deal. If there is anybody (besides the promoter) that has ever made any money with it, it is not recorded in any literature on the subject nor known by anybody in the field. There is no need to go into a lot of detail, but the main flaws are:

- It is impossible to take a catalog, send it to a "cold" list and produce enough revenue to come close to paying for the catalog, let alone making money on the merchandise. We won't count the cost of your time at all. But in addition to the catalog cost and mailing costs, you will have to rent mailing lists which is a minor science and costs quite a bit of money!
- You will sell very little, but — as is usual in the mail-order business — there will be returns, complaints, adjustments, etc. — in all likelihood more than one would usually expect, because now there is a third party (namely your "sponsor") between you and the customer. But you are responsible, you have to refund the entire amount to your dissatisfied customer and it is up to you to try to return faulty or refused merchandise to your "sponsor" and get your money back. You might not find it all that easy.
- If this were such a good deal or even if it were a feasible deal, you might wonder why your sponsor would want to share this bonanza with you. He could just put *his* name on the catalogs, send them out to those fine lists, and get all the profits himself, rather than place expensive advertising in papers and magazines, recruit you and split those profits with you. And, of course. the reason he does not do it is that it can't be done — the way to profits for him is to get *vou* into the picture.
- There is one good feature about this kind of deal, and I think it is fair to mention it. It usually won't cost you more than a few hundred dollars to find out that you have been

had, and you will be a wiser person for it. So you have had a fairly inexpensive education. There are unfortunately many con games around that are much more expensive.

As to the second deal — to buy somebody else's going mail-order business, it is, of course, more difficult to generalize. Let's just say that extreme caution is in order.

In general, unless forced by ill health, old age, or other really weighty reasons, people just don't sell businesses that provide them with a good and pleasant living. Naturally, they might be inclined to do so if they can capitalize their yearly net earnings and cash out very advantageously. Therefore, unless you know what the weighty reasons for wishing to sell are, you must consider the possibility of some hidden joker, obsolete inventory, "imaginative bookkeeping," declining market, or new competition in this business that the owner knows about but does not wish to reveal.

You can probe as much as you wish, but you won't find out what the seller does not wish you to know.

The chance that you will be able to pick up a winner is small. It might be possible to find a small business with some semblance of reality to it. This might be so in case of the owner's sickness or perhaps in case of the owner's having died and his widow's or his estate's wishing to dispose of this business.

Because of the extreme caution required, the only deal you should consider is this:

1. Offer to work as an employee/manager for this business for an agreed-upon period — say three to six months. You should receive a modest, but reasonable salary during that period. You will learn to understand the business in that time, know whether you would really like to own and run it and, most important, you will locate any skeletons that might be rattling around in the closets. If your seller is on the up-and-up, he will agree to this deal, especially if the "employment" period is reasonably short (but three months is minimum) and if your remuneration during the period is moderate.
2. Get an option to buy the business at an agreed-upon price within that period.

3. What should the option price be? A ballpark figure would be 80% to 100% of net worth (assets less liabilities), plus your first year's actual after-tax profits, after having paid yourself a reasonable salary. The first portion (the net worth part) should be payable either immediately or in one or two installments; the second part (first year's profit) might be payable within three months after the end of that year.

This is sort of a basic formula on which all kinds of variants can be played. Your attorney might advise you not to buy the business itself, but just the assets of the business, including "goodwill." "Goodwill" means the name, reputation, mailing lists, etc., plus its value as a "going business." His possible reason for that approach would be that you could not then be surprised and clobbered at a later date with any hidden liabilities or liens, which either were not known or intentionally not disclosed.

Very important, of course, is to verify assets. This means careful checking of inventory by count and value (if cost has gone up, you have a right to insist on the original cost basis) and particularly for obsolescence (check how many of each item have moved in, say, the last six months). If the business has accounts receivable, check their collectability and age. Receivables, however, usually do not play an important role in the mail-order business. Furniture and fixtures at their depreciated values are usually okay — they are generally not a large part of the total package of assets. Do not consider as assets any "intangibles," such as prepared ads, printing plates, etc. You are taking care of all that with the bonus above net worth (first year's profit) that you are willing to pay.

We don't have to emphasize that you need your attorney at one elbow and your accountant at the other for this kind of deal. To repeat: chances to find the right thing are small, and you should be very cautious. But it is possible, and could be of especial interest to you if the line of business is one in which you have previous experience and great personal interest. For instance, if everything else checks out, and if you are an experiences outdoorsman, you might do well with a small mail-order business that handles a line of outdoor hunting and fishing equipment, etc.

And don't forget one thing: after you buy that business, you will still need working capital to operate it, so be sure to make provision for that.

SUMMARY OF THIS CHAPTER

I suggest we stop at this point, before I spin your head with too many details on how to start your mail-order business. We shall come back to business organization — for a going, rather than a start-up business — later in this book. We are going to have a change of pace now. For the next few chapters we shall talk about merchandising and advertising, which are perhaps more interesting than organizational, financial, and legal matters.

Before we go into that, however, and since we have covered quite a lot of ground in this chapter, let's just briefly summarize what we have talked about.

- *Myth Destroyed.* Don't under-finance yourself. Try to have $5,000 to $10,000 available to start your mail-order business. Invest about one-quarter as "equity" and three-quarters as a loan to your new company.
- *Relationship with Bank.* If you already have a bank, use it. If not, you will usually be better off with a small bank. Prepare personal financial statements, be prepared to sign personally for all bank loans, prepare a business plan and financial projections.
- *Business Organization.* You will probably be best advised to start as a "Subchapter S" corporation, and then switch later to a "regular" corporation, as soon as you feel that you are solidly in the black.
- *Attorney, Accountant, Insurance Man.* You will need all three, and you will probably be best off with young, sharp, lean and hungry guys (or gals) who will grow with you and whose inflated overhead you won't have to support.
- *Myth Reaffirmed.* Yes, you can start your mail-order business while you keep your present job. In fact, I urge you to do it, and to keep your job as long as possible.
- *Check Yourself.* Go back over the check list in this chapter, assess your strengths and weaknesses for the mail-order business. Let this help you decide whether you should really go into this at all, whether you should go into it now, or whether you should postpone it or forget it altogether.
- *Name of Company.* Pick a name without specific meaning — geographical names are pretty good. Be sure they sound

good and are graphically attractive. Make sure the name is available. Have your attorney check, if necessary. Register the name.

- *Merchandise.* Start thinking of a line of merchandise. Consider "self-liquidators" as starters. Include bona fide merchandise offers with each package you send out.
- *Customer Services.* From the very beginning, consider the customer "king" (really believe it!). Try not to create situations that make customer correspondence necessary. Answer all correspondence and inquiries promptly and be aware of anxieties of people who send money through the mail. Notify customers immediately about any delays and offer money back.
- *Advertising.* Unless you have such talents yourself, make provision for advertising. Again, your best bet is "lean and hungry" — in this case an arrangement with a small agency or free-lance copywriter and art director with previous mail-order experience. Create a house agency.
- *Credit Cards.* Get affiliated with MasterCharge and Bank-Americard (now VISA). Forget about all the others.
- *Mail-Order Courses — Catalog Deals.* Stay away altogether. There is no way in the world that you can make out on such a deal.
- *Buying a Going Mail-Order Business.* Extreme caution is in order and you should be convinced of soundness of reason for selling. Good and reasonable deals are hard to find. Might be of interest if you have special experience in the product line. Consider only on employment basis, with option to buy.

You may be getting a little nervous or a little confused by now. You know how to organize a mail-order business and how to get started. But, so far, you have nothing to sell and perhaps not even any really good idea of what *kind* of merchandise you *should* deal in. Patience — in the next chapter we'll find out what you are best suited for and we shall learn where and how to find merchandise for your new mail-order business.

Chapter 2

ALL YOU'LL EVER WANT TO KNOW ABOUT MAIL-ORDER MERCHANDISE

The thing that is different in writing a book from what happens in real life or in real business is that publishers like to have their authors tidy everything up neatly, put it into chapters and have one thing follow the other.

It isn't like that in real life and in business. Every housewife knows it: she doesn't just make one dinner dish and then start on the next one. No, everything is sort of stewing at the same time, and in between she might cut her boy's hair, make a couple of telephone calls about the car pool and the PTA meeting, feed the dog and get the table set.

Chances are that you are now employed in some business, and it is the same story, of course: you may be writing a memorandum on a sales meeting, take a couple of phone calls on entirely different topics, field some questions from the boss who just happens to "drop in" (doesn't that man ever take a vacation?), and try to soothe your secretary who is pouting because you gave her a semi-dirty look after her third coffee break before 10:30.

And, of course, the same is true in starting a new business, your new mail-order business. We have talked about how to start and organize your business. In this chapter we are going to talk about how to find the right kind of merchandise, how to create a line of items that people will want to buy from you, that will establish your business identity and that will help you toward your goal of a million dollar business.

THE REAL LOWDOWN ON PROMOTIONAL MERCHANDISE

Obviously, your thinking about merchandise — and many other things that we shall discuss in the following chapters — goes on at the same time as your thinking about your business organization. In fact, it is likely that it even came first. You might have had some pretty fair idea of what you were going to sell in your mail-order business before you started actually to organize it. And as you went ahead with organization, you probably thought more and more in detail about merchandise. Not just about merchandise, but about advertising and much besides.

But in a book, it has to be one thing at a time. So this chapter deals only with merchandise.

We sort of snuck in one thought about merchandise in the last chapter, and that was about "promotional items." (Remember Mack-the-Knife?). Since we have already gotten started on that, let's go into it a little more deeply.

Casting undue modesty to the winds for the moment, let me tell you once more that I pioneered this concept at Haverhill's. It appears almost incredible to me today because it is such an obvious thing. Yet, like many others — how about putting beer in cans? — somebody had to think of and do it first. Telling you about this concept has to be worth several thousand times the value of this book to you if you follow my advice and go into the mail-order business. It is the most simple concept, but even my experienced associates at Time Inc. never fully understood what it was all about.

The principle is this:

- Every mail-order business is based on having customers. These customers must be true "believers," loyal and confident. Once you have gained that confidence, they will believe in your offers and will continue to buy from you.
- It is hard and expensive to gain customers by "conventional" means. By such means, it may cost anywhere from

$1 to $3 to gain a customer that "sticks." Few ordinary mortals have the kind of money to finance the acquisition of, say, 100,000 customers (about the minimum number for a really going mail-order business). Therefore, if you can find a way to acquire a large number of loyal customers directly, at no cost, and in all likelihood at a profit, you can put yourself quickly into orbit and on the way to glory with a very small investment. The way to do this is with *promotional merchandise.*

- Your promotional merchandise must be related to the main thrust of your business. For instance, if you are in the home sewing mail-order business, you don't want to use a paper weight with a picture of a girl in an ill-fitting bikini in it as a "promo." Of if your mail-order business is in outdoor equipment you don't want to use a religious calendar. Your "promo" must be related to your merchandising direction. For the home sewers, how about a thimble or some small travel scissors such as the Hennisnips. And for the outdoors people, how about a set of three "flies" or, of course, Mack-the-Knife.
- There will inevitably be a large number of "deadheads" among the "promo" buyers, those that are interested only in buying a "cheapie," but who will lose all interest when you later on offer them real merchandise. This may be as many as 20 to 40% of all "promo" buyers. We shall talk about techniques of how to get those people off your mailing list. In the meantime, don't worry! You made money on your initial transaction with them and if you follow my advice you'll keep most of it.

I shall tell you in a minute how I started merchandising in the mail-order business. As you will see, your approach will probably have to be different from mine. But, to get ahead of myself just some, my "thing" was the "executive gift" market, and I plowed this field faithfully and thoroughly until I merged with Time Inc. So, until then, my "promos" had to be restricted to items that fit that category. But when I merged Haverhill's into Time Inc., my market became quite literally "the world" because Haverhill's became based on advertising in *Life* (there was still life in *Life*), *Time, Sports Illustrated* and *Fortune.*

So we changed our "image," subtly, but fairly fast, from "Executive Gifts" to "Attractive Merchandise to All the World." There was a niche for almost any good promotion in our hutch.

And we came up with some absolute spectaculars. *Mack-the-Knife* was founder, granddaddy and most productive of the whole family. But he was just first among many. My guess is that we sold 500,000 Macks before the cost went up and we could no longer do it profitably at a dollar. And then we always got extra mileage (dollars) out of Mack because every package contained an offer for a sheath (that cost us $.20 and that we sold for a dollar). The beauty of it was that our fulfillment cost for this bounceback was close to nothing, because the customer filled out his own label and all we had to do was to slap it on the pre-packed jiffy bag that contained the sheath.

After Mack came *Cork Jet* (later re-dubbed "Jet 37"). I had my misgivings about it at first, because I learned that over 50% of all wine in the United States is drunk in California and New York. Therefore, since we were advertising in national mass media, such as *Time* and *Life*, and without any real possibility to carve out regional markets, I feared that we would have so much "wasted" circulation that it would defeat the whole project. It is true, California and New York always were the champs with Cork Jet, but we sold incredible quantities to Iowa, Arkansas, Nebraska and other states that the American Wine Institute may have virtually written off as markets. It is possible that we picked the raisins out of part of the cake with this attractive item, because it almost seemed as though we must have sold Cork Jets to every wine drinker in the United States.

And there were other incredibly successful promotions: there was the *Haverlite,* the *Big Dad* pen, the *Haversnips,* the *Mail Scale* and, almost as successful as Mack, *Havertools* of which we sold several hundred thousand.

In selling these promotional items, we didn't just make a customer and earn a quarter. Each of these promotional items was pre-packed by our manufacturer, and a letter of welcome and a mini-catalog (we shall talk later about techniques for these promotional materials) were included in every package as a "bounceback." We found that, on the average, about 2% of all customers would respond to the bounceback offer and that the average bounceback

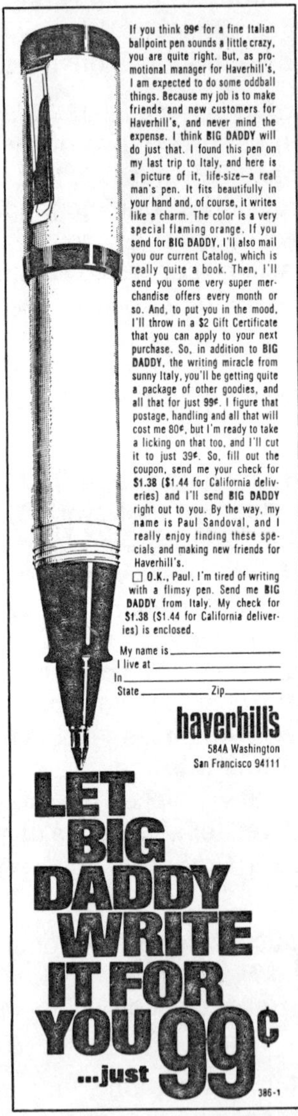

If you think 99¢ for a fine Italian ballpoint pen sounds a little crazy, you are quite right. But, as promotional manager for Haverhill's, I am expected to do some oddball things. Because my job is to make friends and new customers for Haverhill's, and never mind the expense. I think BIG DADDY will do just that. I found this pen on my last trip to Italy, and here is a picture of it, life-size—a real man's pen. It fits beautifully in your hand and, of course, it writes like a charm. The color is a very special flaming orange. If you send for BIG DADDY, I'll also mail you our current Catalog, which is really quite a book. Then, I'll send you some very super merchandise offers every month or so. And, to put you in the mood, I'll throw in a $2 Gift Certificate that you can apply to your next purchase. So, in addition to BIG DADDY, the writing miracle from sunny Italy, you'll be getting quite a package of other goodies, and all that for just 99¢. I figure that postage, handling and all that will cost me 80¢, but I'm ready to take a licking on that too, and I'll cut it to just 39¢. So, fill out the coupon, send me your check for $1.38 ($1.44 for California deliveries) and I'll send BIG DADDY right out to you. By the way, my name is Paul Sandoval, and I really enjoy finding these specials and making new friends for Haverhill's.
☐ O.K., Paul, I'm tired of writing with a flimsy pen. Send me BIG DADDY from Italy. My check for $1.38 ($1.44 for California deliveries) is enclosed.
My name is
I live at
In
State Zip
haverhill's
584A Washington
San Francisco 94111
LET BIG DADDY WRITE IT FOR YOU
...just 99¢
386-1

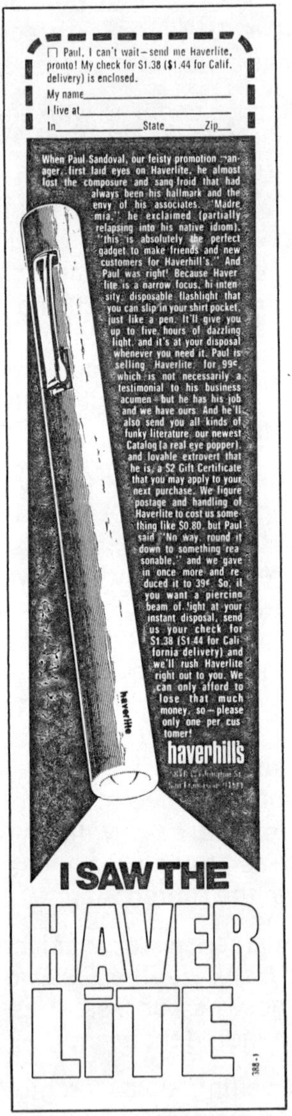

☐ Paul, I can't wait—send me Haverlite, pronto! My check for $1.38 ($1.44 for Calif. delivery) is enclosed.
My name
I live at
In State Zip
When Paul Sandoval, our feisty promotion manager, first laid eyes on Haverlite, he almost lost the composure and sang froid that had always been his hallmark and the envy of his associates. "Madre mia," he exclaimed (partially relapsing into his native idiom), "this is absolutely the perfect gadget to make friends and new customers for Haverhill's." And Paul was right! Because Haverlite is a narrow focus, hi intensity, disposable flashlight that you can slip in your shirt pocket, just like a pen. It'll give you up to five hours of dazzling light, and it's at your disposal whenever you need it. Paul is selling Haverlite for 99¢, which is not necessarily a testimonial to his business acumen—but he has his job and we have ours. And he'll also send you all kinds of funky literature, our newest Catalog (a real eye popper), and lovable extrovert that he is, a $2 Gift Certificate that you may apply to your next purchase. We figure postage and handling of Haverlite to cost us something like $0.80, but Paul said "No way, round it down to something reasonable," and we gave in once more and reduced it to 39¢. So, if you want a piercing beam of light at your instant disposal, send us your check for $1.38 ($1.44 for California delivery) and we'll rush Haverlite right out to you. We can only afford to lose that much money, so—please only one per customer!
haverlite
haverhill's
I SAW THE HAVER LITE
388-1

Two more promos created at Haverhill's and continued at Henniker's. They are the only ones that we did not find in the Orient. They were successful year after year. We created the character of Paul Sandoval, our "premium manager." Sometimes I think that lovable Paul got more fan mail than Betty Crocker.

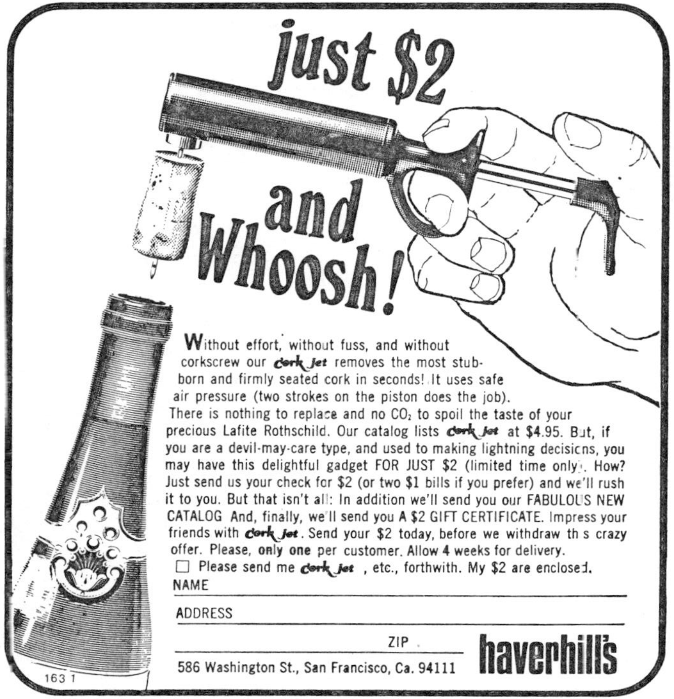

just $2
and Whoosh!
Without effort, without fuss, and without corkscrew our cork jet removes the most stubborn and firmly seated cork in seconds! It uses safe air pressure (two strokes on the piston does the job).
There is nothing to replace and no CO₂ to spoil the taste of your precious Lafite Rothschild. Our catalog lists cork jet at $4.95. But, if you are a devil-may-care type, and used to making lightning decisions, you may have this delightful gadget FOR JUST $2 (limited time only). How? Just send us your check for $2 (or two $1 bills if you prefer) and we'll rush it to you. But that isn't all: In addition we'll send you our FABULOUS NEW CATALOG. And, finally, we'll send you A $2 GIFT CERTIFICATE. Impress your friends with cork jet. Send your $2 today, before we withdraw this crazy offer. Please, only one per customer. Allow 4 weeks for delivery.
☐ Please send me cork jet, etc., forthwith. My $2 are enclosed.
NAME
ADDRESS
ZIP
586 Washington St., San Francisco, Ca. 94111
haverhill's
163 1

how to repair practically everything for just two dollars
Paul Sandoval (our lovable promotion manager) has really outdone himself this time. He's uncorked HAVERTOOLS, undoubtedly his greatest accomplishment to date. Because with HAVERTOOLS you can repair practically everything. Overcome by the spirit that is the constant delight of our customers (and a source of scorn and derision to Fred Spanberger, our doughty controller), he's offering it today for just $2 . . . surely the bargain of the year. Let me tell you about HAVERTOOLS: there's a handle with four different regular and Phillips screwdrivers, a hammer, a set of four spanners, two double wrenches, a 4-inch Crescent, a vial with assorted bolts, and even a polishing rag to clean it all up. So you see, it contains practically all you might need, except perhaps for an electric drill, which Paul somehow neglected to include. Paul will also send you our colorful 64-page Catalog and he'll throw in a $2 Gift Certificate that you can apply to your next merchandise purchase. So, if you want a nice set of tools, fill out the coupon and mail it to us with your check for $2. Paul will send HAVERTOOLS right out to you and he'll even pay the postage.
☐ OK, Paul, old amigo–send me HAVERTOOLS–pronto! My $2 check is enclosed.
Name
Address
Zip
haverhill's
586 Washington St.
San Francisco, Cal. 94111
342 - 2

Two promotional products, dreamed up by ''Paul Sandoval,'' that were invested with special customer acceptance by giving them our own brand name. We did mercifully restrain from calling the cork puller ''Hennijet.'' ''Cork Jet'' (now re-dubbed ''Jet 37'') worked just fine.

order would be about $12.50. Figuring on a 60% gross profit margin, that meant that, in addition to the small profit in the original transaction, we would have an approximate gross profit of $150 in bounceback per thousand promo items sold. The cost of the printed matter was about $60 per thousand, so we had an additional net profit of about $90 per thousand promos sent out. Even $90 is nothing to sneeze at, but by the time you multiply it by the hundreds of thousands that we sent out, you have respectable help with your fixed overhead and contribution to profit. Also, very importantly, you have started the "conversion" of the promo buyer to a "real merchandise" buyer.

Both you and I are clear that promos are not and should not be the "nut" of your business. But you should try to develop a good promo right away. You will make money, you will get positive cash flow, but — most importantly — you will have laid the groundwork for a going business, because you will acquire customers and "believers," and that is what the mail-order business is all about.

Before we leave promos and go on to "real" merchandise, let me quickly tell you where to find those promotional items. Almost without exception, they come from abroad, mostly from the Orient. And in the Orient, it used to be mostly Japan. Now that costs in Japan are beginning to be almost worse than those in the United States, the emphasis shifts to Hong Kong, Taiwan and Korea. And other countries with even lower-priced labor are coming to the fore: The Philippines, Singapore, Thailand. After years of visiting every European trade fair, we have come up with only one solitary European promotional item. It's our *Big Dad* pen. It comes from Italy, and it is a real humdinger — a great product, at the right price (we can make money on it) and something that the customer really likes when he gets it. And that means that we make a friend. But it is slim pickings for Europe, nonetheless.

We had completely given up on ever finding a suitable promo item in the United States. Labor costs are just too high. But then we did find one — in a backdoor sort of way. We had been importing the *Haverlite* from Hong Kong, and were selling scads of them. The *Haverlite* is an expendable flashlight (which means you throw it away after it is exhausted) that is shaped like a pen and fits in your shirt pocket with a clip. A great idea and a great item. Only one thing wrong with it: the batteries were lousy. And instead of having a one year shelf-life, as the manufacturer had solemnly assured us, and giving five hours of intermittent light, quite a few of these flashlights gave up their little electric ghosts on the way across the wide Pacific, in our warehouse, on the way to the customer, or after the overjoyed owner of the spanking new Haverlite had it switched on for 15 minutes or so. It was pretty much of a debacle, we had many unhappy customers on our hands and had to refund thousands of dollars. But then, to our pleased surprise, a manufacturer in Florida wrote and told us that the Hong Kong crowd had "stolen" his product, but had never learned how to make it right. He could deliver it at the same price as the Hong Kong flashlight (which had to carry duty, freight, etc.). His flashlight was equipped with Eveready batteries, and they are the "real thing," of course. So his flashlight would actually do what those from Hong Kong were supposed to, but didn't.

I must just mention two more items of promotional merchandise that have played a big role in the development of Henniker's.

The first are the *Hennisnips,* a really nifty pair of folding scissors. They are, of course, "Son of Haversnips." We sell these at $1.99 (plus postage) each and do a truly tremendous business with them. Since they sell for quite a bit more than $1, they are not truly "promotionals," but occupy a sort of "intermediate" position between "promotional" and "real" merchandise. We must have saturated the United States with these snips, because things are beginning to slow down somewhat. But that was perhaps our most successful promotion (somewhat fewer customers, but much more money and net profit than Mack-the-Knife) than we had ever made.

And then there is the *Organizer*. It is another one of our great successes. And no wonder! It is a very nifty item that our competitors sell for as much as $4.95. With Henniker's it is FREE, and we make sure the customer notes that right away. The $1 postage and insurance charge actually covers that expense and leaves a net profit of about $.25. There is virtually no work involved, because it is all pre-packed in Hong Kong, with all printed matter included. All we have to do is to process the order through our computer, put on the mailing label and take it as "bulk mail" to the post office. We don't have too long a track record yet with this item, but it looks as though it is going to be as big — as a customer getter and as a moneymaker — as Hennisnips.

BE PREPARED
just don't get caught without hennisnips
just $1.99

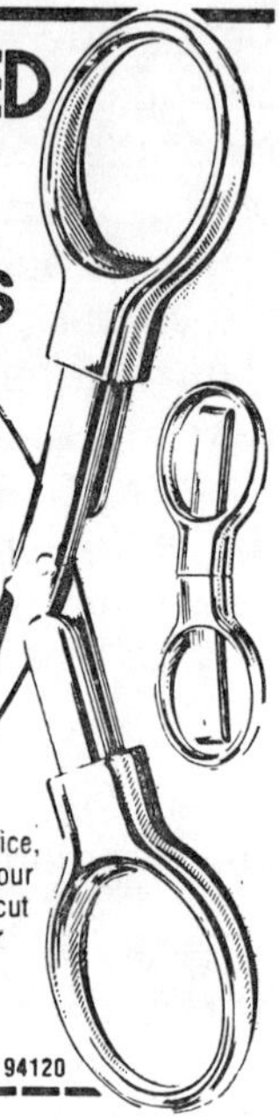

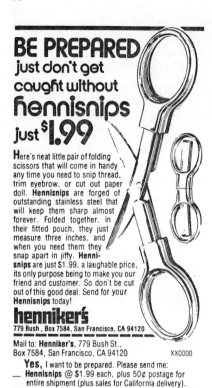

Here's neat little pair of folding scissors that will come in handy any time you need to snip thread, trim eyebrow, or cut out paper doll. **Hennisnips** are forged of outstanding stainless steel that will keep them sharp almost forever. Folded together, in their fitted pouch, they just measure three inches, and when you need them they snap apart in jiffy. **Hennisnips** are just $1.99, a laughable price, its only purpose being to make you our friend and customer. So don't be cut out of this good deal. Send for your **Hennisnips** today!

henniker's
779 Bush, Box 7584, San Francisco, CA 94120

Mail to: **Henniker's**, 779 Bush St., Box 7584, San Francisco, CA 94120 XX0000

Yes, I want to be prepared. Please send me:

__ **Hennisnips** @ $1.99 each, plus 50¢ postage for entire shipment (plus sales for California delivery).

☐ **One dozen** Hennisnips, for a total of $19.99, plus $1 postage for entire shipment (plus sales tax for California delivery).

My name is ____________________

I live at ____________________

City __________ State ________ Zip _____

M148-6

Hennisnips and Henniscales (sons of Haversnips and Haverscales) are two promotionals that we have "branded" with our name. They have been excellent sellers for over ten years. We still use them successfully as "promos" or as premiums with direct mail merchandise.

Get postage right every time with...

HenniScales
just $1.99

With postage rates going up and up, you can no longer afford to guess at weight of your letters and small packages. And, of course, you don't want to annoy your correspondents with having to pay penalty postage either. Most mail scales have same graduation all across, but **Henniscales** have extended reading in ½ oz. to 2 oz. range, which covers 97% of all correspondence. **Henniscales** go to 3½ ozs. and are uncannily accurate over entire range. They weigh less than one ounce themselves, come in flat vinyl pouch and fit snugly in pocket, purse or desk drawer. You can save cost of **Henniscales** in less than one month—so stop giving your money away to Uncle Sam and get your **Henniscales** today!

779 Bush St., Box 7584, San Francisco, CA 94120 **henniker's**

Henniker's, 779 Bush St., Box 7584, San Francisco, CA 94120

Yes, I want to weigh exactly. Please send me:

__ **Henniscales** @ $1.99 each, plus 50¢ post. for entire shipment (plus sales tax for CA deliv.)

☐ **One dozen** Henniscales, for a total of $19.99, plus $1 post. for entire shipment (plus tax for Calif. delivery)

My name is ____________________

I live at ____________________

City __________ State ________ Zip _____

M255

One thing you will have to keep in mind with these "promotionals" (and with most of your "real" merchandise): you will occasionally have to give them a rest and put them on the shelf, or the public will get tired of them. Then, after a while, you can dust them off and sell them again. Also, everybody is looking over your shoulder, watching you, and copying you if you are successful. So it is up to you always to have some new idea up your sleeve, something new brewing. Then you don't have to worry about your imitators copying your last year's ideas. You are always at least one step ahead of them.

Apart from Big Dad and Haverlite, I found every one of my promotional items — and there must have been as many as thirty or forty of them altogether — by careful reading of a number of Far East trade publications and pinpointing likely manufacturers. I would either adapt merchandise that they already had to our specifications or I would ask them to manufacture merchandise that would fit our requirements.

Okay, so much for promotionals; now let's talk about "real" merchandise.

FOR "REAL" MERCHANDISE: THINK OF YOUR OWN TALENTS FIRST

The first thing in determining your line of merchandise is quite simply to make up your mind what your line of merchandise *ought to be.* Does this sound like a trick statement? Really, it is not! Your line of merchandise should be that which your background, your talents, your "special angle," your ability or your interest makes most suitable and most comfortable for you. Or, your line of merchandise should be a line built around the one special product that you have invented, developed, have a special pipeline to, or have an "exclusive" on.

Let's take a few examples: we have already talked about the fellow who is a real outdoorsman. He should obviously concentrate on merchandise in this area, beginning with merchandise in his most narrow field of specialization. Because it is in this field that he will be able to do his best purchasing — he will know value, utility and competitive product, he will be able to assist his customers with advice and guidance.

HOW TO GO Metric

~~JUST $4.95~~

absolutely **free**

H290

You might as well face it: the metric age is upon us. You simply aren't with it if you don't know your liters from your square meters, can't tell what 84° Fahrenheit is in Centigrade, or can't quickly convert ounces to kilograms. Stop fretting — because nifty **Henni/Metric Sliderule Cup** (**H/MSC**, for short) comes to the rescue. Its rotating scales give you all the right answers and quickly convert one unit to another. And it is a dandy desk accessory, because **H/MSC** holds your pens, pencils, glasses, scissors, rulers and whatnots right at hand. But best of all: it's absolutely **FREE!** Why do we give such beautiful things away? Are we bereft of business sense? Not really! We are trying to build our customer list with nice and tasteful people, and this seems to be a good (though somewhat expensive) way to do it. To get your **H/MSC**, please assist us with part of our postage/insurance cost by sending us your $1 bill (no checks, please — our bankers are very uptight about getting avalanches of tiny checks). And here is something extra: to get you acquainted with us, we'll include a **$2 Gift Certificate** with our compliments. How does that grab you? Send for your **H/MSC** today! You will be metricized, organized and delighted, and we hope you will be our friend forever!

773 Bush Street, Box 7584,
San Francisco, CA 94120 **henniker's**

Henniker's, 773 Bush St., Box 7584,
San Francisco, CA 94120

yes, I want to go metric. Please send me one **Henni/Metric Sliderule Cup** (sorry, only one per customer, please). My $1 bill for part postage/insurance is enclosed.

My name is ____________________
I live at ____________________
In ______________ St. ______ Zip ______

HOW TO GET Organized

~~JUST $3.95~~

absolutely **free**

M284

End mess and clutter with nifty **Henni/Organizer.** It lets you stow your knick-knacks, worry beads, and paper clips in its four handy drawers — pens, pencils and whatnots in its open well. **H/O** is 4½'' high and lovably handsome in navy/white cyrolac. Best of all, it's absolutely free. Why do we give things away? Are we bereft of business sense? Not really — we are trying to get new friends and customers, and this seems to be good way to do it. To get your **H/O** please assist us with part of our postage and insurance costs by sending us your $1 bill (no checks please — our bankers are very uptight about getting avalanches of tiny checks). And to get you acquainted with our ''organization'' we'll include a **$2 Gift Certificate**, with our compliments. Send for your **Henni/Organizer** today! You will be delighted.

771 Bush Street, **henniker's**
Box 7584, San Francisco, CA 94120

Henniker's, 771 Bush St. Box 7584, San Francisco, CA 94120

yes, I want to get organized. Please send me one **Henni/Organizer** (sorry, only one per customer, please). My $1 bill for part post./insur. is enclosed.

My name is ____________________
I live at ____________________
In ______________ St. ______ Zip ______

Although the era of the $1.00 ''promo'' seems to be over, we have been able to give it new life with the ORGANIZER and its companion, the METRIC CADDY. The results are astounding. If you are sharp-eyed, you may have noticed that the house numbers given for our address are ''771'' and ''773'' (instead of the real ''779''). The purpose is, of course, to enable us to separate the thousands of promotional orders immediately from ''real'' merchandise orders, thus enabling us to process them separately and speedily.

If his narrowest field of specialization is, say, backpacking, he will offer at first a few well-selected items, such as: padded jackets, boots, socks, outdoor shirts, rain gear, sleeping bags, ground cloths, air mattresses, mosquito repellants, knapsacks and packframes, sewing kits, first aid kits, pocket knives, flashlights eating utensils, and perhaps a few others. He might not want to offer all of it at one time, because this is already a pretty formidable and well-rounded line of merchandise. And once this backpack expert is on his way, he can branch out from there — one by one — into related areas: fishing, hunting, jogging, bicycling, and much more — each one with at least twenty or thirty product possibilities.

You keep your merchandise line fresh and your prices competitive and your own thinking up-to-date by visiting trade fairs in your area of specialization (more about that later) and by religiously (yes, I *mean* religiously) studying the catalogs of your competitors. Don't worry about that: in this business, everybody learns from everybody else. You want to be sure not to plagiarize, but you want to learn and to adapt. The line is pretty fine, but quite clear to the discerning. I have been told by an ex-employee of Neiman-Marcus that, when Haverhill's catalog arrived, Stanley Marcus, the great Dallas, Texas, panjandrum of merchandising, used to closet himself to study it. He would brook no interruption. except if some Texas trillionaire wanted to place a special order for a dozen gift-wrapped plastic his/hers mouse farms at $3,500 each or something like that. So — if you are in this backpack/outdoor interest area, you'll want to make a very thorough study of at least the catalogs of the leaders in this field, who — not intending any offense to those whom I might have left out, are perhaps the following:

- Norm Thompson Outfitters
- Eddie Bauer
- L. L. Bean
- Bill Boatman
- Sportpages
- P & S Sales
- Holubar Mountaineering
- Frostline Kits

- Eastern Mountain Sports
- Damart Thermolactyl
- Cabela's
- Gander Mountain
- Gokey Co.

Let's take another example. Suppose you are a middle-aged ex-GI, who married a nice French girl right after World War II. Even after thirty years she has some trouble with English (which is really fiendishly difficult, although to you natives it seems like a snap). But when she went to that little convent in St. Gervais d'Auvergne, the good nuns taught her a marvelous recipe of how to make a cheese of absolutely heavenly flavor — out of one-third cow's milk, one-third goat's milk, one-third sheep's milk, and a few little extras thrown in that she wouldn't reveal even to you. She knows how to make that cheese in her own kitchen for about $1.22 per pound. You should be able to sell it as "la creme de les fromages de France" for at least $3.50 per pound — just about the right profit margin (look at the ad on the facing page on how to promote cheese by mail) to make you comfortably rich. And after you start your mail-order business around this one cheese, you should have little trouble to expand into other cheeses that you will buy (your petite Francaise won't have to make it) and eventually into other gourmet products — pecans, candies, fruits, preserves, cookies and much more.

I don't want to tire you with examples, but the important principle is that you can always successfully promote your own special line of products and that you can usually build a related line of products around it. Because you now have customers who have proven that they are interested in this kind of product. More important, they have proven that they are willing to buy by mail; and most important: they are now your customers. And with just a modicum of imagination you can branch out. You will have to believe it, because this is part of the thesis of this book: the potential market is so enormous and the branching out possibilities so large, that you will definitely succeed in merchandising your line if you have good products, if you keep your mind on a reasonably even keel, compare and test and check, and proceed cautiously with the introduction of new merchandise.

We'd ship it to France if we had enough of it...

Once you've tried Maytag Blue Cheese you'll agree with gourmets and cheese connoisseurs that it's superior to any domestic and finest imported "blue" or similar cheeses. We have one of country's outstanding Holstein-Friesian dairy herds here in Newton, Iowa, and make delicious, tangy Maytag Blue by painstaking hand process in small batches. We cave-ripen Maytag Blue carefully and don't release single wheel until our cheesemaster, incorruptible hawkeye of old school, gives his ok. This being off-season, we are able to sell small quantity of this incomparable delicacy to new customers. If you want to treat yourself or friends to exciting taste experience, discover Maytag Blue. Our faithful Holstein-Friesians are generous with their bounty, but there's only so much to go around. So, please, don't be left out and order right away!

Mail to: **MAYTAG Dairy Farms**
Rural Route 1, Box 806S, Newton, IA 50208

YES, my friends and I deserve the best.
Please send
______ 2 lb. wheels of Maytag Blue Cheese @ $6.10
______ 4lb. wheels of Maytag Blue Cheese @ $10.30
☐ to myself, ☐ to attached gift list (enclose cards if you wish)

☐ My check for full amount, plus $1 per shipment (to cover partial postage, handling and insurance expense) is enclosed.
☐ Please charge my BA, MC acct.

#______________ exp______

NOTE: BA, MC accounts may call (515) 792-1133 for super-fast service.

My name is______________

I live at______________

in______________ State______ Zip______

Yes, cheese can be promoted in space advertising — very successfully! This is an ad that I created for one of my consulting clients, Maytag Dairy Farms of Newton, Iowa. It ran well in such media as THE WALL STREET JOURNAL and THE NATIONAL OBSERVER.

HERE IS HOW I APPLIED THIS APPROACH TO MY OWN PRODUCT DEVELOPMENT

Finding myself almost "by accident" in the mail-order business (remember, I had only one product that I thought could be sold by mail — but I flunked out with it), I needed to find quickly some new products to keep my just formed business from floundering.

I decided to take stock of what "specialties" and what talents I had to bring to the business of merchandise selection. I found them to be the following:

- A knowledge of foreign languages and personal connections abroad.
- An engineering education and understanding of scientific and technical products.
- An ability to write copy (I had by then discovered that modest talent).
- A knack to take an existing product and to conceive improvements in function, appearance and packaging.
- An understanding of foreign trade, customs regulations and duty rates (much of it acquired by working for a multinational firm in New York after graduating from the Harvard Business School).

So, taking all of these "specialties" together, and trying to find a common denominator for these, I came to the conclusion that my future in the mail order business lay in doing the following:

- Locate small foreign companies that produce one (or several) specialty products. Redesign these products for the U. S. market.
- Package them so as to make them appealing to the U. S. public.
- Secure exclusive U. S. rights to such products whenever possible and promote them with outstanding advertising in space, direct mail and catalogs.

That was my formula, and — I hope you will forgive my lack of modesty — I have done really pretty well with it.

Let me give you a few specific examples of how I used the formula. The key, in every case, was to exclusive rights to the product in the United States.

Emoskop Vest Pocket Optical System: I located this product in Wetzlar, Germany, not being aware that it had already been sold — at the rate of less than fifty units per year, in the United States for the preceding six years or so. I realized that to all those that had previously sold it, it was just another gimmick item in their catalog to which no particular importance was attached. I wrote to Mr. Seibert, the inventor of the Emoskop and owner of Emo-Optik, the manufacturing company. I committed for an immediate 1,000 units, with option to get the exclusive distribution in the United States, as long as we would purchase a minimum of 1,000 units every three months. It turned out that that was no problem at all: once we got going, we never took fewer than 20,000 units per year! We prepared good space ads and an outstanding direct mail piece. Emoskop was the ideal direct mail item, and I promptly recognized it as such. Here's why:

- It's truly a great item — optical perfection in miniature.
- The customer doesn't just get what he expects, but he gets more — he is pleasantly surprised. Therefore:
- The ratio of returned merchandise is very small.
- It weighs very little — package is small and can be shipped inexpensively either by first class or by third class mail.
- It's solid — virtually impossible to be damaged in transit.

We made history with Emoskop. Until I left Haverhill's we sold over 150,000 Emoskops in the course of the years. Can you imagine it — a little vestpocket optical system, and by good merchandising and promotion we sold such a large quantity, equivalent to over $3 million retail sales, in less than seven years!

Monaco Shaver. This is another dilly. I saw this gadget advertised in a European trade publication, wrote to the manufacturer and asked for a sample. I heard nothing. Three months later, I wrote again and I still heard nothing. I waited another three months — still nothing. The factory was located in Monaco, which is sort of a dependency of France. So I wrote to the French commercial consul in San Francisco and told him what unresponsive treatment I was getting from this factory in Monaco. They

The Emoskop and the Monaco Shaver are perhaps the most successful products I have ever developed. They represent well the "niche" that I had carved out for my business. You can ferret out items like these in your area of mail-order specialization and then go with them all the way.

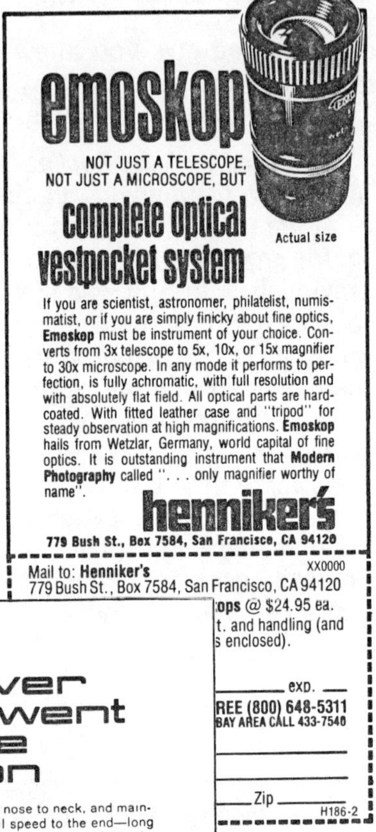

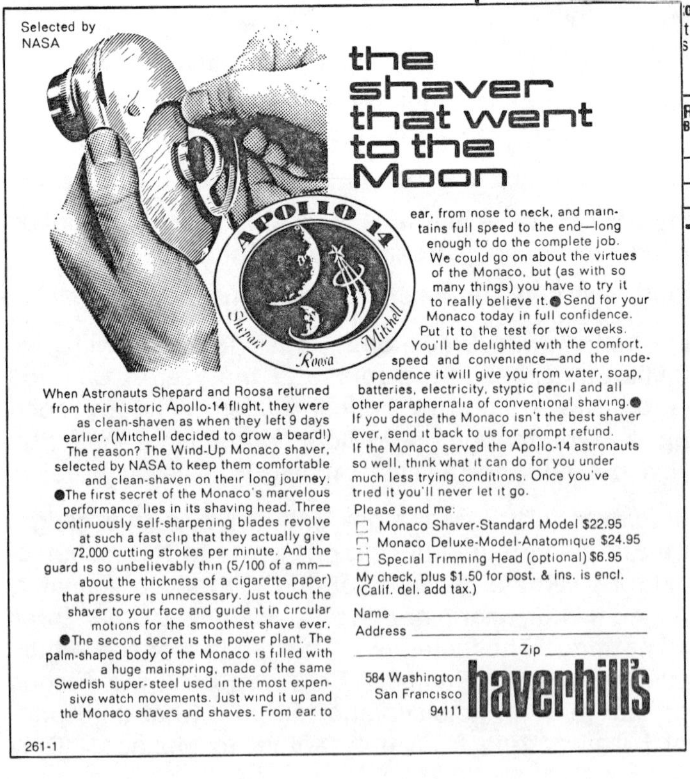

stuck some kind of a needle into the management of the company and presently I received a sample shaver, a letter of apology and an "offer."

I was, as I thought I would be, immediately fascinated by the shaver. I, myself, had been a brush-and-lather man all of my life, but I found that this razor gave me a closer shave than any blade that I had ever used. So I did exactly what I had done with the Emoskop: I contracted for 1,000 pieces, with an option for U. S. exclusive rights if we purchased a minimum of 1,000 units every quarter. The Monaco proved to be my best merchandising decision, because in the course of seven years we sold close to 200,000 units at a price of between $22.95 and $24.95. We also sold large numbers of accessories, which customers either purchased on the spot or in the after-trade. The Monaco had been distributed in the United States before by a number of companies. One of them was savvy Abercrombie & Fitch. Way back, in 1968, my wife and I were manning (or "personing," to use the current term) a booth at the Chicago Premium Show. A gent approached, identified himself as a "top executive" of Abercrombie & Fitch and told us (yes, those were his words) that we must have rocks in our heads to try to sell this shaver. They had had it in their line for years and couldn't move it. Well, we came into the picture and, what do you know — Abercrombie & Fitch and five other firms became our steady wholesale customers for the Monaco, after we had acquired U. S. exclusive rights and began really to promote it in depth.

I shouldn't take all of the credit for the Monaco success myself. There was one event that helped us to move the Monaco shaver from the "great success" to the "fabulous bonanza" category. Here is what happened: NASA had to decide which shaver the astronauts would use on their journeys in space. Every shaver available in the United States was anonymously purchased by NASA for the use and examination of the astronauts so as to evaluate performance and also to assure compliance with the super-rigid components and safety requirements of NASA. We did not know, of course, that NASA had purchased any Monacos and I was totally surprised when I found out. Can you imagine my pleasure, glee and euphoria when I received a call from NASA's public relations department to tell me that the Monaco shaver had been selected for Apollo voyages and for Sky Lab. We got permission to use the NASA emblem in our advertising. It produced incredible numbers of sales and gave the American public a chance to become acquainted with this truly outstanding product.

Multator-4 Calculator. May I ask you to please journey back in spirit to 1967-68. The calculator business was dominated by such formidable names as Friden, SCM, Royal and Monroe. And even the least expensive of the electro-mechanical calculators (the only kind then available) sold for a minimum of $200 — most models for $400 and up.

I located a small factory in Germany and became great friends with its proprietor, Klaus Meuter. After evaluating the calculator business and its potential in the United States, he modified an existing product and came up with a full-function manual calculator that we could sell in the United States at the then incredible price of $89.95 and still make a very respectable profit (our landed cost was about $35). We distributed the machine mostly through business media, such as *The Wall Street Journal,* and had an absolute blast.

Orders came in so fast that the factory couldn't keep up with them and (hang the expense) we decided to air freight all machines, rather than to bring them in by sea. In short, while it lasted, we made so much money with this product that it seemed almost sinful. It was simply a marvelous product.

But, suddenly and brutally, that bubble burst. When electronic calculators appeared on the scene, the utility of the Multator-4 disappeared virtually overnight. Sales simply stopped. If an ad in, say, *The Wall Street Journal* would regularly produce between 200 and 300 orders, it would suddenly produce between 0 and 2 orders. And it was that quick — just about from one month to the next.

Bowmar Calculator. But I have a sequel to the Multator-4 story, and as you will see, it is a very happy one. While Multator-4 was still going strong, I was reading in trade publications about electronic calculators being developed. But they were still Flash Gordon stuff, much more of a dream than reality.

One day — I think it was in the spring of 1968 or 1969 — a Mr. White appeared unannounced in my office. He introduced himself as vice-president of the Bowmar Company of Acton, Mass. — a company that I had never heard of before. He proceeded to pull a gadget out of his briefcase (it was just a "dummy," had no "innards" and, of course, didn't work) which he told me was the prototype of an electronic pocket calculator. He assured me that his company would have it ready for Christmas and that it would have to be sold at a retail price of $240. He had come to us, because he had been following our advertising and promotion campaigns for various technically oriented products and he thought that we could do a great job introducing this electronic pocket calculator to the American market. Did we want to take it on?

Even though I had nothing to look at but a piece of plastic, I immediately saw the fantastic potential of this breakthrough product. I contracted to take it into Haverhill's Christmas catalog and negotiated the exclusive right to mail-order distribution for it. The gamble paid off spectacularly. Until the market "deteriorated" (which means until such time that the calculator which we sold for $240 would decline in price and eventually sell for $19.95 — and that didn't take more than two years) we probably sold more pocket calculators than any other single source. We sold tens of thousands of them — I have lost count. We made a great deal of money with them. In the process, Bowmar, Inc. became the largest gainer on the American stock exchange in 1971. I don't mean to imply that their huge gain was our doing — they had pioneered a wonderful product. They brought it out at the right time and themselves knew how to promote it. But our drumbeat schedule of advertising — in mass media and direct mail — contributed not only to our own revenue and profit, but without question, to the great success of Bowmar, Inc.*

These are just a few examples of how we select merchandise. If you wish, please re-read what I consider the assets that I could bring to bear on merchandise selection and on line of merchandise and see, by just these few examples, how consistent I have been in applying my pinpointed abilities to it. Then review once again your own assets and your own special interests and you will be able to carve out a very successful merchandising niche for yourself.

---

* A footnote is in order: Bowmar, the pioneer in this field, fell from its dizzying heights and came to a bad end — bankruptcy. They were knocked out of the ring when the really "big boys," Texas Instrument, Casio, Rockwell, Commodore, Sharp and others started entering this business, driving prices and profit margins relentlessly down.

Why spend a fortune on a super-electric if Multator-4 can easily handle the job?

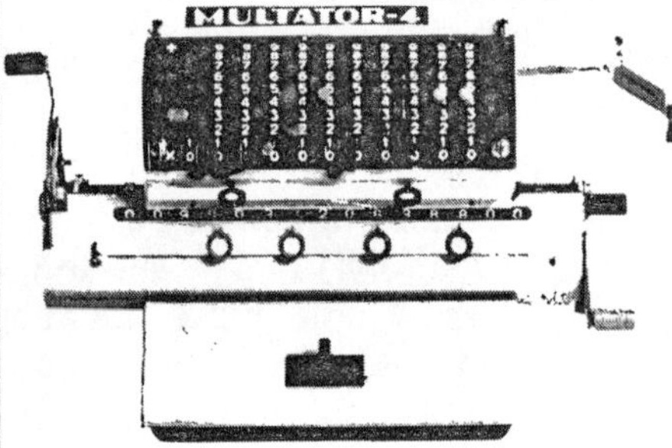

If you are a busy billing clerk, rate computer, claims adjuster, or anybody else whose workday is a succession of computations, you would be foolish using any but the most advanced calculating equipment. But . . . if you are a business-man, engineer, insurance broker, plant foreman . . . anybody who uses a calculator 2 or 3 hours a day or less, you shouldn't waste your money on unnecessarily complex and sophisticated equipment. You don't need it! What you need is a small, rugged, accurate, light-weight, inexpensive calculator and the Multator-4 should be the machine of your choice. Multator-4 multiplies and divides at a brisk clip; but it also performs tricks that even some of those $800 machines haven't learned. It provides automatic re-entry of intermediate products, read-out of credit balances, extracts square roots and has other features found only in the most expensive machines.

Multator-4 is a little, reliable mastermind from Hamburg, weighs less than 4 pounds, and measures 8x7x3½", with 10-digit keyboard and 15-digit read-out. The remarkably low price of this precision portable is possible only because we arc the exclusive importers in the U. S., and sell directly to you. Two-week return privilege. One year Guarantee on parts and workmanship. We maintain total parts and repair servce.

In reliance on your Guarantee, send me:

☐ Multator-4, cover & instructions $89
☐ Foam-lined, blk. vinyl carry-case $10

My check (incl. $2 for post. & ins.) is enclosed. (California resid. add tax.)

584 Washington, San Francisco 94111

Name____________________

Address____________________

________________ Zip________

haverhill's

The Multator-4 was one of the most exciting products we ever promoted. Alas, its life was short — a victim of technological revolution.

Try to be an innovator in your merchandise development, if at all possible. It is a little risky sometimes, but when you hit, you may hit big. The Bowmar Calculator made history — we were the first company to advertise electronic calculators for mail-order sale. This ad shows a price of $119.95, about six months after the $240 introductory price.

HERE IS HOW TO FIND THESE PRODUCTS

Great, you will say, but how did you find all those successful products?

I shall tell you!

There are essentially only three basic sources for products in the mail-order business. If you cultivate all three of them — it is difficult to say which is the most important — you are bound to wind up with a viable, vibrant and profitable product line.

- Consumer media, trade media, periodicals, and competitors' catalogs.
- Trade fairs.
- Manufacturer's representatives.

Let's run through these one by one:

Consumer and Trade Media

Coming back a minute to my own experiences, you will recall that I decided that I did not qualify to specialize in any single "vertical" kind of business, but that my abilities lay rather in "broad spectrum" merchandise, as long as such merchandise corresponded to the criteria that I had established for myself. These were essentially foreign products of small factories that I could develop and package for the American market and that had some technical attributes.

Having pinpointed my target area, I began to put together a list of foreign publications that advertised consumer products. I parked for weeks at the San Francisco Public Library, the Federal Building (the foreign trade section of the Commerce Department) and the library of the San Francisco World Trade Center. I found at least twenty publications that proved invaluable. I located virtually every one of my key products, which over the years accounted for, perhaps, 70% of Haverhill's and Henniker's sales through these publications. In fact, I found every smash hit, except the Bowmar Calculator — an American product that came to me "over the transom" — through these media. Your talents and interests are possibly in quite a different field, but the usefulness of media to you will be the same.

Let's say your special area of interest is photography. If you are not already familiar with them (and since this *is* your field of interest, I would assume that you are) please go to your public library. Let the librarian give you a listing of all periodicals on photography — even those that the library does not carry. Look through all of them and subscribe to those that you feel are related to what you plan to do. Subscribing, if you can afford it, is much better than just reading these publications in the library, because you will then have these publications always available for reference. Reading these publications thoroughly will not only keep you abreast of developments in your field, but, equally important, you will see what other firms — manufacturers and mail-order companies — advertise, what product points they stress and how they price their goods.

In addition to subscriptions to important publications in your field (both trade and consumer oriented) you will, of course, assemble a library in your chosen field. In photography, for instance, *The Life Library of Photography,* published by Time-Life Books, comes immediately to mind. But, of course, there is much more. You will want to look at all of it and select that which is most directly useful to you.

Another quick and quite thorough way to locate consumer publications in your chosen field is through the consumer publications volume of *Standard Rate & Data.* It is available in every public library.

Let's say you have decided to go into the mail-order business dealing with outdoor products. Look into Sections 6 (Boating & Yachting), 8A (Camps, Recreational Vehicles, etc.), 8B (Camping Outdoor Recreation), 9 (Fishing & Hunting), 30 (Men's), and you will find altogether approximately 200 publications. Not all, but quite a few will be most helpful to you. You should subscribe to the most important in your own specific interest area and scan the others, once a month or so, in your library.

You can also go to the fat green Standard Rate & Data book called *Trade Publications.* There are very many such trade publications, most of them dealing in services, supplies and equipment, rather than with consumer products. But do a little digging through the sections that seem to be in your area of interest. Look in your public library at sample issues of those publications that seem to be promising or, if not available, get a sample issue from the publisher.

Let's go back to consumer publications: you may wish to disregard some or perhaps most of them right away, because they simply don't "target" on what you are trying to do. But you will be left with a fistful of others that should interest you. As to trade publications, you can get subscriptions to almost any one of them without any payment at all, because most of them are so-called "controlled circulation" publications. This means that they are being *given away* to people in the trade — the publications exist only by their advertising revenue. You can write to the publisher, tell him what you are doing, also tell him that you are a potential advertiser (this is *not* a white lie, but a fact, and he'll just love to hear it) and ask that you be put on the "complimentary subscription list" (which is, of course, all there is).

Things are a little more complicated with consumer publications. You may also introduce yourself as a serious advertiser, a statement that would be more plausible if you had advertised already in a competitor's publication. You will then in all likelihood be put on the complimentary subscription list.

In addition, you will want to request catalogs from all firms in your field (your competitors, if you wish) so that you can see what *they* feature as "specials" and what *they* charge for their merchandise. You can usually get a catalog by just writing and asking for one. Some companies are a little "selecive" and request that you pay them $.50 or a dollar for their catalog. Go ahead and pay it — it's a good investment. In fact, my advice is to make a small purchase from each of your competitors. You will be on their mailing list for anywhere from two to five years and your investment in the small purchase will yield you great dividends in information.

Remember the fellow from a few pages back who, with his French wife, had gone into the cheese business by mail order? Suppose that is you. You should turn to the consumer publications volume of Standard Rate & Data. In this case, sections 17A (Epicurean), 24 (Home Service & Home), and 49 (Women's) would be of interest. And you would follow the same routine that we have just described.

And, of course, you would also have to have catalogs, be on the mailing lists of firms already in your business. If you are in the gourmet business, you will have plenty to choose from. There are many of them, but you should keep abreast, at least, on what the following firms are doing:

- Wisconsin Cheese Maker's Guild
- The Swiss Colony
- Harry & David
- Figi's
- The Wisconsin Cheeseman
- Frank Lewis Grapefruits
- Maytag Farms
- Bachman Foods
- Pepperidge Farm
- Collin St. Bakery
- Paprikas Weiss
- Day & Young Gourmet Foods
- Cheese Lovers International
- Omaha Steaks International

Trade Fairs

When I ran Haverhill's, and of course now Henniker's, I would never miss a trade fair that I considered to be of importance to the line of merchandise approach that I had taken. At first I was intrigued with so-called "gift shows," but I found very quickly that they were pretty useless for our purposes. They are mostly a hodgepodge of gimcrackery, primarily with the retail store business in mind. I can't recall ever locating one single worthwhile item in these gift shows.

The shows in the United States that were important for us, that were most productive and that supplied a constant stream of new ideas and new merchandise were the New York and Chicago Premium Shows (May and September) and the Chicago Housewares Show (January). The Housewares Show is somewhat misnamed, because it covers a very broad spectrum of all kinds of merchandise, not just restricted to "housewares."

In addition, we would make our yearly rounds of certain European trade fairs. The ones that we find most productive for our purposes are the Fiera de Milan (the Milan Trade Fair), the Basel Fair and Hanover Fair. They have the added advantage of being timed so that you can visit one right after the other, and everything in Europe is pretty close together. Once every other year or so, we would visit either the Cologne or the Frankfurt Housewares Fair. The Frankfurt Fair is a little more suited for our purposes; it has the further advantage that it runs at the same time as the Offenbach Leather Goods Fair — Offenbach being a suburb of Frankfurt.

As you perhaps suspect, this visiting of foreign fairs isn't all work (although there is lots of that), but also a little play. The IRS, generous as ever, allows you to deduct your ("reasonable") fun-and-play expenses for weekends, as long as these weekends are sandwiched between working Fridays and working Mondays. And don't kid yourself that your friendly "revenuer" won't come around and scrutinize your expense account. They have a wide open weather eye for those who want to take a foreign vacation under the guise of a business trip. So you want to be sure and keep a pretty meticulous diary of what you are doing — with special emphasis on hard work on Fridays and Mondays!

We got audited by the IRS every year — just as regular as clockwork. And we always had a little fun with our IRS man. Because the one thing he would invariably latch on to ("aha" was his exact word) was the routine side trip to Monte Carlo. He thought he really had us there, and he was already whetting the blue pencil and the "DISALLOWED" stamp — until we explained to him that one of our most important suppliers was located in Monte Carlo, namely the manufacturer of the Monaco shaver. It always took a little convincing, it was almost too good to be true, but naturally, we always prevailed.

What kind of shows should *you* go to and how do you find out what is of interest to *you*. Simple: read the publications of your specialty — domestic and foreign, and they'll have a listing of trade fairs in your field. Of course, you can't attend them all — some of these shows go from city to city and are rather repetitive. You will quickly learn, however, which are the "must" ones in your field. Many trade publications are considerate enought to keep you from guessing and put the important and really worthwhile fairs in boldface type.

Talking about trade shows, I must confess to my regret and shame that I have never attended a single trade show or fair in the Orient. I don't really know why and I am sure it was a mistake. I just never got around to it. I gravitated toward Europe, because I felt "at home," because I could speak the principal languages and could negotiate without help, right on the spot. I felt, perhaps, that I would be at the mercy of intermediaries and therefore a little helpless if I went to the Orient. Please do not emulate me: it's in the Orient — Japan and Hong Kong and Taiwan, primarily, where much of the exciting merchandise of today and tomorrow is being generated. Sure, we have always had permanent agents in Japan and Hong Kong, but it isn't quite the same as being on the spot yourself.

Sales Representatives

The mail-order business is not much different from any other. At first nothing happens to you, nobody comes to see you, and you are an unknown. But once you begin advertising, once you begin writing to trade sources and, especially, once you begin to visit shows and fairs and start dropping your business cards around, you will start being on all kinds of people's lists. Before you know it, you will receive visits from sales representatives who wish to sell you merchandise and services.

At first you will think of these visits as welcome interruptions from a perhaps somewhat drab and leisurely routine of stamp licking and money counting and you will be glad to give each of these chaps a full hearing. After a while, however, you will find that these visits can take up an ever increasing part of your day. So you will have to learn to discern quickly which are of possible importance to you and which are time wasters. And you will have to learn to develop techniques to cut those visits as short and make them as productive as possible. Because, for some reason that I have never quite understood, salesmen and representatives seem to have unlimited amounts of time. If you give them half an opportunity they will easily stay in your office most of the day.

But businesslike brevity does not mean brusqueness. You will want to be invariably friendly and courteous to these men. They go from place to place, keep their eyes and ears open, do a fair amount of gossiping and you will not only be exposed to scads of merchandise, you will learn about trends, about what is coming up, what is new, what is being phased out, what response other firms and other mail-order houses get to which products, what price changes are in the wind, and much more. And all of this "free" information is in addition to the merchandise they will show you.

There is an observation about "reps" (or as they used to be called — "drummers" or "traveling salesmen") that we have made and find confirmed over the years. These men are almost without exception, gregarious, helpful, friendly, reasonably tough-skinned and really interested in people and in helping their customers. I suppose it is these personality traits that made them gravitate into that kind of work in the first place and kept them in it after they got started. So, in making friends with them, in getting known in your industry as a pretty good egg yourself, you will get lots of good information, free advice (not all of it good, necessarily) and even an occasional lead to some "special deals," close-outs or other goodies.

Are you getting a little tired hearing about merchandise? There are just a few more things.

ALL MERCHANDISE IS NOT CREATED EQUAL

In developing and running a "typical" mail-order business, you will find that merchandise falls into three groups. The lines between these groups are sometimes a little fuzzy and there is some "movement" between them. You will always look for items with "upward mobility," but in the majority of cases, merchandise will stay in its original slot.

Catalog Merchandise

Within a year or so after you have started in business, you will have to have a catalog. It is essential to the success of your business. We shall talk about catalogs in full detail later on.

In order to make your catalog viable you will have to have at least, say, 16 pages of merchandise and, let's call it, 100 to 150 items. You will find it almost impossible — I know that I did — to find that number of "world beater" merchandise items. So your catalog will have to feature your super winners, together with a substantial number of items which you expect to be profitable in the catalog, but which have not sufficient oomph, sex appeal and pulling power to make it on their own — either in space advertising, let alone in direct-mail. So, in order to fill your catalog with attractive and profitable merchandise, you will need exposure to lots of it, and that's where your visits to fairs and shows and your visits with reps come in.

Space Merchandise

This is merchandise that you determine to be sufficiently attractive, non-competitive, unique and with enough profit margin to be able to run in space ads — i.e., in magazines, newspapers, Sunday supplements, etc. We are now talking only about "real" merchandise, and not about "promos," which, although advertised in space, serve a different purpose altogether.

Such items are not at all easy to find. Even after you have found them, you will learn that only about three or four out of every ten of your "discoveries" are viable and sufficiently attractive to be profitable in space. And that is if you are pretty good! The other six or seven you will run once or twice and then conclude that they won't make it. You must then decide whether their performance is so dismal that you should forget about them altogether or whether there is enough life in them to allow you to relegate them to the catalog, where they can lead a less glamorous, but at least profitable existence.

But by digging your way, adding and discarding, you will be able to develop a family of space ads that will be profitable and that may stay so for a very long time. Earlier in this chapter, I told you about the Emoskop and about the Monaco. I have run both of these items regularly for over ten years, in all kinds of media, and always successfully. And in all these years, we hardly changed the ads at all, except that we added the NASA emblem to the Monaco ad and changed the copy to tie in with the space program theme.

There were other items besides these two, of course — at least a dozen "evergreens" that we could successfully advertise in space year after year — several dozen of them altogether. And there were many others that were successful for perhaps a couple of years or so and which then declined and had to be set aside. But these are just the successes. Please be prepared to accept occasional defeat gracefully. Not everything you will do will come up roses. You will have your share of "bombs." There were many items and many ads on which we lavished care, money and many expectations, that dudded out so completely on the first go-around that they had to be relegated to oblivion immediately. I emphasize this once more so *you* won't be discouraged. If you can get three or four winners out of ten space tries, you are a very good mail-order operator.

But perhaps the important point here is this: if you have a winner, you can ride it for all it is worth — spread it into other publications and expose it with continuing profit to millions of prospective customers. If you have a dud, you will usually know after having run just one test ad, at comparatively little outlay. And if it fails, you can quietly bury it. We usually do our testing in the Southwest edition of *The Wall Street Journal*. A test can be scheduled in about 48 hours. It's quite inexpensive. And usually you have the "verdict" of the market place, good or bad — in just about a week.

Space merchandise will usually take more digging than catalog merchandise. You're most likely to find it in trade publications (preferably foreign) or visits to trade fairs. And every so often a rep will offer you an item that is so obviously attractive that you think it will work in space. The *Sanyo PF Flashlight,* branded item and, therefore, conventionally a no-no for space advertising, is a successful example in that category. So is the *Nivometre.* And, of course, there have been many others over the years.

Another source for space advertising merchandise is your own catalog. As you go along selling from the catalog, you'll find that certain items are so "hot" that you should give them a try in space. Among the items that "graduated" from Henniker's catalog to space were the *Z and X Chairs,* the *Dynalight Flashlight* and the *ExerGym.* All of them turned out to be as successful in space as their unexpectedly brilliant performance in the catalog led us to hope. One memorable "sleeper," the most successful item by far in Haverhill's 1974 Catalog (which appeared at Christmas 1973) was the *Nixon Candle.* It was a large candle, about 13" high, sculpted into a pretty good likeness of Richard Nixon. He was, of course, still president at the time. That was long before Watergate, but he wasn't the most admired and beloved man even then.

I didn't really want to put it in the catalog, because I thought of it as being of questionable taste. Further, it was heavy and bulky

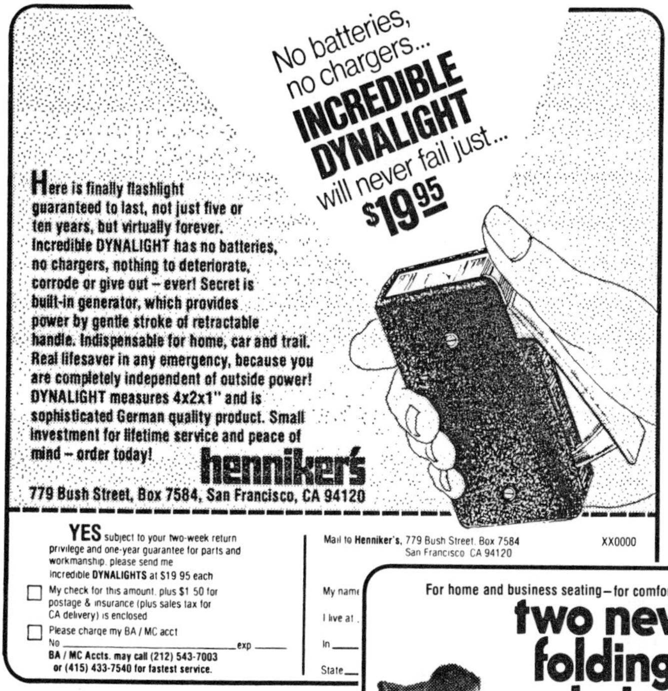
No batteries,
no chargers...
INCREDIBLE
DYNALIGHT
will never fail just...
$19.95
Here is finally flashlight guaranteed to last, not just five or ten years, but virtually forever. Incredible DYNALIGHT has no batteries, no chargers, nothing to deteriorate, corrode or give out – ever! Secret is built-in generator, which provides power by gentle stroke of retractable handle. Indispensable for home, car and trail. Real lifesaver in any emergency, because you are completely independent of outside power! DYNALIGHT measures 4x2x1" and is sophisticated German quality product. Small investment for lifetime service and peace of mind – order today!
hennikers
779 Bush Street, Box 7584, San Francisco, CA 94120
YES subject to your two-week return privilege and one-year guarantee for parts and workmanship, please send me
incredible DYNALIGHTS at $19 95 each
My check for this amount, plus $1 50 for postage & insurance (plus sales tax for CA delivery) is enclosed
Please charge my BA / MC acct
No exp
BA / MC Accts. may call (212) 543-7003 or (415) 433-7540 for fastest service.
Mail to Henniker's, 779 Bush Street, Box 7584 San Francisco CA 94120
XX0000
I live at
In
State

Dynalights and Folding Chairs were two items that performed so well in the catalog that we "promoted" them to space advertising, a more demanding category. The Dynalight does well in almost all media, despite its rather steep price. The Chairs work only in selected media.

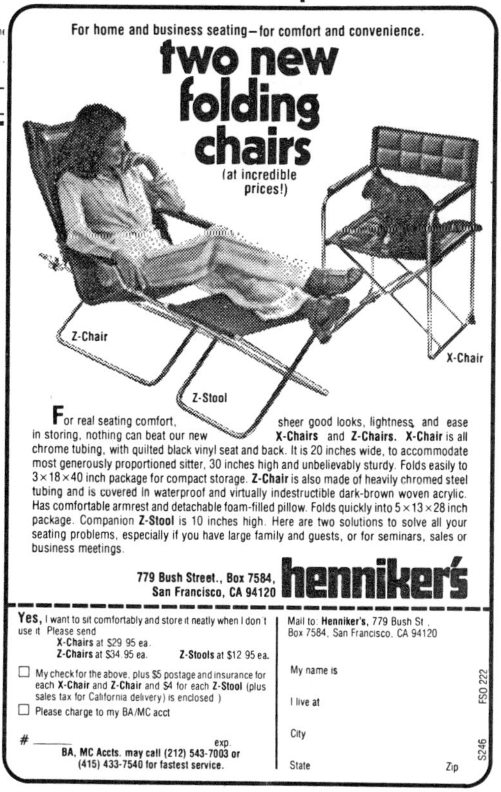
For home and business seating—for comfort and convenience.
two new folding chairs
(at incredible prices!)
Z-Chair
X-Chair
Z-Stool
For real seating comfort, sheer good looks, lightness, and ease in storing, nothing can beat our new X-Chairs and Z-Chairs. X-Chair is all chrome tubing, with quilted black vinyl seat and back. It is 20 inches wide, to accommodate most generously proportioned sitter, 30 inches high and unbelievably sturdy. Folds easily to 3×18×40 inch package for compact storage. Z-Chair is also made of heavily chromed steel tubing and is covered in waterproof and virtually indestructible dark-brown woven acrylic. Has comfortable armrest and detachable foam-filled pillow. Folds quickly into 5×13×28 inch package. Companion Z-Stool is 10 inches high. Here are two solutions to solve all your seating problems, especially if you have large family and guests, or for seminars, sales or business meetings.
779 Bush Street., Box 7584, San Francisco, CA 94120
hennikers
Yes, I want to sit comfortably and store it neatly when I don't use it Please send
X-Chairs at $29 95 ea.
Z-Chairs at $34.95 ea.
Z-Stools at $12 95 ea.
My check for the above, plus $5 postage and insurance for each X-Chair and Z-Chair and $4 for each Z-Stool (plus sales tax for California delivery) is enclosed)
Please charge to my BA/MC acct
exp.
BA, MC Accts. may call (212) 543-7003 or (415) 433-7540 for fastest service.
Mail to: Henniker's, 779 Bush St., Box 7584, San Francisco, CA 94120
My name is
I live at
City
State
Zip
FSO 222
S246

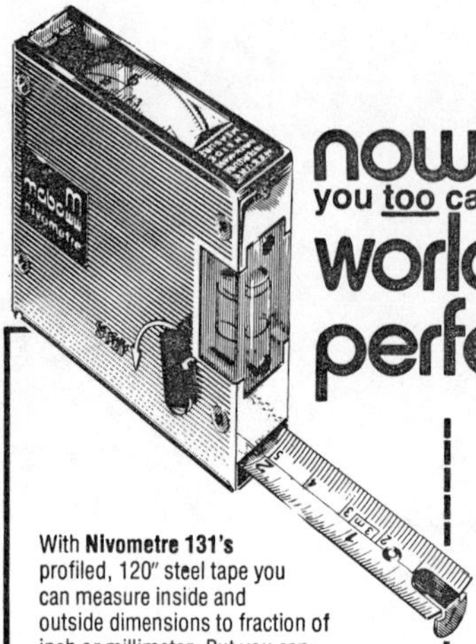

now
you too can work with . . .
world's most perfect tool

With **Nivometre 131's** profiled, 120" steel tape you can measure inside and outside dimensions to fraction of inch or millimeter. But you can perform many other nifty tricks. Lock in place and draw circles and parallels. Built-in levels lets you hang doors straight, and keep chairs from wobbling. **Nivometre 131** comes from France and is all chrome, stainless steel and acrylic. You measure things every day—so why not use the best and most versatile tool?

henniker's
779 Bush St., Box 7584, San Francisco, CA 94120

Mail to: **Henniker's,** 779 Bush Street, Box 7584, San Francisco, CA 94120
Please send me:
____ Nivometres 131 @ $12.95 each.
○ 3 Nivometres 131 for $35.95
____ Belt-looped cases @ $2.95 each
☐ My check for this amount, plus $1 for postage/insurance (plus sales tax for Calif. delivery) is enclosed.
☐ Please charge my BA, MC acct.
____
exp. ______

or for fastest service call **TOLL FREE (800) 648-5311**
[IN NEVADA (800) 992-5710] IN SF BAY AREA CALL 433-7540

We found both the Nivometre and the Sanyo PF Flashlight through sales representatives. They did not just offer these items from their broad selections, but we plucked these two because we thought they had unusual qualities and promotional possibilities. We were right: they have run successfully for years.

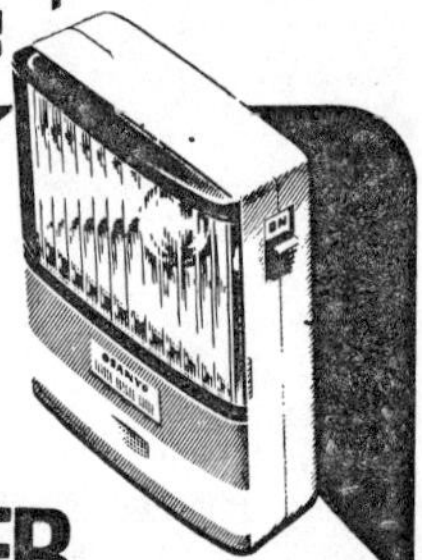

light that NEVER fails...

Trouble with ordinary flashlights is that they often don't work when you need them. Because chances are their batteries are dead. This can't happen with **Sanyo PF (Power Failure) Flashlight.** It's the **light that never fails.** Keep it plugged into any socket, if you wish, and its powerful NiCd batteries will stay at peak charge, providing soft night light at same time. But let power be interrupted—and **PF Light** automatically turns itself on, providing brilliant area illumination until power is restored. Unplug it, and it's a hand lantern of unusual brightness. **PF Light** is a "must". It packs a triple wallop: 1. nightlight, 2. automatic emergency floodlight, 3. great rechargeable flashlight—it will **never fail!**

henniker's
779 Bush St., San Francisco, CA 94108

Mail to: Henniker's, 779 Bush, San Francisco, CA 94108
Please send me:
____ Sanyo PF Flashlights @ $15.95 each
☐ 3 Sanyo PF Flashlights for $44.95 ☐ 6 Sanyo PF Flashlights for $85.95
☐ My check for this amount, plus $1 for postage/insurance (plus sales tax for Calif delivery) is enclosed.
☐ Please charge my BA, MC acct. # ____________ exp. ____
BA, MC Accts. may call (212) 543-7003 or (415) 433-7540 for fastest service.
I understand I have 2-week return privilege & 1 yr. guarantee parts & workmanship.
My name is ____________
I live at ____________
City ____________ State ______ Zip ______
SF0706 D 149-3

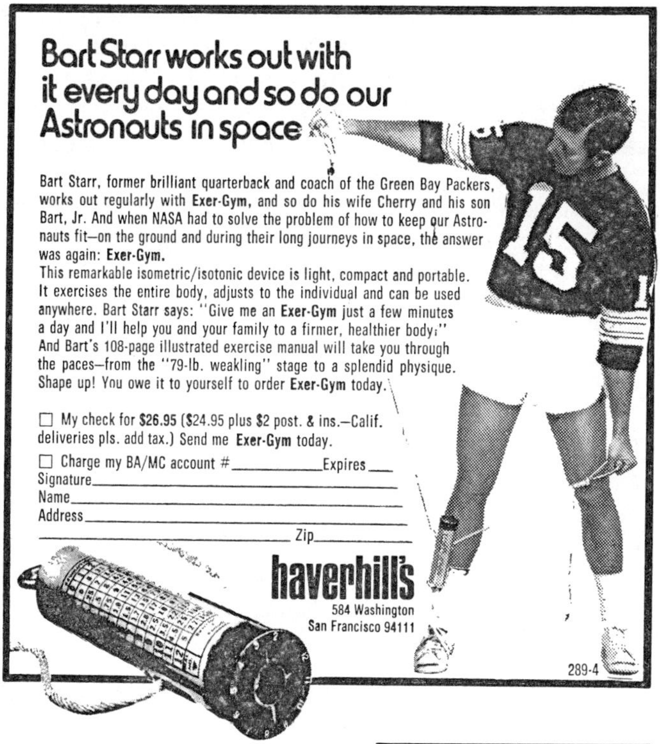

Bart Starr was also "promoted" from catalog to space and has done well for many years. President Nixon was a "sleeper." His likeness as a candle was a star attraction in our catalog. Though he would have qualified for "space status," we decided to forego it.

and somewhat fragile. My wife was Haverhill's merchandising manager and she insisted that we put it in. So we did. It was such a fantastic success that I couldn't believe it and thought that we had a computer error or something. But we didn't. It was the darndest and most surprising thing I had ever seen. I cannot give you the precise sales figures (they belong to Time Inc. and are confidential), but the Nixon Candle had an *index of 25,* which means that it produced 25 times as much profit per catalog space used as the average of the entire catalog. Naturally, I got ready to prepare space ads on this fantastic item, immediately after the Christmas rush. But about that time, lots of things happened to Mr. Nixon and I decided to leave it alone. Some people cashed in with Nixon watches and other such things, but I just didn't feel like going on with it.

Before leaving this subject: contrary to what you may have believed until now, space advertising is definitely not what the mail-order business is about. This may come as a great surprise to you. We shall talk about it in detail later in the book, but I thought I should briefly mention it now.

Direct Mail Merchandise

Please remember that the lines are not all that clearly drawn, but direct mail merchandise is the highest expression and has to fill the severest requirements of this business. A piece of merchandise may do marvels in your catalog, it may be a real winner in space advertising — and yet it may not be powerful enough to sustain a direct mail campaign. Because a direct mail campaign is not only very expensive in terms of the creative and technical cost of producing it, but also because the offer to the individual customer may cost as much as $.15 to $.25 each. And if you think of just a $5,000 production cost (easy) and a sample mailing of just 100,000 pieces at $.20 each, you have a quick crap shot of $25,000. This, as they used to say, "ain't hay," and you can't make very many mistakes and still stay alive. Compare that with a 2-column x 10" black/white ad in *The New York Times Sunday Magazine,* which will set you back something like $1,500. Nothing to sneeze at either, of course, but we don't have to emphasize the difference.

Promotion by direct mail is, however, one of the main pillars of your successful mail-order business. The risks are great, but the rewards for successful promotions are very large. The successful mail-order marketer will, therefore, be constantly on the lookout for suitable direct mail merchandise. He will attempt to create a "stable" of merchandise and mail pieces that he can successfully promote to his own list and to other lists.

I wish I could put into a formula or into a few pithy phrases what makes a good direct mail item. If I could really do that, I wouldn't have just the secret of how to make a million dollars, but I could probably position myself somewhere between Nelson Rockefeller and J. Paul Getty.

But let me try:

- Your direct mail product must be as closely attuned to your own buyers' list (and to those outside buyers' lists that you will select) as possible. The offer should hit them right in the solar plexus.
- While the item should find response within your customer group, it should have unusually wide appeal within that group. For example: if your established market, your mailing list, is women who sew, offer them a can't-resist-your-proposal sewing machine (with every conceivable gadget and attachment), rather than a handloom.

  If your market is buyers of office accessories, offer them a portable dictating machine, rather than an automatic drafting device. In both cases you have broad appeal, rather than appeal to a narrow subgroup. Sounds elementary? Of course, but you'd be surprised how often even "sophisticated" mailers throw this simple precept to the wind. They go ahead and sink a bundle (and lose it) by promoting an item that even within their niche of the market has too narrow an appeal.
- The price must be "right." After you have thanked me for this piece of wisdom, let's see what we can do with this generalization. It really means two things:

  First, the obvious, that the customer has to recognize *value for his/her money.* Most people, even if they are not inveterate shoppers or price comparers, know pretty well what things should cost. They will not accept an offer that does not correspond to their conception of value. And even if they should take your "bait," they will find out sooner or later that this was a poor deal. They will feel that they have been "had," and you will lose them as customers. Your million dollar business is absolutely based on gaining and keeping satisfied customers, so this would be a pretty poor bargain.

Second, the merchandise has to be in a *suitable price range* to have a chance at success in direct mail. There are exceptions, either way, but if I would have to generalize, and excepting installment sales offers, I would say that a successful direct mail offer should be in the $20 to $100 (maximum) range. The main target area, perhaps, should be between $40 and $60. We shall have much more to say about the "why's" later in the book

- The item should not be trademarked and should be "reasonably exclusive" to you. (I always shudder when I hear about "reasonably exclusive," but it's a term used in this business. It is somewhat analogous to "my wife is reasonably faithful" or "my bookkeeper is reasonably honest" — but don't let's fight industry practice). Reasons are obvious. If it is a trademarked item, you can bet your bottom French franc that some discount house is going to offer it for $10 less. You will hear most vociferously from those customers who have bought from you at full price. It isn't worth the annoyance, trouble, aggravation and bad customer relations. And if it is not at least "reasonably exclusive," your customer may be more induced to step into his friendly neighborhood hardware store and pick the thing up, rather than send you a check. He will have to wait for it to arrive, he is not 100% sure that it will work and that he can return it and get his money back if he isn't satisfied.
- The profit margin has to be "right." Direct mail is an expensive medium, and it is almost impossible to be successful if you don't have an adequate profit margin. What is "adequate" is a matter of feel, because it involves the interplay of likely volume of sales, costs, and sales price level.

  If I were under the gun and had to put it into arithmetic form, I would say that in the price range that we are considering, "minimum adequate" profit margin would be $5 plus 50% of sales price. Thus, your profit margin on a $20 retail item should be $15 to be suitable for direct mail. This means that your cost of the item should be $5. For a $50 item, your profit margin should be $30, or your cost should be $20. For an $80 item, your profit should be at least $45. Obviously, this, like any such generalized formulas, should be taken with several grains of salt and there are always "special cases" (but not too many) that warrant exception. But this rule-of-thumb formula will show you what to shoot for.

I guess I could formulate a few more "Joffe's laws" for direct mail items, but let's leave it at this. You have the general idea.

Where do you find these paragons of direct mail successes? Again, I wish I could reveal the magic secret, but I can't. It's important to develop a habit of looking at each piece of merchandise that crosses your path and consider it in terms of its possible suitability and success as a DM (direct mail) item. Remember the guy in high school who looked at every girl wondering "will she or won't she?" He made out all right — actually a whole lot better than his buddy who thought of all his distaff schoolmates as though they were just that, his classmates. The analogy may be far-fetched, but that's the way it is. You'll have to keep your eyes open, ask yourself, "will it or won't it" (make a good DM item) and keep looking and questioning all the time.

At Haverhill's, at Henniker's, and I suppose this would be a universal fact of life in the mail-order business, we produced some of our most spectacular and long-lasting DM successes by locating a piece of merchandise — either through publications, through our foreign agents or through foreign trade journals. Usually, a product as we found it, would not be quite suitable for the American taste. We would redesign it, re-engineer it and repackage it to fit the critical demands of the American market. These "spectaculars" had to fulfill every one of our requirements. Beyond what can be put into words, they had to have a certain "smell of success" about them. The most spectacular winners that we found in this way were the *StationMaster Clock* (which we virtually developed from the ground up and which is now a staple on the American clock market), the *No Hips Binoculars* and the *La Peppina Expresso Machine.*

And then there is what I call the "ascension route," namely the migration from a catalog item to a space item and, if it continues to be successful in that category, to a direct mail item. We

is handsome reproduction, faithful to every last detail, of 19th century railroad clock Case of StationMaster is crafted of solid hardwood (not veneers) lovingly hand-rubbed to antique sheen Pendulum and all metal parts are gleaming brass And you can absolutely depend on clockwork. It's 31-day chime movement, all brass, make that's renowned for sturdiness and reliability. Chimes peal full and half hours, and red calendar hand points to date, just as in clocks of yore. We guarantee StationMaster unconditionally for one year. In unlikely case that you are not delighted you may return clock within two weeks for prompt and courteous refund Our large purchase and assembly contracts make our astonishingly low price possible Grace your home with this outstanding reliable clock and exquisite example of Americana. Order StationMaster today!

You can produce direct mail successes by locating a piece of merchandise, and re-design or "re-package" it to fit the American market and the American taste. These three items were great direct mail products and also performed beautifully in the catalog and in space.

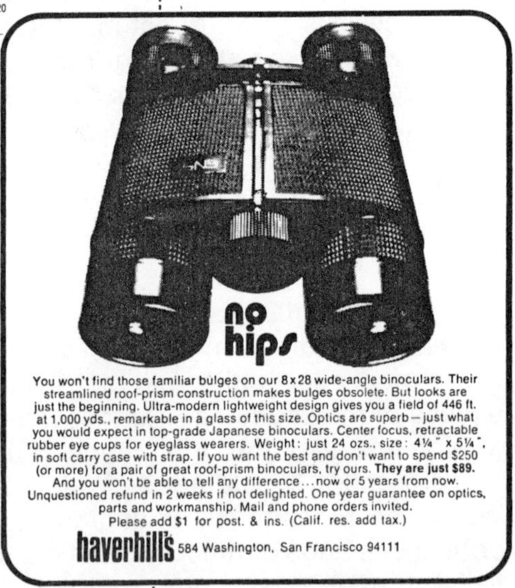
no hips
You won't find those familiar bulges on our 8x28 wide-angle binoculars. Their streamlined roof-prism construction makes bulges obsolete. But looks are just the beginning. Ultra-modern lightweight design gives you a field of 446 ft. at 1,000 yds., remarkable in a glass of this size. Optics are superb—just what you would expect in top-grade Japanese binoculars. Center focus, retractable rubber eye cups for eyeglass wearers. Weight: just 24 ozs., size: 4¼" x 5¼", in soft carry case with strap. If you want the best and don't want to spend $250 (or more) for a pair of great roof-prism binoculars, try ours. They are just $89. And you won't be able to tell any difference... now or 5 years from now. Unquestioned refund in 2 weeks if not delighted. One year guarantee on optics, parts and workmanship. Mail and phone orders invited.
Please add $1 for post. & ins. (Calif. res. add tax.)
haverhill's 584 Washington, San Francisco 94111

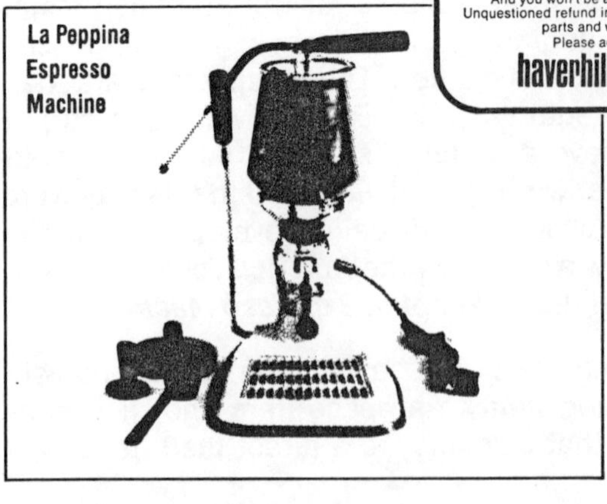

Espresso

have had quite a few of those. The ubiquitous Emoskop and Monaco were among Haverhill's consistently successful mail pieces for six or seven years and continue to perform beautifully for Henniker's. And there were others: the *Henniscope,* the *Ranger* (range finder) and the *Rondo Clock.* They all worked their way up from catalog space to direct mail.

PUT YOUR OWN "STAMP" ON YOUR MERCHANDISE

I must now tell you about a technique that has grown extremely successful for me over the years. I introduced this technique at Haverhill's — I don't think it had ever been done before on any systematic basis — and I am now doing the same thing, with similar success at Henniker's.

It is the technique of applying your name or part of your name to your merchandise. You accomplish four principal purposes with that:

- You avoid possible infringement of other people's names and trademarks.
- Every piece of merchandise that is in circulation carries your name. It is therefore an advertisement for your business and for your merchandise.
- You now have *branded* merchandise (your own distinctive brand), instead of unbranded (or branded with a brand that does nothing for you), undifferentiated merchandise that is carried by many others. You can avoid price pressure and price comparison.
- You are creating a family of products, each of which is supporting and promoting every other.

We stumbled into this technique partly by accident and partly by necessity. The necessity came about after having unwittingly infringed on trademarks of others and either having to change names of products (which can be very expensive and which loses most of the goodwill previously created for the item) or worse — being sued for alleged money damages by those who felt thus infringed.

The most painful example I can give you is that of the Monaco Shaver, which, when we first introduced it, and for the first three years or so, was known as "Riviera." One day we got a letter from

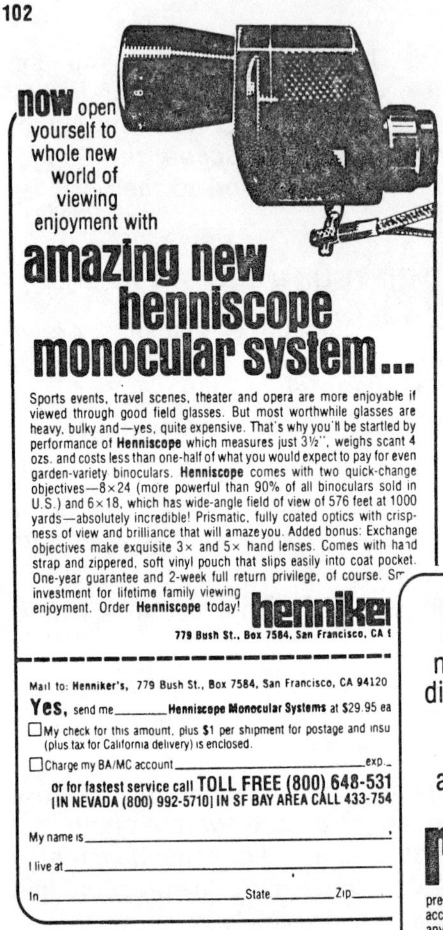

now open yourself to whole new world of viewing enjoyment with
amazing new henniscope monocular system...
Sports events, travel scenes, theater and opera are more enjoyable if viewed through good field glasses. But most worthwhile glasses are heavy, bulky and—yes, quite expensive. That's why you'll be startled by performance of Henniscope which measures just 3½", weighs scant 4 ozs. and costs less than one-half of what you would expect to pay for even garden-variety binoculars. Henniscope comes with two quick-change objectives—8×24 (more powerful than 90% of all binoculars sold in U.S.) and 6×18, which has wide-angle field of view of 576 feet at 1000 yards—absolutely incredible! Prismatic, fully coated optics with crispness of view and brilliance that will amaze you. Added bonus: Exchange objectives make exquisite 3× and 5× hand lenses. Comes with hand strap and zippered, soft vinyl pouch that slips easily into coat pocket. One-year guarantee and 2-week full return privilege, of course. Sm
investment for lifetime family viewing enjoyment. Order Henniscope today!
hennike
779 Bush St., Box 7584, San Francisco, CA
Mail to: Henniker's, 779 Bush St., Box 7584, San Francisco, CA 94120
Yes, send me ______ Henniscope Monocular Systems at $29.95 ea
My check for this amount, plus $1 per shipment for postage and insu (plus tax for California delivery) is enclosed.
Charge my BA/MC account ______ exp.
or for fastest service call TOLL FREE (800) 648-531
(IN NEVADA (800) 992-5710) IN SF BAY AREA CALL 433-754
My name is
I live at
In ______ State ______ Zip

These three items worked their way up "all the way" from catalog merchandise, through space, to direct mail. Henniscope and Ranger still survive after ten years or more. The Rondo Clock is a relic of the past.

One of America's Nobel Prize winning physicists developed and patented this incredible precision optical instrument that lets you determine distances quickly and accurately from 6 inches to almost as far as eye can see. Simply "shoot" any target of approximately known size—person, golf flag, boat—yes, even the moon, and with just turn of graduated dial pinpoint distance quickly in read-out window. And you can read it in feet, yards, miles (nautical or statute) or even metric units—it's all the same to Ranger. With just few minutes practice you should get accuracy of 98% or better over any distance. Ranger is indispensable for golfer, yachtsman, hunter, photographer or just anybody who wants to know quickly and accurately
from here to there. You may even use with compass for surveys
rain. Get best and most advanced instrument of its kind,

Ranger today!

ant to know quickly and accurately how far it is from here to there.

Rangers @ $26.95 each

additional saving: Six (6) Rangers for $148.95

an attorney, who informed us that we were infringing on the trademark of his client (he was right!) and to change the name immediately.

We had no choice — we had to do it. It was pretty much a debacle, because we had to change the tools for the plastic housing of the shaver, prepare completely new promotional material, devise new packaging, make new ads, and much more. It cost us a bundle. And what's more, the goodwill that we had built for the Riviera name was lost. We renamed the shaver the "Monaco" —fortunately no one has yet come out of the woodwork with a claim to that name.

The next case involved a little optical instrument that we called "Miniscope," We really should have known better. It's such a natural name for a small optical instrument that somebody was bound to have preempted it. And sure enough, somebody had. He thought he had made his fortune when he found that we had infringed on his trademark and he was "going to sue you for all you're worth." He got calmed down, we settled for a few hundred bucks, but we had to give up the name "Miniscope."

I was not going to let this happen again, so I came up with a list of about five likely names and had my patent/trademark attorney check them out one by one. The so-called preliminary check on a name costs approximately $50, and since every one of the names that I had thought up belonged already to somebody else, it was clear to me that we could spend a lot of time and even more money chasing down a name for a product.

Then it came to me in a flash: why not call the instrument "Haverscope?" The name, Haverhill's, was registered to us, so nobody could possibly assail "Haverscope." And, of course, I was right. It was a beautiful accident and a good insight, because I accomplished all the purposes that I had set.

The *Haverscope* (which by now has graduated to *Henniscope*) was only the first in a long line of distinctive merchandise items that carried the "Haver" name. It was followed in fairly quick succession by the *Haverwatch,* the *Haverlite,* the *Havershaver* (rechargeable shaver, stablemate yet competitor of Monaco), *Haverdryer,* the *Haverdigit* (a digital watch), *Haversnips* (little travel scissors), *Haverclock,* and others. It worked out extremely well. Each piece of merchandise looked distinctly ours. We didn't just give it a name and provide it with a distinctive logo, but we usually

Don't step off pavement without . . .

henniCamper $10⁹⁵

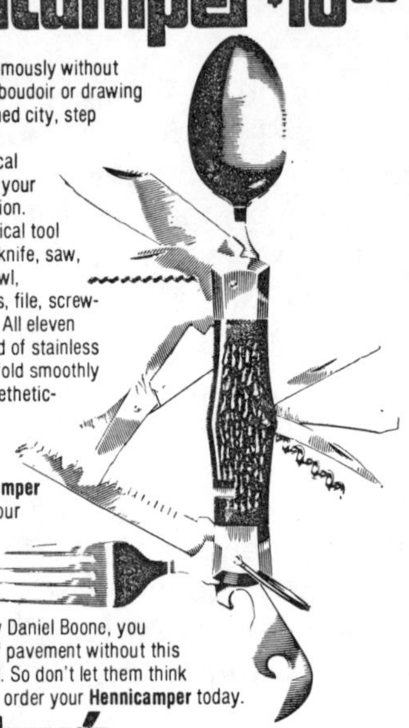

You may get along famously without it in big-city office, boudoir or drawing room. But once you shed city, step off pavement and into great outdoors, practical **Hennicamper** must be your indispensable companion. This lovable and practical tool contains fork, spoon, knife, saw, small drawing knife, awl, bottle opener, scissors, file, screw-driver and corkscrew. All eleven instruments are forged of stainless and carbon steel and fold smoothly into **Hennicamper** synethetic-horn body. And there is real leather belt-looped pouch that lets you stow **Hennicamper** away, yet puts it at your ready reach. Whether you are scout-master, fisherman, camper, casual picnicker or latter-day Daniel Boone, you just shouldn't step off pavement without this universal outdoor tool. So don't let them think of you as city slicker: order your **Hennicamper** today.

henniker's

779 Bush Street, Box 7584, San Francisco, CA 94120

Henniker's, 779 Bush St., Box 7584, San Francisco, CA 94120

Yes, I want to be prepared. Please send me:

__ Hennicampers with leather belt-looped pouch @ $10.95 each

☐ For special savings. Three (3) Hennicampers for just $29.95.

○ My check for this amount, plus $1 for postage, insur. (plus sales tax f

○ Please charge BA / MC account # ______

or for fastest service call TOLL FREE (800) 6

[IN NEVADA (800) 992-5710] IN SF BAY AREA CALL

My name is ______

I live at ______

In ______ State ______ Zip ______

whoops time is up!

You'll never, never again be caught flat-footed (or worse) by expired parking meter, overcooked roast, untaken pill or overslept siesta. Because **Hennichron** is reliable pocket alarm that can be set from one minute to two hours. And when time is up it will buzz-buzz like a mad hornet, wake you up, shake you loose and remind you of chore to be done. If you are a doer and not a foot dragger, **Hennichron** should be your monitor and conscience. Comes with nifty chrome chain and keyring. Set yourself on the road to action: order your **Hennichron** pocket-alarm today!

779 Bush St., Box 7584, San Francisco, CA 94120 **henniker's**

Henniker's, 779 Bush St., Box 7540, San Francisco, CA 94120

YES, I don't want to be a sluggard. Send ______ **Hennichrons** at $9.95 ea.

☐ My check, plus $1 for postage/insurance expense (please add sales tax for Calif. deliv.) is enclosed.

☐ Charge my BA., MC acct.

______ exp. ______

or for fastest service call TOLL FREE (800) 648-5311

[IN NEVADA (800) 992-5710] IN SF BAY AREA CALL 433-7540

My name is ______

Time at a glance just $14⁹⁵

Hennidigit tells you at glance **exactly** what time is . . . not somewhere between 3:00 and 4:00 o'clock, but 3:27 on nose. This exclusive import from Switzerland features Roskopf movement to keep it running smoothly and accurately for many years. Comes in silver-toned, brushed aluminum case, with sporty tropical strap. Choose from man's or lady's model, both incredible bargains at just $14.95 each. And you can buy his/hers pair for extra saving. **Hennidigit** is guaranteed for one year and you may return it within two weeks for full credit or refund if you are not delighted. Make **sure** what time it is: Order **Hennidigit** today!

henniker's

779 Bush St., Box 7584, San Francisco, CA 94120

Mail to Henniker's 779 Bush St., Box 7584, San Francisco, CA 94120

YES, please send me:

☐ **men's Hennidigits** @ $14.95

☐ **ladies' Hennidigits** @ $14.95

☐ **his/hers Hennidigit pairs** @ $27.90

☐ I enclose my check in this amount, plus $1 per shipment for postage and handling. Calif. deliveries, please add tax.

☐ Charge BA, MC acct. # ______ exp. ______

BA, MC may call (212) 543-7003 or (415) 433-7540 for fast service.

My name is ______

I live at ______

In ______ State ______ Zip ______

H195-1

Three successful items to which we lent "personality" by investing them with the "Henni" brand. All of them are good merchandise, but investing them with a brand name game them a special uniqueness.

redesigned appearance and packaging sufficiently to make it truly different from anything else on the market. Naturally, we are doing the same thing very successfully now at Henniker's. I illustrate a few examples of such naming and packaging. And even in those cases in which we decided to keep the original name, such as the *Swiss Army Style Knife,* we usually always give the item our distinctive stamp by designing our own package and instructions for it.

This is a technique that I cannot recommend too strongly to you. There are three points to think about:

- You can't really afford to do this kind of thing until you are ready to commit for reasonably large quantities of merchandise. For instance, if you want to buy watches with your own brand and dial, you'll have to commit for perhaps 10 dozen. If you want to put your name on a small radio you might have to take 500 to 1,000 pieces. And, of course, it takes planning, money and time. They can't pull merchandise with your name on it and with your package right off the shelf.
- You don't want to overdo it and you don't want things to sound ludicrous. For instance, you wouldn't want to call something the Henni-Electric Alarm Clock. I am sure you get the idea. In general, you want to do it only with merchandise that you expect to sell in large quantities. While certainly not restricted to it, it is probably most indicated for promotional merchandise.
- We all make mistakes, and a piece of merchandise that you believe to have carefully tested, can turn out to be a dud, a lemon, a return hassle and source of customer dissatisfaction. This annoyance of shoddy merchandise is greatly aggravated if it carries your name, because, naturally, you will achieve an effect completely opposite from that which you had intended. So be very careful with what you put your name on, or as Zenith puts it: "The quality goes in before the name goes on."

A WORD ABOUT THE GOLDEN NOSE

You may be getting a little exhausted about merchandise by now, but before we close this chapter, let me tell you about the

You shouldn't just stop at naming your product — you should go a step further and invest time, effort and money in designing special proprietary packaging for those products that you feel you should really put your weight behind. Here are examples of packages that we have developed at Henniker's for some of our most popular products.

"golden nose." One of my good friends is Dr. Christian Heine, son of the founder of Heinrich Heine, the foremost specialty mail-order house in Germany. They have a "Golden Nose" award — it is an actual trophy — for that member of their merchandise committee who in any year has been most successful in "smelling out" successful merchandise. For some reason that I don't quite understand, they call their award "le Prix de le nez d'or" rather than (as they should) "Der Goldene Nasenpreis." At Henniker's we simply called it "golden nose prize." It was won three years in a row by Priscilla, my wife, and then we retired it. But seriously, the ability to "sniff out" good merchandise for mail order is very much of a gift. If you have it, cultivate it. If you don't have it, but have somebody on your team that does, treat him or her very gently. This is one of the very valuable (and almost indispensable) persons in your million dollar mail-order business.

At seminars and lectures across the country, I have often been asked what characteristics a "good mail-order item" should have. The first time I heard the question, I stammered, stuttered and improvised. But in case this happens to be *your* question, and considering that we talk in generalities, let's see what we can come up with:

- It should be such that the customer will get, not just what he expected, but something a little better. It should be an obvious value for money spent.
- It should be of wide appeal.
- It should be light in weight (less than 1 lb. — so it can be shipped by third class mail), should neither be bulky nor fragile.
- It should be an item on which you have a "reasonable exclusive."
- It should be unbranded merchandise.
- It should give you an "adequate" margin of profit (we have discussed what that is).
- It should be of such quality and good construction that it won't konk out during its 1-year guarantee period (which is customary in this business) and hopefully for some reasonable time beyond that. This suggests merchandise that either has no moving parts or, if it has moving parts,

that they be hermetically sealed against probing fingers of would-be adjusters of the mechanism.

Since, as you will inevitably find out, returned merchandise is the greatest pain in the neck (and other dorsal parts of the anatomy) in this business, I had at one time formulated an additional requirement for a good mail order item:

- It should immediately disintegrate, vaporize and disappear into thin smoke if the purchaser thought of returning it. Since my fairy godmother steadfastly (and I suppose, rightly) declined to accede to this request, I gave up on that and decided to concentrate on the first seven requirements. It worked out pretty well.

We have covered quite a bit of territory in this chapter about mail-order merchandise. Before we go on, let's summarize what we have talked about.

NUTSHELLING WHAT YOU SHOULD KNOW ABOUT MAIL-ORDER MERCHANDISE

- Try to create one or several promotional items — as list builders *and* moneymakers. "Promos" should have tie-in with the general thrust of your business.
- Pick *real* merchandise to fit your chosen line of merchandising activity. This line should be something for which you have talent, experience or to which you can bring something to bear. Expand your line from your narrow specialty into widening circles of related merchandise.
- Find products by faithfully reading all pertinent literature — consumer and trade publications and competitors' catalogs. Visit trade fairs, get yourself known in your industry and cultivate manufacturers' representatives.
- Distinguish between the promotional possibilities of merchandise. You may decide on different classifications, but the division into catalog, space and direct mail merchandise is helpful. Categories are not completely fixed. Merchandise can "migrate" upward — and downward.
- Price merchandise properly.

- Keep your eyes open at all times. Subject, in your mind, all merchandise that you come in contact with to the question as to whether it would make a good item for your business. There are certain requirements as to what makes a "good mail-order item." Go back over the list a few pages back.

- Consider putting your own "stamp" on your merchandise.

Now we know what to look for. Our next problem is how to promote and sell merchandise. The first thing you'll have to learn is how to be successful in space advertising. So let's talk about that in the next chapter.

Just before going to press, and after re-reading this chapter for the last time, I thought I should give you another piece of *specific* information. I should give you the names of what I think of as the most important foreign trade magazines that cover general merchandise. You should consider subscribing to some or all of them — it will pay you great dividends in merchandise information. Here goes:

- *The Importer,* c/o East Asia Publishing Co., 2-11 Jingumae, 1-Chome, Shibuya-ku, Tokyo 150, Japan — $20/year
- *Hong Kong Enterprise,* 3rd fl., Connaught Centre, Central Hong Kong — $20/year
- *Asian Sources,* c/o Trade Media Ltd., P. O. Box K-1786, Kowloon Central, Hong Kong — $25/year
- *Made in Europe,* P. O. Box 174027, D-6, Frankfurt/Main, 17 W. Germany — $30/year

And as long as we talk about publications, by all means subscribe to the "bible":

- *Direct Marketing,* c/o Hoke Publications, 224 7th St., Garden City, NY 11535 — $18/year

That is all about merchandise for now. We know what to look for and where to find it. Our next problem is how to promote and sell merchandise. The first thing you'll have to learn is how to be successful in space advertising. So let's talk about that in the next chapter.

Chapter 3

HOW TO CREATE GREAT SPACE ADVERTISING

You will start your career in the mail order business by making sales and getting customers through advertising in "space." "Space," in case you are not familiar with the term, is not the void between the planets, but it is magazine and newspaper space. You may also call it advertising in print media.

WHAT ROLE DOES SPACE ADVERTISING PLAY IN THE MAIL-ORDER BUSINESS?

Most beginners in mail order believe that space advertising is what this business is all about, but this is definitely not the case. There are mail-order businesses, some of them seemingly quite successful — that do really nothing but space advertising and a little "bounceback" (patience, that comes later). They do not engage at all — or hardly at all — in any direct mail effort, and they do not mail out catalogs.

So, obviously, it can be done. I assure you that it is very much the exception. In your success-oriented business, space advertising should play a role — a very important one at the beginning, but one that should gradually decline in importance as your business progresses.

The reason that its importance should decline is that space advertising is, unfortunately, quite risky and the "crap shots" are usually rather large. In order to do things professionally, you have to put quite a bit of money at risk. Unless you think in terms of very tiny ads in small publications or of classified advertising, you usually have to take quite a gamble. Normally, you have to buy the whole circulation of any publication in which you advertise. Sure, some of the larger publications have "regional" editions," and you can buy the "regionals." But even the regional editions are usually quite formidable in circulation and cost. What is more, the "cost per thousand" (we'll learn more about that later) will normally be a lot higher in the regional editions than in the full edition of the publication in which you advertise.

Naturally, there is another way in which you can decrease your cost, and that is by taking small space ads rather than large space ads. You certainly should do that in the beginning, until you are very sure of what you are doing. Even so, there are certain limitations, beneath which you won't want to go, or really cannot go. Because if your ad is too small, it will "get lost" on the page — and it is, of course, much easier even to get lost on a large newspaper page than it is on a magazine page. Also, your illustration — and you definitely need that, and your coupon — and you most definitely need that also, will not allow you to go below a minimum size.

Well, you'll ask, if space advertising is so risky and so difficult, why should I fool around with it at all? The answer is that there is really no other reasonable way to get started in this business. You need to build a mailing list of satisfied customers, and the only rational way to do that in the beginning is by space advertising.

I shall try to teach you how to conduct your space advertising so "scientifically" and so carefully that you will build a large mailing list by such advertising. And I shall teach you how to do it at minimum expense.

I shall teach you methods by which you will not just do that, but by which you will also make money in the process. And I shall show you how you can build a mailing list fast, so that you can reduce your reliance on space advertising as quickly as possible. You will then be able to put an ever-increasing proportion of your advertising budget into media that you "control," namely your own direct mail, your own catalogs and your own bouncebacks.

A CLARIFICATION ABOUT "COST OF ADVERTISING"

Let me just say a word about the "cost of advertising" in a mail-order business. Most businesses think of advertising as an "expense," and they think in terms of "our advertising budget is

20% of sales, 25% of sales" or whatever. They consider advertising as something that in tough times can be cut out or at least reduced.

I know that this — if advertising made any sense to begin with, is fallacious reasoning in any business. But most businesses can probably get by with this fallacy for quite a little while before they feel the effect of their poor judgment. In the mail-order business, it would obviously be a fatal error to think this way. If you are inclined to such reasoning, you should free yourself from it as quickly as possible.

Because advertising *is not an expense* in the mail-order business. It is *"input."* And the question to ask is not: "What percentage of sales is advertising expense. The question to ask is: "How many dollars of sales — what multiple — does each dollar of advertising input produce?" You may say it amounts to the same thing, just stated in reverse, but it does not. The way you pose the question, the way you approach the problem, what you consider cause and effect make all the difference in the world.

And when things get tough, you won't be tempted to reduce your advertising. You will look for ways to *improve* your advertising and to make it more successful and more effective. Instead of making each dollar of advertising input produce $3 in sales (which others may look at as a "33% advertising expense") you will bend every effort, and use your wit and knowledge, to make every dollar of your advertising input produce $4 in sales (suddenly your "advertising expense" is reduced to 25%). And you will try to invest more dollars successfully in this manner.

I just cannot stress this point enough. It sounds perhaps like a minor quibble. But really, it is the mental attitude needed to be successful in the mail-order business. It is very important. You must try to accept this way of thinking and you should never forget it.

Advertising is not an expense.

It is your input, it is your electricity, it is your engine, the wind that turns your mill and — it is what makes your business go. And the better you can use advertising — space, which we talk about in this chapter — and in its other forms, the quicker and more directly will you go to success.

A Few Technical Points

Let me get a few "technical," but rather simple things out of the way before we go into the "how to" of space advertising.

There are different kinds of space in which you will wish to advertise. The most important are the following:

- *Standard magazine page.* Measures 7" x 10" and is divided into 3 columns. Each column is 140 lines deep. (A "line," in printers parlance is 1/14th of an inch — it sounds a little crazy but that is the way it is, and if you don't want to sound like a beginner, you'd better learn it).

  Space is usually purchased in the following sizes: full pages; two columns (2/3rd pages); one column (1/3rd page, vertical); 2 x 1/2 columns (2 columns x 70 lines, also called 1/3rd page square); 1/6th page (1/2 column); 1/12th page (1/4 column — 2-1/2", 35 lines).

  In many magazines, you need not buy these "standard formats," but simply the number of lines you need. You should, however, discipline yourself from the very beginning to prepare your advertising in standard formats. This will enable you to move your ads from one magazine to another, without any bother. Also, if you use non-standard ads, you will be relegated to the boneyard of the book — the back pages, and that will most unfavorably influence your pull.

- *Sunday Supplements.* You are familiar with them — they are *Parade* or *Family Weekly,* (which are syndicated publications that run in many cities on Sundays) and which have very large circulation. Large dailies have their own Sunday supplements. The best known (and the best) of these is *The New York Times Sunday Magazine,* followed by *The Chicago Tribune Magazine, The Los Angeles Times Magazine* and several others.

  Their page size is 10" wide. The page is divided into 5 columns, of 1-15/16" (if this doesn't seem to add up you are correct — the difference is accounted for by the spaces between columns). Each column is 170 lines deep (figure it out, that is just a little over 12"). You usually have to buy a standard format (and again, you should discipline yourself to prepare your ads in standard formats) — these "standards" being multiples of 1/20th of a page. Thus, since the page is 5 x 170, or 850 lines, the smallest standard unit is 1/20th of a page — 42 1/2 lines. A popular small ad size is 1/5th page, 170 lines which is usually taken as two columns x 85 lines.

- *Newspapers.* You don't have to worry about the size of a full newspaper page, because you are not likely to ever buy that. What you are concerned with is the width of the columns so that you can prepare your artwork properly. Unfortunately, this is a matter that is somewhat in flux. Quite a few newspapers are in the process of narrowing their columns and to schedule more advertising columns per page. This, supposedly, saves paper, but mostly increases revenue. You should get information from each individual paper (initially, probably only your home town paper) as to their exact mechanical requirements. But it is probably correct to say that most U.S. newspapers have a 1-7/8th inch width advertising column. There is one notable (and as far as I know singular) exception: it is *The Wall Street Journal.* They stoutly continue the custom of six columns per page. This makes each column 2-1/4 inches wide, and therefore, compatible with a magazine column. *The Wall Street Journal* used to have a stablemate, *The National Observer.* It had the same generous column width. But, alas, it expired, and that leaves *The Wall Street Journal* as one of its kind.

  Newspapers usually have few size limitations, so you can run any size ad you want, as long as you adhere to the column width. The only conditions are usually that you must run your ad of minimum depth if you go beyond one column — more depth required the wider your ad. Also, once you go beyond a certain depth, you may have to buy the full depth of the column. But this is not really anything you should be very much concerned with — surely not at the beginning.

- *Digest Sizes.* You know what they are — primarily *The Reader's Digest* and *TV-Guide.* The former has little interest to mail order advertisers. It simply is not a good medium. To make things worse, it is a monthly, and that takes very long scheduling.

- *TV-Guide* is a different kettle of fish altogether. It is the largest circulation magazine in the country, and you can test any ad in a small fraction of their total circulation. The page size is 4-1/2 x 6-7/8 inches. It is divided into two columns. It is a very difficult market since the very vastness of the audience makes it somewhat unresponsive. There is no real selection of the audience, no common denominator, except that they like to look at television. But if you hit on something that clicks, something that works with this enormous audience, you can make your fortune very quickly. It is a weekly and the circulation numbers (and *possible* profits) are truly fabulous.

There is one other "technical matter you should familiarize yourself with, and that is the different methods of printing. For our purposes, there are really only three important methods:

- *Offset.* Most magazines and newspapers are printed in this manner. Printing is done with a "flat plate" which is treated by special means to make ink adhere to those portions that are meant to print, and not to those that are not meant to print. The ink on the plate is transferred to another cylinder that "offsets" it to the paper. The preparation of such printing is easy — all you have to supply is your paste-up or a good positive copy of it, a so-called "reproduction proof."
- *Letterpress.* This is a process that prints with regular metal plates, usually zinc or copper. Quite a few magazines, especially those that pride themselves on their detailed reproductions, print in this manner. Your cost is somewhat higher, because you will either have to supply the plates to the publication, or you have to pay them to make a plate for you.
- *Rotogravure.* This is the printing method used for Sunday supplements and similar publications. Technically, the rotogravure process is almost the exact opposite from the letterpress process. Because the areas to be printed, instead of being raised as with letterpress, are depressed and ink is deposited in those depressions. Just as in offset, all you have to supply to the publication is your artwork, or "reproduction proof." They will make their own plate from your material. That step is included in the space cost.

So much for that. The preceding few paragraphs obviously don't make you a printing expert. But if you had no previous exposure to printing, these are perhaps the most important printing fundamentals you should be familiar with. You will learn all that you need to know as you go along.

All the foregoing, by the way, refers only to black/white printing. Color is a different story altogether. But in all likelihood, for the first few years of your business life in mail order you won't be involved with anything but black/white printing for space ads. So why concern ourselves with anything else? We'll have to touch on color printing when we talk about direct mail and about catalogs. But that can wait.

THOUGHTS TO KEEP IN MIND IN PREPARING AN AD

Also, purposely, don't let's talk at this time about the "mechanics" of preparing an ad, the personnel needed, etc. That will also come later. Let's just talk in this chapter about how you should go about creating a super ad, that will create customers, sell merchandise, and generate profits beyond the cost of producing the ad and beyond the cost of the space that it occupies.

This is not quite as easy as it sounds, because space is expensive. And in talking about making a good ad, we already assume two things:

1. That you have selected attractive merchandise, and
2. That your "proposition" is attractive. The "proposition" is your entire offer — the price at which you offer the merchandise, your return privilege, your Guarantee, and any bonus or discount.

In preparing an ad, you have to keep in mind the thousands of advertising impressions to which each reader is constantly subjected and the hundreds of advertising impressions in any medium that compete with yours for the reader's attention. Once the reader has turned the page, you have lost him or her forever. Therefore, you usually have to "grab" him in the fleeting instant that your ad (hopefully) catches his or her eye. And if it catches his eye, you have to persuade him to start reading what you have to say. That isn't all that easy to do.* More difficult even is to make the

* For simplicity's sake and in order to avoid having to say he and she, his or her constantly, we shall unisex the reader and use, for the sake of convenience only, the masculine pronoun. Naturally, one does not have to be "liberated" to realize that women are possibly more important in this business than men. The use of the masculine gender is just a simplifying device.

customer *act* on what he has read and accept your proposition. None of this is a snap. Just think of it: everybody keeps his wallet pocket tightly zipped. And here you are, probably several thousand miles away, communicating with a person who has possibly never heard of you before and who certainly has never seen you. Your job is to persuade him to accept a proposition, from a total stranger, from somebody who might as easily be a highbinder as an honest person, and be so convincing that he will actually pull out his checkbook and write a check in your favor. Now that you think about it, doesn't it sound like a tall order? Well, it is!

THE "STANDARD" FORM OF A SPACE AD

While there are variations on the theme, my advice to you is not to depart from the "standard format" of a space ad until you are very sure of what you are doing. And after you are very sure of what you are doing, you will probably decide that the standard format is best.

The "standard" format mail-order ad has the following components:

- Lead-in or "call-out"
- Headline
- Illustration
- Body copy
- Coupon

Before we think about these, one by one, remember once again that all of your wit, your talent, your fine art and your clever words will come to nought if you don't catch the reader's attention. It is true, sometimes publications seem to make it purposely difficult for even your own mother-in-law to find your ad because they have stuck it away in the gutter (that's the part closest to the fold), on Page 180. But even then it is still up to you to catch the reader's attention (if it can be done at all).

It is very hard (let's call it impossible) to catch the reader's attention with the body copy or with the coupon. So that leaves you with the lead-in or call-out, with the headline and with the illustration. Naturally, you will want to make all three elements really "grabbers," so that you will have as much as possible working for you. Let's have a look:

Lead-in or call-out. This is one element of the standard format that you may be able to dispense with from time to time. But generally you should have it. It can consist of one or two parts. The *call-out* is the attention-getter and consists of such corny and shopworn, but nevertheless, very effective words, as: "New," "Now," "How to (Start, Avoid, Improve)," "What You Should Know About," "Special," "Last Days," "Award-winning," "Fantastic Savings," etc.

Some advertisers use at least one of these phrases in every ad. My personal feeling is that, while you do have to call attention to your ad, this whole thing can very easily be overdone and you run the risk of being too strident. And if you want to impart a quality image to your merchandise and to your business, you should endeavor to call attention and still avoid stridency.

I have usually been able to overcome this dilemma by incorporating the "call-out" word, in the lead-in, perhaps accenting it by underlining, or by special graphic touches. Look at our Nivometer ad. The lead-in reads, "Now you too can work with world's most perfect tool." The call-out, *"Now"* is part of the lead-in. The word, "Now," boldfaced, and positioned at the very top of the ad, catches the reader's eye, and leads him smoothly into the headline, "World's Most Useful Tool," into the copy and, hopefully, into the proposition, the coupon and the purchase.

The *Nivometer* ad has been very successful. I showed you a reproduction of this ad in the preceding chapter. We sell so many of them that we are importing them directly from France in our own package, and our own execution. We don't sell them just by mail order, but have a thriving wholesale and premium business in this item. More about that later.

I have followed an almost identical pattern with the *Ranger Distance Measurer,* a steady standby of my Haverhill's business and now again at Henniker's. Once more, take a look at the ad and notice how the "Now" call-out draws the reader into the ad. The lead-in tells the reader and potential purchaser quickly what the ad is all about.

Headline. Having caught your reader's attention with your lead-in, you now must quickly tell him, with your headline, what the ad is about. You have to further rouse his curiosity and interest and

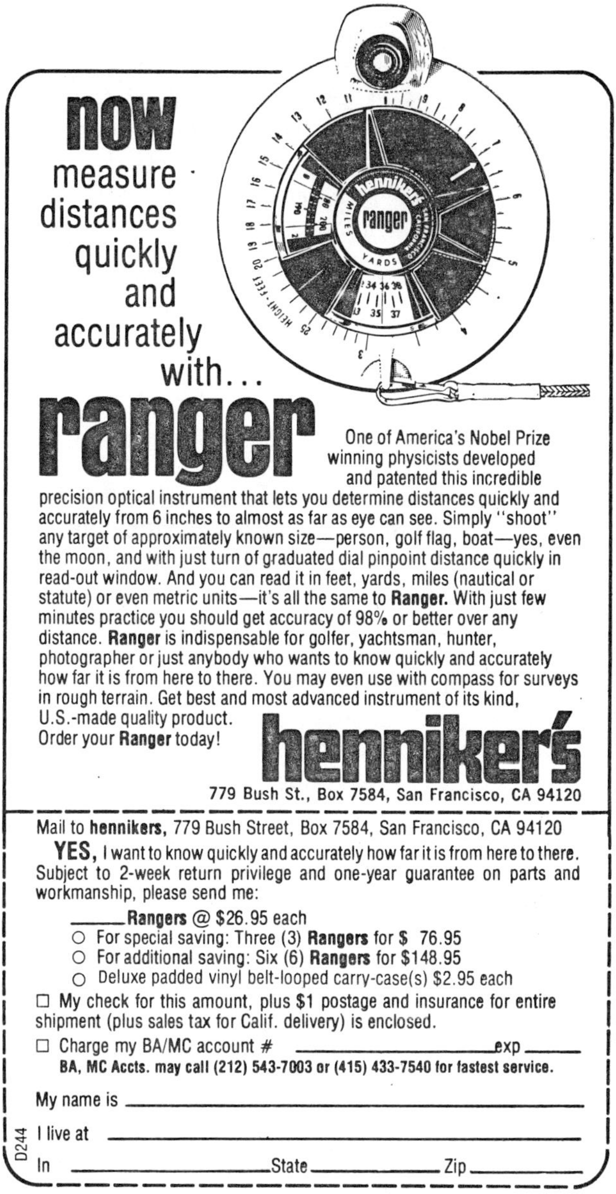

The Ranger ad has run successfully for years with Haverhill's and with Henniker's. The "Now" call-out draws the reader right into the headline and — hopefully — into the copy and into the "proposition".

lead him into the body copy, in which the product will be clearly discussed and your proposition put forward. I find that, with a good lead-in *and* a good illustration, the name of the product itself often makes a good headline. This may not be very imaginative, but it is usually quite effective. It is most appropriate if the name of the product itself explains its function and, for best balance and economy of space, if the lead-in is fairly long.

If you think that the price of the product is exceptionally attractive and that it may move the reader to be even more interested in the product and in the ad, then be sure to put it right in the headline.

These points are, I think, well brought out in our *Quadriloupe* ad. I think it is one of our really great ads.* It has a good lead-in, its own self-explanatory name is the headline, and the very attractive price is part of it. There is a little extra fillip. We thought we might get extra mileage out of the $4.44 price (rather than $3.95 or $4.95, which were the alternatives) because it seems to tie in so well with the "4-in-1" theme of this optical instrument.

There are many things "right" with this ad. Be sure to look at it again when we talk about illustrations, copy and coupon. We are extra proud of this one. It is one of the products that we developed single-handedly. It is packaged under our name in Germany. It is an item that we control exclusively in the United States, and for which we have built up a very large mail order, retail and premium business. The Quadriloupe is a real success story, and I am sure that the good ad we made for it helped very much in positioning it in a leadership role in optical goods.

Another real success story is that of *Henni/HiGrips* which is also a product that we helped develop (a new and much better version of an old concept). We departed from standard procedure on this one, by doing three "unorthodox" things — throwing the rule book away, you might say. Here is what, intentionally, and with some hesitation, we did "wrong."

---

* Just before going to press, I learned to my pleasure that other professionals share my high opinion about this ad. It was included, as an example of good direct response advertising, in "Understanding Modern Media" (by Azveda, Margolies and Reynolds). This is a standard textbook, primarily designed for high school and college students. I can heartily recommend it. It is published by Laidlaw Bros. (Div. of Doubleday & Co., Inc.).

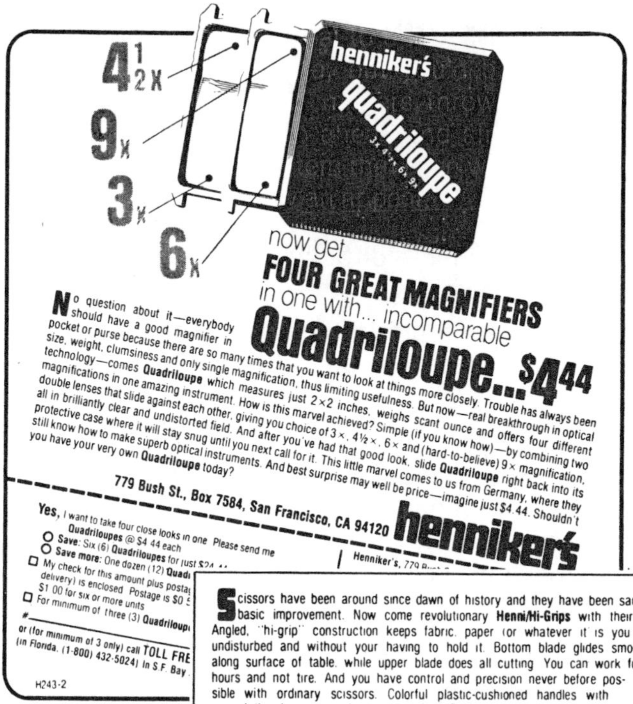
4½x
9x
3x
6x
henniker's
quadriloupe
now get
FOUR GREAT MAGNIFIERS
in one with... incomparable
Quadriloupe...$4.44
No question about it—everybody should have a good magnifier in pocket or purse because there are so many times that you want to look at things more closely. Trouble has always been size, weight, clumsiness and only single magnification, thus limiting usefulness. But now—real breakthrough in optical technology—comes Quadriloupe which measures just 2×2 inches, weighs scant ounce and offers four different magnifications in one amazing instrument. How is this marvel achieved? Simple (if you know how)—by combining two double lenses that slide against each other, giving you choice of 3×, 4½×, 6× and (hard-to-believe) 9× magnification, all in brilliantly clear and undistorted field. And after you've had that good look, slide Quadriloupe right back into its protective case where it will stay snug until you next call for it. This little marvel comes to us from Germany, where they still know how to make superb optical instruments. And best surprise may well be price—imagine just $4.44. Shouldn't you have your very own Quadriloupe today?
Scissors have been around since dawn of history and they have been same ever since. There has been no basic improvement. Now come revolutionary Henni/Hi-Grips with their new and se..ible design. Angled, "hi-grip" construction keeps fabric, paper (or whatever it is you wish to cut) undisturbed and without your having to hold it. Bottom blade glides smoothly along surface of table, while upper blade does all cutting. You can work for hours and not tire. And you have control and precision never before possible with ordinary scissors. Colorful plastic-cushioned handles with special thumbrest, provide extra comfort. Blades have adjustable pivot-screw, are 8½ inches long and let you handle even heaviest material with ease. Incredibly sharp stainless nickel-steel for lifetime of heavy-duty service. If you own only one pair of scissors, it should be Henni/Hi-Grips. They are boon and absolutely indispensable to anybody who does any tailoring or dressmaking. Why work with outmoded tools? Order Henni/Hi-Grips today!
779 Bush St., Box 7584, San Francisco, CA 94120
Somebody finally had a better idea: Henni/Hi-Grips...just $6.95
YES, I want to cut with ease. Please send me
hennikers
H243-2

Save: Three (3) Henni/Hi-Grips for just $19.95
Save more: Six (6) Henni/Hi-Grips for just $36.95

The Quadriloupe and Henni/Hi-Grips ads are two of our most successful ones. Everything seems to be "right" with the former, and textbooks have featured it as an example of good space advertising. A number of things are "wrong" with the Henni/Hi-Grips ad, but it works and I am kind of reluctant to tamper with success.

- We didn't put the lead-in and headline on top of the ad, but right in the middle. This is "wrong" because the reader has to make an effort to go back to the top of the ad — the flow of sight is not smooth.
- We used script rather than type for the headline, which is "wrong," because it is more difficult to read and therefore puts up another obstacle against the reader's attention.
- The headline and lead-in are in the same typeface, which likely is "wrong" because it can be a little confusing.

But this ad is one of the most productive and successful we have ever made. It is a consistent big money maker. In fact, we sell so many of these shears that the factory can literally not keep up with us. It is one of the few products in which success has led to some trouble. Before we had quite realized what a fantastic ad we had created, we were overwhelmed with an avalanche of orders that we couldn't fill and that created a serious back-order situation.

While you're always happy, of course, to see big sales, and knock-out response to a space ad, back orders are a big headache, and potential trouble. Naturally you want to avoid them by all means. Sometimes I wonder whether we are so successful with Henni/HiGrips because of our breaking the "rules" or in spite of it. But, while I do like to experiment, I have decided, at least for the time being, not to change the ad. I prefer not to tinker with success and to leave well enough alone.

Here are a few more interesting things about headlines:

We have a book division at Henniker's, Advance Books. We are not as active in it as we would like to be, mostly, I suppose, because our merchandise activities keep us hopping. But let me just give you two examples of what I think of as good lead-in and headline writing for mail-order ads. The first is for a book, *How to Get 20% to 90% Off on Anything You Buy.* I don't care how harried or tired the reader may be, when he leafs through his magazine or newspaper — this headline, "Stop Ripping Yourself Off!" and the graphic treatment must grab him as with a meathook.

The second, *Don't Buy Another Dime's Worth of Insurance* is the most successful book promotion we have ever had. It is on a book by Dr. Herbert Denenberg, who used to be Insurance Commissioner of Pennsylvania. He is quite a feisty guy and quite a

STOP

RIPPING YOURSELF OFF!

You are throwing your hard earned money away if you don't get 20% to 90% off on everything you buy.

THE crunch is on. With double-digit inflation, many of the things that we had so long taken for granted are suddenly beyond our reach. Inflation is actually eating into our ability to provide the bare necessities — food, shelter, and medical care.

•

Wouldn't it be great if we could buy things wholesale, get rebates, knock-offs, and special insider deals? But where to turn for those "specials"? Most of us don't know, and we pay through the nose for everything we buy, every service we need. And we deprive ourselves of what we could afford if we just knew how to buy like insiders do.

Don't Give up — Get up to 90% Off on Everything

Impossible you say? Well, we don't blame you for being dubious. But it is true, and you can learn how to put it to your own enormous advantage. A remarkable couple, Jean and Cle Kinney, have spent years of research on how to **beat the soaring cost of living and how to make every dollar do the work of four or five.** And they've put all of their experience into the most amazing book — a run-away bestseller — now in its 14th up-to-date printing:

HOW TO GET 20% TO 90% OFF ON EVERYTHING YOU BUY.

Show me, you'll say. OK, the Kinney's will show you. You'll learn how you can buy clothing at 45% off its regular list price. Just think how that will help your budget. And they show you how to buy furniture at just about one-fifth of its regular price. How does that grab you for saving money?

S-T-R-E-T-C-H Every Dollar

You would be crazy to pay more than rock bottom for anything you buy — daily necessities and luxuries. And the Kinneys show you HOW, not dry theoretical advice and platitudes, but names, addresses and facts you can put to use right away. You'll learn such amazing things as how to buy an honest-to-goodness mink stole for $45, how to buy a 2-year old sports car for $185, how to buy a $90 man's suit for $13, a woman's girdle for 25¢.

Where this book **really** shines is in groceries. If you are a housekeeper you know that groceries are what you most worry about, your greatest single headache. You probably dread the weekly trip to the supermarket. But the Kinneys have "beaten the system". They show you how you can slash your grocery bill to less than half. Would you like to cut your meat bill by 45%? Would you be interested in peaches at 50¢ a bushel, tomatoes at 30% off, or 80% off on strawberries? This book shows you how!

But That isn't All

Naturally, the emphasis of this how-to-live-the-good-life book is in the basics — clothing, medical, housing, groceries, because that is where most of our money goes and where we need most relief.

But what to do with all the money we'll save and that we'll now have left over? Delightful dilemma! The Kinneys show you how to put your extra funds to good use. How to buy fine French Champagne and imported perfume at half price, how to make eye-boggling savings in appliances, office equipmen, candy, baby clothes, hi-fi equipment, and just about anything you can think of.

But, you'll say, there is one big category of my monthly money drain that I am absolutely stuck with and those are my "fixed expenses". And here is perhaps the best surprise the Kinneys have prepared for us. They have discovered that "fixed expenses" aren't really "fixed". You'll learn to save money on things you'd always thought had no "give" in them at all. Yes, you'll find out how to cut down on your phone bill, your gas and electric bills, your medical, dental and drug bills. You'll even learn how to cut down on your monthly rent or mortgage bill (and just think what it will mean to you to be able to lighten that millstone around your neck!), and how to cut down on your cost of daily transportation.

The whole object of the Kinney's book is to teach you in down-to-earth language **how you can make your money go a whole lot further and how to live a richer, more fulfilling life, free of money worries.**

An Encyclopedia of Money Management

The nuts-and-bolts information on how to slash your household budget is the main part of this remarkable book, but there is much more. Because, if you read the Kinney book you'll become a better household and money manager than you ever believed you had in you — you'll not only have more things and better things, but you'll also become a better and more competent person and have a better organized and happier family. Most of the information that the Kinneys have so painstakingly researched is summarized, saving you detailed reading, if that is what you prefer. Turn to page 80 for instance for the **10 most important money-saving tricks.** Or to page 61, for the **10 basic things you can buy wholesale wherever you may live.** To page 238 for **how to save $$'s on gifts that everyone will appreciate.** You'll find the **13 basic techniques to save a small fortune travelling,** on page 227. And two very important topics for women: Turn to page 189 for the **cardinal rules on how to be "best dressed" at thrift shop prices,** and to page 175 for **30 key points on how to slash your food budget.**

But all of this is just the tip of the iceberg. This fantastic book is so full of information that you'll read and re-read it and will keep it at your elbow for ready reference.

Only You Can Help Yourself to a Better Life

You want to provide a better life for yourself and for your family. You don't want to squander your money, you want to make every dollar count. But only **you** can help yourself to a better life — and this book will show you how to do it. The cost is so small that it's really nothing compared to what it will do for you. Just as an example: if you are the average householder, **we absolutely guarantee** that just the tips on three surefire ways to save on drugs and cosmetics (page 64) will **repay the cost of the book over ten times in the course of one year.** If you decide that just this one claim isn't 100% correct, return the book for immediate full refund.

•

You are cheating yourself and your family if you don't follow these step-by-step money-saving techniques that the Kinneys have researched for you. That's why we say: **Stop ripping yourself off,** because that's what you're actually doing if you throw your money away and don't learn how to **get 20% to 90% off on everything you buy.**

GUARANTEE

We know it sounds almost unbelievable, so we'll make you this unprecedented offer and Guarantee:

Be doubtful, but go ahead and order the Kinney book today. Look through it and be amazed. If, at the end of two weeks you conclude that you cannot **save the cost of the book at least 100 (one hundred) times in the first year,** return it to us for immediate and courteous refund. There will be no quibbling and no questions. You are the only judge.

But if you want to cut your bills by 20% to 90%, if you want to provide a fuller and richer life for yourself and for your family, order this revolutionary book today. Remember, with our no-questions-asked money-back guarantee you take no risk at all. This may be the end to your money worries, your key to a much better life. Act now!

advance books

Mail to:
ADVANCE BOOKS
779 Bush St., Box 7584
San Francisco, CA 94120

☐ Yes, send me Jean and Cle Kinney's book **How to Get 20% to 90% off on Everything You Buy.** I may return the book in two weeks if I don't believe that it can **save me its cost at least 100 times in the first year.**

☐ My check for $8.95 ($7.95 plus $1.00 for postage and insurance—New York residents please add sales tax) is enclosed.

☐ Please charge my BA, MC Account

#__________ exp.______
BA, MC Accts. may call (212) 543-7003 or (415) 981-7137 for fastest service.

My name is__________

I live at__________

City__________

State__________ Zip______

G 167

You might think of it as less than subtle, but this is certainly an "arresting" headline. You haven't won the battle just by stopping the reader, but if you don't stop him, you are sure to have lost it.

DON'T BUY ANOTHER DIME'S WORTH OF INSURANCE

(WITHOUT FIRST READING THIS EYE OPENER OF A BOOK)*

YES you may be making a serious mistake if you pay another premium or buy another insurance policy. For **your** sake and for the well-being of your family, take three minutes to read this vital information about insurance. It may well be the most important reading you've ever done.

Your Most Important Asset

If you are like most of us, chances are that you don't give insurance a lot of thought. More than likely, you have group insurance on the job, car insurance, and perhaps some life insurance that somebody sold you a few years ago. And again, if you are like most, you probably believe that your most important asset is your home—but that isn't so! The most important thing you own—or should own—is your insurance coverage. If it's adequate—with the right companies, and purchased at the right price—it provides protection for almost all contingencies that can befall and will take care of your family in case of your death. But many of us are under-insured, unprotected against hazards that can wipe us out. Or we may be "insurance poor"—paying an arm and a leg, a bigger bite out of our monthly pay than we can afford, for coverage we don't really need or that could be obtained at a fraction of what we are paying now.

And there is really no way that the average person can determine just exactly what he needs in insurance coverage—it's too complicated—or rather the insurance companies made it that way (remember, **they** invented "the fine print"). And your insurance agent makes his living by selling. Human nature being what it is, that doesn't necessarily make him the best judge of your needs.

Enter Herbert Denenberg

Dr. Denenberg, until recently Insurance Commissioner of Pennsylvania, was recommended to this post by no less an advocate for consumer protection than Ralph Nader himself. While he was in this job, he made history and has saved Pennsylvanians hundreds of millions of dollars. He forced insurance companies to live up to stringent codes, ordered them to make disclosures and publish comparable rates, and by widespread educational campaigns. TIME says that "no facet of insurance has escaped him." Another weekly calls him a "mover, shaker and maker of waves, who has few equals in public life." A national newspaper proclaims that "he out-Naders Nader." We think that Dr. Denenberg is the man who should advise **you** on **your** insurance needs. He has no ax to grind. He is the agent of the public—he is your agent! And, luckily for all of us, he has put all of his technical and practical knowledge, all of his down-to-earth wisdom on insurance into one brilliant book!

THE INSURANCE TRAP
unfair at any rate?

What This Book Can Do for You.

In his no-nonsense manner, and without ever using any fancy insurance double talk that only a lawyer could understand, Dr. Denenberg takes you through the "insurance jungle" and teaches you:

- **How to buy insurance** — Should you "shop" around, what traps to avoid, what to look for in a company.

Let Dr. Denenberg be **your adviser on your insurance needs.** Remember, Ralph Nader called him ". . . most outstanding insurance commissioner this country has ev had."

- **How to select an agent** — The 10-point check list to separate the knowledgeable pro from the fast-buck charlatan.
- **How to buy auto insurance** — How much coverage, what kind, what most motorists overlook, 11-pt. check list for saving many dollars.
- **How to buy health insurance** — Learn not to "trade dollars", what about mail order plans, dove-tailing with your coverage on the job, how to avoid catastrophic expenses.
- **Should you get disability insurance** — Who should and who shouldn't, what to watch out for, length of coverage, how to cut your premium to a fraction.

*

Mail to:
RUSSELL BOOKS

Please send me THE INSURANCE TRAP by Dr. Herbert Denenberg. I understand that I may return the book within two weeks of receipt for full credit or refund if I am not completely satisfied.

☐ My check for $8.95 ($7.95 plus $1.00 for postage and insurance, California delivery please add tax) is enclosed.

☐ Please charge my BA or MC account

#__________ exp.______

My name is:__________

I live at:__________

City:__________

State:__________ Zip______

BA, MC accts. may call (415) 989-6987 for fastest service.

R199

- **All about life insurance** — The most important part of the book, perhaps. Types of policies, amount of coverage needed, how to "shop", what about double indemnity and waiver of premium, borrowing on policy and much, much more.
- **What to do when you are turned down** — Dr. Denenberg shows you six "tricks" by which you can get coverage even if you thought you were uninsurable. This chapter is invaluable for the peace of mind it can bring you.
- **How to insure your home and possessions** — Different types of "homeowner's policies" (do you know which one **you** have?), what about such catastrophes as floods and earthquakes? Should you have "floaters" and what kind? Could an "umbrella" be the answer to protect you against **real** disaster?
- **How to collect on insurance** — What records you should keep to get "quick action", what to do if you get the "run-around."

This partial list can only give you the flavor and barest outline of the compenhensive coverage Dr. Denenberg gives the subject — with only **your** interest in mind, and speaking directly to **you** and about **your problems.**

Appendix May Be Most Valuable Part

An appendix in any other book may just be a dry collection of sources and references, but not in THE INSURANCE TRAP. Because it's in the Appendix that Dr. Denenberg gives numbers and names. You will get a full "Shopper's Guide to Life Insurance", that shows in complete detail the comparative cost of life insurance policies of the fifty largest companies. You will learn with amazement that "Company A" will sell you exactly the same coverage at 170% higher premium than "Company B." (Can you imagine what that runs up to in 20 years?).

And, you may find that a company that you believed to be in the pink of condition has a "financial stability rating" too low perhaps for real comfort.

Let Dr. Denenberg help you with your most important asset. You need expert advice from a disinterested and unimpeachable source. And, that is what Dr. Denenberg is. In today's environment **you have to know** whether you are properly insured. Remember, inadequate insurance can result in law suits that can take away every penny you have or can result in bills that only millionaires could pay without going broke. And you have to know whether you are paying the right price for what you are buying and whether you are dealing with reliable and financially stable companies. **The Insurance Trap** will give you every answer you need. For your own peace of mind, for the well-being and security of your family, order this brilliant and extraordinary book today!

russell books

779 Bush St., Box 7584, San Francisco, CA 94120

Another headline stopper, aided by Dr. Denenberg's bemused gaze. This book has been one of our steady sellers, in many media, year after year.

crusader. We bought up and took an option on the entire remainder stock of this book and it turned out to be a very lucrative business for us.

There are many other things "right" in this ad, of course. One of these is the last thing I want to talk about in connection with headlines, namely the use of the human form or, better yet, the human face, about which we will talk in more detail when we discuss illustrations.

Dr. Denenberg's face is looking right at you. In looking at this ad, you are not just grabbed by the headline, but also slightly "hypnotized" by Dr. Denenberg's gaze, which, while not exactly part of the headline, is right underneath it.

We have created a few ads in which the human face has been an integral part of the headline. In these ads the reader is stopped by both the headline and the face.

Take, as an example, our *Bicentennial Watch* ad, our greatest success, perhaps, in 1975/1976. The headline and illustration are, of course, a spoof or take-off on the famous World War I recruiting poster, with Ben Franklin replacing Uncle Sam. We ascribe a great part of the success of this campaign to Ben's pointed finger and his penetrating gaze, together with his admonition of "I want you (to buy this watch)."

The same principle is illustrated by our *Black Jade Jewelry* ad, the "Mystery Stone of the Orient." We decided that we could not say anything too startling in the headline about a piece of jewelry, so we decided to use an attractive Eurasian model as part of the headline, looking straight at the reader, leading him into the (rather lengthy) copy and, hopefully, have him take us up on the proposition. An interesting and unexpected sidelight about this ad was that it pulled excellently in men's media such as *The Wall Street Journal,* but did not do too well in the media in which the proportion of women readers was high. I suppose, in retrospect, it is clear why it should be that way. The model is attractive to men, but that does not necessarily "turn on" women.

Illustrations. We have talked about illustrations briefly along with headlines, but these were special cases. Keep in mind what we have said about the human figure and the human face. It is what most attracts attention. Not surprisingly, babies or very young children are almost irresistibly attractive to women.

Ben Franklin's pointed finger, stern gaze and his "I want you!" admonition turned out to be sure-fire stoppers. This ad was perhaps our greatest success during the bicentennial year. The "$1 lay-away plan" was an inspired response to the shortage of watches that developed as consequence of the great demand. We sold so many watches that our factory in Switzerland simply couldn't keep up with us. This ad ran well across the entire spectrum of media — from THE NEW YORKER to THE NATIONAL ENQUIRER.

the mystery stone of the orient

incomparable black jade...

From time immemorial, Jade has been one of world's most coveted jewels. Sacred to many peoples in the Orient, this mysterious stone comes in a nearly endless variety of shades—from almost snowy white, rose, green, to pitchest black. It is that pure-black jade, without even a trace of any "off" color that almost all women who were ever lucky enough to own jewelry made of it think of as the most beautiful and the most flattering.

Now **you** can own this fabulous jewelry . . . at a price that is scarcely believable! Henniker's has been able to commission a large run of two exquisite pieces of Black Jade jewelry—a necklace and a bracelet.

Our **Black Jade Necklace** consists of 41 absolutely perfect jade beads, each one 10 mm (just under ½ in) in diameter and each one hand-polished to such perfection and such sheen that you can literally mirror yourself in its black surface. This necklace is strung (in traditional Oriental fashion) on unbreakable catgut filament. And there is added safeguard in the clasp, because it just can never come unhooked.

The **Black Jade Bracelet** is perfect circlet, 3½ inches in diameter, and full 8 mm thick. It has gold-filled, finely filigreed hinge and clasp and is secured by a lovely gold-filled chain. It is of the same superb finish as the companion necklace, polished to deep mirror perfection and exhibiting at its best that mysterious luster that has made Black Jade so admired and beloved since the dawn of history.

Here are two pieces of jewelry that are simply exquisite. Both can be worn at almost any occasion and with almost any outfit. Black is always right. Black is always flattering, and black will go with most anything. It looks good on young girls and mature women. Unlike other jewelry, Black Jade is no fad. It is a jewel that will be as "modern" tomorrow as it is today and as it was 1000 years ago. And the classical timeless design of these two pieces is further assurance that you will wear and treasure them for the rest of your life and will wish to pass them on to your daughter and granddaughter.

**And here is Wonderful News—
best surprise of all**

If you have ever priced jade in a big city specialty store, you know that cost of unflawed Black Jade jewelry is quite hefty. Even a small piece—a pendant or broach, can cost a good deal. Our best surprise, therefore, is the incredible price at which we are able to bring this jewelry to you—directly from our exclusive manufacturer in the Orient, and without going through platoons of middlemen who add layers of cost and profit every step of the way. The **16" Necklace** is a hard-to-believe $19.95, and the exquisite **Bracelet**, with its handsome gold-filled fittings, an equally astonishing, $24.95. But there is more and even better: If you buy both pieces you can get another large saving, because we will give you the pair for just $39.95! And with that, we'll also give you, with our compliments, a beautiful large, fully sculpted **Jade Heart** that you may wish to wear for casual, carefree or romantic occasions—or that you may wish to give as a present to a very dear friend.

You take no risk at all, because our Guarantee is foolproof and ironclad.
But what if I am not as pleased with this jewelry as I thought, you may ask. What if I don't like the quality or the workmanship? What if it doesn't suite me? We are pretty sure that none of this will happen, but you deserve a straight answer to these questions, so here is our

Guarantee: You must be thrilled, 100% satisfied, and the jewelry must in every respect come up to and surpass your highest expectations. If it does not, you may return it within two weeks of receipt for immediate refund. And if you bought both the Necklace and Bracelet and got the Heart Pendant as our present, you may keep it with our compliments—our way of saying "thank you" for your courtesy and for your confidence.

Here is your chance to buy some of the most beautiful jewelry you may ever own. Two exquisite pieces of Black Jade—at a price that is almost unbelievable and that we can guarantee only until our present stock is exhausted. Order today and adorn yourself with Black Jade, the most beautiful jewelry of all.

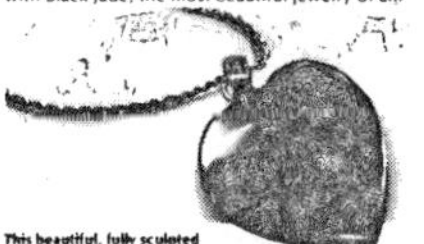

This beautiful, fully sculpted Black Jade Heart Pendant (1½" across) is our complimentary gift to you if you buy both the Necklace and the Bracelet. And you may keep it with our compliments in the unlikely case that you wish to return the jewelry for refund. Note: gold-plated chain is included with the Pendant.

Yes, I wish to avail myself of your offer, subject to your no-questions-asked 2-week return privilege. Please send me

16-inch **Black Jade Necklaces** (10 mm beads) @ $19.95 each

3½ inch **Black Jade Bracelets,** with gold-filled fittings @ $24.95 each

Necklace/Bracelet combinations @ $39.95 each

I understand that I am entitled to one free Jade Heart Pendant for every Necklace/Bracelet pair I buy, and that I may keep Heart if I decide to return the jewelry for any reason at all

☐ My check for the above plus $1.50 postage and insurance for entire shipment (plus sales tax for California delivery) is enclosed.

☐ Please charge my BA/MC account
____ exp. ____

For fastest service call TOLL FREE (800) 327-8912
(IN FLORIDA (1-800) 432-5824) IN SF BAY AREA CALL: 433-7540

My name is ____________
I live at ____________
City ____________
State ____________ Zip ____________
W50506 H24

779 Bush St., Box 7584,
San Francisco, CA 94120 **henniker's**

I am afraid that this is not one of our really "classy" ads, but it was quite successful and ran well in such media as THE WALL STREET JOURNAL, which surprised me at first. The soulful look of the Eurasian beauty is a stopper.

Unfortunately, perhaps, you may not have too much occasion to use the human figure or the human face in your space advertising illustrations. In the first place, not too many things lend themselves to be shown with models — mostly clothing perhaps and jewelry. In some cases, when the human figure could be used, there is the danger that it might overwhelm the merchandise itself, more so it if is a rather small object. Thus, you might be accomplishing your first purpose, namely to attract the reader's attention. But you would, in all likelihood, not make a sale because your merchandise is not clearly and fully visible. Also, you always have the problem of space, which is expensive. And although you may consider it desirable, you simply can hardly "afford" to show anything but the merchandise itself.

I have often overcome that, especially with small objects, by showing just one part of the human anatomy, namely the hand holding the object. This does not only give the merchandise an "alive" quality, but also clarifies size and proportion.

Take, for instance, the *Map Measurer* ad, which shows a hand actually operating the instrument. Frankly, I had my serious doubts whether we could make a relatively inexpensive gadget (and one with limited application) work in such a large space. But we did, and continue to do extremely well with it. The headline and copy may, perhaps, not be the greatest, but the illustration, brought to life by the hand holding it, is first class. I believe that it is largely responsible for the steady good sales of this item.

Another example of the hand in action is our ad on the granddaddy of all of our successes: the *Monaco Shaver* (that's the one that went to the Moon). Please turn back to the reproduction of this ad in the preceding chapter. The illustration, showing the shaver and both hands, makes it clear, better than any words could, just exactly what the special features of the shaver are, namely that it is wound by hand and that it needs no outside power. Naturally, it isn't just the illustration that made this shaver such a success: the headline is super, the Apollo 14-NASA emblem doesn't do it any harm either (we received special permission to use it) and the copy is quite good.*

---

* One reason, apart from its steady success, that I am so proud of this ad is that **Advertising Age** (the "bible of the industry") selected it a few years ago — I believe it was in 1972 — as one of the five best consumer products ads of the year.

KNOW IMMEDIATELY HOW FAR FROM HERE TO THERE WITH

MAP MEASURER

JUST $6.95

This clever gadget should be in your car's glove compartment and in your knapsack on any hike. Just run **MAP MEASURER** along crookedest road on any map – scale makes no difference – and read off immediately and exactly how far it is from point A to point B. Certainly beats asking local farmers or surly gas station attendants. In case you are really lost, compass on back side will steer you to destination. Hikers, campers or motorists: get this nifty tool today!

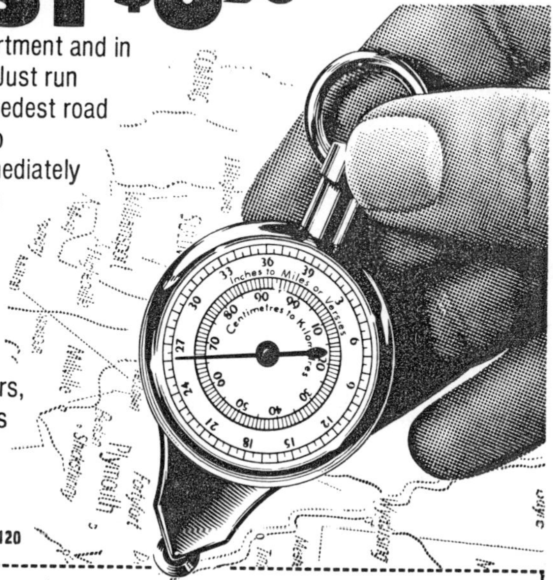

henniker's

779 Bush St., Box 7584, San Francisco, CA 94120

YES, I want to know how far it is . Please send me:

____ **Map Measuers** at $6.95.

○ **Save:** Three (3) **Map Measurers** for just $19.95.

○ **Save more:** Six (6) **Map Measurers** for just $35.95.

☐ My Check for this amount, plus postage (plus sales tax for California delivery) is enclosed. Postage is $0.50 for fewer than six units and $1.00 for six or more units.

☐ For minimum of three (3) **Map Measurers**, charge my BA / MC account

____________________ exp. ______

or (for minimum of 3 only) call TOLL FREE (800) 648-5311
[IN NEVADA (800) 992-5710] IN SF BAY AREA CALL 433-7540

Mail to: **Henniker's,** 779 Bush St., Box 7584, San Francisco, Ca 94120

My name is____________________

I live at____________________

In____________________

State__________ Zip______

H238-2

Small objects are often successfully shown being held and operated by the hand. It lends identity, dynamics and scale of the item. Usually, so much space for such an inexpensive and somewhat "secondary" item is not warranted and does not pay. But it works with the Map Measurer although we alternate it with a half size (1/6 page) version.

We shall have occasion to refer to the *Monaco* ad and to the *Black Jade* ad later in this chapter — in an entirely different context.

There are really only two fundamental ways in which you can illustrate: one is by photography and the other is by drawings. You will read and hear as "conventional wisdom" that photography is always to be preferred, because it makes things look more "natural" than drawings. But I can't quite subscribe to that, although I must admit that for most conventional reproductions, photography is probably more suitable. You should probably stick with it until you find a really good illustrator/artist.

Again, while this is not an absolute truth, you are probably always better off to show clothing in photography, rather than in drawing, and the same may be true for food. In "gadgets," equipment and many other inanimate products, a good draftsman can often do things the camera cannot quite bring out. The draftsman can subtly emphasize points, bring out highlights, show attractive features, and suppress distracting details. That cannot be readily accomplished with photography, except by extensive (and fairly expensive) retouching.

Another "disadvantage" of photography is that it has to be "screened" in order to reproduce in printing. Look closely at an illustration on a newspaper page and you will see the rather coarse printing dots. You might need a magnifying glass to see these dots on a magazine page, but they are there and they do tend to fuzz detail in reproduction. In drawings (graphic illustrations) no such "screening" is necessary. It is "line art" and will print as is. That can often make a dramatic difference, especially in reproduction in newspapers. They are printed on inexpensive newsprint and on high speed presses, and demand a coarse screen.

Also, if you find a good artist to draw your merchandise (they are not easy to find, not too inexpensive and should be cherished and treated well), you may be able to give your advertising an individuality, a personality and an instant recognition that would not be otherwise possible.

I have, from the very beginning of my career in mail order — with Haverhill's and Henniker's — worked with drawn illustrations for space advertising and have used photography only in very exceptional cases.

I was fortunate in being able to establish in the early days of Haverhill's, a connection with a studio in England that specializes in a drafting technique known as "scratch board." This is a technique that, in my opinion, is superior to any other. Please have a look at some of the examples shown and see how vividly and clearly each detail is brought out. This art form is pretty expensive, but you can get lots of mileage out of it. When you look at the same subject side by side, once well photographed and retouched and then rendered by scratch board, you can really tell. There *is* a difference. I think that this type of graphic rendering really pops out and hits the eye much better than a photograph would. That little difference may well be what it takes to overcome the customer's buying resistance.

Keep in mind, please, that — even more perhaps than your lead-in or your headline — your illustration must arrest the reader's eye, stop him and make him want to read your proposition. Therefore, your illustration, whether you ultimately decide on photography or graphic rendering, is certainly not the place to save any money. In the area of illustration, more perhaps than in anything else you do in this business, you are most likely to get what you pay for.

Body copy. So far, you haven't done any selling. All you have done, and it's been a pretty big order, is to stop the reader long enough to have at least a look at what you have to say. Your selling job starts now.

There are quite a few "formulas" about the elements that the body copy of an ad should contain, but perhaps in most general and simplest terms, you should have the following — in this sequence:

What is new, different, attractive about your product. This should include (either at this point, or later on in the copy) all the product information the customer should have — such as size, material, color, is it a wind-up item, does it run on batteries, house current or both — or anything else that might be pertinent. This is pretty tricky and you must be careful. Because, naturally, the customer needs and wants to know what he is going to get, and there should be no unanswered questions or later disappointments. But remember, you are trying to create a mood and to build a buying decision, which is essentially an emotional one. A listing of technical specifications is not conducive to creating this emotional

Photography

Scraperboard

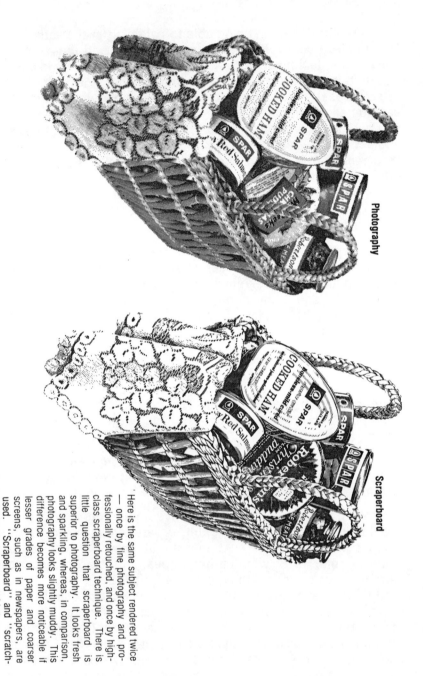

Here is the same subject rendered twice — once by fine photography and professionally retouched, and once by high-class scraperboard technique. There is little question that scraperboard is superior to photography. It looks fresh and sparkling, whereas, in comparison, photography looks slightly muddy. This difference becomes more noticeable if lesser grades of paper and coarser screens, such as in newspapers, are used. ''Scraperboard'' and ''scratchboard'' are interchangeable terms.

mood. So be careful: give the information that is needed, but do not go overboard into detail.

Why should the reader buy it, even though he may have something now that does a similar job? In other words, you have to *create desire* to buy something that will make the prospective customer's life a little more pleasant, a little easier, perhaps. This part of the copy — the creation of desire and mood — is obviously the heart of the ad, and also the toughest.

The "Proposition." If it is not already contained in the headline — and even then it may do no harm to repeat it — is the "call to action," namely to place an order. This may be subtle or straightforward and direct.

Many people in the mail-order business write very good copy and are able to put the stamp of their personality on each of their ads. If you have this knack or if you can develop that by constant practice, you have a great advantage. If you decide that it is not your thing, however, don't feel bad about it. There are competent mail-order copywriters who will do it for you. But, whether you can do it yourself or not, I hope I have given you enough insight into what to do and what to look for.

If you have an outsider write your copy, you should now know enough to judge whether you are getting a topnotch professional copy job or whether you have fallen into the hands of a humdrum hack. I would say that untalented people abound more in copywriting than in most other fields, because it isn't quite as easy to put one's finger on the deficiency and incompetence. But, in order to be successful and to build your business, you must learn to recognize talent and be alert to it and to the lack of it.

Coupons. First let me make one flat statement: every mail order ad must have a coupon. I have done it without, tried to save money on space, or rather used the space for more copy and illustration. It simply does not work. Don't let anybody tell you differently. I make only two exceptions to this ironclad rule:

1. We run occasional small space ads in media in which our contracts call for so many insertions per year. We call such ads "rate holders," because they help us fulfill our advertising commitment and assure us the lowest rate. I give you a couple of examples. These ads, simply do not

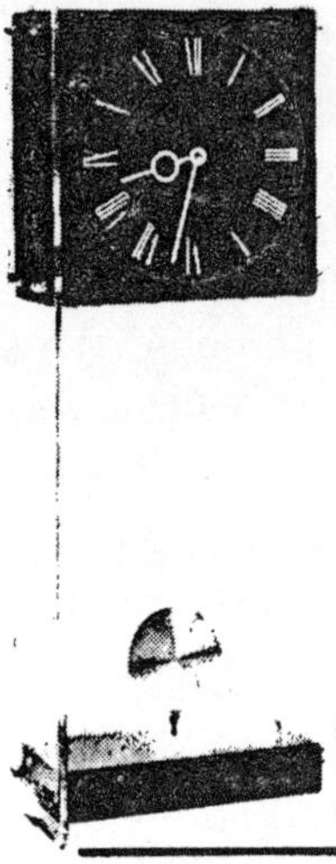

acrylic clock

is 20 inches high and constructed entirely of heavy-gauge clear and black acrylic. Stunning accessory for home or office. Exquisite battery movement runs for one year on alkali D-cell (included). Attractive white graphics. Anodized aluminum pendulum allows adjustment to one minute per month. **$59.95**. Add $1 for mail order (and sales tax for Calif. delivery). BA / MC may call TOLL

Area call: 433-7540

hennikers

Dept. YN, 779 Bush St., Box 7584, San Francisco, CA 94120

A rule that should (almost) never be broken: every mail-order **must** have a coupon. But we break this rule for these 35-lines "rate holder" ads. We are happy if they make a few dollars or just break even.

VERTICAL CAR COMPASS

Useful automobile accessory, with futuristic airplane styling and vertical 2½" dial for full 360° view. Great for night driving, because lights at touch of button. Fastens to dash with no-mar adhesive. Can be fully compensated for car's magnetic field. **$12.95.** Add $1 for mail order (and sales tax for California delivery). BA / MC may call (212) 543-7003 or (415) 433-7540 for fastest service.

hennikers

Dept. YN, 779 Bush St., Box 7584, San Francisco, CA 94120

Gold Plated Bobby Whistle

Children snap to attention, cabs come to screeching halt and baddies run for cover at first blast of **Bobby Whistle**. But above all, it's snappy piece of jewelry – faithful copy of real London police thing. 12-kt. gold-plated, with 18-inch gold-plated chain. **$12.95.** Add $1 for mail order (and sales tax for CA. delivery) BA / MC may call TOLL FREE

Area call: 433-7540

hennikers

Dept. YN, 779 Bush St., Box 7584, San Francisco, CA 94120

produce very well because of the absence of coupon. We are usually quite satisfied if we make just a few dollars beyond break-even.

2. Ads in our hometown newspaper, *The San Francisco Chronicle/Examiner.* We used to run coupon ads, just the same as in other publications. But we found that we can do much better by eliminating the coupon and running hometown advertising for promotion of our retail store. Sure, even without a coupon, we get many mail and phone orders, in fact we do quite well. But the main emphasis is on promoting the store. This increases store traffic, leads to additional sales, and creates a special relationship with our shopping area customers that we feel could not quite be achieved with a coupon ad. This is a conclusion we have reached after much experimenting and I am satisfied that we are right.

Mostly, the ads in *The San Francisco Chronicle/Examiner* are of the "omnibus" variety. They show an assortment of merchandise usually under one single "theme," such as "travel," "automotive," "gourmet," etc. We try to promote the store, but of course, there is always the invitation to order by phone or mail.

Your coupon should be quite straightforward and, after some experimenting, you should arrive at a standard format. In addition to being in the coupon, your firm's logo and address should also be in the body of the ad itself. The reasons are that, after the coupon is detached, your customer has a record of to whom he has sent his order and, somebody might pick up the publication in which your ad appears, *after* the coupon has been clipped. Naturally, you would want him to know where to send an order.

- *"Mail to" information.* This is important. The customer may have clipped the coupon and may be carrying it around in his wallet or purse. Unless name and address are given on the coupon itself, the customer might not know where to send it.
- *"Guarantee."* Although you may have already spelled out in detail in the body of your ad just what your guarantee is, *do* repeat it in the coupon. Mail-order customers need assurance. Just as you could not tell your mate too often that you love him/her, so can you not reassure your potential

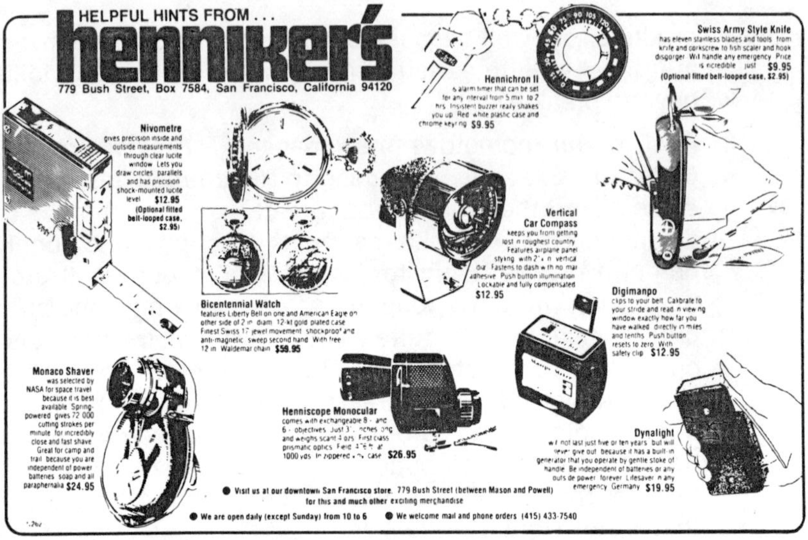

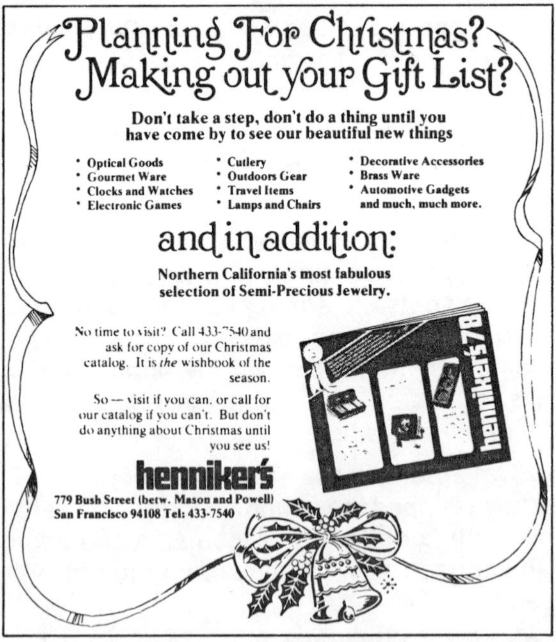

In contrast to mail-order ads, you should not have coupons in the ads of your hometown paper, because your main purpose should be to promote your store. Your coupon would distract from that. The top ad is one of the "theme omnibus" ads that we run regularly in the SAN FRANCISCO CHRONICLE-EXAMINER. The bottom ad, although it does invite the reader to come to the store, is somewhat of a "hybrid" because it also promotes the catalog.

customer too often that you guarantee your product and that you will refund promptly if he is not satisfied. And the time to repeat it and nail it down is now that he is in the process of taking that all important, crucial step: to take out his pen, fill out the coupon and write out the check.

- *The "action."* We like to start this off with a boldfaced "Yes." It is a visual focal point and an affirmative statement. Then request fill-in of how many to send (thus you suggest sales of more than one), repeat the cost and state your Guarantee.
- *If you can possibly make a "Special Offer"* for instance "Three at Special Savings," do it here. But do not clutter coupon and confuse your customer by giving too many different options from which to choose.
- *Give customer a choice* of more than one method of payment, including (very important!) toll-free phone order information (more about that later).
- *Name and Address Block.* We find that we establish a nicer rapport with our customers by saying "My name is ____," "I live in ____," etc. rather than simply "Name," "Address," "City." It is somewhat impersonal. Every little bit you can do to establish additional contact with your customers helps.

Your coupon, except perhaps for the lead-in line — the phrase following the boldfaced "Yes" — should be quite standardized and is therefore the easiest part of your ad to write. But do give your coupon all the thought it deserves. It is your mini-order blank, and its purpose is not just to make it as easy as possible for the customer to order, but, if that can be done at all, to induce him to order more than he had originally planned. Finally, the coupon should be designed in such a way and enough room must be left to hold all necessary information. This will make it as easy as possible for your office staff (that's going to be you and your wife at first, I can assure you) to get the needed information and to fill the order cleanly and without error.

Two final points about coupons, which may be self-evident to you. They are:

1. The coupon belongs on the bottom of your ad, and no place else.

2. The coupon should be limited by straight lines.

As to the first, several years ago, I was reading David Ogilvy's book, *Confessions of an Advertising Man.* Mr. Ogilvy is somewhat of a guru in the advertising business, and everything he writes has to be listened to carefully. Well, he flatly declares in this book that a mail-order coupon should be *on top* of the ad. I was so impressed with this "insight" that I ran right out and redid a few of my ads, so as to conform to this dictum. It was a complete disaster. I wrote Mr. Ogilvy about it. He replied and was gracious enough to admit that this particular "inspiration" had been a bad error. I don't really know how he ever got the idea in the first place.

As to the second — you may be tempted to put your coupon into some cute shape other than straight lines. The heartfelt advice from this corner is to resist such temptation with all might. Remember, you want to make it as easy as possible for your customer to buy and the easiest cut to make is a straight line, and not cutting out some intricate pattern.

TWO WAYS TO TELL THAT YOU ARE DOING THINGS RIGHT

There is one obvious and incontrovertible way to show you that you are doing things right in the mail-order business and that is when you are making money with it. Obviously, you have done things right if you create propositions in space ads that people will "bite on" sufficiently to give you a high return on your space advertising investment.

But there is another way (although it usually goes hand-in-hand with the first). And that is when people begin to imitate you, copy you or — to put it more bluntly — start plagiarizing you or ripping you off.

I am not quite as temperamental as I was ten years ago, but I must confess that I still get more annoyed than flattered when I see my friendly competitors bodily lift work that I have created.

Naturally, I understand that everybody wants (and needs) to "make a buck." I also understand that we must all learn from one another. In fact, I have advised you to study what your competitors are doing — to see what merchandise is being advertised and how to promote and how to price it. But there is a whale of a difference between that and actually stealing someone's work. The only consolation when people start stealing from you is that they, too, recognize that you are doing things right and that they would therefore rather steal your work than take a chance and create their own.

I have a whole collection of such things, but let me just give you a few examples. In all of these (at the suggestion of my attorney) I have obliterated the name of the offending company. Let me just say here that they are all "big boys" — firms with large "creative (?) departments," and not some poor guy who needs to engage in a little larceny to meet the payroll.

Remember the *Black Jade* ad a few pages back? Well, here's our old friend again, but this time by one of the country's largest mail-order houses. I wrote the president of the company about it. He claimed that they had never seen our ad — that it's just one of those "funny coincidences" — what do *you* think? Or take our ad on *Amethyst Jewelry,* one of our all-time great successes. Look at our ad and the other company's ad (yes, one of the major jewelry mail-order houses of the country) side by side. They even lifted the type-face on this one!

Another one is the *Monaco* ad that I showed you a few pages back. Well, one of our colleagues thought it was a pretty good ad too and decided to lift it almost bodily — headline, illustrations and copy. One of the comical aspects of this one is that we had a typo in the ad and talked about the shaver giving "72,000 cutting strokes per minute." That is a whole lot of strokes — it should have read 7,200 strokes. But wouldn't you know it — those 72,000 strokes and everything else showed up in that plagiarized ad.

I tell you these things not to vent my spleen, but to tell you, annoying though it may be to you, that you know you are doing very well when people start stealing from you. You might not grin, but you will have to learn to bear it, because there isn't really anything you can do about it. At least, you have the reassurance (if you need it) that you are doing well.

But, if I may "moralize" for a minute: please try to conduct your own mail-order business in such a way that you will keep your eyes open and learn from others, without feeling the need to rip off other people's work and intellectual property. Because if you were reduced to doing that, you would not really be successful. You would always be a Johnny-come-lately and would try to promote something which probably had already run its course. Also, you

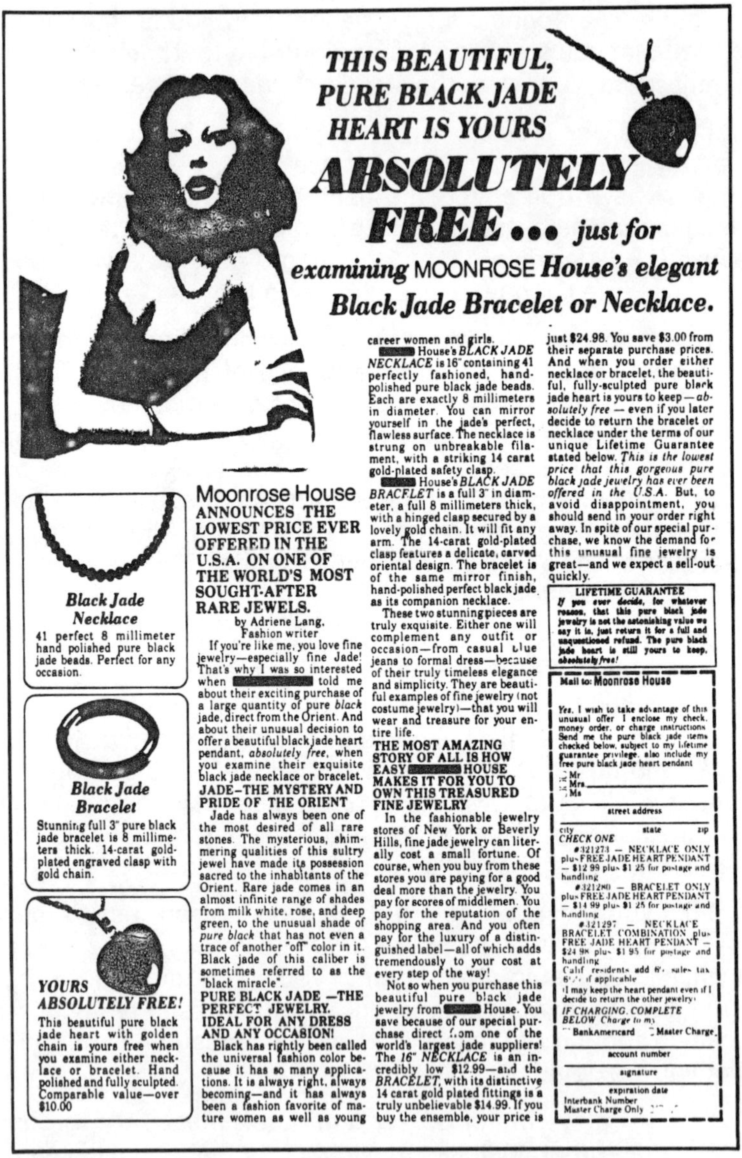

THIS BEAUTIFUL, PURE BLACK JADE HEART IS YOURS **ABSOLUTELY FREE** ••• *just for examining* MOONROSE *House's elegant Black Jade Bracelet or Necklace.*

Black Jade Necklace

41 perfect 8 millimeter hand polished pure black jade beads. Perfect for any occasion.

Black Jade Bracelet

Stunning full 3" pure black jade bracelet is 8 millimeters thick. 14-carat gold-plated engraved clasp with gold chain.

YOURS ABSOLUTELY FREE!

This beautiful pure black jade heart with golden chain is yours free when you examine either necklace or bracelet. Hand polished and fully sculpted. Comparable value—over $10.00

Moonrose House
ANNOUNCES THE LOWEST PRICE EVER OFFERED IN THE U.S.A. ON ONE OF THE WORLD'S MOST SOUGHT-AFTER RARE JEWELS.

by Adriene Lang,
Fashion writer

If you're like me, you love fine jewelry—especially fine Jade! That's why I was so interested when [redacted] told me about their exciting purchase of a large quantity of pure *black* jade, direct from the Orient. And about their unusual decision to offer a beautiful black jade heart pendant, *absolutely free*, when you examine their exquisite black jade necklace or bracelet.

JADE–THE MYSTERY AND PRIDE OF THE ORIENT

Jade has always been one of the most desired of all rare stones. The mysterious, shimmering qualities of this sultry jewel have made its possession sacred to the inhabitants of the Orient. Rare jade comes in an almost infinite range of shades from milk white, rose, and deep green, to the unusual shade of *pure black* that has not even a trace of another "off" color in it. Black jade of this caliber is sometimes referred to as the "black miracle".

PURE BLACK JADE —THE PERFECT JEWELRY. IDEAL FOR ANY DRESS AND ANY OCCASION!

Black has rightly been called the universal fashion color because it has so many applications. It is always right, always becoming—and it has always been a fashion favorite of mature women as well as young career women and girls.

[redacted] House's *BLACK JADE NECKLACE* is 16" containing 41 perfectly fashioned, hand-polished pure black jade beads. Each are exactly 8 millimeters in diameter. You can mirror yourself in the jade's perfect, flawless surface. The necklace is strung on unbreakable filament, with a striking 14 carat gold-plated safety clasp.

[redacted] House's *BRACELET* is a full 3" in diameter, a full 8 millimeters thick, with a hinged clasp secured by a lovely gold chain. It will fit any arm. The 14-carat gold-plated clasp features a delicate, carved oriental design. The bracelet is of the same mirror finish, hand-polished perfect black jade as its companion necklace.

These two stunning pieces are truly exquisite. Either one will complement any outfit or occasion—from casual blue jeans to formal dress—because of their truly timeless elegance and simplicity. They are beautiful examples of fine jewelry (not costume jewelry)—that you will wear and treasure for your entire life.

THE MOST AMAZING STORY OF ALL IS HOW EASY [redacted] HOUSE MAKES IT FOR YOU TO OWN THIS TREASURED FINE JEWELRY

In the fashionable jewelry stores of New York or Beverly Hills, fine jade jewelry can literally cost a small fortune. Of course, when you buy from these stores you are paying for a good deal more than the jewelry. You pay for scores of middlemen. You pay for the reputation of the shopping area. And you often pay for the luxury of a distinguished label—all of which adds tremendously to your cost at every step of the way!

Not so when you purchase this beautiful pure black jade jewelry from [redacted] House. You save because of our special purchase direct from one of the world's largest jade suppliers! The *16" NECKLACE* is an incredibly low $12.99—and the *BRACELET*, with its distinctive 14 carat gold plated fittings is a truly unbelievable $14.99. If you buy the ensemble, your price is just $24.98. You save $3.00 from their separate purchase prices. And when you order either necklace or bracelet, the beautiful, fully-sculpted pure black jade heart is yours to keep—*absolutely free*—even if you later decide to return the bracelet or necklace under the terms of our unique Lifetime Guarantee stated below. *This is the lowest price that this gorgeous pure black jade jewelry has ever been offered in the U.S.A.* But, to avoid disappointment, you should send in your order right away. In spite of our special purchase, we know the demand for this unusual fine jewelry is great—and we expect a sell-out quickly.

LIFETIME GUARANTEE

If you ever decide, for whatever reason, that this pure black jade jewelry is not the astonishing value we say it is, just return it for a full and unquestioned refund. The pure black jade heart is still yours to keep, absolutely free!

Mail to: Moonrose House

Yes, I wish to take advantage of this unusual offer. I enclose my check, money order, or charge instructions. Send me the pure black jade items checked below, subject to my lifetime guarantee privilege, also include my free pure black jade heart pendant.

Mr
Mrs. ________
Ms

street address

city state zip

CHECK ONE

#321273 — NECKLACE ONLY plus FREE JADE HEART PENDANT — $12.99 plus $1.25 for postage and handling

#321280 — BRACELET ONLY plus FREE JADE HEART PENDANT — $14.99 plus $1.25 for postage and handling

#321297 — NECKLACE BRACELET COMBINATION plus FREE JADE HEART PENDANT — $24.98 plus $1.95 for postage and handling

Calif. residents add 6% sales tax 6½% if applicable

(I may keep the heart pendant even if I decide to return the other jewelry)

IF CHARGING, COMPLETE BELOW Charge to my

BankAmericard Master Charge

account number

signature

expiration date

Interbank Number
Master Charge Only

Remember that ''Black Jade'' ad from a few pages back? Here it is reincarnated by the ''creative department'' of one of our very large competitors, let's call it ''Moonrose House''. You want to learn from your competitors, but you certainly don't want to plagiarize. To the discerning the line is clear.

Another example of "creativity": this, by the "Blackroom Company", national jewelry mail-order house. They even lifted the typeface off the word "Free" and the characteristic asterisk. You can do this sort of thing once or twice, but then people will get wise to you. You cannot be successful in this business if your colleagues do not respect you and they won't if you steal their ads. Also, if you are inclined to do this sort of thing, you will usually be too late: in many cases, the particular promotion will have run its course.

would become known in your industry as a plagiarist, as one who hopes to build his business on other people's work — and that won't make you many friends.

I am a firm believer that business should be conducted for profit *and* for fun. And it just can't be much fun to work in an industry in which your colleagues and competitors think of you as a thief and therefore can't have much respect for you.

A WORD ABOUT SUCCESS

Before we close this chapter on space advertising, I must tell you, if you have not already suspected it, that I have spoken so far only about successes. There have been many failures along the way, some of them quite spectacular. And you know what? The spectacular failures are almost better than the "borderlines" because on the *real* busts you give up right away. With the so-so's you attempt to fiddle around with and improve. And that may cost you more money. I mention failures (perhaps even too casually), because I want you to brace yourself to expect them now and then, and not to be disappointed when they come.

You *can* get rich and you *will* get rich in the mail-order business. And you will do it despite your failures. You will be a success and *you will make a bundle, if only one out of every five ads that you come up with is a real success.* Why is that? Simple: you will try the failures once, then perhaps once more, and then forget them. The successes can be expanded into publications of ever larger *circulation* and very large sales and profits can result. And they can go on and on and on. There are ads that I first ran with Haverhill's fifteen years ago and which, in slightly updated format, I still run at Henniker's. There are ads which I run every week of the year in many media, year in and year out. And there are ads that I created two or three years ago and that I predict will run successfully ten years from now. That is the beauty and one of the sources of the great potential of this business: you can cut your losses and run with your winners. And it doesn't take too many winners to make you a real success.

Remember how, at the beginning of this chapter, I told you that space advertising is not really what this business is all about? It isn't, but it is the inevitable starting point to build your business and your million dollar fortune in the mail-order field. Because it is *the* way to get started selling on a small but increasing scale. Most importantly, it is the way to build a mailing list, a lot of loyal customers in a reasonable time.

SOME GENERAL GUIDELINES ON SPACE ADVERTISING

You should know, however, what to look for and what to expect from space advertising. Let me give you a few general guidelines:

- You should shoot for a 50% return on your investment with every space ad you run. Here is what I mean. Suppose you have an item on which you have a 60% gross profit margin. That means, for instance, that it costs you $4 and you sell it for $10. Thus, on each unit that you sell, you make $6 "profit."

  Suppose you run this ad in space that costs you $500. In order to reach your goal of 50% return on your investment, you would have to recover that investment, namely your $500 in space cost, plus 50% of that, namely an additional $250. This makes a total of $750. Since you make $6 gross profit per unit, you have to sell 125 units to meet your goal of 50% profit on space investment.

  You will find quite a few ads that don't make that 50% profit margin and it is then a matter of judgment whether you should go on running them or not. Perhaps you can make some slight improvement. Perhaps a change in price would help. Perhaps you could modify your proposition by adding a premium or by some other means to jack up response. I believe that you should not consider continuing to run anything that gives you less than 25% return on your investment.

- If you turn into a good operator, that means that you select good merchandise and present it effectively, you will also come up with quite a few ads that will yield substantially more than 50% return on your investment. We have created ads that have given us 100% return on investment for months and years. In the example I've given, this would mean that you would have to sell about 165 units to reach that magic figure of 100% return on your investment.

- But, to repeat an important point, space advertising has a much broader purpose than just to make you some money in the initial stages of your mail-order business. The main purpose of a sound mail-order operation is to use space advertising to create customers. The fastest way to do this is to sell some quality product at a relatively low price — say, not over $4.95 — that is likely to generate high-volume sales. With one good item like the Henni/HiGrips, Mack the Knife, or the Organizer, you should be able to build a respectable mailing list of 25,000 or 30,000 names during your first year of operation. And you will make money in doing it. Those less experienced than you and I will actually make an *investment* in creating customers. That means that it will cost them $1, $2 or more, for every bona fide customer they get on their list. But you shouldn't have to do that. You now know how to spot a good promotional item, and how to make a good promotional ad. You should be able to make at least a 50% profit margin on such a good "promo," make high sales, good profits and generate many customers.
- During your first year of operation, the crucial year and the most difficult year in almost any business, put approximately one-half of your space advertising money into promotional ads and the other half into regular merchandise ads. If you follow my suggestions and if you play the game right, you should be making a 30-50% average return on investment on all the ads you will run during the first year. You will have made some money but, more importantly, you will have created the basis of a sound business and a good solid mailing list.
- But, to repeat, space advertising is not what this business is about. Space advertising is a means to *build your business.* It is a rather expensive means of advertising and getting more so as space rates relentlessly increase year after year. As you progress, you will phase out of it more and more, and will begin to rely on promotions that are more cost effective and that use the "rifle," rather than the space advertising "shotgun" approach.

In the next chapter, we shall talk about direct mail, which puts us right in the middle of the *real* mail-order action.

Chapter 4

HOW TO WRITE DIRECT MAIL PIECES THAT SIZZLE

If you have read the last chapter with the attention it deserved, you will now know how to produce first-class mail-order space ads. You will know how to make "promotional" ads and how to make "real merchandise" ads. If you have followed the guidelines that I have given you, you will, after a few false starts perhaps, be able to produce space advertising that will fairly consistently come up to, and hopefully exceed, the "50% return on investment" profit goal that you have established for yourself.

But you will also remember what I have told you and what may have come as a surprise to you: space ads are *not* the essence of the mail-order business. They are the almost unavoidable way to get started and to create a mailing list. And, after you have created a reasonably sized mailing list — I shall take a stab and say that 100,000 names would be about the "ignition point" — then you can (and should) relegate space advertising to a secondary role. Its primary role will be simply to keep your name in front of the public — sort of "institutional advertising," to generate new customers (though at a less frantic pace than in Phase 1) and, of course, to have an additional source of profit. Because if you follow my guidelines, you will always make money on space advertising — it will simply assume a less important role as your business matures.

And now I am going to show you how to make all that hard work and those many hours of sweat of that initial phase pay off for you. Until now *you were building* a business. Now that you have a mailing list of 100,000 names of satisfied customers, you are truly in the mail-order business. And this business consists of dealing with, "massaging," "harvesting" the customers you have created.

Your customers are next to your own family, the most important people in the world. Don't take them for granted. Also, never forget that besides being your customers, they are also many other things. In fact, they hardly ever think of themselves in that role (or if they do, it is a quite incidental part of their lives). But *for you,* it is their common denominator and the most important attribute they have and share. You don't really care whether they are black or white, Southerners or New Englanders, Episcopalians or Zen Buddhists. They have one great thing in common: they have had one or more satisfactory dealings with you. They recognize your name, they believe you and they trust you. And you are going to get very rich by mining this mother lode of confidence. You are going to circularize them regularly by direct mail and by catalogs. They are going to respond to your appeals and your promotions, because these promotions are going to be very attractive and they are going to be irresistibly presented.

There may be other ways to slice this pie, but, for our purposes, let's consider "direct mail" falling into three categories:

- Direct mail "solos."
- Package inserts and "bouncebacks."
- Catalogs.

In this chapter we will talk about solos and bouncebacks (although, as you will see, the latter are sort of a hybrid critter and don't perhaps entirely belong in this classification.

EXACTLY WHAT IS A DIRECT MAIL PIECE?

The "classical mail piece" consists of four parts:

- Outside envelope
- Letter
- "Folder"
- Return medium

There are variations on this formula. For instance, the letter may be omitted or combined with the "folder." Or sometimes the return medium may be combined with the letter or other such shortcuts. Believe me — it doesn't work too well. All of these variants have been tried, but the "tried and true" 4-part formula has always come out the winner.

But there *is* one exception and that is very fortunate. Because there is one serious problem with the classical mail piece: it is quite expensive on a per unit basis if run in small quantities — and let's consider for our present purposes everything under 100,000 units as "small quantities." It is so expensive, in fact, that any such mailing would almost be bound to be a failure. As you will find out, the "trouble" with all artwork and all printing is that the cost of production, the "going-in cost" is exactly the same whether you print 1,000 pieces or 10,000,000 pieces. And if you print 10,000,000 pieces, the "going-in cost," although it may be a good deal of money, becomes a trivial amount per each single unit, hardly anything to worry about. But if you print only, say, 25,000 pieces, that cost may well become prohibitive on a per unit basis.

THE "POOR MAN'S MAIL PIECE"

And if there were no other way of doing it, you could not possibly mail to your list unless you had at least, say, 200,000 good names. Even then, it would be a very iffy proposition. But there is a way how you can start mailing to your list by the time you have about 20,000 or 25,000 names. And here's how you do it: you use a *single piece mailer* which has a built-in envelope that the customer can detach and mail. These kinds of mailers are usually patented forms and can be purchased from and printed by quite a few specialized printing companies.

When I built Haverhill's, I used this type of mail piece exclusively in the early stages, simply because I could not afford to go "all the way" with conventional 4-part mail pieces. Some of these mail pieces, for instance, that on our *Emoskop Vest Pocket Optical System,* were so successful in that format, that I used them for many years. I only did some minor "face lifting," but without changing their basic format. Call it inertia or call it not wishing to tinker with a successful product — I just kept on using it and it just kept on working for me. I show you some Henniker's versions of these single piece mailers, among them the updated and face-lifted Emoskop mailer. Just as at Haverhill's, they were used as "starters" in Henniker's poor-boy stage. But they are so successful that we shall, in all likelihood, continue them for a long time, with only minor modifications that may be needed as time goes by.

Another successful mail piece of this nature — call it "the Poor Man's Catalog" if you wish, is our *Omnibus Mailer.* It

This Emoskop mailer is one of the granddaddies of our direct mail pieces. We have run it successfully for over ten years — naturally, we updated it from time to time. It does consistently so well in this ''Poor Man's Mail Piece'' that we never gave it the ''full treatment.'' The simple mailer seems to lend itself particularly well to this small, compact optical item.

This ''Omnibus Mailer'' of which I show you just the merchandise display portion worked well for us. Select the eight or ten best pieces of **your** merchandise and you will be able to compose an effective mail piece to your own and to selected outside lists. We have discontinued this type of mailer and use ''mini-catalog'' inserts instead.

features at any time about ten of our most successful merchandise items. We mail it to our own list and to test outside lists. This has always been successful, but we have slowly phased out this particular piece and don't much use it any more. We have superseded it by our "mini-catalog" package insert (bounceback), which we use now in our own packages and insert in those of others. More about that later.

You will notice that both mailers have the same basic design. Both are printed in black and one color — bright yellow in the case of the *Emoskop* and a golden buff in the case of the *Omnibus Mailer.* There is an eye-catching piece of art on the cover and a "teaser" that leads (at least I hope it does) the recipient to open the piece and to see what is inside.

ANATOMY OF SINGLE PIECE MAILER

Let's open the Emoskop mailer and look at what is a typical and successful "formula" treatment for this kind of single piece mailer.

First, there is the headline, which picks up the theme from the cover and thus provides a smooth transition, easing the reader to go on. Remember, just as in space ads, you have to keep your reader's attention in order to make him go all the way to your proposition (and then, hopefully, make him act on it). So you have to keep leading him all the way, and you must see that one element flows smoothly into the next.

While your customer is reading the headline, his attention is caught simultaneously by two elements, namely, the excellent main illustration (no expense spared here — it has to be top-notch, very detailed, looking as though it might jump right out of the page) and the boldly stated price. The price, in the immediate vicinity of the illustration, makes it clear that this is an attractive bargain and now leads the customer to read the letter that runs alongside the illustration.

The letter, by necessity, is quite short and to the point. It describes the main features, points out the advantageous price and closes, of course, with the buying proposition. At that point, we also mention the "Free Bonus," which is an important part of the whole proposition.

This is the inside of our successful Emoskop mailer. It illustrates well all the elements that you should have. The only possible "objection" (and that would be an artistic one) is that the piece is perhaps a little too crowded, a little too "busy."

In addition to the main illustration, we have, in the case of the Emoskop, a number of "vignettes," carefully executed line drawings. Each of these illustrates one of two functions of the instrument. These line drawings really make the explanatory copy come alive and add interest to what might otherwise be pretty dry reading, namely the description of technical functions.

In some cases in which we "solo" a product, we use one single bold illustration, surrounded by so-called "call-outs." Look at the treatment we have given our *Swiss Army Style Knife* in this same type of mailer. Every detail is explained by these "call-outs." Since the customer cannot see nor touch the merchandise, we do the next best things:

- Provide a super illustration, and
- Demonstrate every feature, exactly what it does, almost just as though the customer were in our San Francisco store and getting personal attention from trained sales personnel.

Below the heavy dash line there is the order form on the left, which, just as we do in our space ads — starts out with the affirmative **YES.** It is really pretty much like a space ad coupon, complete with the "Special" (three for $27.95), charge information and toll-free telephone number.

The right side contains the "bonus box," showing a picture of the "freebie" and telling the customer how to go about getting it, namely by ordering *right away* ("within 7 days — no exceptions, please!"). It is an important part of the mailing. This little extra, the "free lunch," the chance to get something for nothing, is what will make a so-so mailing a success and a success a smash. On offers of this kind, don't ever forget that a bonus may make all the difference!

There are two other important features on this side of the mailer, namely address correction information and Guarantee. The first helps to keep your list "clean" and up-to-date (we'll have a lot more to say about your list later on). As for the Guarantee, please do read its wording. Just as it says, it is simple, namely the customer is the only judge. He can return the merchandise if he doesn't like it and it is guaranteed to work and to perform.

I just cannot emphasize too much the importance of the Guarantee. Please remember that you are dealing with a person who has never seen you. He may be thousands of miles away and you are asking him to entrust his hard-earned money to you, just on the strength of your fine words. You owe it to him and you owe it to yourself to tell him exactly what you will do for him if he is not happy. And then *be very sure* to do just exactly what you have promised him if the case should arise — and to do it very quickly!

As you may have gathered, the customer detaches the portion right below the dashed line and puts his check in the envelope, folds it over, then moistens and seals it. Glue is already supplied.

Let me clarify a couple of points. In order to facilitate address correction, we work with so-called "peel-off" or "self-adhesive" labels. The customer is invited to remove this label from the address side and adhere it in the space provided, *even if there is an error.*

This has several advantages:

- It "involves" the customer. I am not entirely sure how much there is to it, but studies apparently have proven that response increases if the customer gets to do something, if he gets "involved." This may be punching out a token, marking a "yes" or a "no" box, or some such. In our case, we involve him by letting him unpeel and then adhere his label.
- If the name and address are indeed correct, we are less likely to make a mistake in the filling of the order, because everything is already neatly printed, and we don't have to rely on handwriting that many times is difficult to read.
- If either name, address, or both, are wrong, and having invited the customer to peel off and adhere the label anyway (and to write corrections in the space we have provided) we have a quick way to enter the correction on our computer master file. The top line of the label (consisting of 13 letters and numerals) is this customer's very own "match-code." All we have to do is feed that match-code into the computer, make the proper corrections — and, presto, we have this customer on our list *right* and, just as importantly, he will be on the file only once.
- We get "keying" information. We do a great deal of testing, of course, of mailing through other people's lists. And the

easiest way to know which list (our own list or which outside list) this customer comes from and which proposition he has responded to, is by printing the "key" right on the label and to have it in front of us when we enter the order.

In the *Casio CQ-1* mailing I show you what the complete package looks like when you receive it. It doesn't make much difference how long you have been in this business, but there is no greater thrill than having the mailman come to your place of business and dropping a bundle that you can tell contains maybe 250 of these beautiful envelopes and knowing that each one contains a check, close to $30 in the case of the Emoskop and over $50 in the case of the Casio CQ-1. Really there is hardly a prettier sight in the world!

Let's turn the mailer around. We have already seen two of the panels, namely the front and the return envelope portion, which is covered up by the front when the piece goes out. The third panel consists of two important elements: the story about the FREE GIFT and the Endorsement. The FREE GIFT story has, of course, already been told. But it is possible that a customer chances to look at this side of the mail piece first. And if he does, he sees two things that greatly interest him, namely FREE and DELIGHTED — two very powerful and important words.*

LET'S TALK ABOUT TESTIMONIALS

How about them? If you have a good item, your satisfied customers *will* write to you and tell you how they liked your product. You should immediately acknowledge such letters and ask permission to use any portion of those letters for future promotion. I have never found a case in which such permission was withheld. But *do* be sure to get it in writing and to keep it. If you go ahead without such release, you could find yourself involved in nasty legal action — I have had it happen, I know what I'm talking about.

Such letters of endorsement come in spontaneously. But we have developed a technique to "produce" endorsements that we find particularly useful in the introduction of a new product. Now, quite often, when we launch an important new promotion, we send

---

* As you will notice, we occasionally switch the "Guarantee" and the "Endorsement" panels, especially if we have many good endorsements that we want to quote.

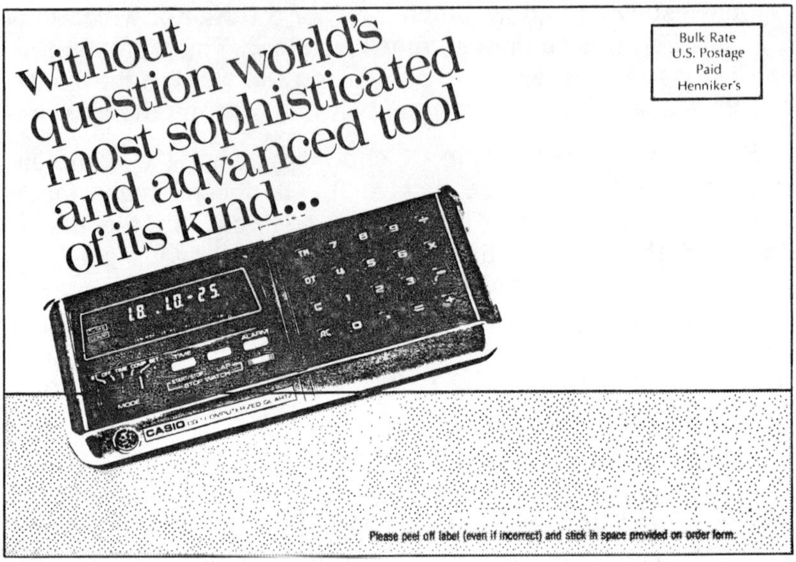

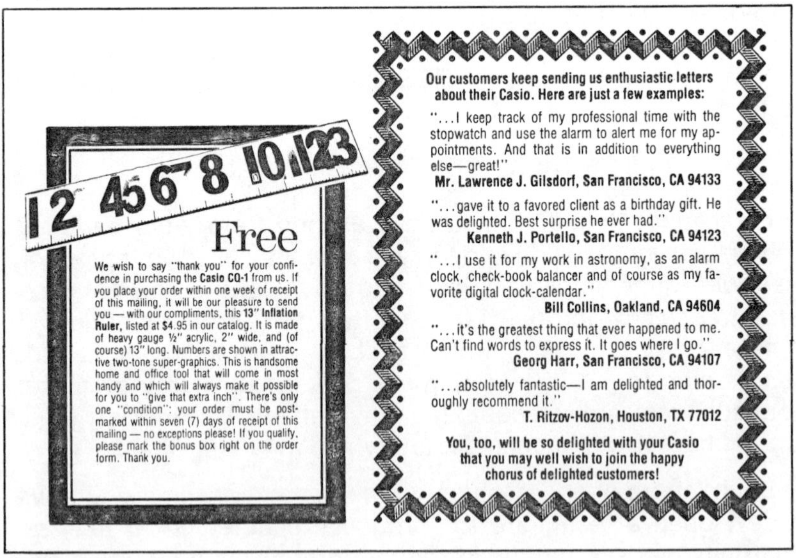

Front and back of a simple mail piece for a sophisticated electronic consumer product. We did not quite as well with it as we had hoped. And the answer is perhaps that for such a relatively expensive item, a product of high technology, more elaborate treatment, the full-color complete direct mail package might be required.

about 100 letters of inquiry to randomly selected purchasers of this product, asking for opinions — bouquets or brickbats. I show you one of these letters sent to a customer and returned to us. It is rather typical. We learn many things about our products and we do get usable quotes. And, believe me, people aren't shy at all if they think brickbats are in order. If there are too many brickbats, we try to remedy the feature the customers find objectionable. If that is not feasible or too difficult, we might forget about the whole thing. The product is not well accepted and might possibly be more grief than it is worth. It is much easier to pull the plug at this stage, rather than after having spent much time and money.

The absolutely greatest and best endorsement a product or service can get is personal word of mouth. Think of yourself and your reactions! When a friend tells you that he has found a movie entertaining it is 100 times more effective than the advertisement of the movie proclaiming it "the smash hit of the year." The same is true, of course, with products. For a national mail-order company (in contrast to, say, a local bakery) it is almost impossible to produce word-of-mouth endorsement. So, the second best thing (thought admittedly a quite distant second) is to have testimonials. They are not person-to-person endorsements, but they do tell in believable terms how people feel about your product.

JEWELRY SELLS SUCCESSFULLY WITH SINGLE PIECE MAILER

I want to show you one more of the single piece mailers. It is one of my favorites because I believe it is exceptionally well executed and because it is very successful.

I must confess that I approached the sale of jewelry through this rather inexpensive means and to a fairly sophisticated audience with much trepidation. We first tried it with a less expensive piece of jewelry, an Amethyst Necklace, that retailed for $19.95. It was successful. So then we took the plunge and launched the Garnet, a rather more expensive piece of jewelry. It fulfilled our fondest expectations, and we were able to roll it out successfully to outside lists.

The Garnet mailer is meant to be just an example of what can be done and done successfully with an inexpensive single piece mailer. While it did work for us, I am pretty sure that this is not the best way to sell jewelry by mail. Jewelry really deserves the "full

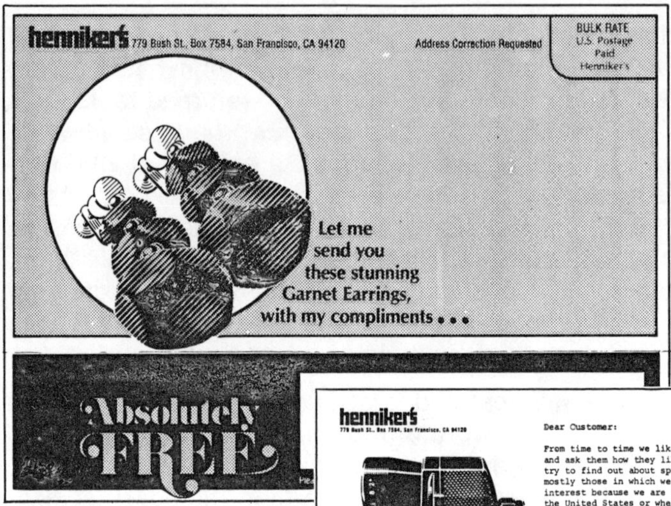

henniker's
779 Bush St., Box 7584, San Francisco, CA 94120

Dear Customer:

From time to time we like to "poll" our customers and ask them how they like our merchandise. We try to find out about specific pieces of merchandise, mostly those in which we have a great personal interest because we are the exclusive distributors in the United States or when the merchandise is being manufactured to our specifications.

The HENNISCOPE SYSTEM is one of those items. Our printout shows that you purchased one of these within the last three months and you are one of the customers that we selected at random for your possible evaluation and opinion.

If you don't mind, why don't you please take a minute and write me, in not more than 50 words, what you think of the HENNISCOPE SYSTEM, your experiences, the kind of use you put it to, how it helps you in your personal and professional life. In short, anything at all you think would be of assistance to me, to Henniker's and to our other customers.

In replying and in giving me your comments, I shall assume (unless you specifically disallow it) that I may publish all or any part of your statement in any future promotion that Henniker's might make on the HENNISCOPE SYSTEM. I have no immediate plans for it, but it is possible. If we were to publish all or part of your statement, we would use your name and your city, but not your address.

I would be really grateful if you would cooperate with me and give me the benefit of your opinion. A prepaid envelope to my personal attention is attached. And, oh yes, if we should use your quote for any promotional purpose, we would send you a little present, our way of saying "thank you".

I do appreciate your help. Thank you very much.

Sincerely yours,

Gerardo Joffe
President

This is my comment on the HENNISCOPE SYSTEM

I have found the Henniscope to be a wonderful instrument for the home with a view--children, especially, are delighted to use it without fear of dropping, and can manage it any age. I am sure there are many uses for it, but, in San Francisco, where views abound I can think of nothing more useful than a Henniscope to enjoy them.

☒ I allow possible use of my statement as proposed in this letter.
☐ I will not allow any use of my statement as proposed in this letter.

signed ________ date 11/3/77

Name (Mrs.) Anne M. Schmid Address [redacted] State SF Zip 94122

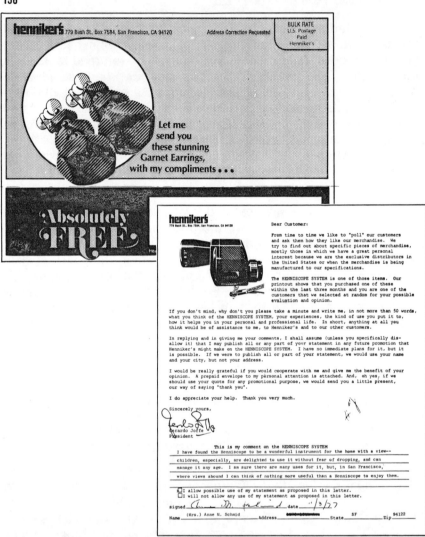

I approached the sale of jewelry through an inexpensive mail piece with some trepidation. But this mailer and a similar mailer on amethyst jewelry worked very well. Even so, there is little question that jewelry can be sold more successfully through a standard 4-part mail piece.

Your customers will let you know what they think of your product and of your service. But you don't have to stand and wait for things to happen — you can **do** something about that. This kind of letter will elicit a surprising percentage of response. You will learn things about your product that you didn't know before, you will get good copy ideas and you will get excellent endorsements.

treatment" — color, good paper and all. We are re-working these jewelry pieces now and we are confident that they will be even more successful in their reincarnation.

HOW TO GET STARTED WITH DIRECT MAIL

By the time you are about a year into your mail-order business, you should have created four or five mail pieces of this kind. By all means, prepare an "omnibus" mail piece of your best merchandise, very much like the one we have just discussed. If you have picked your merchandise well, it will always be a winner. Then take three or four of your best items, those that have really sold well in space advertising, on which you have the right price and the proper margin, and prepare solos on those. Usually, you should not attempt to make a solo mailing on an item that sells for less than, say, $20 — it is almost too difficult for the arithmetic to come out in your favor. But there are always exceptions — the *Swiss Army Style Knife* is one of them. True, it sells for just $9.95, but it has a number of "extras" going for it:

- It is an extremely attractive item that appeals to a wide audience.
- Our profit margin is quite a bit higher than usual.

This, as I just told you, is a very successful mailing, but it is an exception at this price level. Usually, it is very difficult to find items that are relatively inexpensive and that can make a profit by direct solo mail.

FROM "POOR BOY" TO "STANDARD" MAIL PIECE

Let's now talk about an honest-to-goodness "standard" mail piece, the kind I described in the very beginning of the chapter. This will be your regular mail piece once you really get going (except those extra-special good ones from the "poor boy" stage that you decide to retain). And that will be after you have a mailing list of not fewer than about 200,000 established customers — customers whom you have acquired pretty much "the hard way," namely by space advertising.

Just as I told you in the preceding chapter about space advertising, there are many thorns among the roses — many failures among the successes. Again, that's the beauty of mail order —

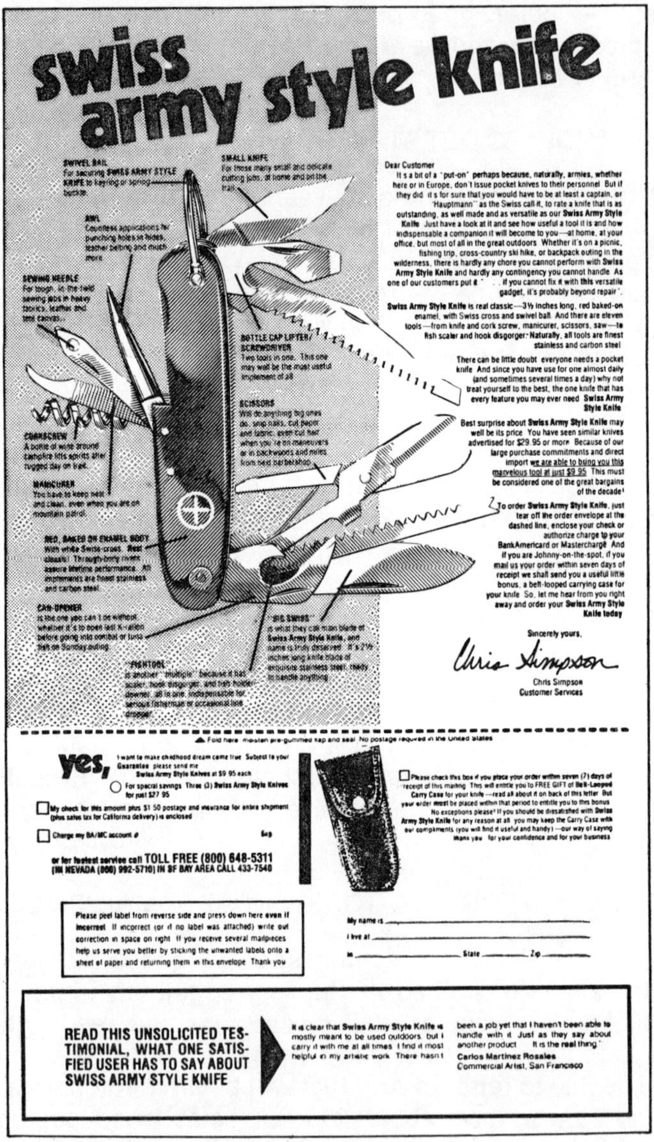

A simple mail piece of the Swiss Army Style Knife. We made up for the inexpensiveness of the mailer by using an excellent illustration, with many "call-outs" explaining each feature. This mailer works well, but, as a rule of thumb, it is almost impossible to sell such a low-priced item successfully by direct mail.

whether it be in space advertising, in direct mail, or catalogs. You can cut your losses and ride your winners. I have had my share of losers. If I had been batting 1.000 all along, or anything close to it, I might be working on my tenth million dollars now, instead of just on my second.

ANATOMY OF A "STANDARD" MAIL PIECE

The "standard" mail piece that I am going to talk about is that of the *StationMaster Clock.* It was one of our all-time great successes. Fashions in merchandise come and go, and it now seems to have run its course. This mail piece worked extremely well, with our own list. Much more importantly, it was so successful that it could be almost infinitely expanded to produce profits with many quality outside lists. This, of course, to use the hackneyed phrase, is "the name of the game."

The success of the StationMaster Clock, needless to say, was not just based on the quality of the mail piece. It was primarily based, of course, on the *attractive proposition,* which offered an extremely fine piece of merchandise at an almost incredibly low price — a 31-day calendar/chime clock, made of select tropical hardwoods, for less than $100! But, naturally, no matter how attractive the proposition, it has to be well presented and attractively and intelligently sold. I think we were doing all that extremely well with this mail piece.

Let's have a look at the four elements of this mailing:

1. *The 6" x 9" Outside Envelope.* This features an "engraving" of an old-fashioned locomotive, thus setting the tone of the entire mailing, its connection with an old-time railroad. And the "teaser" line: "Bring Beauty and a Touch of America's Romantic Past into your Home with . . ." complements this motif and leads the reader to open the envelope. Remember this is your first and most important task, a hurdle to overcome: to have your reader open the envelope. If he doesn't do that, everything else is lost. You have struck out right there.

2. *The Letter.* This is the second piece your reader will see. Its lead-in sentence, in bold-face, ties right in with the motif we have begun on the envelope. This is important — you must not jar the reader, but must lead him smoothly from one step to the next.

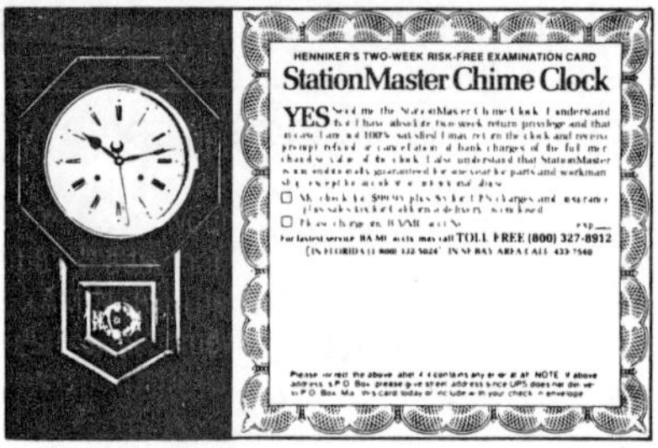

henniker's

This Bicentennial Year . . .
Bring beauty and
touch of America's
romantic past into
your home with
StationMaster Chime Clock

Dear Customer

If you have ever priced American antiques you know that it is almost beyond the reach of the average person to get anything worthwhile. That is why we are so pleased to be able to bring you StationMaster Chime Clock, which, while not a "genuine antique", is the closest thing to it: a loving and faithful reproduction of classic 19th century North Carolina railroad clock. The kind of clock that hung in every stationmaster's office and in many a schoolhouse, in the more leisurely days of our country's first century and a half.

You may think that it is difficult or perhaps impossible to improve on an "original" but we think that we may have done just that. The most important improvement perhaps is in the cabinetry. We certainly lay no claim that our craftsmen are more skilled or lavish greater attention than the cabinetmakers of yore. But these old cabinetmakers could not always use the finest hardwoods; and if they did, could use it only in veneers. StationMaster Clocks are built entirely of solid tropical hardwoods, very similar and superior perhaps to finest American walnut, with the richness and variety of grain you would expect only in the most expensive furniture. Most remarkable perhaps is that these are not veneers. StationMaster is solid hardwood through and through.

The cabinet is lovingly hand-rubbed to a matte gloss -- real antique sheen, so as to bring out every whorl and every detail of the exquisite wood. It is a handsome piece of furniture that blends beautifully with traditional decor and contrasts strikingly and handsomely with the most modern furniture.

> The clock face is truly beautiful. It is protected by glass and hinged door, with brass rim and brass fittings, features found in the most expensive 19th century clocks. The finely patterned hands and the carefully detailed Roman numerals are true reproduction of late 19th centruy American taste in workmanship. The handsome solid brass pendulum swings in its "caboose", visible through a pane that is gold-decorated in a 19th century American motif.

Will you please open the attached folder and look at this stunning clock. While you do that let me tell you a little more about it. The clock is octagonal in shape with a pendulum "caboose". It is 24 inches tall, 15 inches wide and

(please turn page)

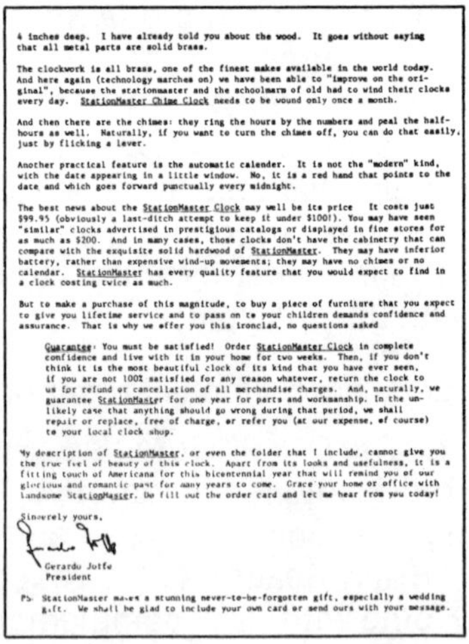

4 inches deep. I have already told you about the wood. It goes without saying that all metal parts are solid brass.

The clockwork is all brass, one of the finest makes available in the world today. And here again (technology marches on) we have been able to "improve on the original", because the stationmaster and the schoolmarm of old had to wind their clocks every day. StationMaster Chime Clock needs to be wound only once a month.

And then there are the chimes: they ring the hours by the numbers and peal the half-hours as well. Naturally, if you want to turn the chimes off, you can do that easily, just by flicking a lever.

Another practical feature is the automatic calender. It is not the "modern" kind, with the date appearing in a little window. No, it is a red hand that points to the date and which goes forward punctually every midnight.

The best news about the StationMaster Clock may well be its price It costs just $99.95 (obviously a last-ditch attempt to keep it under $100!). You may have seen "similar" clocks advertised in prestigious catalogs or displayed in fine stores for as much as $200. And in many cases, those clocks don't have the cabinetry that can compare with the exquisite solid hardwood of StationMaster. They may have inferior battery, rather than expensive wind-up movements; they may have no chimes or no calendar. StationMaster has every quality feature that you would expect to find in a clock costing twice as much.

But to make a purchase of this magnitude, to buy a piece of furniture that you expect to give you lifetime service and to pass on to your children demands confidence and assurance. That is why we offer you this ironclad, no questions asked

> Guarantee: You must be satisfied! Order StationMaster Clock in complete confidence and live with it in your home for two weeks. Then, if you don't think it is the most beautiful clock of its kind that you have ever seen, if you are not 100% satisfied for any reason whatever, return the clock to us for refund or cancellation of all merchandise charges. And, naturally, we guarantee StationMaster for one year for parts and workmanship. In the unlikely case that anything should go wrong during that period, we shall repair or replace, free of charge, or refer you (at our expense, of course) to your local clock shop.

My description of StationMaster, or even the folder that I include, cannot give you the true feel of beauty of this clock. Apart from its looks and usefulness, it is a fitting touch of Americana for this bicentennial year that will remind you of our glorious and romantic past for many years to come. Grace your home or office with handsome StationMaster. Do fill out the order card and let me hear from you today!

Sincerely yours,

Gerardo Joffe
President

PS. StationMaster makes a stunning never-to-be-forgotten gift, especially a wedding gift. We shall be glad to include your own card or send ours with your message.

Three parts of a ''standard'' mail piece. This is for our very successful StationMaster Clock promotion, which we ran for about two years of Haverhill's and continued at Henniker's. This illustration shows the outside envelope, order card and the promotional letter. This version of the promotion did well during the bicentennial year.

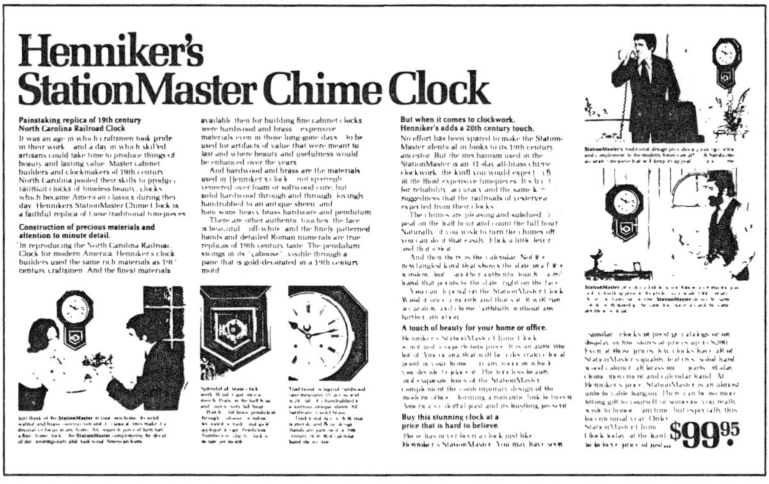

Both sides of the "folder" of the StationMaster mail piece. Opened up, it measures 11 x 17" and folds down to fit into a 6 x 9" envelope. It is printed on heavily coated paper that assures best color reproduction. You can usually afford such a mailing if you have a list of no fewer than, say, 200,000 names or if you can see your way clear to mail your piece to at least 200,000 reasonable prospects.

The letter is one sheet of paper printed front and back. People often ask me how long a direct sales letter should be. I can only give you the somewhat trite answer that it should be as short as possible but as long as necessary to make your point and to tell your story. You must have heard the story about President Lincoln, when somebody asked him how long a person's legs should be. He answered, "Long enough to reach the ground." Well, it's pretty much the same with a direct mail letter. It should be long enough to make your point.

I have seen great sales letters that were just two or three paragraphs long. But there are real classics, all mail order pros know about them, that run twelve single-spaced pages to tell their story. They are so well written, give much-needed information that you simply cannot get bored by them — on the contrary, you will be stirred to action. So perhaps one cardinal rule about these letters (easier said than done): don't bore your reader. Trim, cut, squeeze all unnecessary fat and water out of your letter. Write in short sentences, and avoid over-long words. Most important, no matter how proud you may be of your letter — have somebody else read it and criticize it. That "critic" must be somebody who has good judgment, who can put himself into the position of a prospective customer, and, most important perhaps, who does not mind telling you what he really thinks.

The StationMaster letter is just straightforward. It creates the mood and sets the tone, and then proceeds to talk about the general features of the clock. It refers the reader to the *illustrated folder* (the next piece), talks about the price, (and why this price is very attractive), states the Guarantee, and closes with appeal to action. The intended action, of course, is to get the reader to fill out the order card, to mail it to us and to buy the clock.

It is almost an article of faith in this business that every sales letter should have a P.S. Naturally, you have to say something meaningful and worthwhile in your P.S., but it really works. I have tried using the same letter with and without a P.S. and there is a noticeable difference in response. So, try to think of a good afterthought to leave your reader with and put it into a P.S.

Let me come back once more to the Guarantee. You will notice that we spell it out very clearly, and we give it importance graphically by indenting the entire paragraph of the Guarantee. You define the Guarantee once more in the folder, and also on the order card. Repetitious? Sure! Unnecessary duplication? Certainly not! Because remember — you are dealing with a person who has never seen you before and who might have never dealt with you before. He needs and deserves reassurance before you can expect him to part with his money. So your Guarantee is very important. It should be clear and straightforward and should be repeated wherever it might do some good.

3. *The Folder.* It again takes up the same theme that we had begun on the envelope, and continued in the letter. We repeat that here is something which is a genuinely American antique, and an especially significant purchase during this Bicentennial Year, (when this promotion was written). Open the folder: there is a glorious, highly detailed picture of the StationMaster Clock. This is one of those expensive pieces of scratchboard art I told you about in the last chapter. It costs quite a lot of money, a whole lot more than a photograph would. But there is no comparison: it pops out of the page, shows every feature in minute detail, and creates desire in the reader's mind to have this beautiful clock in his home or in his office.

Open the folder once more, and we now have a double spread. We recreate once more the mood of 19th century America. We then go on to give as much technical and specific product information as a customer would like to have. This is a little tricky, because you do want to tell everything that is important, but must not bore your customer with unnecessary detail. So you will need a sure sense of balance. We wind up the folder copy by once again talking about the price of the clock and by comparing it with clocks that have fewer quality features, and cost a lot more. The attractive price of $99.95 is boldly printed. Thus, even if your reader is in a hurry and does not feel like reading your whole offer, he will be stopped by this startlingly low price. Naturally, illustrations are an important part of the story.

We have already shown a full view of the clock itself. Here we have three "mood" shots, showing the clock in three different settings, and have two close-up shots of important detail. This, by the way, is perhaps a good time to make a point: any illustration should have a caption, should explain what it is. It may be perfectly clear to you, you may think no explanation is necessary. But remember, your reader is not as familiar with your product and with your thinking as you are. He has no time to guess. You have to make things easy for him and tell him exactly what he is looking at.

In the back of the folder, the last panel features some more "sell copy." This panel should really be used for the "free gift" which usually should be part of any mailing. For a number of internal reasons, we could not offer a gift with this version of the mailer (although we previously offered an attractive art book on railroading). But the most important part of this panel is to state once more the ironclad Guarantee: that the clock can be returned if the customer is dissatisfied for any reason, and that the clock will be repaired free of charge if anything at all should go wrong within a year.

One point here: while a "standard" mailing is designed in such a way that all pieces complement each other and do the complete selling job, each component should be able to stand on its own feet, give all pertinent information, and do the selling job if necessary. Look at the letter once more. If you have lost everything else, you still have enough information to buy the clock. That, of course, is also true of the folder and, as you will see, of the order form.

4. *The Order Form.* This is the last piece of the 4-part mail package. In this particular mailing, we chose a card. In others, we might prefer to use an envelope. Each has its advantages and disadvantages. If your business runs heavily to credit cards and telephone orders, a card may be preferable, because all the customer has to do is to fill in his credit card information and drop it into a mail box (unless, of course, he prefers to use the toll-free phone). Naturally, if he wishes to send his check with the card, he has to use his own envelope. This is a slight complication, which would not arise if we had provided a business reply envelope. I think it might be a matter of experimenting with what works best with your customers and from case to case. Chances are that it won't make a great deal of difference.

The copy on the order card should be to the point and once more should repeat the Guarantee. Here is the final moment of truth, the time when your customer is making his final decision to send you a check or to authorize a charge to his account. So this is definitely the place where you want to state what your commitments are and what assurances you are willing to give.

The reverse of the card is the business reply portion. Also, it has a detachable panel, which your customer can keep as a reminder. It tells him whom to talk or write to in case anything at all goes wrong with his order.

A final point about order cards and order envelopes: like most mail-order businesses, we use business reply cards (or envelopes), which means that we have to pay the post office ($.16 at this writing) for any reply we receive. There have been quite a few tests run to find out whether the difference in response is significant if the customer has to put his own stamp on this reply envelope, or when he may use the prepaid business reply card or envelope. I have done quite a bit of testing myself. The surprising and, it appears, conclusive answer is that it doesn't seem to make any measurable difference in response at all. So if one has a fair volume of response one might save quite a few dollars by eliminating business reply mail. This, however, is one area of this business in which I have, at least until now, let my "gut feeling," rather than my head, be my guide. And it seems as though most mailers, having the same information, do the same. We are just too afraid to lose even a few sales for lack of a postage stamp. And rather than run this risk, we don't mind paying the post office for this business reply mail. As you can imagine, this is the most pleasant expense in your entire business. For every $.16 you pay the postman, you make $8, $10, $20 or more. That, of course, is much fun, and fun and money are what this business is all about.

An important point about your mailer: you must use it as a "list cleaning device." Just about 10% of all Americans move every year. Therefore, if you don't "clean" your list periodically, you will very soon have a "phantom list," a list of people most of whom do not live at the address that is in your file. You can remedy this by printing the endorsement "address correction requested" right under your own return address. The Postal Service will return the piece to you, with the customer's new address if it is available. Then you can correct this customer's address on the list and remail the piece to him.

Until recently, we sent every single piece of mail with this endorsement. This service used to cost less than a dime, so it was a pretty good investment. As of this writing, the cost per return piece and forwarding address is $.25(!) and that can run into a lot of money. So now we do the "cleaning" every third or fourth month. This keeps the cost down and still maintains the list quite clean.

TECHNICAL POINT ABOUT LIST CLEANING

How do we do this every third month cleaning? Simple! We divide our list into three almost exactly equal parts. For our list, the first third goes from zip cycle 000XX to 268XX (West Virginia); the second third to 714XX (Louisiana); and the third third through the end of the list to 999XX (Alaska). Naturally, your own divisions may run somewhat differently. We are weighted heavily in favor of California, of course, and of the metropolitan eastern sea coast.

We mail to our customers regularly every four weeks, except for the period between the drop of our Christmas catalog (in early October) and Christmas. We have, at all times, four tested mail pieces and two "trial balloons" circulating through the list. One of the tested pieces carries the "address correction requested" endorsement and thus cleans the whole list over a 4-cycle (16-week) period.

If we call the tested mail pieces A, B, C, and D and the "trial balloons" a and b, we'll have a schedule something like this:

	1st month	2nd month	3rd month	4th month
First third list	A*	D	B	b
Second third list	B	a	C	A*
Third third list	C	A*	D	B

Only mail piece A happens to carry the "address correction requested" endorsement. From this schedule it is clear that the entire list is "swept" by this mail piece in four cycles (16 weeks — call it four months).

This is one reason to be systematic in your mailing schedule — naturally, that is not the only, or even the most important, one.

SOME COST AND PROFIT FIGURES

This is a good time perhaps to talk about general cost and profit expectations in direct mail. Naturally, both cost and response figures vary all over the lot. What I am telling you here can only be the broadest of "ballpark" outlines.

Cost, of course, depends very much on the total quantity of pieces that you print and mail. Early in this chapter, we talked about the "going-in" costs, the preparation and production costs, which are quite independent of the total number of pieces printed and mailed. Also, quite apart from those fixed going-in costs, long print runs are usually less expensive than short print runs. The printer can put your work on a high-speed press and effect certain economies in the purchase of paper. The only thing that you cannot save any money on, no matter how many pieces you run, is on postage. It is always the same. Indeed, the postal service, in a noble gesture to your start-up and budding mail-order business, gives you a special break on the bulk rate of the first 250,000 pieces you mail in a year. Thus, since we are still talking about a stage of your business at which you are not likely to exceed this figure, you are getting, in fact, a small but welcome subsidy from Uncle Sam. It is something that the big boys have to do without.

Let me give you some rough cost figures for direct mail on the approximately 100,000 unit level. The simple mailers that we talked about in the first part of this chapter should cost approximately $120 per 1000 pieces, if mailed to your own list, and about $160 per 1000 if mailed to an outside list. This includes printing, postage, "fulfillment" (which is for labelling, zip code sorting, bundling and delivering the pieces to the post office). In case of outside lists, it also includes the cost of list rental which, for quality lists, will vary from $30 to $50 (and sometimes even higher — but don't use them!) per 1000 names.

On a standard 4-piece mailer, as the one described for the StationMaster, the total in-the-mail cost would be perhaps $180 for your own and $220 for an outside list per thousand pieces. We are now thinking in terms of approximately 200,000 mailings. And we're talking about 2-color work — usually black and one color.. You cannot even consider "real" color, full process color, for runs as short as 200,000 pieces at a reasonable price and still get a quality job.

WHAT CAN YOU EXPECT?

What can you expect in response or, perhaps equally important, *what must you have* in response in order to break even and make a reasonable profit?

Let's look at the arithmetic of the "simple" mailer, the one that costs us $120 per 1000 pieces, if mailed to our own list, and $160 per 1000 pieces to an outside list.

Let's assume that the offer is for a single item that retails for $20. And let's assume that your *gross margin* (that is the difference between your sales price and the actual cost of the merchandise) is 60%. That means it costs you $8 to put it into your warehouse, and that you make $12 *gross profit* on each item sold.

It is clear that you would have to sell 10 units per thousand pieces mailed, or 1%, to break even. This means that you would have to attain this in order to recover your $120 outlay per 1000 pieces mailed. On mailings to outside lists, you have to recover $40 more per thousand to break even. This means that you would have to sell just over 13 units per thousand with the same proposition. Please keep in mind that, in doing this, you haven't yet made any money — no profit at all; you have just recovered your investment, and you are definitely not in this business in order to just break even. You might scrape by, by making very little profit on space advertising — remember, you were building your business and your mailing list. But you are now supposed to be in the first pay-off phase of your business and you *must* make money at this stage.

What is a reasonable amount to shoot for in direct mail? Naturally, opinions will vary, even among "experts." As in most things, generalizations are difficult. But I shall give you a good rule of thumb: to have a *good* mailing, you should *make a gross profit of about $100 per thousand pieces mailed* to your own list. To have an *acceptable mailing, you should make about $50 per thousand,* mailing to your own list.

Using our previous example of cost of $120 per 1000 and a $12 gross margin per unit, you would have to sell 18+ units per thousand to your own list to have a good mailing and 14+ units per thousand to your own list to have an acceptable mailing.

WHERE THE REAL MONEY IS IN DIRECT MAILING

The distinction between "good" and "acceptable" is more important than you might think at first. Sure, it is better to make a lot of money than to make just a little money, but the real difference is this: suppose your own mailing list is now at the 100,000 level and you have developed a mailing piece that we consider to be "acceptable." This means that it will give you about $50 profit contribution per thousand pieces mailed. You send this mailing to your entire list, and you will have made a profit contribution of $5,000. That's nothing to sneeze at, for sure. But once you have made this mailing, you are virtually through with it. You may be able to repeat it to your own list in about six months or so (with somewhat diminished results). But the *real payoff* in any mailing, is *mailing to millions of outside names on other people's lists.* And with an "acceptable mailing," this opportunity is not yet available to you.

Why is that? The inexorable reality of arithmetic comes into play. First of all, *you have to rent* those outside lists (you may occasionally be able to exchange names with other firms, but that can never be a major factor in your mailing program). The rented names, we have already found, cost just about $40 per thousand, so there goes your cost per 1000 from $120 to $160. But wait: that, unfortunately, isn't all. You will find that even the best outside list won't give you more than say 80-85% of the response you get from your own list. The reason, of course, is that your customers know *you,* they have already done business with *you,* and have confidence in *you,* and *your business.* If you use other people's names, there just isn't that confidence, and that will definitely be reflected in diminished pull.

Accept these two facts of life about outside lists:

1. your mailing to outside lists is going to cost you $30 to $40 per thousand more than to your own list;

2. your pull to outside lists is going to be at best 85% of what it was when you mailed to your own list.

What happens? It is this: instead of selling 14+ units per thousand (remember that's what you did when you made $50 per 1000 profit), you will (with good outside lists) probably sell only about 80 to 85% of that, say 12 1/2 units per thousand. That will give you a *gross profit* of $144 instead of $180 to your house list. But your cost per thousand is now $160. And in consequence, the *acceptable* profit of $50 per 1000 turns out to be a *loss* of $16 per 1000 by mailing this same piece to an outside list of roughly the same quality ("demographics") as your own. And that, of course, would be the quick way to the poorhouse, and not to success.

If you have created a *good* mailing, namely one that gives you a good profit contribution of about, and not too much less than, $100 per 1000 pieces mailed to your own list, things look much more promising.

Following the same reasoning again, you will find that, with a cost to outside lists of $160 per 1000, you may be able to sell 15+ units (namely about 80-85% of the 18+ units you achieved with your own list) to outside lists. This will yield you a profit contribution of about $20 per thousand pieces mailed. Not a whole lot, you will say, and in a way you are right. Certainly, it is quite a comedown from the $100 per 1000 you make on your own list. But, the enormous difference is that you can "roll out" to a very large number of potential customers, instead of being confined to your own small "universe" of perhaps 100,000 names or so. As the saying goes, you make it up by volume. Work with your list broker, tell him exactly what results you have attained with your own list and he will lead you to good, compatible lists to test. With his help, you may find several lists of 2 or 3 million names that will work for you with these results. You can figure out for yourself what that can mean to you in terms of total profit, even if you make a profit contribution of only $15 or $20 per thousand pieces mailed.

In the next chapter (Catalogs), we make a more sophisticated analysis of the true costs, the marginal cost of mailing to outside lists. That is important information — do try to understand it and to master it. You may then wish to apply these tools to your analysis of direct mail pieces. And you may find that certain mailings — perhaps in the upper regions of the acceptable category — those that you might not have considered for outside mailings — may indeed work for you on a roll-out to outside lists.

You should take these numerical examples with a grain of salt. Certainly, not all outside lists will give you exactly 85% of the response of your own list. Some will do worse, and some will "bomb" completely, and some may do a little better. It may even be possible that some outside lists will pull better for you than your own list. It could, but I have never seen it (or heard of it), in all the years I have been in this business. Your list — your own proven customers — invariably perform better for you than anybody else.

What I'm trying to show is the important principles that are involved. *You have to develop good mail pieces* — that is where the money is. From time to time you will develop mail pieces that won't even work for your own list. Obviously, you will drop these even faster than that proverbial hot potato. And you will develop quite a few that will be "acceptable," that will work for your own list, but not sufficiently well for outside lists. That will be fine, because they will be making money — it's just that you will have to come up with something new right away in order to be able to roll it out. But every so often, just as we did with our Emoskop mailer, our Garnet mailer and with our StationMaster mailer, you will come up with something that will be good, really good. You will be able to mail it to a very large number of outside lists. You will make a good deal of money with that, and it will point you toward the success and profit that this book is all about.

In case you don't know where to go for the outside lists, that is easy. There are quite a few competent list brokers, most of whom are in New York. Perhaps your best bet would be to write to the *Reporter of Direct Mail Advertising* (*"Direct Marketing"*), the "bible" of the industry. They are at 224 Seventh Street, Garden City, New York 11530. Tell them what your product is, and they will give you a list of good brokers to deal with. The people in these brokerage firms are usually very savvy. They will look at your mailing and will give you good suggestions for list testing.

NOW IS THE TIME FOR YOUR TOLL-FREE ORDER LINE

Remember when, in the chapter on Business Organization, we talked very briefly about the toll-free order line? We decided at the time that we needed access to credit cards right away, but that we could and should wait for that toll-free line until the volume of our business warranted it.

Well, this is the time! I would say, almost as an article of faith, that you *must* have such a service in order to be successful in the direct mail phases of your business and, of course, in mailing out catalogs.

As a rule of thumb, operators of toll-free services won't take you on unless you can assure them of a minimum level of service. This may vary from firm to firm, but perhaps a good average would be that you should have at least, say, 50 orders per week to make it at least remotely worth their while. And even at that level, they will take you on mostly buoyed by the hope that you will grow quickly and hopefully give them several hundred calls per week within a reasonable period.

What does this service cost? As of this writing, the average cost for taking an order is about $.75. This includes a (hopefully nice and attentive) person answering the phone in your firm's name, taking the order, the customer's name and address, the customer's bankcard number, the source (where does the order come from), and verification of this information. If you are very lucky (but don't count on it — they will all tell you that they will do it, but it doesn't work out) they will even offer additional merchandise to the caller. Once a day, the orders will be forwarded to you and you fill out the charges and send out the orders. You can also buy additional services, such as their filling out the charge cards, etc., but that starts getting a little expensive and you should really do that yourself.

Naturally, in order to assess the value of this service, you would have to know whether the additional cost is justified by the additional orders you receive. That, unfortunately, is almost impossible to determine exactly, because you don't really ever know who would and who would not have ordered if that service were not available. You have to go a little by hunch. But let me give you this piece of information: about 20% of *our* business comes over the phone. My guess is that we wouldn't be getting perhaps one-half of that were it not for the toll-free line. So my conclusion is that the toll-free line adds about 10% to our business. Do a little pencil pushing yourself: if our average order is $20, and we spend an extra $.75 per order, even if we have to spend that same $.75 on the same number of customers who would have ordered without it — that makes it quite worthwhile doesn't it? Go through the same reasoning with your own business and with your own numbers and you will see that it works out for you.

Where do you find such services? Look in your yellow pages or, better yet, in order to get really good people, those who are used to working with national mail-order firms, write to the *Direct Marketing Magazine.* I have given you their address.

VERY IMPORTANT: PACKAGE INSERTS

I cannot close this chapter without talking, at least briefly, about package inserts. They are not, strictly speaking, direct mail, but I think it is as good a place as any to talk about them.

Each package and each letter that goes out of your place of business *must* carry, absolutely, at least one package insert.

Unless its inclusion increases the weight of your package so as to put it into a different postage bracket (something that you should try to avoid by all means) the cost of your package insertion is virtually zero, because it includes only the very small outlay for printing the piece. Your customer receives this new offering when he is opening a package that he has just received from you and (I hope) when he is very pleased with what he finds. Better yet, he may even be getting a little more than he had expected. And while he is feeling good about you and about dealing with you, right there, before his eyes, is another attractive offer from you. This is, of course, the best time for you to sell him. Even if he doesn't buy right then, (many do — that is why we like to call these inserts "bouncebacks") he may well put your offer away and come back to it later.

We use all kinds of inserts from time to time. One of our most successful ones is a "mini-catalog," which has now become one of our standard inserts. Remember the Omnibus mailer? This is the outgrowth of it. Naturally, we change it and update it. I show you here a fairly recent version, in which we feature over 30 pieces of merchandise.

By the way, the mini-catalog does not really "compete" with our regular catalog. The catalog is an expensive piece and is printed in long runs. Therefore, when the customer gets it, it is likely to be ever so slightly "out of date." The mini-catalog, on the other hand, is a "cheapie," a quick print job, and can always feature the newest, hottest merchandise.

Then, for specific merchandise, we use "targeted bouncebacks." Have a look at the offer that we include with every one of our Henniscope systems, promoting a telescope lens attachment and a tripod. It is very successful.

Or have a look at the bounceback for an amethyst bracelet that we include with each piece of amethyst jewelry (necklace and earrings). The response is astonishing: just about 25% of all jewelry buyers take us up on that one. You can figure out for yourself how this adds to the overall profitability of this proposition! And we do exactly the same with other jewelry that we sell — such as garnet or agate. It works with all of them.

Do you remember the *Organizer* which we mentioned when we talked about "promotionals?" We give it away for "FREE" (just charge a dollar for postage and insurance). Naturally, we cannot

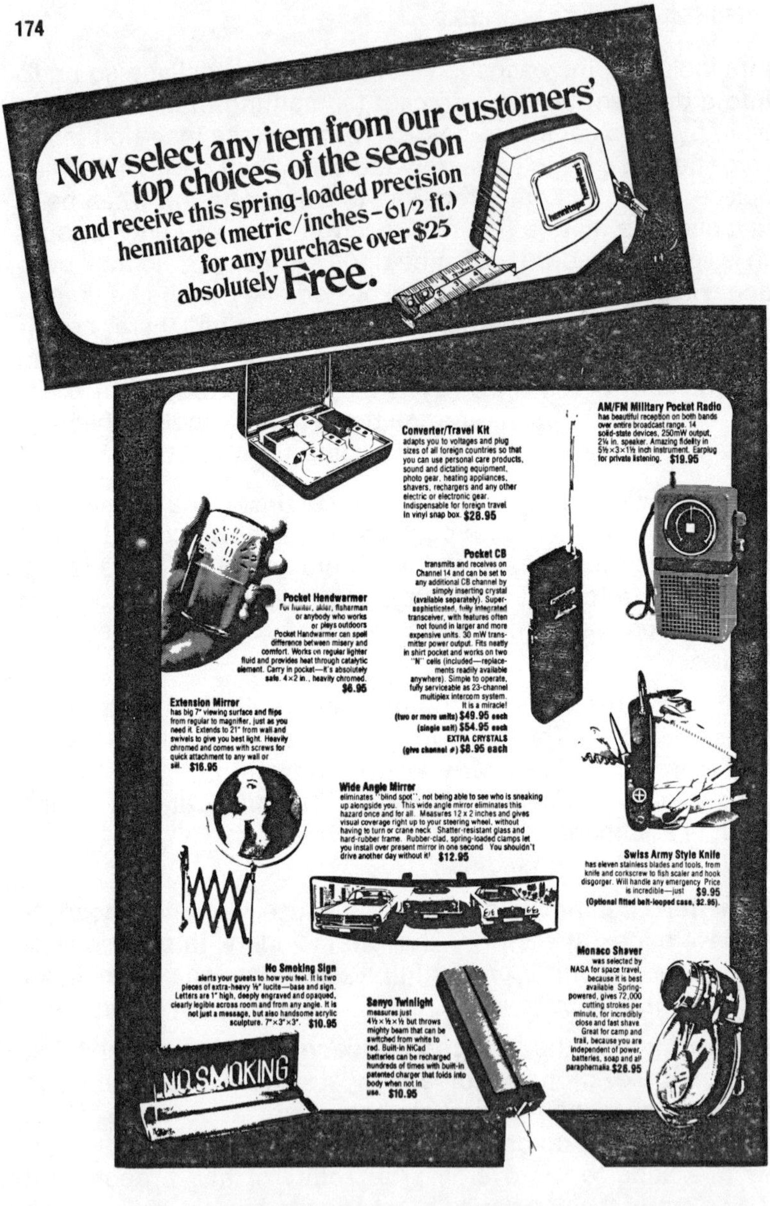

A rule never to be broken is that every package, every communication that leaves your business must carry one or several inserts. This "mini-catalog", an evolution of the omnibus mailer we saw earlier in this chapter, is an all-time champion. This illustration shows only a portion of this insert, which features over thirty pieces of our best and most current merchandise. You will always make money with such a mini-catalog. It measures 11 x 17" (open) and folds down to fit into a #10 (business size) envelope or into any package.

afford to spend much time and effort with each individual Organizer since we move them in such large quantities. So, in order to reduce our work to virtually nothing, except to putting on the label, the Organizer is completely pre-packed in Hong Kong, with three bouncebacks that we have printed right in Hong Kong and included in the factory. We don't make too much money in the original transaction (netting about a quarter on the dollar postage, with which we defray our space advertising cost and make a small profit), but that bounceback program really makes the cash register hum. And then, of course, we have a new good customer on our master file.

You might say that the Organizer promotion is essentially a self-liquidating program to put sales literature in the hands of qualified people and to generate new customers. We consider it very successful. Try to do something like it yourself. Try to locate a nice little gadget with a raw cost of $.30 to $.40 that you can afford to "give away FREE" — just charge $1 for postage and insurance. The results will amaze you. Read trade magazines from the Orient. They are full of things like that. Try to find the right one and "romance" it up, just as we did with the Organizer.

Another interesting minor idea that we developed with our bounceback program and which is a good time/money saver is to have the customer write his own label. Look at the front and back of such a label. You will get the idea. In this case, we don't even run the order through the computer. We already have this customer's name; we don't need it for our master file. And by not running it through the computer, we save the cost of data processing (which may be as much as $.25 per order and which would, of course, be a large fraction of such a small bounceback). What's more, with this system we can give immediate turn-around service. The jiffy bags containing these bounceback purchases are already pre-packed (Yes, they too contain bouncebacks!). We put on the label that the customer himself has written, and the package gets bounced right out of the warehouse.

Another extremely successful insert, one that I stumbled upon almost by accident, is one for records and tapes, that has now become a staple with us.

As you can see, this program runs in connection with *Columbia Musical Treasuries* — a branch of *Columbia Records.* We do not stock any tapes or records at all — it is all "drop shipped"

hennikers
779 Bush St Box 7584 San Francisco CA 94120
Tel (415) 433 7540

SPECIAL ANNOUNCEMENT TO
HENNISCOPE OWNERS

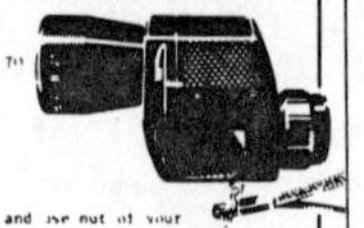

Dear Customer:

We hope that you are getting every bit as much enjoyment and use out of your Henniscope as you expected. It is a remarkable instrument that holds astonishing optical power in a very small package. And you will agree that the quality of Henniscope is outstanding.

We have developed a truly amazing attachment for the Henniscope which adds an entirely new dimension of optical application and perfection to it. It is a 35 power lens that you may substitute for the regular 8x or 6x objectives. This lens is 13 inches in length, with a 2-1/2 inch objective. It combines exquisite resolution and absolute distortion-free viewing with great light-gathering capacity. It transforms your Henniscope in an instant to a powerful 35x terrestrial telescope --- into an instrument for which you would expect to pay well over $100 if you were to purchase it separately. Yet, during this introductory period, the 35x lens cost only $35.95.

With the 35x lens attachment, the Henniscope is too powerful to be hand-held. A tripod is mandatory. If you have a tripod, you may use it because the 35x lens is provided with standard tripod fittings. If you do not have a tripod, we can suggest our deluxe floor tripod, 3-sectional, all-aluminum, with panning and locking-in vertical and horizontal planes.

If you enjoy your Henniscope and if you enjoy fine optics, this will bowl you over. It's something you will enjoy the rest of your life.

Sincerely yours,

Chip Stanyon

Chip Stanyon
Customer Services

PS: It goes without saying that our usual return privilege and one-year guarantee applys to these accessories.

Please clip coupon and return to us with your check or with your charge authorization.
Mail to Henniker's 779 Bush St., Box 7584, San Francisco, CA 94120

Yes, I want to avail myself of your offer. Please send me:

35x lens......................$35.95
Deluxe floor tripod............$24.95
35x lens/tripod................$55.95 (for special saving)

☐ My check, plus $2 for post. & insur. (plus tax for Calif. delivery) enclosed.
☐ Please charge my BA, MC Acct. No. ____ ____ ____ Exp. ____
Note: If you have BA/MC acct. you may call (415)433-7540 for fastest service.

My name is
I live at
City State Zip

hennikers 779 Bush St Box 7584 San Francisco CA 94120

Dear Customer:

Here is your Amethyst Jewelry. I hope you are as pleased with it, or perhaps even more, than you expected.

We have designed an Amethyst Bracelet, after many of our customers had asked about such a companion piece. We went through a number of trials, but weren't entirely happy. Finally, an outstanding jewelry designer came up with a bracelet we really liked (and all customers whom we have sent it to so far seem to agree). The bracelet consists of four links of stones and three links of tiny gold-plated balls. We think it is stunning -- a perfect complement to your new jewelry.

The above sketch can give you only a rough idea of the really good looks of this bracelet. I wish you could see it for yourself or wear it. You would agree.

We do not sell the Amethyst Bracelet separately because it would not be economically feasible. We include it only as an option with new orders.

If you wish to purchase this bracelet (subject to your usual return privilege, of course) simply print or type your name on the coupon, include your check for $9.95 (plus $1 for postage and insurance and sales tax for California delivery) or authorize charge to your BA/MC account.

If you wish to take advantage of this offer, please do so now. We shall not repeat this offer, nor shall we advertise the bracelet in our Catalog or in any media. If you like your jewelry, you'll love the bracelet.

Sincerely yours,
Chris Simpson

...ts

...ip coupon and return with check of charge ok in enclosed envelope

...l me___Amethyst Bracelets @ $9.95 each.
...or this amount (plus $1 for postage and insurance, plus sales tax ...nia delivery) is enclosed

...rge my BA/MC acct. #____ ____ ____exp.____

____State____ ____Zip____

Dear Friend of Mack-the-Knife

Now that you are proud owner of this masterwork of cutler's art you may wish to make it even more useful and practical with our special **belt-looped Mack Sheath**, made of extra-heavy vinyl, stitched and riveted for lifetime rugged service. If you want the sheath, please write clearly or type your name including zip code on reverse (front side of label) and send it to us with a $1 bill (no checks please, unless you order more than one, because our bankers don't like to handle it) and we'll shoot it right out to you, even pay for the postage. Yours for better pickle snatching, frog spearing and rabbit skinning. Chris

Chris Simpson, Customer Services

"Bouncebacks" are usually very productive, because they refer to the specific piece of merchandise that the customer has just received. The amethyst bracelet bounceback pulls an incredible 25%! Note the back of the mailing label for Mack-the-Knife: the customer fills in his own name and address and we have virtually no processing expense at all.

This is our only insert for "o.p.m." (other people's merchandise), but notice how we "appropriate" it by linking our name with Columbia Musical Treasuries. All artwork (in full color) is provided, we supply the "customized" type and do the printing. The backside contains additional offers and the coupon. We run this same piece over and over again and net about $50 per thousand inserts. You should try something like this. Everybody seems to love music, and has confidence in the well known stars and reputable brands such as Columbia.

directly from Columbia. So that makes it attractive in itself. But the most attractive part of it are the profits. Let me give you a few figures:

• Approximate cost per 1000 inserts, one side full-color, back side black/white	$ 50
• Approximate sales per 1000	$150+
• Profit Margin	65%(!)
• Approximate Gross Profit per 1000 inserts	$100
• Approximate Net Profit per 1000 inserts	$ 50

This is just about representative of what you should do with a good package insert. We do quite a bit better, however, with our own mini-catalog and other inserts. We use the Columbia insert only to add variety to our merchandise offerings, and because it does not compete with our own merchandise. Also, we do not have the expense and trouble of having to carry inventory.

With our own inserts, we generate approximately $90 net profit per 1000, and figures look about as follows:

• Approximate cost per 1000 inserts, colored stock, black and one color	$ 60
• Approximate sales per 1000 inserts	$250
• Approximate Profit Margin	60%
• Approximate Gross Profit per 1000 inserts	$150
• Approximate Net Profit per 1000 inserts	$ 90

We include about three assorted inserts in each package. We send them out — with promotional (such as the Organizer) and with "real" merchandise. We figure that we average about $70 net profit contribution (conservatively) per any thousand inserts sent out or about $200 for every thousand packages. At this writing, we send about 3000 to 4000 packages per week. This is not a very large operation as mail-order houses go. But the little wrinkle of inserts adds a minimum of $600 to $800 per week right to the bottom line. I assure you that this comes in very handy!

INSERTS TO OUTSIDE LISTS

But that is really only part of the story — the best is yet to come.

Quite a few of the very large mailers, firms that mail hundreds of thousands of packages every month, solicit as a source of revenue to them, "ride alongs" — inserts from other mail-order houses. The cost for that is about $20 - $30 per thousand (in some cases less, if you commit very large quantities). There are usually size and weight limitations, but these are easy to comply with.

With a list compatible with your own, you should be able to achieve sales of not less than 75% as those to your house list. Take our mini-catalog, for instance. With a compatible list (and there are quite a few large ones that have customer "profiles" pretty close to ours) we get typically $200 per thousand inserts (instead of the approximately $250 to our own customers). But let's be conservative and call it $175 of sales per 1000 inserts.

Let's see what the arithmetic looks like:

• Approximate cost per 1000 inserts	$ 60
• Ride-Along charge per 1000 inserts	$ 25
• Total cost per 1000 inserts	$ 85
• Approximate sales per 1000 inserts	$175
• Profit Margin	60%
• Approximate Gross Profit per 1000 inserts	$105
• Approximate Net Profit per 1000 inserts	$ 20

I assure that this is very heady stuff. If you develop a good insert — such as our mini-catalog, you should have no problem in placing, say, 100,000 inserts per month. You will, of course, not be able to do that right away, but you can work up to it and do even better. Yes, you're right, 100,000 inserts per month to outside lists would add about $2,000 per month to profits. Not bad, what? And, of course, all these customers that purchased from you through outside inserts are now *your* customers and you will be able to keep selling to them and make profit. Naturally, while the money and profit are fun, all of this involves a great deal of extra work. In the example just given, we are talking about an additional $17,000 to $20,000 in sales per month. And, for a small company, that is quite a bit of extra work, especially with the mini-catalog, because so many different items are involved. The point is this: one thing is to generate sales, and the other is to be prepared to handle them.

Coming back once more to the Columbia Record/Tape insert. These numbers don't look quite so good. Without going through the arithmetic in detail, you will find that the net profit contribution in mailing this piece to outside lists works out to about $8 to $10 per 1000. This makes the margin rather slim because it could easily tilt into the loss column. But with this kind of mailer, and if you select your list carefully, you still should be able to add $500 to $1000 to profit per month, which, of course, is not bad at all. The beauty, however, is that you have virtually no work with it, except recording the order, getting the customer on your master file and forwarding the order to Columbia. They take care of the rest.

To summarize: while a somewhat secondary aspect of your mail-order business, package inserts — to your own list and to outside lists — are substantial moneymakers. Don't neglect them — learn all about them and put them to work for you!

I really hope that I have given you insight in this chapter into how to create direct mail and at least a passing glance at package inserts. It is a rather broad subject, and I know you will understand that I have not been able to cover it completely. But you should have learned enough to make acceptable or good mail pieces yourself — or to supervise others who do it and know how to judge their work.

And you also know about the numbers that are involved, when to abandon, when to pull in the reins, and when to let it all hang out.

In the next chapter, we shall talk about catalogs. They are the capstone of your promotional effort and quite likely the most important tool for your growing mail-order business.

Chapter 5

CATALOGS WILL PUT YOU OVER THE TOP

Now that you know how to make space ads to sell "promotional" and "regular" merchandise, and now that you have learned how to make "solo" mail pieces to send to your own and to outside lists, you are well on your way to being "all the way" into the mail-order business. But, in reality, you are not really quite there yet at all. You may be one-half of the way, or two-thirds of the way. The most important ingredient, the vital spark, is still missing.

WHY YOU MUST HAVE A CATALOG

The fact is, you are not really and completely in the mail order business until you have a catalog.

Let me say quickly that there are exceptions that confirm the rule. Just as there are mail-order firms that get by without ever sending out direct mail pieces to their own customers (let alone to outside lists) so are there mail-order firms that do not send out catalogs either. They conduct their business entirely by running newspaper and magazine ads. I think it is a very hard way to make any kind of success in this business — but it has been done.

There may be another reason why certain of these companies decide not to publish a catalog. I don't suggest that it is necessarily the case, but — since I assume that people conduct their business on a rational basis — the thought has crossed my mind. And the possible reason is this: the success of a mail-order catalog is primarily based on having customers who have had one or more satisfactory transactions with you before. Then, when they get your catalog, they know you, they have confidence, they know you will deliver (in every sense of the word). And they know that your merchandise is up to snuff. If a company knows that they have not fulfilled one or several of these expectations, they will also know that no purpose is achieved in sending out catalogs to their customers. These customers have been disappointed in their first dealing, they feel they have been "burned," and they are not likely to purchase again. These people are essentially in what I call the "hit and run" end of the mail-order business. Sometimes these firms can make lots of waves, but I have never seen one survive for any length of time.

I don't want you to be in that kind of business. I want you to build a solid, going business, with an increasing base of satisfied customers, who identify you with service and with good merchandise. And, in order to accomplish that (and as you will see, for other reasons), you simply have to have a catalog.

I have told you in a previous chapter, that the normal development of a typical and well-structured mail-order business is to decrease reliance on space advertising and to shift promotional emphasis more and more to direct mailing and to catalogs. Most "mature" mail-order businesses operate in this manner — maintain just enough space advertising to keep their name in front of the public and to increase their customer file.

HOW MUCH OF YOUR PROMOTIONAL DOLLAR SHOULD GO INTO CATALOGS

When I owned Haverhill's, before its acquisition by Time Inc., I had reached a level of approximately $2 million sales per year. My promotional input was about $500,000 (a very acceptable 4-to-1 ratio). Of that $500,000, about 50% was in direct mail, 30% in catalogs and about 20% in space advertising.

That was about my fifth year of operation — from a standing start. In retrospect, the ratio was still a little lopsided. At that stage of the game, the catalog should have been perhaps 65%, direct mail 20-25%, and space advertising not more than 10-15% of total advertising or promotional input. Now, having learned my lesson, I am more rapidly approaching these ratios in my new Henniker's business.

Naturally — coming back to my Haverhill's experience — the "normal" development of my mail-order business changed radically when I merged Haverhill's with Time Inc., the largest publisher of books and periodicals in the United States.

My merging with Time Inc. gave me immediate large-scale access to space in their publications at very favorable "house" rates. Having this resource at my disposal shifted the emphasis back to space advertising. In almost complete reversal of "normal" development, space advertising reached as much as 70-80% of my total promotional budget. This was almost entirely in Time Inc. media, which at that time still included *Life.*

But this was an unusual, and not a typical case. You are not likely to merge with a publisher. So prepare yourself to be very much in the catalog business. In fact, get used to the thought that your catalog (or rather catalogs) are going to be the most important selling tool that you will have..

HOW TO SELECT MERCHANDISE FOR YOUR CATALOG

You would not be too far off if you thought of catalogs as just a specialized form of direct mail. Remember, how I told you in the last chapter about our very successful "Omnibus" mailer. That Omnibus mailer was, in a way, really a small catalog, featuring ten of our most successful items. And you also remember that "bounceback" package insert, which featured over 30 of our best items. While not in booklet form, nor presented in the "conventional" way, both of these were already close to being true catalogs.

Because that's really what a catalog is. A presentation of all of your merchandise, or at least those items of your merchandise that have proven to be good sellers or that you expect will become good sellers.

There are many important things to keep in mind in preparing a successful mail-order catalog. The most important, perhaps, is the proper selection of merchandise, which fits *your customers,* the audience to whom the catalog is primarily addressed. It sounds elementary, but in selecting the merchandise, you have to have a pretty clear picture as to who exactly your customers are, what you represent to them, and what they expect from you.

Naturally, if you have created a specialty mail-order business, your choice of merchandise is fairly clear-cut. If you have specialized in, say, camping and trail equipment, and if you have solicited your customers through advertisements in such publications, you have reached the people interested in such activities and your choice of merchandise will be governed by that. You will stick to merchandise in that field — backpacks, tents, field cooking gear, hunting knives, and so forth. You certainly would not want to include such things as gourmet food in your catalog, although you may wish to include a line of dehydrated foods for outdoors people. But you would want to be very careful before including clothing, except that which would be especially geared to your market, such as ponchos, parkas, hiking boots, and so forth.

Or if you have staked out the gourmet food business, you want to be sure not to include anything in the catalog that is not related to that. Remember, your customers, whom you have recruited through space advertising and by sending direct mail promotions to related lists, look to you for gourmet food. They won't buy optical goods or automotive accessories from you. You may think that you have a captive audience, and that you might as well "throw something else at them," while you are at it. Resist the temptation! You will confuse your customers and you will weaken your over-all impact and sales.

Again, a grain of salt: naturally, in order to grow, you have to expand your merchandise line. A natural direction of such expansion is to promote related items. You should do that, but do it slowly, very carefully and keep constant watch whether this new, "related" merchandise carries its own weight (which means that it makes money) and whether it supports or weakens the sales of what, up to now, has been the principal thrust of your business.

For instance, going back to your camping and trail mail-order business, you may try a few fishing items in your catalog, or perhaps some hunting equipment. If you are in the gourmet food business, you may wish to include some gourmet cooking utensils, some selected table items, or things of that nature. You get the idea.

HOW MANY CUSTOMERS DO YOU NEED TO PRINT A CATALOG

Let's just talk right now about your first catalogs, because you won't need my guidance on this when you are three or four years down the road.

The first question is: how many customers should you have before you publish your first catalog. Since you have a right to look to me for answers, I shall stick my neck out (knowing that some of my colleagues may disagree).

My rule of thumb is that you should have at least 25,000 customers before you should attempt to publish a real, honest-to-goodness catalog.

The reason for this is that to make a real catalog (even a modest one) is quite a project. Once you have designed it and have it ready for the printer, it makes no difference whether you print 5,000 copies or half a million. Even if you are willing and able to do the work that catalog preparation takes — just as in direct mail (only more so) — the "going-in" cost is fairly high and cannot easily be justified for a catalog being mailed to fewer than 25,000 customers.

We shall go into the financial end of the catalog business later on in this chapter. But for the moment, consider that for a catalog, even carrying only 100 items of merchandise, art direction, copy writing, photography (or drawings), headlines, body copy, veloxes, stats and sundry odds and ends, will cost you at least $5,000 before you can turn the job over to the printer. We are now talking about your very first catalog, and everything has to be done from scratch. In later catalogs, you will, of course, be able to pick up material from previous catalogs.

Your printer's make-ready for what, with 100 items of merchandise, may be a slim 18-page catalog, may well be on the order of $1,000. Printing costs for 25,000 catalogs (we assume that you do it in black and one color, in standard 8-1/2 x 11 format and on regular paper) will be on the order of $.10 each. Postage and fulfillment will cost about another $.10 each. Add it all up and you will find that your 25,000 catalogs will cost you about $11,000 altogether in the mail, or roughly $.44 each.

If you work on a gross profit margin, of say, 55%, that means that you must sell not less than about $.80 of merchandise per catalog sent out — about $20,000 altogether in order just to break even. I assure you that this is a pretty tall order. You will find that even at that 25,000 catalog level, your first catalog will in all likelihood be pretty much a labor of love, just about a break-even situation. But don't worry about that — you are in the start-up phase, this is your first catalog, and you do not yet expect to make too much money. You are still building business. Next year you will have 50,000 customers. Most of your work for your next catalog will already be done (you will be able to pick up art and copy from the first year) and your in-the-mail cost will be drastically reduced. You should and will make substantial money on your catalogs in the second year.

TESTING YOUR CATALOG TO OUTSIDE LISTS

Can I not increase my catalog print run, you may ask, and thus effect economies by mailing to lists other than my own — to rented lists? The answer is that you may, but be slow and very careful. The same principle applies that we discussed talking about direct mail. It will cost you approximately $.04 per catalog more to mail to an outside list (the cost of list rental).* For reasons that we have already agreed upon, your response, even from the best and most related lists, should not be expected to be more than 85% of what you get from your own list. You can work out the arithmetic yourself. Find out what the pull of your own list has to be in order to do mailings to outside lists with any expectation of profitability.

In other words, before you plunge headlong into "wholesale" mailing of your catalog to other people's customers, you will want to be very sure that you know what your catalog will produce from your own list.

This does not mean that you can or should not do some cautious testing every time you mail your catalog (or anything else, for that matter) to your own list. As a matter of routine, I never mail out anything to my own list without, at the same time, mailing to representative samples of outside lists that have in the past proven to work for me. For instance, if I make a test mailing of, say 100,000 pieces to my own list, I will usually test five outside lists of 5,000 names each at the same time. This is a risk I am able to handle and it gives me a quick reading of how this catalog or this mailing will perform, not just to my own list, but also to those that are representative of best outside lists. But I test; I do not plunge headlong.

You should afford to do the same with your first full catalog mailing. As a general rule, if you mailed to 25,000 names of your

---

* We'll see later that it is really a little more complicated than that and that the true cost of sending your catalog to others is not as high as you may think at first.

own, you may be able to risk 5,000 names each from as many as three carefully selected outside lists.

Let's see what this will do to your cost, based on the assumptions that we have made before. Your preparation cost ("going-in cost") and your printer's "make-ready" will be the same, about $6,000. Your printing, postage and fulfillment costs will also be the same, on a per unit basis, about $.20 each, or about $8,000 for the whole run of 40,000 copies. Thus, before paying for your 15,000 outside names, your cost in the mail will be $14,000, $.35 per catalog — almost a dime less than when you only printed 25,000 units. Now, again assuming a gross profit factor of 55%, your break-even sales to your own list will be about $.64 — a little easier to attain than the $.80 we had before. Mailing to the three outside lists will cost $.04 more per catalog (the cost of list rental) — $.39 per catalog, with a break-even of about $.70 per catalog.

THE CONCEPT OF "MARGINAL COSTING"

A good case can be made, for purposes of analysis, that this is not the right way of looking at cost. You could, quite properly, apply the concept of "marginal costing." This would mean that the cost of the original 25,000 catalogs, which we found to be $11,000, does not get "magically" reduced by printing additional catalogs over which the fixed cost is distributed. For purposes of analysis whether or not to mail to outside lists, *only the additional cost* should be considered, since all other costs are already "sunk." Thus, to print and mail 15,000 *additional catalogs* will cost you $.24 each, or $3600 for the full additional run. On a 55% gross margin basis, this would mean that each of the catalogs mailed to outside lists should sell a minimum of $.24/.55 = $.44 to break even. That for *analytical purposes* is your go/no-go figure. Notice how it differs from the previously arrived-at cost and break-even figures of $.39 and $.70, respectively, for outside lists. The difference comes about, of course, by distributing or not distributing fixed cost over the additional catalogs. In reviewing the costs and respective contributions of all catalog segments mailed, it is proper to distribute all fixed costs across the board. But, in order to make a decision whether an additional list can profitably be mailed, this should not be done, because the new list, in order to break even, really has to carry its own cost only. This is perhaps a somewhat complex point, but it is very important that you truly understand and master it. You will never be able to make proper yes/no decisions of this nature if you do not apply this concept of marginal cost and marginal profit.

This is such an important concept and, I believe, so little understood, that we shall deal with it in greater detail later in this chapter.

YOU MUST MAIL A CATALOG AT CHRISTMAS

Whatever else you do or don't do, you absolutely *must* mail a catalog (or equivalent) to your customers at Christmas time. I cannot say that they will be waiting for it with bated breath or that they will be deeply disappointed if they fail to hear from you. But you are not really in business if you don't mail at Christmas. And when you get back in touch with your customers at a later date, without having mailed to them at Christmas, they will have that vague feeling that you were not there when you should have been, namely, offering your wares for Christmas shopping.

But, apart from these somewhat philosophical ruminations, there is a very practical reason why you absolutely *must* mail at Christmas. It is obvious: it is the one *sure chance* in the year to make good money. People *want* to buy, and this is your opportunity to sell them. And if you don't make them an offer at Christmas, you have obviously blown the most important opportunity in the entire year.

What do you do then if Christmas rolls around, and you have fewer than the 25,000 customers which we have agreed is a minimum level for catalog mailings? Here is your answer: take your Omnibus bounceback package insert that we talked about in the last chapter and transform it into a Christmas mailer. Naturally, you can change a few pieces of merchandise, take out those that have not sold too well, and replace them with some fresh merchandise, especially of the "gifty" kind. Then change the front of the insert to make a mailer out of it, even supplying it with a Christmas motif if you wish.

As an example of what I have in mind, please look back once more at the example of a mini-catalog bounceback that I gave you in the last chapter, and just visualize it transformed into a "mini Christmas catalog."

We are too large now to use it as our Christmas catalog, of course, but we use essentially the same piece as a trial balloon to prospective outside catalog lists. All we do is to change the cover so it can be used as a mailer.

You can send this mailer, instead of a catalog, to your own list if you have anywhere between 10,000 and 25,000 customers — and I certainly hope you have that by the time your first Christmas rolls around. With a print run of 10,000 pieces, and with most of your preliminary work done, (remember you already have your insert — all you have to do is to make a few changes and rearrange the cover), you should be able to put this in the mail for not more than \$.20 each. Again, with a gross profit margin of 55%, you need to sell about \$.35 of merchandise to break even and about \$.65 in sales per catalog to make a \$.20 profit contribution per catalog, or \$2,000 on the whole run of 10,000 pieces. You can do it!

SPECIAL POINTERS IN CATALOG PLANNING

But let's go ahead and assume that you have attained that "magic figure" of 25,000 customers and that you can afford to publish your first reasonably complete catalog.

In addition to the guidelines for merchandise selection, there are other things to consider, for instance:

WORK WITH YOUR PRINTER

After you have selected your merchandise — I would suggest not fewer than 100 and not more than 200 items — get the advice of a knowledgeable printer, one who has experience with merchandise catalogs, and get his advice regarding pages, format, kind of paper, etc. With a run of 25,000, you will in all likelihood work with a sheet-fed press printer. Once you get over 50,000 or so, a so-called web press may give you a much less expensive job.

SHOULD YOU USE COLOR?

Forget about full color. You simply cannot afford it at your size of press run. Full color is very expensive, because color separations have to be made. They are tricky (if they are not first class, you are much better off without any color). Their cost is such that it should be spread over a run of at least 200,000 to 300,000 catalogs to make it economical.

Use black and one color instead. It is not much more expensive than just black and white and much more effective. Depending on the kind of press you are using, you may even use different colors for different pages without much additional cost.

If it should be desirable, you can obtain additional color effects by differential "screening" of your single color. One word of caution: discretion in the use of color is usually advisable. An "accent" of color here and there is often better than splashing it all over the place.

HOW TO SELL WITH YOUR COVERS

Use the front and back covers of your catalog to sell merchandise. It is really your most valuable space. This is a case of "do as I say, don't do as I do," because I had not followed my own advice for many years. In all of my catalogs at Haverhill's and in my first full catalog at Henniker's, I used the front cover strictly for "institutional" purposes — to promote the company name and to make a good graphic impression. We accomplished that and got much praise for good design. But I thought even then that it was a mistake, because we did not sell anything in that space. Sort of as an afterthought, we used one-half of the back cover to promote a chair set. It became one of our "gold star" sellers. While the merchandise was great, I think the position helped it a whole lot.

But then I became intrigued with the selling power of the covers. In my second (and in all subsequent) Henniker's catalogs, I used both front and back covers for some of our most attractive and most "representative" merchandise. My hunch was amply borne out. The merchandise on the covers (both front and back) sold much more than we had expected, judging from their previous performance. So this is very valuable space. Don't squander it. Use it for your "star" items. It will repay you very well!

PICK A CATALOG "FORMAT"

Unless you decide to go into the loose "silhouetted" format that we saw in our mini-catalog bounceback insert, you may consider a "modular" format. In the "modular" catalogs that we used, illustrations, on an 8-1/2" x 11" page, make up an area of 7.3" square on each page. This area is divided into 4 x 4 = 16 "modules." Some illustrations take up one module, some two vertical or horizontal modules, or in some cases (although not on the page shown) even four or six modules.

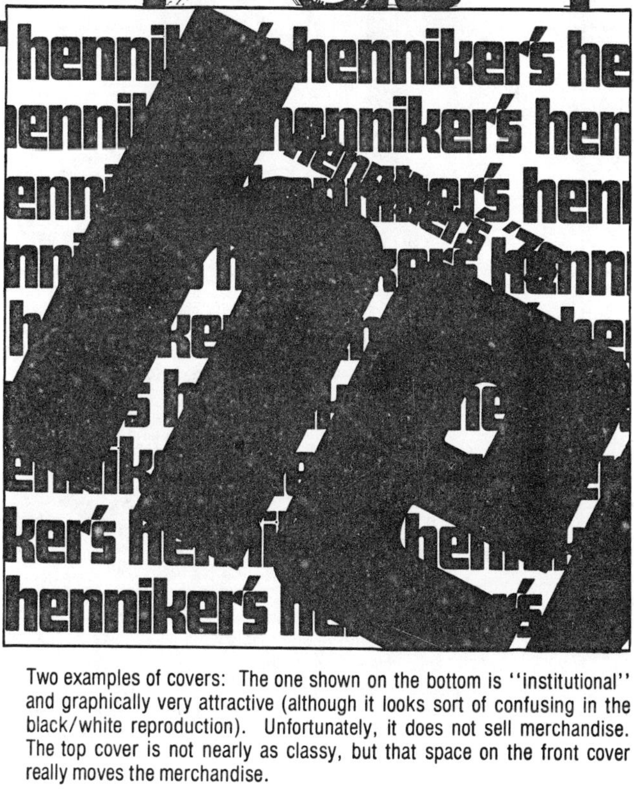

Two examples of covers: The one shown on the bottom is ''institutional'' and graphically very attractive (although it looks sort of confusing in the black/white reproduction). Unfortunately, it does not sell merchandise. The top cover is not nearly as classy, but that space on the front cover really moves the merchandise.

Two ways of selling with your back cover. This space is almost more valuable than the front, because it contains the label with the customer's name — and that is what people like to look at. The chairs (on the back of the "institutional" cover in the previous illustration) sold exceptionally well. That was our first experiment with using the back cover for selling. Now we routinely surround the address area with merchandise, and never feature fewer than four items on the back cover.

This system has a number of advantages:

- You can prepare all of your artwork uniformly, without having to "fit" it on the page.
- The customer gets a sense of orderliness — the merchandise is neatly displayed.
- Since you allocate profitability of each item in the catalog on the basis of space occupied (we will talk about that in detail later), all calculations regarding space occupied are very easily made — there are so many modules, each module costs so much, and that's that.
- Most important, in any reprinting of the catalog, you can unceremoniously pull out anything that hasn't produced on the first run and replace it with another single module or two-module unit, depending on how big a "hole" you have created. You don't have to look for something that "fits" in the hole; since all holes are standard you will have no problem.

There is, however, one serious disadvantage to this kind of layout, and I now incline to believe that it outweighs all the advantages listed. It is this: the copy (captions to the illustrations) are removed from the illustrations themselves. The customer has to "hunt" to correlate picture and copy. On the page shown, for instance, there are four different binoculars and several other optical instruments. We are putting somewhat of a burden on the customer to find his way. There is one maxim in this business: make it as easy for the customer as you can. And this layout is not entirely easy.

Compare tnis with the example of the non-modular catalog page that features quite similar merchandise. One would have to do a little "jiggling" to take out a piece of merchandise and put another one in, but of course, it can be done. Also, it is perhaps a little more difficult to determine accurately what fraction of a page an item occupies and that makes cost calculations a little more complicated. But these are minor points. There is, however, one great advantage, namely that copy is clearly related to merchandise. The customer leafs through the catalog, sees something he likes, and without strain and without possibility of error can immediately relate copy to illustration and find out what he wants to know.

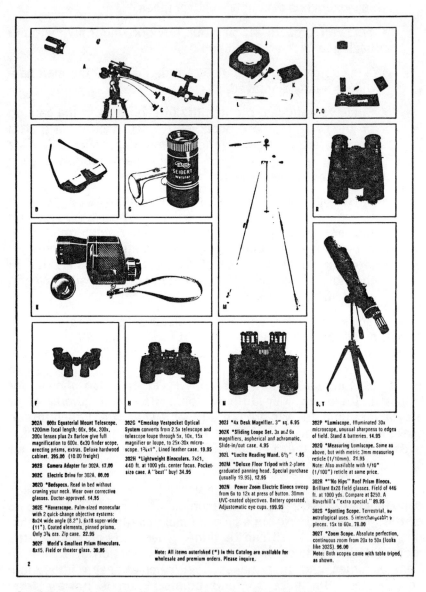

302A 600x Equatorial Mount Telescope. 1200mm focal length; 60x, 96x, 200x, 300x lenses plus 2x Barlow give full magnification to 600x. 6x30 finder scope, erecting prisms, extras. Deluxe hardwood cabinet. **395.00** (10.00 freight)

302B Camera Adapter for 302A. **17.00**

302C Electric Drive for 302A. **80.00**

302D *Bedspecs. Read in bed without craning your neck. Wear over corrective glasses. Doctor-approved. **14.95**

302E *Haverscope. Palm-sized monocular with 2 quick-change objective systems: 8x24 wide angle (8.2°), 6x18 super-wide (11°). Coated elements, pinned prisms. Only 3¾ ozs. Zip case. **22.95**

302F World's Smallest Prism Binoculars, 6x15. Field or theater glass. **30.95**

302G *Emoskop Vestpocket Optical System converts from 2.5x telescope and telescope loupe through 5x, 10x, 15x magnifier or loupe, to 25x-30x microscope. 1¾x1". Lined leather case. **19.95**

302H *Lightweight Binoculars. 7x21, 440 ft. at 1000 yds. center focus. Pocket-size case. A "best" buy! **34.95**

302J *4x Desk Magnifier. 3" sq. **6.95**

302K *Sliding Loupe Set. 3x and 6x magnifiers, aspherical and achromatic. Slide-in/out case. **4.95**

302L *Lucite Reading Wand. 6½" **1.95**

302M *Deluxe Floor Tripod with 2-plane graduated panning head. Special purchase (usually 19.95). **12.95**

302N Power Zoom Electric Binocs sweep from 6x to 12x at press of button. 30mm UVC-coated objectives. Battery operated. Adjustomatic eye cups. **199.95**

302P *Lumiscope. Illuminated 30x microscope, unusual sharpness to edges of field. Stand & batteries. **14.95**

302Q *Measuring Lumiscope. Same as above, but with metric 3mm measuring reticle (1/10mm). **21.95**
Note: Also available with 1/10" (1/100") reticle at same price.

302R *"No Hips" Roof Prism Binocs. Brilliant 8x28 field glasses. Field of 446 ft. at 1000 yds. Compare at $250. A Haverhill's "extra special." **89.95**

302S *Spotting Scope. Terrestrial, su astrological uses. 5 interchangeable e pieces. 15x to 60x. **78.00**

302T *Zoom Scope. Absolute perfection, continuous zoom from 20x to 50x (looks like 302S). **98.00**
Note: Both scopes come with table tripod, as shown.

Note: All items asterisked (*) in this Catalog are available for wholesale and premium orders. Please inquire.

2

Page from a modular catalog. There are advantages and disadvantages to this format. It is easy to do, and things are very orderly. But copy may be difficult to relate to the merchandise, especially, as in this case, if items are quite similar.

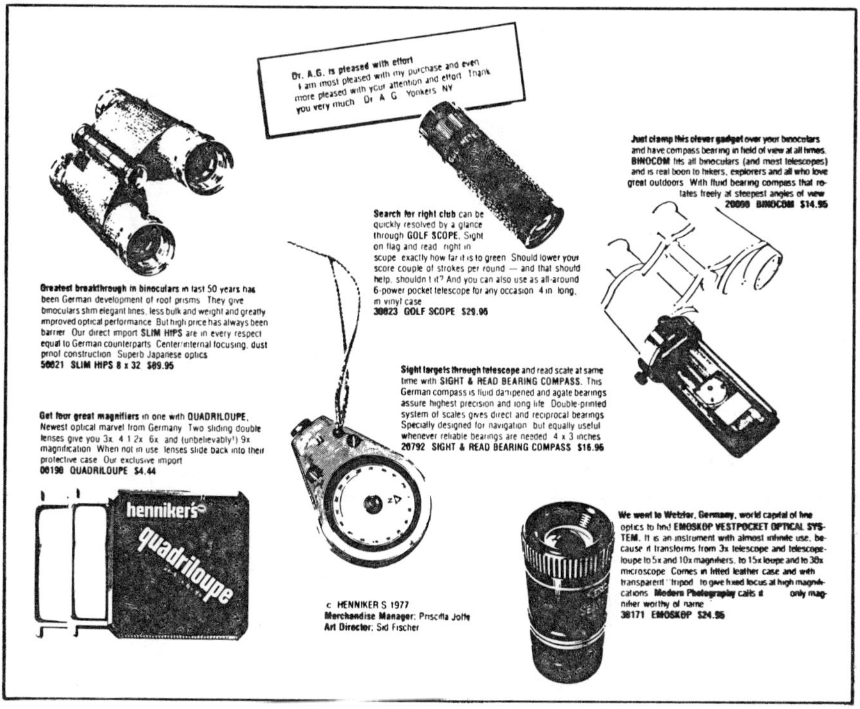

Dr. A.G. is pleased with effort
I am most pleased with my purchase and even more pleased with your attention and effort Thank you very much Dr A G Yonkers NY

Just clamp this clever gadget over your binoculars and have compass bearing in field of view at all times. **BINOCOM** fits all binoculars (and most telescopes) and is real boon to hikers, explorers and all who love great outdoors With fluid bearing compass that rotates freely at steepest angles of view
20090 BINOCOM $14.95

Search for right club can be quickly resolved by a glance through **GOLF SCOPE**. Sight on flag and read right in scope exactly how far it is to green Should lower your score couple of strokes per round — and that should help, shouldn t it? And you can also use as all-around 6-power pocket telescope for any occasion 4 in long, in vinyl case
30823 GOLF SCOPE $29.95

Greatest breakthrough in binoculars in last 50 years has been German development of roof prisms They give binoculars slim elegant lines, less bulk and weight and greatly improved optical performance But high price has always been barrier Our direct import **SLIM HIPS** are in every respect equal to German counterparts Center/internal focusing, dust proof construction Superb Japanese optics
50821 SLIM HIPS 8 x 32 $89.95

Sight targets through telescope and read scale at same time with **SIGHT & READ BEARING COMPASS**. This German compass is fluid dampened and agate bearings assure highest precision and long life Double-printed system of scales gives direct and reciprocal bearings Specially designed for navigation but equally useful whenever reliable bearings are needed 4 x 3 inches
20792 SIGHT & READ BEARING COMPASS $16.95

Get four great magnifiers in one with **QUADRILOUPE**. Newest optical marvel from Germany Two sliding double lenses give you 3x 4 1 2x 6x and (unbelievably!) 9x magnification When not in use lenses slide back into their protective case Our exclusive import
00198 QUADRILOUPE $4.44

We went to Wetzlar, Germany, world capital of fine optics to find **EMOSKOP VESTPOCKET OPTICAL SYSTEM**. It is an instrument with almost infinite use, because it transforms from 3x telescope and telescope-loupe to 5x and 10x magnifiers, to 15x loupe and to 30x microscope Comes in fitted leather case and with transparent "tripod" to give fixed focus at high magnifications **Modern Photography** calls it only magnifier worthy of name
38171 EMOSKOP $24.95

c HENNIKER S 1977
Merchandise Manager: Priscilla Joffe
Art Director: Sid Fischer

Similar merchandise displayed on a non-modular page gives a less "constricted" impression and has copy right next to each illustration. There are disadvantages too, but we now favor this type of page and I think you might also find it best suited to your purposes.

HOW TO MAKE ONE CATALOG DO THE WORK OF TWO

An interesting point in connection with a typical catalog page: this is from the very first catalog that I made at Haverhill's. I had been in business for just about a year — the stage I have in mind for you right now. We had exhausted our catalog run at Christmas and decided to reprint. We had no reason to change merchandise, because all items had done fairly well. We did feel, however, that some change was needed. We did two very inexpensive things:

- We changed the color of the catalog from a (Christmassy) red to olive green. This was not a particular improvement, but it helped us distinguish the two editions of the catalog and gave those customers who had already received the first version the illusion that they were getting something new.
- But please look closely for the real improvement. You have the same page that we had before, but we have now silhouetted every piece of merchandise, taken away the flowery frame around the headline and removed the (somewhat senseless) color overlay from the shaver. What an improvement! It is as though the merchandise had been "liberated." It pops right out of the page.

A FEW THINGS TO STAY AWAY FROM

Until you are a real expert or have very good reasons to the contrary, by all means, stay away from "composite" pictures. Catalog designers love them, because they look very pretty, win plaudits from their colleagues and possibly even design awards. But they are murder for you. Everything is wrong with them:

- They are as expensive as the dickens to set up. Believe it or not, the art director and a photographer can spend a whole day setting up one of these composite shots. They cost a fortune and if models are included, this can drive you to the verge of ruin.
- Merchandise is usually not clearly displayed and some things are so puny that you can hardly see them. The poor customer who may be interested in buying has to hunt through the beautiful "artistic arrangement" to find it.

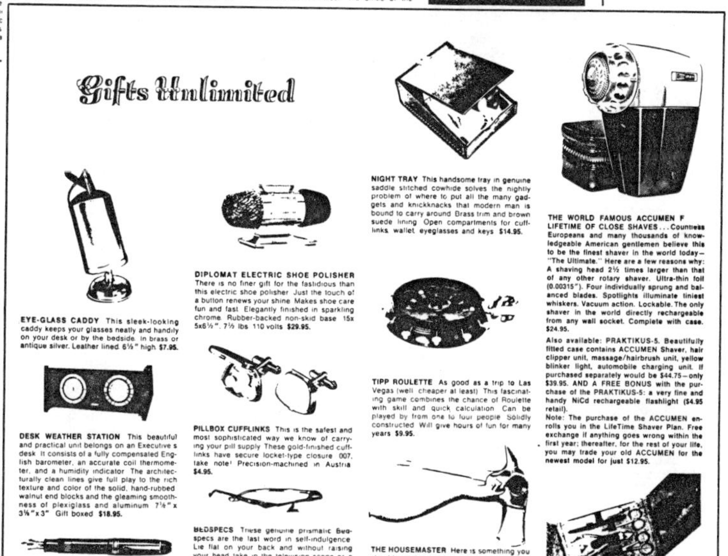

Gifts Unlimited

EYE-GLASS CADDY This sleek-looking caddy keeps your glasses neatly and handily on your desk or by the bedside. In brass or antique silver. Leather lined. 6½" high. **$7.95.**

DIPLOMAT ELECTRIC SHOE POLISHER There is no finer gift for the fastidious than this electric shoe polisher. Just the touch of a button renews your shine. Makes shoe care fun and fast. Elegantly finished in sparkling chrome. Rubber-backed non-skid base. 15x5x6½". 7½ lbs. 110 volts. **$29.95.**

DESK WEATHER STATION This beautiful and practical unit belongs on an Executive's desk. It consists of a fully compensated English barometer, an accurate coil thermometer, and a humidity indicator. The architecturally clean lines give full play to the rich texture and color of the solid, hand-rubbed walnut end blocks and the gleaming smoothness of plexiglass and aluminum. 7¼" x 3⅛" x 3". Gift boxed. **$18.95.**

PILLBOX CUFFLINKS This is the safest and most sophisticated way we know of carrying your pill supply. These gold-finished cufflinks have secure locket-type closure. 007, take note! Precision-machined in Austria. **$4.95.**

MONTBLANC "DIPLOMAT" FOUNTAIN PEN The Montblanc 'Diplomat' has a **lifetime guarantee.** Beautiful continental design with 14 karat gold point enhanced with edged facing. Longtime favorite of discriminating doctors, lawyers, engineers and others in the family. Superbly balanced. Specify [illegible]

BEDSPECS These genuine prismatic Bedspecs are the last word in self-indulgence. Lie flat on your back and without raising your head take in the television scene or a page of a book at one glance. Invaluable for invalids. Lie on the beach and watch the passing parade without raising your head. Precisely aligned ground glass prisms. Streamlined demi-blond frame. Can be worn with corrective glasses. Approved by leading ophthalmologists. Plush lined leatherette snap case. **$14.95.**

NIGHT TRAY This handsome tray in genuine saddle stitched cowhide solves the nightly problem of where to put all the many gadgets and knickknacks that modern man is bound to carry around. Brass trim and brown suede lining. Open compartments for cufflinks, wallet, eyeglasses and keys. **$14.95.**

TIPP ROULETTE As good as a trip to Las Vegas (well, cheaper at least). This fascinating game combines the chance of Roulette with skill and quick calculation. Can be played by from one to four people. Solidly constructed. Will give hours of fun for many years. **$9.95.**

THE HOUSEMASTER Here is something you should not be without: almost a complete tool box in one single piece. Everything you need around the house, the office or the car. The Housemaster, a fine product of famous Dreizack-Works in Solingen (Germany) is an all-in-one hammer, pipe wrench, cutters, hatchet, screwdriver and nail lifter. What will they think of next! All steel and heavily chromed. Height 6". **$10.95.**

THE WORLD FAMOUS ACCUMEN F LIFETIME OF CLOSE SHAVES... Countless Europeans and many thousands of knowledgeable American gentlemen believe this to be the finest shaver in the world today—"The Ultimate." Here are a few reasons why: A shaving head 2½ times larger than that of any other rotary shaver. Ultra-thin foil (0.00315"). Four individually sprung and balanced blades. Spotlights illuminate tiniest whiskers. Vacuum action. Lockable. The only shaver in the world directly rechargeable from any wall socket. Complete with case. $24.95.

Also available: PRAKTIKUS-5. Beautifully fitted case contains ACCUMEN Shaver, hair clipper unit, massage/hairbrush unit, yellow blinker light, automobile charging unit. If purchased separately would be $44.75—only $39.95. AND A FREE BONUS with the purchase of the PRAKTIKUS-5: a very fine and handy NiCd rechargeable flashlight ($4.95 retail).

Note: The purchase of the ACCUMEN enrolls you in the LifeTime Shaver Plan. Free exchange if anything goes wrong within the first year; thereafter, for the rest of your life, you may trade your old ACCUMEN for the newest model for just $12.95.

GENTLEMEN'S NAILCARE KIT This luxurious set from famous Dreizack Works contains everything a gentleman might need for nail care. Implements are finest steel. In black calf. **$29.95.**

A page from Haverhill's very first catalog. We made one catalog do the work of two. We changed the color and changed the cover, and we "liberated" the merchandise by removing overlays and eliminating the somewhat tacky frames. You can often make a "new" catalog by making very slight changes — perhaps just in color, covers and arrangement of pages.

CAMEL HAIR SPORT JACKET
Handsome for the fall and winter scene Superb camel hair material is a camel-hair wool blend Two button front with flap pockets and center vent in back It s lined
N952-1. Jacket 38-46 Regular $100.00
N952-2. Jacket 38-46 Long $100.00
NAVY HOPSACKING BLAZER
The classic navy blazer for fall well tailored with 2-button close flap patch pockets center back vent In wrinkle resistant Polyester wool
N953-1. Blazer 38-46 Regular $60.00
N953-2. Blazer. 38-46 Long $60.00
THE CORDUROY JACKET
Comfortable well tailored a man s jacket in every sense of the word Two button styling n midwale cotton corduroy Flap pockets, lining center vent in back
N951-1. Jacket. 38-46 Reg $50.00
N951-2. Jacket 38-46 Long $50.00
THE HERRINGBONE JACKET
A classic for men Has 2-button front, flap pockets center vent in back 100% Wool, fully lined perfect with our gray flannel slacks Very good looking
N954-1. Jacket 38-46 Regular $60.00
N954-2. Jacket 38-46 Long $60.00
SHETLAND WOOL CREW-NECK SWEATER
Easy fitting, downright comfortable to wear. Has the popular crew neck, rib-knit sleeve tips and hem
X416-6 (Beige). X416-3 (Blue). X416-5 (Navy).
X416-9 (Gray). Sizes MD. LGE. XLG $24.00
CASHMERE SWEATER IN FOUR COLORS
Luxuriously soft cashmere in V-neck styling a classic sweater to wear to treasure for years to come
Cashmere Sweater X401-3 (Blue). X401-6 (Barley).
X401-9 (Gray). X401-5 (Navy). MD. LGE XLG $45.00
JIMMY'S LAMBSWOOL CARDIGAN
Relax in the comfort of a 100% lambswool button-front cardigan For those autumn days outdoors
X402-6 (Barley). X402-5 (Navy)
X402-9 (Gray). Sizes MD. LGE XLG $32.50
CUNNINGHAM
ROYAL STEWART
GORDON
BLACK WATCH
DRESS CAMPBELL
CORDUROY SLACKS: THREE COLORS
Comfortable medium-wale Cotton corduroy for the country gentleman Side and hip pockets
X302-7. Olive Corduroy Slacks. 32-42 $25.00
X302-6. Wheat Corduroy Slacks. 32-42 $25.00
X302-3. Blue Corduroy Slacks. 32-42 $25.00
WOOL PLAID SLACKS
These Wool worsted slacks have side and hip pockets belt loops This is a superb choice with sport jacket or sweater Muted plaid is in good taste
X308-0. Plaid Slacks 32-42 $37.50
JOHNNY APPLESEED'S TARTAN SLACKS FOR GENTLEMEN
We have imported a brand new material for these popular slacks Wool/Polyester with belt loops, side and hip pockets Choose from the above, left to right
X303-1 (Cunningham). X303-2 (Black Watch). X303-3 (Royal Stewart). X303-4 (Dress Campbell). X303-5 (Gordon) Sizes 32-42 $30.00
ON ALL SLACKS: State inseam measurement if you wish slacks finished. State with or without cuffs. Not returnable if tailored.
11

Congratulations to Johnny Appleseed! They sell a large quantity of fine clothes at very good prices and they manage to display a lot of merchandise on every page. They accomplish that by doing away with models and they save a great deal of money in doing that. This page won't win any design awards at the Art Institute, but that probably wasn't its purpose. Its purpose was to move merchandise, and I am pretty sure it did that.

- If any of the items in this composite picture should bomb, if the manufacturer discontinues it, or if you wish to take it out for any reason — you cannot. You are stuck with it, unless you want to throw the whole elaborate concoction out. I give you one particularly gruesome example in which my art director (no longer with me!) managed to cram fourteen distinct pieces of merchandise into one single illustration. Beautiful things, too! The only trouble was that nobody could find anything or when they finally did find it, could get any idea of what it really looked like. It was terrible and this page really bombed badly. The disaster was compounded by another abomination that certain designers adore — "reverse type." This means white type on a black page. Be stronger than I was — put your foot down and insist you simply won't have it, regardless of how many tears flow and how much your art director stomps his foot. Please believe me: it will not sell merchandise.
- If at all possible, stay away from models. I have nothing against models, but they are very expensive, and if you have that short run, those 25,000 catalogs that we are talking about, they can run up your cost something fierce.

I also believe that unless you sell clothes, you can do a better job without models. Very often they detract from the merchandise by focusing attention on themselves rather than on the merchandise. Remember the chairs on the back cover we looked at a few pages back? We did a good job with that, but I am now convinced that we could have done even better if we had left the pretty girl and the pussycat at home. (This, apart from the fact that it took a day and a half and almost hypnosis to get that cat to stay on that chair.) The point is that people are interested in what the chairs look like and that is not accomplished by people or animals sitting on them.

Even mail-order firms selling clothes have learned to do almost completely without models. One of my favorites and, I believe, one of the best examples is that of a page from the catalog of Johnny Appleseed's, one of my wife's favorite shops. There are no models at all. Nothing detracts from the clothes — the prospective purchaser knows exactly what he or she is getting.

WHAT KIND OF ILLUSTRATIONS TO USE

Try to make up your mind early what kind of illustrations you

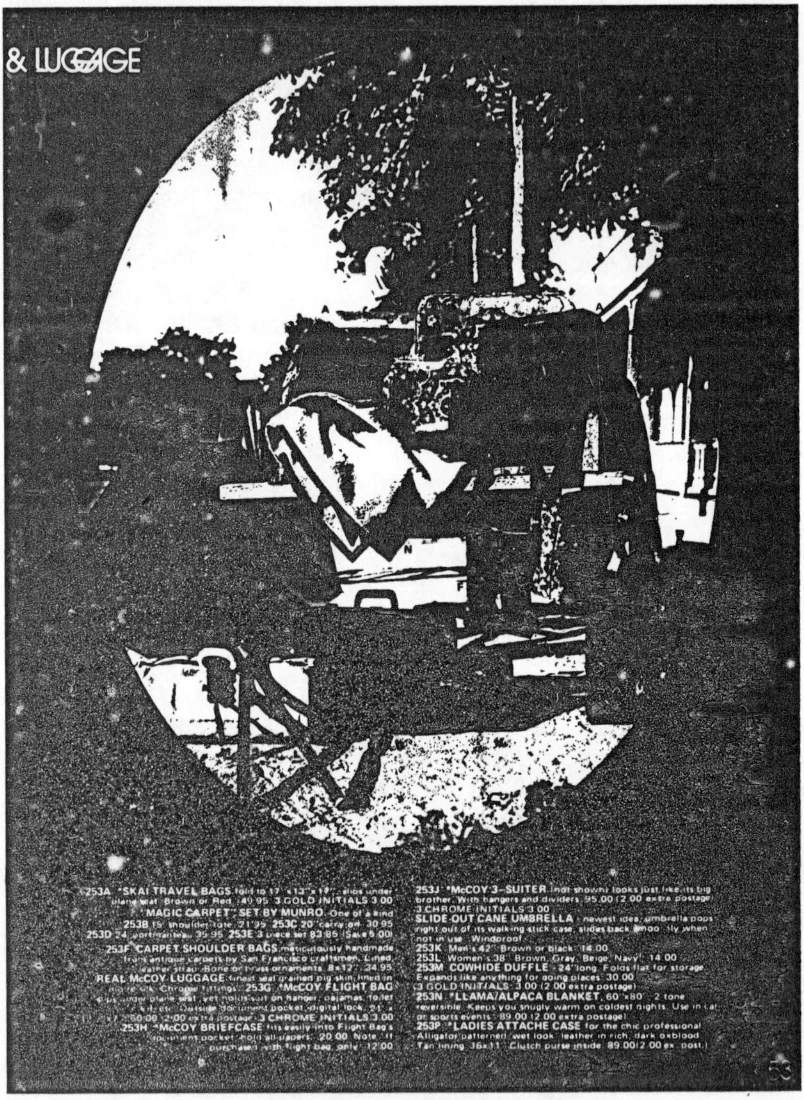

A rather gruesome example of a ''composite'' catalog page. We all make mistakes — you will, too! Almost everything is wrong, and of course, it bombed badly. Composites have their place, but my advice is to stay away from them for the first few years, unless you really know what you are doing.

are going to have in your catalog, whether drawings or photographs. Remember, by the time you are ready to launch your catalog, you will already have a fairly sizable collection of illustrations — perhaps as many as 40 or 50, from your space advertising and catalog inserts. So, if you have decided to feature, say, 150 items in your catalog, you may have to produce as many as 100 additional illustrations. That will take some time (especially if you have decided on drawings and working with just one artist) and will take a fair amount of money. As a general rule you may figure that each good illustration (and you shouldn't consider anything else) will cost you between $30 and $50, depending on complexity. That is part of the "production" money we have been talking about. It is a substantial amount of money. But you must think of it, not as an expense, but as a capital investment. Because if you have chosen your merchandise well, and have found a good illustrator, you will be able to use most of this art for many years. We have talked about that before and I told you about the longevity of some of the art that I have produced over the years.

With any illustrator or photographer, before you commit yourself to him, ask for two or three samples of his work *on your own merchandise.* You are not interested in what he has done for other people. Photography, although it looks easy to all of us who have ever snapped a picture with a Brownie, is a very tricky business. Lighting is all-important, the positioning of merchandise, avoidance of shadows. Many photographers think they are very great. But let them show you what they can do. *You* have to be happy, *you* will have to live with that art for many years.

Usually it's not too successful to mix drawings with photographs. But, naturally, if you already have an investment in both, you should not be expected to discard one or the other for the sake of "artistic unity." We have found a neat solution to the problem, by making what turns out to be essentially line work from photographs. The standard way of doing this is by screening the photograph, to make a so-called "velox," which produces a "halftone" image. But this still looks like a photograph. We often superimpose special circular or line screens on photographs and that gives them the effect of line art. Look at the *Sight and Read Bearing Compass* in the catalog a few pages back. It shows the use of this technique. It is something to remember.

CRYSTAL CORDIAL SET

Charbonnet glasses are beautifully faceted, handsomely shaped. An elegant addition to any bar. Perfect for favorite Liqueurs and Cordials. Gift boxed. Set of six.

12A Crystal Cordial Set **$10.00** (2.50)

DELUXE BAR CADDY

Our handsome Lucite Tray/Caddy holds two distinquished Crystal Decanters each with special dispenser spouts. An attractive way to keep and display your "Private Stock".

12B Deluxe Bar Caddy **$50.00** (2.50)

DELUXE JUMP ROPE

The "in" exercise program needs a jump rope. Our Deluxe model has an exclusive digital counter in the handle which easily monitors daily programs. Heavy nylon cord with protective end prevents cord from wearing out. Adjustable length. With carry case and instructions.

12C Deluxe Jump Rope **$10.00** (1.50)

CASINO TUMBLERS

The unique feature is sealed at the base of each glass. Roulette, Craps, Big Six and Jackpot—games are actually played while drinking your favorite beverage. Add fun to any bar. Tumblers are stackable, thick crystal clear acrylic. Set of four assorted.

12D Casino Tumblers **$14.00** (1.50)

12 Personalized items—allow 3-4 weeks for delivery.

A page from the catalog of Stern's of Atlanta, a very fine and well reputed firm. The entire catalog features the identical four modules per page. It seems to work well for them. I personally consider it too restrictive, because every piece of merchandise occupies exactly the same space — regardless of its size.

By the way, manufacturers will often supply you with their artwork, which you may use if you wish. It is hard to believe, but there isn't one manufacturer in ten who has photographed and retouched (oh yes, most photographs will have to be retouched) his merchandise so that it can be successfully used. Since this is often their only product or only one of very few products that they make (especially in smaller firms) you would think that they might want to spend a few dollars to make some decent reproducible pictures of their merchandise. But don't count on it: most of what they will give you is not usable, and you will have to do it yourself if you want to get it right.

HOW TO WRITE CATALOG COPY

If you have reasonable command of the English language and if you know your merchandise, you should be able to write your own catalog copy. I recommend this, even though I would advise you to shy away from writing direct mail letters or space ads (unless you have some real talent for it, and have worked on developing it or until you have really good, solid experience in doing it). But catalog copy is much easier, straightforward and concise. Since you know your merchandise better than anybody else, you should be able to write catalog copy.

In thinking what to write, keep your customer in mind at all times. What would *you* like to know if you were he or she? You would like to know the facts, of course. So, never mind the cleverly turned phrase and the fancy adjectives. Tell what the merchandise will do, how it is constructed, how it operates (on batteries, on household current or by solar power, or do you wind it up?), what size it is, what special features are included, just what and how does it perform. Very often, you will get help from the manufacturer, because he knows the merchandise even better than you do. He will usually supply you with "spec sheets" from which you can get most of the facts you need and usually some good copy ideas.

When I advise you to stick with the facts and dispense with the "pretty words," I certainly do not mean that you should not do a selling job and create desire to buy. After all, you are writing copy for a consumer catalog (many call it a "wish book"), and not an industrial catalog. But you must not overdo it. You want to be pretty brief, and to the point. You have about 250 items in your catalog. If you expect your customer to read all or most of it, you should not wear him out before he gets all the way through.

One insider trick: it is usually a good idea to write copy immediately as you decide that a piece of merchandise should go into the catalog. As you make that decision, you have just looked at all the features, have studied the manufacturer's literature, and are as familiar with the merchandise as you will ever be. Sit right down and write copy. All the pertinent facts are clearly in your mind. You feel well about the product — you have sold *yourself,* and will therefore be better prepared to sell others. You will also save a lot of time, because if you have to go back later to write copy, you have to get the product file, re-acquaint yourself with the facts, and rekindle your own enthusiasm. And if you have 50 or 80 pieces of merchandise staring you in the face, for which you have to write copy all at one time, you can get pretty tired, and the copy on your last 30 pieces or so may turn out to be somewhat less inspired than it could have been.

Let me give you two examples of catalog copywriting, each in two versions, which were used in two subsequent catalogs. The first version in each case is very factual, the second a little more expansive and "mood creating."

A.

1. *Emoskop Vestpocket Optical System* converts from 3x telescope and telescope loupe through 5x, 10x, 15x magnifier or loupe, to 30x microscope. 1¾ x 1". Lined leather case.
2. *We went to Wetzlar, Germany,* world capital of fine optics to find EMOSKOP VESTPOCKET OPTICAL SYSTEM. It is an instrument with almost infinite use, because it transforms from 3x telescope and telescope loupe to 5x and 10x magnifiers, to 15x loupe and to 30x microscope. Comes in fitted leather case and with transparent "tripod" to give fixed focus at high magnifications. Modern Photography calls it " . . . only magnifier worthy of name."

B.

1. *Wind-up Monaco Shaver* that went to the moon with Apollo 14, kept astronauts Shepard and Roosa as clean-shaven as

when they left 9 days earlier. Just wind up. Self-sharpening.

2. *When our Apollo astronauts went to the Moon,* they took the best shaver available, because they wanted to stay neat and clean even in outer space. MONACO WIND-UP SHAVER is powered by Swedish super spring and shaves from ear-to-ear, nose-to-chin as cleanly as finest blade. 72,000 cutting strokes per minute. No blades, no batteries, no soap, no water, no electricity — you're independent, have no further expense and get greatest shave you've ever had.

I suppose it is a matter of preference, but I have drawn away from the first copy style which may be too short and too factual, and I am now more inclined toward the second style. It seems to work.

One final word about copy: I encourage you once more to write it yourself, if you think you can pull it off (and *I* think you can). It is a very good idea, though, to have somebody (preferably somebody quite literate — your friend the schoolteacher?) look it over and correct any spelling and grammatical errors. You don't want to make any glaring boo-boos in your catalog, and while your proofreader is at it, she (or he) should also carefully check each fact (give her the files) and, very importantly, the prices. There have been times when a $12.95 item has erroneously been listed in the catalog at $2.95 — and believe me, that is not a happy event.

HOW TO MAKE A CATALOG ORDER FORM

You definitely should bind an order form into your catalog. Have a look at the front and back of one of our recent Henniker's order forms.

This is a format that we have evolved over the years and that serves our purposes best. We find that it makes it as easy and unconfusing to the customer as possible, and yet gives us all the information that we need. We work with self-adhesive labels, which the customer peels off the cover and then places in the position shown. There are several advantages for doing it that way:

- You have customer's name exactly as it appears on your master file.

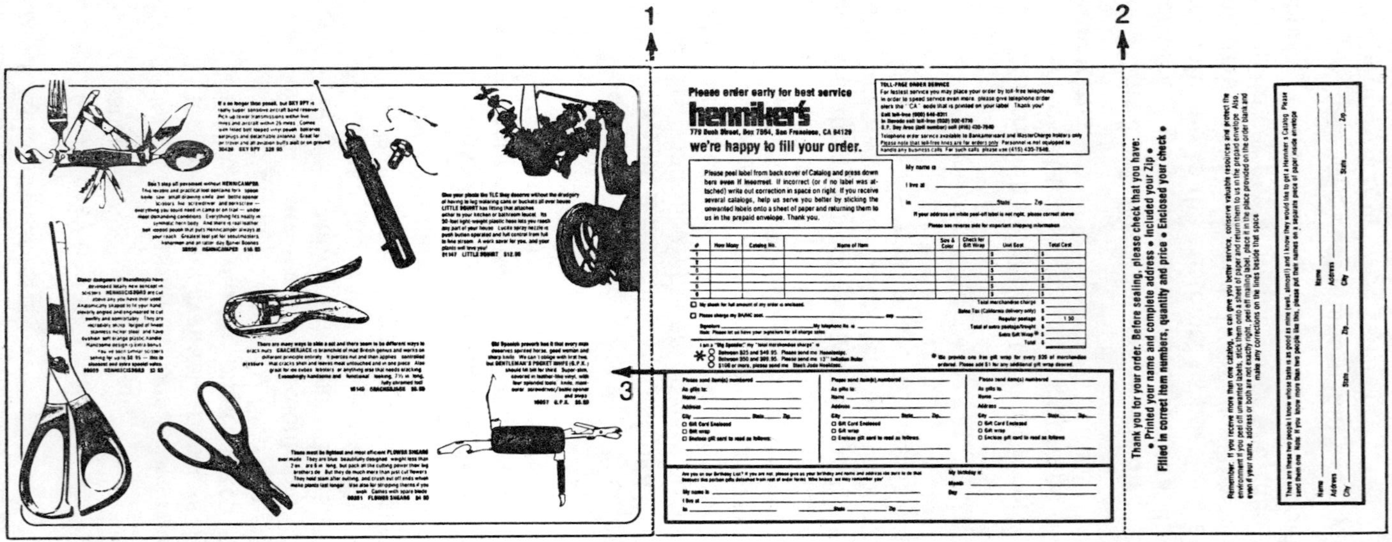

Front part of Henniker's order envelope, a style which we have developed after some trial and error. The form is bound into the catalog on Arrow 1. Customer applies the peel-off label in the place shown, fills in the information requested, tears the form on Arrows 1 and 2 and folds the order with his check in the pre-formed envelope that has glue already provided. By all means, stay away from envelopes that the customer has to form himself! It creates anxiety. To the left of Arrow 1 is the "tail." It is valuable merchandise display space.

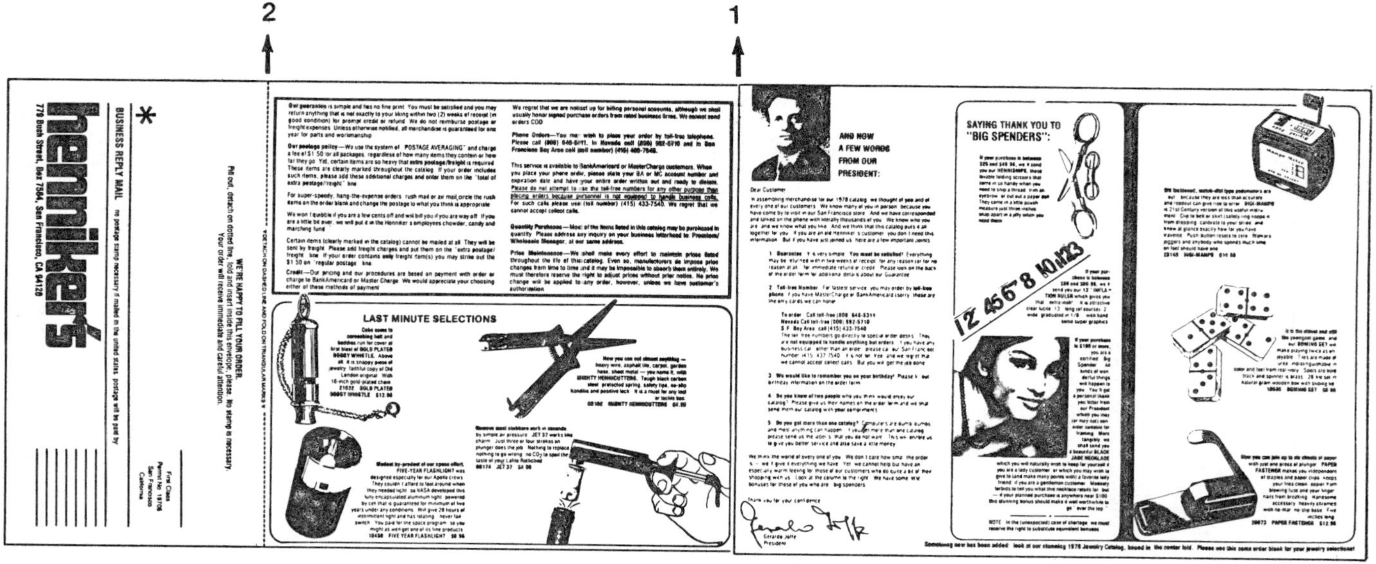

The backside of the order blank carries the President's letter. It is a somewhat corny custom perhaps, but I think it is important because it does really lend a sort of "personal touch." Then we display the bonuses for "Big Spenders" and show more merchandise. The back of the order form itself spells out company policies', gives special information and shows some "Last Minute Selections."

- You have it neatly typed and don't have to decipher handwriting, especially during your rush season.
- If there is an error in the name or address, the customer is shown how to correct it, and will usually do it.
- Corrections are easily accomplished because you have the original label, which contains the customer's "match code" (we have talked about this before).
- The customer gets "involved" by the act of removing the label and re-positioning it. "Involvement" is very big. I am not sure as to how much is real and how much mumbo-jumbo. But "everybody is doing it" (some kind of involvement devise), so I guess it can't hurt.

There is information about the toll-free telephone number for the placing of orders, a clear order schedule and charge card information. You will note that we depart somewhat from what seems to be the usual practice in that we use "standard postage," which doesn't put the burden on the customer to add up several individual postage charges, figure out his mailing zone or go through other mental exercises. Always make it as easy on your customer as you can! Sometimes we make a few pennies on postage and sometimes we lose. But it all evens out pretty much, and our customers seem to like it.

Then there is information about gifts, gift wraps, etc., which is pretty straightforward.

One wrinkle that has stood us in good stead over the years (and I have done it since just about the very beginning) is the birthday information that we request on the bottom of the order form. About 70% of our catalog customers will fill out this information and send it to us with their order. We tabulate this and send the customer a nice little present, together with a letter of congratulations from the entire staff, on his or her next birthday. The goodwill that we create with this is remarkable. People write us constantly, marvelling how we found out their birthday (very few remember that they gave it to us themselves) and thanking us very much for our thoughtfulness. It is a technique that I can heartily recommend to you. You are in the business of making friends and creating loyal customers. Thoughtful gestures like that will do it.

The right-hand part of the order form is the envelope. It gets detached at the dashed line and sealed. It folds over the form on the dashed line when it is bound in the catalog. When the customer wishes to order, he tears out the entire form, fills out the portion to the right of Arrow (1), then tears off the envelope portion at the dashed line by Arrow (2). The portion to the left of Arrow (1) is the "tail." When the whole order form is bound into the catalog, this "tail" opens on a different page. Typically, in our 32-page catalog, we will have the "tail" between Pages 4 and 5 and the order form and envelope themselves between Pages 28 and 29.

In my opinion, the envelope order form is the only way to go. Stay away from order forms that the customer has to fold himself in some artful manner so as to make an envelope out of it. It is not the real thing! It creates anxiety in people that this jerry-made envelope will come open in the mails, that their check and instructions will fall out, or that some other dreadful misfortune may happen to delay or totally foul up their order. There are enough anxieties in this business. Do everything in your power to re-assure your customer and to make it easy for him. Having him "construct" his own envelope is not the way to do it.

Have a look at the inside envelope copy. First, there are last minute reminders to the customer. You would be surprised how many customers do actually forget to give vital information. So it doesn't hurt to ask them to have one last look to make sure. We also ask the customer's assistance in avoiding duplications. Finally, we ask for the names and addresses of two people to whom we may send a catalog with the customer's compliments. These are usually close friends or relatives. Naturally, when we send the catalog to this third party we tell him or her exactly at whose suggestion the catalog was sent (many mail-order firms neglect to do that). If we didn't do that, it would be just like a "cold" mailing. But giving the name of the person who had suggested it is almost like that person's endorsement. It is a very successful approach, and you should follow it.

Let's have a look at the "tail." We use it for "Special Offers," possibly merchandise in which we are overstocked or perhaps any special merchandise category that we had not included in the body of the catalog. The "tail," which the printer can supply in any width, serves, of course, the primary purpose of holding the order form in place. But we decided to make a virtue of necessity, and to use this space to sell merchandise. That is prime space, as it turns out, and

HAPPY BIRTHDAY

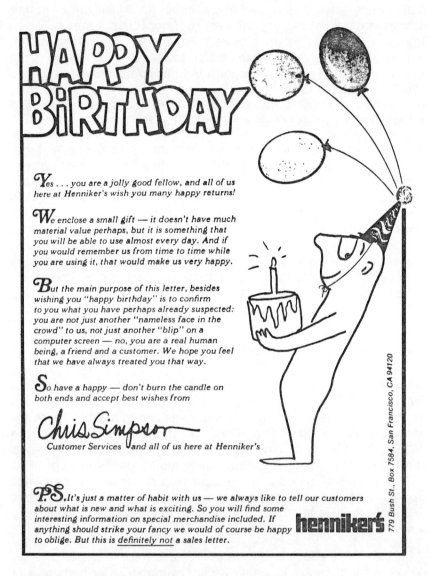

Yes . . . you are a jolly good fellow, and all of us here at Henniker's wish you many happy returns!

We enclose a small gift — it doesn't have much material value perhaps, but it is something that you will be able to use almost every day. And if you would remember us from time to time while you are using it, that would make us very happy.

But the main purpose of this letter, besides wishing you "happy birthday" is to confirm to you what you have perhaps already suspected: you are not just another "nameless face in the crowd" to us, not just another "blip" on a computer screen — no, you are a real human being, a friend and a customer. We hope you feel that we have always treated you that way.

So have a happy — don't burn the candle on both ends and accept best wishes from

Chris Simpson

Customer Services and all of us here at Henniker's

P.S. It's just a matter of habit with us — we always like to tell our customers about what is new and what is exciting. So you will find some interesting information on special merchandise included. If anything should strike your fancy we would of course be happy to oblige. But this is ***definitely not*** *a sales letter.*

henniker's

779 Bush St., Box 7584, San Francisco, CA 94120

Look carefully at the very bottom of the order form in which we ask for the customer's birthday. Almost all catalog customers will respond, but very few will remember that they have given us this information. We never fail to send each such customer a small birthday present, and we include the letter I show you here. Our customers are really pleased with this gesture, and I am quite certain that it "pays" in loyalty and in increased sales.

it really moves the goods. One of the reasons for this being such valuable space is that the catalogs will inevitably open to the page into which the tail is bound. So your customer will see what you have to offer. Therefore, we cut the tail to the same width as the page itself. Here, without much additional cost, is our chance to display seven more pieces of merchandise — all good movers.

Now look at the reverse of the order blank. Over on the right is the reverse of the tail, which is what the customer sees following page 4. First is the President's letter. You may think it is a little corny to have one's picture there and write a personal letter, but I have always felt that it is very important to establish as much personal contact with your customers as you possibly can. A picture, looking the customer straight in the eye, and telling him over your own signature just how you are conducting your business is very helpful. I get literally hundreds of letters (and telephone calls) from customers — brickbats and bouquets, as a result of this and other personalized communications. My customers really find that they know me and, frankly, I think I know them too.

Next to the President's letter comes the presentation of the "Free Gift." Do you, as I do, shudder at the expression of "Free Gift" — as though there were any other kind? But let's face it, the "Free Gift," just like the "True Fact," is here to stay. And the true fact is that the "Free Gift" is the most powerful tool to raise the average sale of your catalog. Since only a small number of the recipients of your catalog will send you any order at all (we'll go into some of the numbers later), it is of the greatest importance to you to increase your sales to those who have decided to favor you with an order.

The "Free Gift" works beautifully. See how we reward customers who order $25 or more, $50 or more, and $100 or more of merchandise, respectively. Naturally, the gifts change from year to year. This is an idea that really works, that you should use as a matter of routine. It may raise your average sale by 5%, 10% or more. And, as you will see in a minute, that makes a disproportionate difference in the net profit that you will derive from your catalog.

Next to the "Free Gift," we display three more pieces of merchandise. It is a good spot — merchandise displayed here always sells exceptionally well.

Now let's look at the left side. The center portion, which is the back of the order form, has a statement of our Guarantee and of our basic policies. We will talk later about customer service policies. Let me just say that we are very "liberal" and decide almost any "dispute" in the customer's favor. Even so, it is important to have written policies that define your responsibilities, so here they are.

We used to offer a Gift Certificate service, but we decided to do away with it. We just didn't have too much call for it in our business. Frankly, I am not too surprised. Very few people like to give such a Certificate. It is sort of a testimonial to their own lack of imagination and, somewhat embarrassingly, it reveals the exact amount spent on the gift. The Gift Certificate was immediately under the "policy" copy. We have taken it out and have been able to put four "Last Minute Selections" in this spot. It was a good idea!

On the extreme left is a standard business reply envelope. I have told you in the previous chapter about my doubts on this point. It may be an unnecessary expense to pay extra postage and associated fees (especially since cranks, nuts and other sickies love to use prepaid envelopes for hate mail), but I have always been too chicken to do away with business reply mail. Who knows, in the next edition of this book I may tell you that I have finally done it and that it works. This envelope portion folds in, of course, when it is bound in the catalog.

Extra Order Blanks

Some of my colleagues bind more than one order blank into their catalog, hoping that this will result in more than one order from the same catalog. I have much question about it. Since binding in an order form is reasonably expensive, we don't want to waste it. Also, I have always thought that the customer might be a little confused by seeing two order forms bound into the same catalog and might think of it as a "mistake." Lord knows, we do make our share of mistakes, but we surely don't want to do anything which, however subliminally, gives the customer any impression of fallibility.

We think we have solved the little problem of what happens if the order form has been removed and the customer wants to reorder. We simply reprint the top portion of the order form — the main portion (to Arrow[3]) on the inside back cover of the catalog, inviting the customer to use it if the main order form has been detached. Frankly, we don't get too much response from that form. But I am not too surprised, really, because I don't think (although I wish it were different) that people keep our, or anyone else's, catalog lying on their living room coffee table month after month. In the great majority of cases they only order once from any catalog, they order pretty much right away, or they don't order at all.

How Many Catalogs To Print?

This depends on three things:

1. How fast are you growing, or rather, how many new customers approximately will you acquire per month;
2. How many times a year will you mail; and
3. To how many outside lists should you mail, and to how many names of each.

Let's say you are about to mail your first catalog. You will drop it in late September or early October, and let's say you have 25,000 customers. And let's also assume that you are acquiring new customers at the rate of about 2,500 per month. At your stage of the game, you should mail two catalogs a year — the one that you are dropping now and the next one, which you should drop in April of the following year. At the rate you are going, you will need approximately 40,000 catalogs for your own list to last through April.

On this first round, you shold mail to three outside lists of 5,000 names each, so your total run should be 55,000, let's call it 60,000 copies. Naturally, when spring comes around, you will have a much better reading as to which outside lists will work for you. You will either have to pull in your horns (I hope not — if you have to, something is wrong and your catalog may need a little remedial work). Or, you will feel confident to act a little bolder, by testing additional lists and by sending catalogs to larger test groups of those outside lists that worked for you on the first round.

How Many Catalogs Per Year Should You Mail?

We have just decided that in your early stages — say your first and second years — you should mail two catalogs per year. Your Christmas catalog should be mailed in late September/early

October; your Spring/Summer catalog should be mailed in late April/early May.

You will recall that we have agreed that direct mail pieces and catalogs will become more and more important as your business matures and that your reliance on space advertising and the budget allocated to it will gradually decline. In the kind of mail-order business that I envision for you, you will have four yearly catalogs, beginning with your third or fourth year. You will add two mailing dates: 1. On or about January 10, to hit about three to four weeks after Christmas, and 2. On or about July 10 to take up the "slack" between the end of summer and the mailing of your Christmas catalog.

We shall talk about numbers in more detail in just a minute. But let me just get this one piece of information out of the way: you should expect about 75% to 80% response from your three "off-season" catalogs, as compared to your Christmas catalog. Thus, if we assume that your Christmas catalog sold about $.85 per unit mailed, your off-season catalogs (assuming there is no major change in format) should sell about $.65 to $.70 per catalog.

Offhand you may think that it would be an almost intolerable amount of work for a small firm to prepare as many as four catalogs a year. But once you have your first catalog on the road it isn't bad at all, and here is why:

- You will maintain the essential format of your catalog so that no completely new design will be necessary. You will change your covers, you will change colors, but you will not change the over-all format. To the customer's eye, it will be a completely new and different catalog from any he had seen before; and yet, because of the unchanged format, it will be recognizably *your* catalog.
- You will retain a large portion of your merchandise from catalog to catalog. You may perhaps discard 20% and put in the same number of new merchandise items. And you can have illustrations and copy for those prepared as you go along. You will re-arrange the merchandise and you want to make especially sure that you feature fresh merchandise on the covers and in the early pages. But all these are essentially "cosmetic" changes and don't take all that much work.

Thus, formidable as the task of making up four catalogs per year appears at first, it isn't really quite as bad, once you break it down into what is actually involved.

WHAT CATALOG MAILING IS ALL ABOUT: THE FAMOUS BOTTOM LINE

Let's just restate what we've said before: the catalog is the heart of your business. You must succeed with it, or you will have a difficult time. We have also acknowledged that there are mail-order businesses that are successful without a catalog or for whom the catalog plays a quite secondary role. It *can* be done, but I assure you that it is the hard way and very much the exception.

The easiest way to talk about what I expect you to accomplish and what you should expect of yourself, is to talk in terms of sales in dollars per thousand catalogs mailed out. That is, of course, the product of the number of orders per thousand catalogs and the average dollar value of all orders. Both of these are quite variable. If you deal in relatively low-priced merchandise, you will get more orders per thousand, but fewer dollars per order. If you deal in fairly high-priced merchandise, the opposite will be the case. Therefore, dollar value of merchandise sold per 1,000 catalogs (or per catalog) is perhaps our most useful, all-around measuring tool.

Please go back to the beginning of this chapter, where we briefly talked about cost. To recap quickly: we said that the type of catalog you should produce as your first effort should cost you overall $6,000 in production and make-ready, plus $.20 per catalog including postage (to your own list).

Mailing your catalog to an outside list will cost you about $.04 more per catalog because you have to rent the outside list at about $35 to $40 per thousand — call it $.04 per name. But please wait for a few pages, and we'll have our detailed analysis of marginal cost and marginal profit.

I will stick my neck out and make some bold statements: you should shoot for $1 sales per catalog to your own list, but chances are that you won't reach that on the first try. But if you have gone along with me, step by step, you should be able to sell, say $.85 of merchandise per catalog to your list and about 85% of that, say $.72 to good outside lists. This depends to a considerable degree on your having a good list broker, who understands what you are doing and who is able to assist you in carefully selecting lists.

We have assumed that we make an average of 55% gross profit on sales.* With all these asumptions, let's see what happens.

Mail-Order Business
Projected Results of Catalog Mailing

(Distributive Costing)

List	Number Mailed	Cost Per Catalog	Total Cost	Sold Per Catalog	Total Sold	Total Gross Profit	Gross Profit Per Catalog	Net Contribution Per Catalog	Total Contribution
House	45m	$ .30	$13,500	$ .85	$38,250	$21,037	$ .46+	$ .16+	$7,537
Outside	15m	$ .34	$ 5,100	$ .72	$10,800	$ 5,940	$ .39+	$ .05+	$ 840
Total	60m	$ .31	$18,600	$ .818	$49,050	$26,977	$ .45	$ .14	$8,377

If you can accomplish something like this, and there is no real reason why you should not, you are very much in business. At first blush, you may be overjoyed at the results of the catalog mailing to your house list. You made over $.16 profit contribution per catalog, more than $7,500 altogether. Compared to that, the barely $.06 per catalog profit that you made to outside lists — a paltry $840 altogether, looks rather insignificant. You are just about prepared to forget about all these other people out there and concentrate on your house list.

But wait, hold everything! You are about to make a very serious mistake. Even if your net profit per catalog to outside lists were "only" $.06, it would still be a potential gold mine. Because chances are that among the lists you have tested there are some with several million names. And once you start working with really large numbers, these "only 6 cents per catalog" can run into a great deal of profit very quickly.

In reality, however, things look much better than you thought. Now it becomes of utmost importance to apply the refined tools of

* You may recall that we spoke in terms of 60% gross profit when we talked about direct mail. In direct mail, if you select one single item, you are usually able to achieve a higher profit margin than when you deal with 100 or 150 items, some of which have higher and others lower gross margins of profit. Therefore, in considering catalogs, a lower gross margin usually applies — 55% is about right.

marginal analysis. Here is what happens: in the above tabulation, we distributed the fixed cost among all catalogs — those mailed to our house list and those mailed to outside lists. Had we mailed only to our own list, our total cost would have been $6,000 plus 45,000 x $.20 = $15,000, or $.33 per catalog. By printing 15,000 additional catalogs to be mailed to outside lists, we have, in this initial analysis, "unburdened" the fixed cost of the catalogs mailed to our house list by one-quarter and burdened this cost onto the outside lists.

But a moment's thought will make us realize that this is not the proper approach. It is obviously not correct that the catalogs that we are in any case committed to send to our house list (and thus, really represent a "sunk cost"), become less expensive as if by magic, just because we have decided to add some other lists. No — the reality of the situation is, for purposes of decision and analysis, that the cost of the catalogs mailed to our own list does not change at all. It is independent of what else you decide to do. It remains the same. But all additional lists should, for purposes of analysis, be totally unburdened of any fixed cost, because that fixed cost is already committed, regardless of whether we decide to mail to additional lists or not.

If you skimmed over the last few paragraphs or if the concept isn't entirely clear, please re-read it and really try to understand it. It is a powerful concept. It is important that you really grasp it, use it in your analysis and work with it.

Working with the figures that we have used, the total cost of each catalog mailed to an outside list is the cost of printing and mailing it ($.20), plus the cost of the rented name ($.04), i.e. a total of $.24. That is a whole dime less than the cost we arrived at by the distributive method. In fact, we find that the cost of mailing to outside lists (after having already committed a mailing to the house list) is less than mailing to the house list. That is a little difficult to grasp at first, but that is the way it is when such relatively small numbers are involved.

Let's see what results the powerful tool of marginal costing gives us, instead of the cruder (and inaccurate method) of distributive costing.

Mail-Order Business
Projected Results of Catalog Mailing

(Marginal Costing)

List	Number Mailed	Cost Per Catalog	Total Cost	Sold Per Catalog	Total Sold	Total Gross Profit	Gross Profit Per Catalog	Net Contribution Per Catalog	Total Contribution
House	45m	$ .33+	$15,000	$ .85	$38,250	$21,037	$ .46+	$ .13+	$6,037
Outside	15m	$ .24	$ 3,600	$ .72	$10,800	$ 5,940	$ .39+	$ .15+	$2,340
Total	60m	$ .31	$18,600	$ .818	$49,050	$26,977	$ .45	$ .14	$8,377

Once more, please re-read the preceding and truly try to understand it, because it may well be one of the most important lessons in this whole book. You have seen that you can make just about as much (or perhaps even more) money mailing catalogs to outside lists as mailing to your own, by projecting reasonable figures and reasonable ratios of performance between your own list and good outside lists. And the reason is that you have properly allocated the fixed cost where it belongs and do not burden your tests and "roll-outs" to outside lists with such costs.

I shall make another bold statement in this connection: successful mail-order houses are those that mail out large numbers of catalogs to outside lists. In many cases, the number of catalogs mailed to outside lists is much larger than that mailed to the house list. Usually such catalog mailings to outside lists (in a successful and well-run mail-order business) are profitable. Sometimes they are very profitable, approaching the house list in profit per catalog. Sometimes they are only fractionally profitable. But that is all right too, because the volume is very large, and even "fractions" add up. And, of course, each customer secured from an outside list becomes now a part of the house list.

If you have picked your test lists prudently, you will have used only such lists that have large "universes," several hundred thousand or perhaps several millions of names. In our example, we lumped all three lists together, but, naturally, you will maintain and analyze the results of each list separately. And it is entirely likely that one or two of the three test lists, if not all three, will perform so as to encourage you to remail, say, another 10,000 catalogs to those lists that you tested with 5,000 names on the first round.

Now you can readily see where *the really big money* in this business is:

- Test your catalog on outside lists. With reasonably good selection (luck plays no role) you should find several lists that are expandable into large mailings and that will produce large sales volume and predictably large profits.

That is it. That is how to be successful in the mail-order business. This is what we have been building up to.

Don't forget a few cardinal rules about testing:

- Always have several tests going at the same time.
- Test list segments large enough so that you can get significant results on which to base analysis. For catalog testing, 5,000 is a good minimum number.
- Keep meticulous records as to what comes from where. Your tests are useless if your results are not properly and carefully tabulated.
- Be careful when you expand the test. Your first results may have been affected by some fluke, you may not have gotten a true cross-section or some (less than scrupulous) list owner may have thrown you a curve by giving you 5,000 names that are the cream of his buyers, rather than the true cross-section. (Sad to relate, but it *does* happen.)
- If you have good results from the first 5,000, test 10,000 on the next round. If everything is still as it should be you may go to 25,000 or 50,000 next time out.
- Don't risk too much on one list—you don't have to get rich in one big swoop. Try always to have several tests running, and to test a few new lists on every round of mailing.

Let's come back to something that we had mentioned before: do you remember our talk about the "Free Gift" a few pages back? You may wish to play with the figures and see what impact a 5% or 10% increase per average order will have on your profit picture. Go back to the tabulation on Projected Results of Catalog Mailings on the page preceding. It is based on distribution of the Free Gift to "Big Spenders." Now assume (not unreasonably) that overall sales would be decreased by 10% had you not offered this Free Gift. Your cost, of course, would remain unaffected. Your sales might, however, decrease from $49,050 to, say, $45,000 and your Total

Gross Profit to $24,750. Cost remains fixed at $18,600, and your Total Contribution reduces to $6,150 from $8,377. This is a *reduction in profit of over 26% as a result of decline in sales of just 10%!* So you see — up or down — the leverage of change in sales on overall profitability is substantial. It really pays to try to get the average order as high as you possibly can. And the "Free Gift" is one of the best ways to accomplish it.

In the preceding few paragraphs, we have talked about what is, so far at least, the most important point — the essence of the whole mail-order business. You have built your own customer list as a base. You have generated these customers one by one "the hard way," mostly through space advertising. Now, you have your first catalog. You mail it to your own list, of course. That's where your bread and butter will come from, for the payment of your rent and your overhead and for whatever small salary you decide to pay to yourself. But the essence of this whole business lies in creating *catalogs that will pull to outside lists* and that can be mailed to ever-widening circles of customers — quite a few of whom will, of course, become your own customers and become part of your ever-increasing house list.

I don't want to get you too excited, but there are quite a few mail-order firms that began as I did and as you will, from a standing start, and that mailed in just a few years as many as a million catalogs — in some cases as much as 90% to outside lists. You might not do quite as well. But you will work in that direction. And you will build a sound business and ever-increasing profits.

In the last three chapters, we have been dealing with techniques of advertising: space advertising, direct mail, and, most importantly, catalogs. You should now know how to get your business started and keep it rolling, how to select good merchandise and how to promote that merchandise through the various media that we have talked about. You are well on your way to being a seasoned mail-order operator. In the next five chapters, we shall talk about certain operating techniques that are peculiar to the mail-order business and that you must familiarize yourself with. And then we shall wind up by finding out how we put all of this together to create a business that we shall eventually be able to sell for at least one million dollars. I have done it, and I shall tell you exactly how I did it. And as you will see, there are quite a few who have done a whole lot better. There is no reason why you should not be able to do the same thing.

Between Chapters

GETTING READY FOR THE FINAL PUSH

There are some special things you need to know in order to run a mail-order business.

In the preceding chapters we have discussed really everything that is important and distinctive about the mail-order business. We have learned how to merchandise and we have learned how to produce effective promotions in all print media.

Really, you should now know just about as much as the most seasoned pros. All you need is practice and experience.

But, besides merchandising and promotion you still have to "run the business." And if you have no prior experience in running any business at all, you will have to acquaint yourself with standard business procedures.

Since you will start on a very small scale and only grow gradually, this should not be a special problem. Perhaps you would be well served in reading one or several standard books on how to run a small business. The Small Business Administration, for instance, has a number of excellent pamphlets available for the asking. They are well written and easily understandable. It might be well worth your while to visit the closest field office of the SBA and see what is available. Or, if you don't have access to such an office, write to them. They are eager to help.

You should also, perhaps, acquire a small library of books on business in general. One of my all-time favorites is *Up Your Own Organization* by Don Dible which you can buy directly from the publisher, Entrepreneur Press, Vacaville, CA 95688. One of the features of Mr. Dible's book is an excellent reference index to business literature. Once you have read that and have really absorbed it, you should be pretty much able to run any business of your own.

Another favorite book of mine is *Accounting for Non-Accountants* by John N. Myer, published by New York University Press. This is an excellent volume to give you a good grasp of bookkeeping and accounting, without having any ambition of becoming an accountant yourself. But, unless you already have that knowledge, it is really necessary for you to understand the main functions of bookkeeping and fundamentals of accounting. It is a "must" to run a successful business to keep track of and to plan for cash, to control profits (and avoid losses), and to be able to spot profit sources and profit wasters.

There is one other book that I believe belongs in the library of every progressive small businessman. It is *Successful Small Business Management* by Leon R. Wortman, published by Amacom (a division of American Management Association). This book is really comprehensive and deals in depth with planning and controlling; accounting and finance; and marketing and sales. If you have only one business book, this might well be the one.

Another thing about running a business, any business — is the handling of personnel. You have to acquire the knack to find the proper people, to train them, to motivate them, and to keep them properly compensated and happy with their work. If you have spent all of your working life until now as an employee, or working all by yourself — let's say as an independent salesman — this will be an interesting experience. Chances are that you will start out just by yourself or perhaps with only one or two family members. So you might not need this skill immediately. But it is something that you will absolutely have to learn as you go along. You can't run a business of any size without good people and without being able to hold them and to motivate them.

Since I seem to be in the process of "pushing" books, I might tell you about one of my favorites in the personnel field. Naturally, the number of books on personnel management is virtually limitless. But my favorite — and I think you will agree — is *McMurry's Management Clinic* by Robert N. McMurry. It is a Simon & Schuster book, and you might find it a little difficult to locate a copy, because it came out quite a few years ago. In contrast to so many other books on the subject, it gives case after case — and practical solutions — of the kind of situation that you are likely to run into in your business. Very little theory, hardly any philosophy — just good solid lessons from actual business situations.

I have been promising myself — and I think I have promised you earlier in the book — to give you some guidelines about the staffing of your mail-order business two or three years down the road. But I think I shall not attempt to do this in too much detail, because there are infinite variants of what is needed. They depend primarily, of course, on how your business will evolve and what functions you yourself (and your spouse) will fulfill. But, in the most general terms, the following will probably be your principal "management pillars."

- President, General Manager
- Merchandise Manager
- Purchasing Manager
- Accountant (Treasurer, Controller)
- Creative Director (Art, Copy)
- Customer Service Manager
- Operations Manager
- Office Manager
- Warehouse/Shipping Manager
- Retail Stores Manager

All of these positions will have to be filled, in almost any mail-order business that has attained a certain size. Then, of course, the specifics of your business might necessitate other slots to be filled. But these ten would seem to be the most standard, without whom you could not properly function.

Now, when looking at this formidable list of high-powered executives, you might get a little concerned when you think of the swollen payroll that you will be confronted with. But things aren't quite that bad, because at the stage of business that we are talking about here — and though all positions have to be covered — people must be able to double (and sometimes triple) in brass.

Take our own situation at Henniker's for instance. The President (that is I) is not just General Manager and overall factotum, but also fills the job of Treasurer, Controller — and Copywriter. The positions of Office Manager and Purchasing Manager are covered by one extremely efficient lady. The Merchandise Manager is also in charge of the retail stores, although, of course, assisted by sales personnel. "Operations" is shared by the Warehouse Manager (and she is already slightly overburdened) and by the Office Manager — and so it goes. The key is that you have to have people who are smart, flexible, self-starters, broad-shouldered and are willing to take on work and responsibilities.

But that is really all that I can generalize about the staffing of your *going* business, in contrast to the start-up personnel we talked about earlier in this book. The important thing is to surround yourself with capable people and to set the tone of performance and accomplishment that you expect.

But back to the topics that we shall deal with in the rest of the book. It is not really our scope or purpose to talk about general business management. We have decided that there is ample literature on the subject, and that you can read up on that. What we really want to talk about are those things that are peculiar to the mail-order business. I have picked out a number of areas that *are* special and that you should know about.

Therefore, the topics that I think we should talk about in the following chapters are:

- How to run a successful retail store.
- How to control inventory.
- What to do about the wholesale and premium business.
- How to put data processing to best use.
- How to run a successful customer service department.
- How to keep good records.

After we have mastered these techniques, which are specifically tailored to your evolving mail-order business, we come to the "pay-off" — the last chapter on *How To Make The Big Score.* So read on, the best is yet to come!

Chapter 6

HOW TO RUN A SUCCESSFUL RETAIL STORE

You may be surprised that I am bringing this up as a topic. After all, we did decide to go into the mail-order business, and not into the retail store business. So what is the importance, or even the need to talk about a retail store? It is a good question, and you may be somewhat surprised about the answer.

CUSTOMERS WANT TO KNOW WHERE YOU ARE

First of all, in order to run a mail-order business, you must *never* rely on a post office box as your address. It is one of the most deadly things that you can do. People instinctively mistrust anything that does not have a given street address that they could not go visit if they chose to, and where they could not (if they felt like it and if they thought it were necessary) look the owner/manager in the eye and punch him in the nose if required. Naturally, you will eventually have to have a post office box, because we expect that the volume of your mail will be such that it cannot be conveniently delivered to your business address. But if you do have a post office box, it must always be mentioned together with your street address. For instance, Henniker's address is 779 Bush Street, Box 7584, San Francisco, CA 94120. With such an address, all mail is automatically delivered to the post office box at the main San Francisco Post Office, where we pick it up every morning. But as far as the customer is concerned, our address is 779 Bush St., and (as you will see from several retail ads that I shall show you in a minute) when we advertise locally, we leave the post office box off altogether.

Having once decided that you absolutely have to have a street address, in other words, that you cannot work with the post office box alone, you will find that within just a very few days after your first ads appear, people will start wandering into your office. They will hold a coupon in their hands and tell you such things as "I never buy anything by mail, so I thought I should come by and have a look at this"; or, "I just happened to be in the neighborhood and wanted to look at it myself," etc., etc. Even at the smallest, most modest level of operation, you will find that anywhere between five and ten people might come in and visit you every day.

At first, you will be very pleased about these somewhat unexpected customers, because almost all of them, once they have gone to the trouble of visiting you in person, will make a purchase. And that, of course, is extra money in your pocket — just what you are looking for.

But then you will come to the realization that these wonderful people are also somewhat of a nuisance, because every time any outsider comes into your small office, practically all work stops. If you are by yourself, you can't do anything else. If you have two or three other people working, they will also stop, visit, and interrupt whatever they are doing. Another disadvantage of people coming into your office is that you have checks, money, merchandise and all kinds of papers lying around that you don't necessarily want outsiders to see. Also, quite frankly, just like the kitchen of the finest hotel, the "back room" doesn't always look too tidy and does not, therefore, convey quite the impression of your business that you wish.

You will then, inevitably, come to the conclusion that your best bet is to move into some downtown ground floor location, where you can conduct a regular retail store business, and have your office and your shipping facilities all at the same location.

At first, this will be entirely a defensive maneuver. In othe words, you simply want to keep your office work away from the walk-in trade. But then you will begin to realize that the store car be a very lucrative adjunct to your business. In fact, you will quickl find that it is one of the most profitable things that you are doing dollar for dollar. The reason for that is that your *additional overhea* to run the store is quite small. We shall hear more about that in a minute.

HOW TO LAY OUT YOUR STORE AND BUSINESS SPACE

The kind of location you should be looking for — I am now assuming that you are in a city of some size — things are somewhat different if you are in a very small town — would be one pretty close to downtown, but not necessarily in the prime shopping district. The reason you may wish to stay away from the prime shopping district is that you will find rents inordinately high. Also, usually, the landlord will insist on a percentage lease, which is really a "piece of the action." Since you will eventually conduct a fairly high-volume business, of which only a fraction is actually store trade, such a lease may give rise to disagreement and argument.

But there is a more important reason. You really have to "compromise" between several needs. Remember, as important as the store is to you, it is essentially only an adjunct to your real business, a "front." The "real action" takes place in the back room and, usually, in the basement.

Thus, you would be looking for a location with, say, 25 feet of street frontage, and perhaps 60 to 80 feet deep, i.e. somewhere around 1,500 to 2,000 square feet all together. You should have a full and easily accessible basement underneath. By that I mean that merchandise can easily be transported to and from the basement, and that people can work in the basement comfortably, and in accordance with safety and fire rules.

Put yourself into the hands of a reliable commercial real estate agent who specializes in commercial property and you will quickly find what you need. The kind of space I described is readily available in most cities.

Let's assume that you have found such a place, namely about 25 feet of store front and about 60 to 80 feet deep. It is possible, of course, that you are lucky and that the previous occupant had divisions and fixtures that you can use. But suppose that you have an empty shell and that you have to make your own store and office installations. Here is what you should keep in mind.

For the kind of operation that I expect you to run, you should have a store of about 600 square feet, which means that you should have a divider, or curtain wall, at about 25 feet from the front. And behind that would come the "bull pen" which is the general office and working area. Let's assume about 750 square feet for that. This would put another divider at 30 feet beyond the first one or about 55 feet from the front.

If we have 80 feet depth altogether, we would now have about another 25 feet of depth left, which we could perhaps divide into two of those offices. One of these should be your art department. You will, within quite a short time, have at least 2 or 3 people working full-time in your art department. So they would need the entire width, say 25 x 12 feet or 300 square feet. The remaining 12 or 13 feet of length could be made into one or two offices, let's call them your "executive" and merchandising offices. (I use the word "executive" somewhat tongue-in-cheek, because you will find that there aren't going to be any "executives" in the accepted sense of the word). Have a look at the sketch of the layout; it is pretty clear.

Naturally, this is simply a rough idea of what should be done. The actual layout will vary with the space available and with its shape. I am in my second such business, and a variant of the layout that I am showing you here has served me both times.

Let's assume that you have a full basement in which case you would have another 1,500 or 2,000 feet of working space. The most convenient layout is to have access from the basement to an alley. The second best choice would be to have a freight elevator that takes you to the basement. But do not consider the space if you don't have either of these two. You will find it impossible and back-breaking to move boxes of merchandise up and down a narrow stairway. You won't want to do it, and your employees won't want to do it and won't stay with you.

For the first couple of years or so, or let's say, until your sales exceed $1,000,000, you should easily be able to store all of your merchandise in your basement, and do all of your packing and shipping from there. While it doesn't take a great deal of imagination to design a warehouse and packing facility for the size of operation that you are going to run, you might take a look at how our basement at Henniker's is arranged. Again, it is just about the same kind of layout that we had at Haverhill's. It was most adequate until sales reached about 1.0 to 1.5 million dollars per year.

At Henniker's we are now beyond the volume of sales that would allow us to do all of our storage in this location. We have rented additional merchandise storage space, but it will take some time before you will have to worry about that.

But let's come back to the store itself. You should not be stingy with expense to make your store attractive and inviting. Keep in mind that people *will* come and visit you — and that the impression that they have about your business will be confirmed or perhaps even formed by what they see in the store.

You don't have to spend a whole lot of money, but you should have clean, functional fixtures and counters (much of it can be bought second-hand and made to look like new with just a little elbow grease and a few cans of paint). The premises should be well-painted, preferably in a light color, and all the merchandise should be attractively displayed on clean and orderly shelves. You should provide adequate lighting — preferably of the "track" variety.

By the time you get through, you will have spent a little money, but it will have been worthwhile. You will have an attractive store that will become an important profit center in its own right. Sales, at first, will be primarily "fallout" from your mail-order advertising. But, as time goes by, and unless you are in a very out-of-the-way location, you will generate more and more walk-in traffic.

By the way, you will find that your most important expense will be electrical installations. Therefore, it would be worth your while to find out beforehand what wiring is, or is not, available. If you find that too much electrical installation will be required, you should perhaps disregard the location. Most of the other things, like painting, carpentry, you should be able to do yourself.

WHY YOUR STORE WILL BE PROFITABLE FOR YOU

Just let me show you why this store, which we decided at first was only a "defensive" maneuver, will be very profitable for you.

It is difficult to determine exactly how much of your store business will come as a result of advertising that you have placed in media, catalogs or direct mail, or how much will simply be walk-in trade. It is a combination of both, and both reinforce each other. You may also make the assumption that quite a few of the people who saw your advertisements in some magazine or newspaper would have bought from you even if you didn't have the store. It has been my experience with Haverhill's and also at Henniker's — and this experience seems to be shared by most people in this business,

Typical layout of a combination store/office floor for a mail-order business. This kind of space is readily available in most localities and will serve all purposes for the first three to five years in the normal growth of such a business.

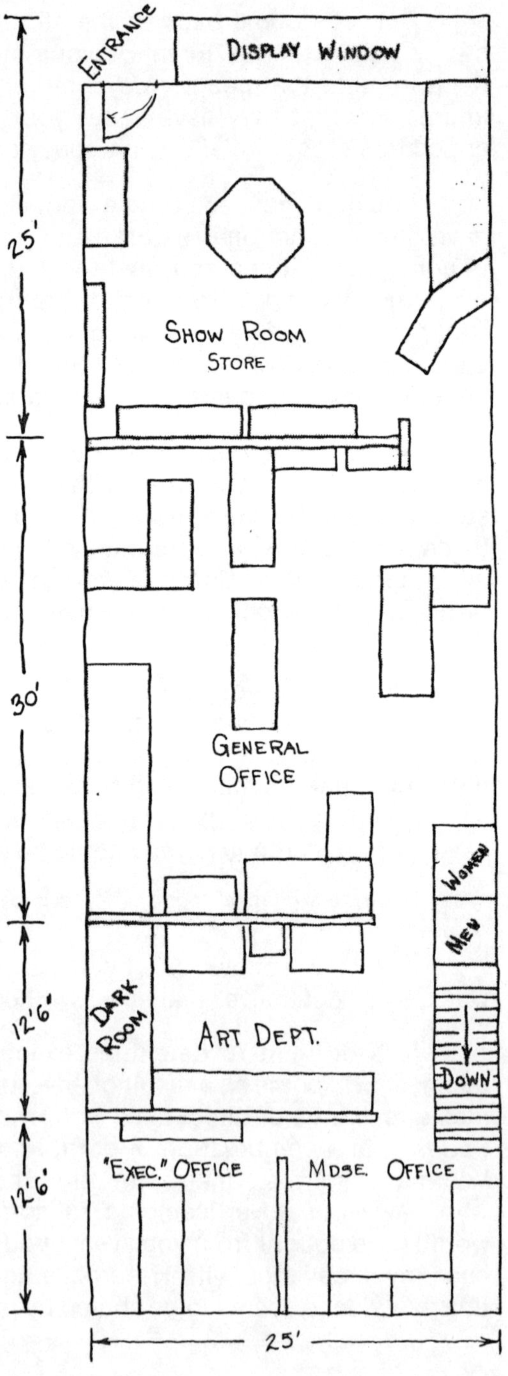

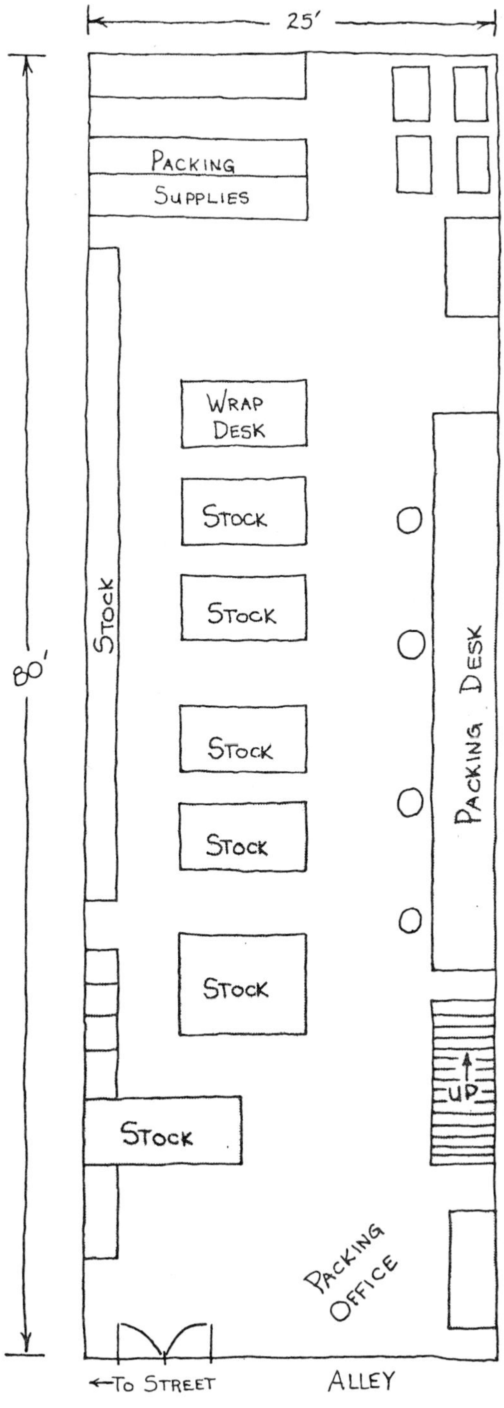

To serve the all-around purposes of a mail-order business that also operates a retail store, a full basement that can be used for storing inventory, packing and shipping is indispensable. This shows a typical layout of such space. Ground floor locations for this purpose are either not readily available in metropolitan areas or would not be economical.

that a retail store such as I describe, will account for anywhere from 5 to 10% of your total business.

Let me show you why our retail store is so profitable — and why yours will be too.

Let's assume that you are now in the third year of your business and that your total sales are $1,000,000 per year. And let's assume that 6% of that, or $60,000 per year, is done through your retail store. Let's further assume — and I think that is reasonable — that you would not have got about 75% of that business if you did not have the store; in other words, that you have $45,000 of additional business, by just having the store.

Remember, we have decided that we are going to have a profit margin of about 55%. Therefore, the $45,000 in sales that you gained by having the store (and wouldn't have otherwise) account for about $25,000 in gross profits. That is "extra!"

What are the expenses that you have with this retail store? You will find that they are quite small. In the first place, it is proper that you amortize the money that you have invested in the store, and that you do it over a reasonable period. Let's assume that you went pretty much all out, and that you spent $6,000 on store improvement and that you amortize that over five years. This would give you an expense of $1,200 per year to be charged against the store.

Let us further assume that you pay, say, $600 rent per month, and that you should, therefore, allocate, say, $250 per month to the store for rental purposes. (After all, it is the choicest part of your premises, and it should therefore, "pay" a small "premium.") Rental, therefore, would account for another $3,000 per year.

And then, of course, you need an employee, usually a sales girl. She will draw a salary and benefits in the neighborhood of about $150 per week. Call it another $8,000 per year.

Thus, between amortization of improvements, rental and employee, we have a cost of, let's say, $12,500 against a gross profit of $25,000. This means that your store will put you about $12,500 ahead of the game.

I assure you that you will find that $12,500 "extra profit" to be a nice help.

The above is fairly in line with reality, although there are, of course, quite a few variants to that. For instance, the sales girl will not be very busy at first, and she will have much time on her hands. You will find that she will be able to do quite a bit of your clerical work, for which you might otherwise have to hire a full-time or part-time person. At the early stages of your business, you might even discreetly put a typewriter in the store, and she can do quite a lot of your light typing, or even correspondence, if you wish. When I first started with Haverhill's — on very much of a shoestring budget, I was fortunate in finding a most capable young woman who ran the store, handled all clerical details of the mail-order busines, and was my secretary at the same time. Admittedly, this did not last too long. We had to split off some of the work pretty soon, but what I am trying to show you is that the expense of the salesgirl is really not just for the store alone.

"FEEDBACK" YOU WILL GET FROM YOUR STORE

Another aspect of the store is that there is a great deal of "feedback" that is not immediately apparent. The mere fact that you have a store will make people more comfortable in ordering from you by mail. Henniker's customers from all over the country often include notes telling us that friends of theirs had come by our store in San Francisco and how pleased and impressed they were wlth what they had seen. Having the store, then, turns out to be much more than the defensive maneuver that we thought of at first. It turns out to be a substantial source of profit. But it is also a source of prestige and a means of giving credence and structure to your business that would otherwise be more difficult to attain.

At Henniker's, we have gone further with the concept of the store and consider it now even more important in profit contribution than we used to. We create special store ads that we run in our local newspaper. This is an innovation that I can recommend to you. We didn't use to do that, but simply ran mail-order ads from time to time in our local newspaper — the same ads that we run nationally. But we have determined that creating special retail store ads is profitable and substantially increases the traffic in the store.

Have a look at some of our typical retail ads. There are different types: First, an "omnibus" ad, a version of which we run about every other week in the Sunday supplement of the *San Francisco Chronicle,* and which features anywhere from 6 to 10

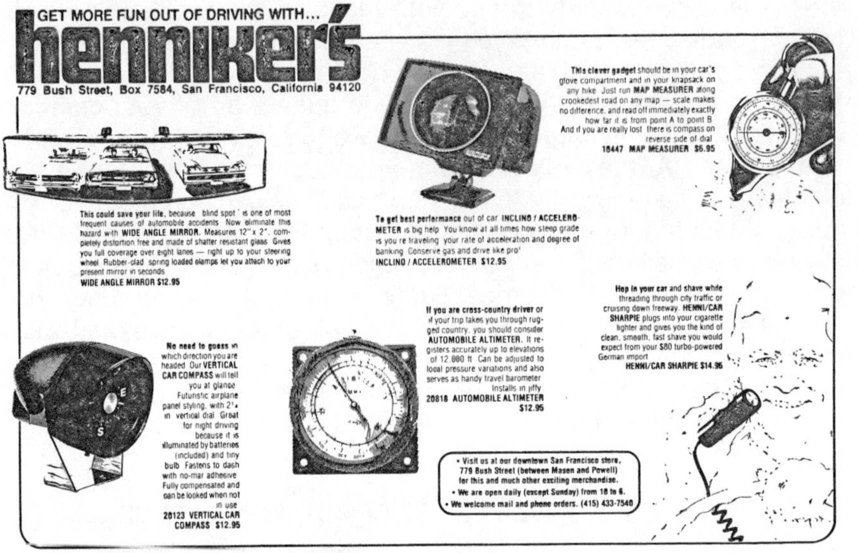

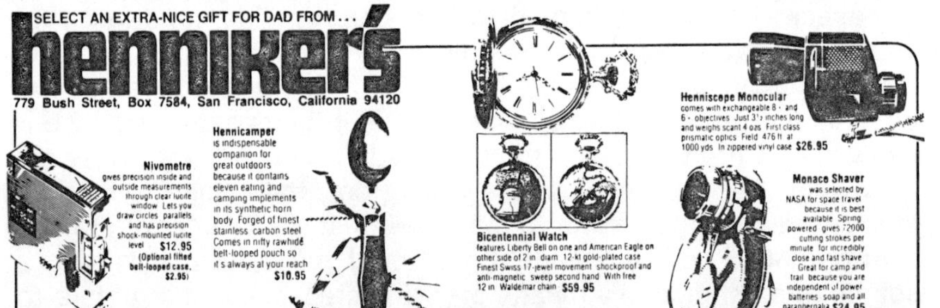

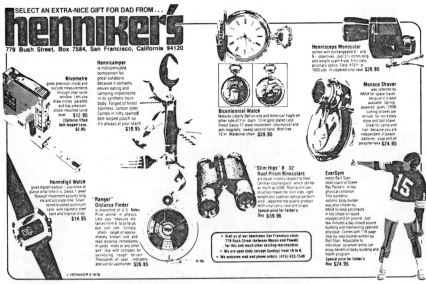

I feel strongly that every mail-order ad must have a coupon, but the opposite is true for ads in your hometown paper. We advertise at least once a week in THE SAN FRANCISCO CHRONICLE-EXAMINER. Our main purpose in this advertising is to promote the store, although the ads also produce a good volume of phone and mail orders. These are "omnibus" ads that usually have a unifying theme. The upper ad features automotive accessories, and the lower ad is a special Father's Day promotion. We run these half-page ads about every other week. Your hometown customers are very important and your store should be a prime profit center. Special attention and special ads are in order!

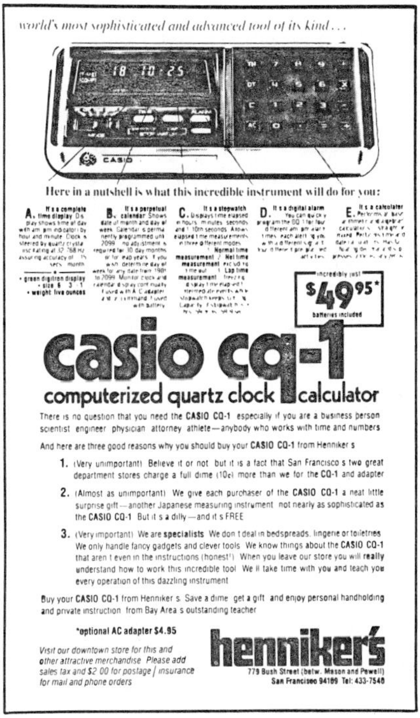

These are typical store ads of a different type. The Exer-Gym ad is a special promotion, a 1-week Sale. We do about one or two of these "mini-sales" a month. They are usually quite successful and create store traffic. The Casio CQ-1 ad is perhaps typical of what a good store ad on one item should look like. We did this ad in nose-to-nose competition with our two large department stores and didn't come out too badly.

For yourself or for that "super person" on your list, This year's ultimate gift . . .

FIREBALL! Pinball Computer by Bally

LOOK AT THESE EXTRA FEATURES

- Programmed for 1 to 4 players — separate score kept for each
- Can be adjusted to individual skill levels
- Regular scores, bonus scores, extra balls, announced by seven special tunes. Volume can be controlled.
- Multi-colored lights flash, producing spectacular light/sound effects
- Tilt feature (tune: 'The Party's Over) stops game.
- Digital read-out of all scores
- Completely computer controlled
- Weight 160 lbs.; size: 2x4 ft.; comes ''knocked down'' into three parts and can be assembled in five minutes (really!)

SERVICE AND GUARANTEE

- **Fireball** is U.S.-made, product of **Bally** (in business since 1931 and now world's largest manufacturer of pinball machines).
- Designed to have practically no service requirements since most components are modular plug-ins, which are not subject to mechanical deterioration.
- Self-diagnostic trouble shooter (in case of any problem, push service button and read-out will tell you which plug-in part has failed).
- Fully stocked part warehouses and repair centers all over the U.S. (closest is in So. San Francisco).
- 2-week return privilege and one year full guarantee.

$699

Make this the greatest Christmas ever with **Fireball Pinball Computer.** Put it in your home or in your office or plant (where it may be tax deductible and will raise the gusto and efficiency of your employees to unprecedented levels). You can see and play **Fireball** in our downtown store. If you order before December 17, we can assure you of Christmas delivery (or we'll immediately refund your money). We are fully stocked, but this is **very hot,** so don't miss out. **Fireball** is just **$699** (plus $10 freight in Bay Area.

henniker's
779 Bush St. [between Powell & Mason],
San Francisco, CA 94108,
Telephone: 433-7540

We were very proud of this store ad, but I must confess that it was not ''successful'' — we didn't sell one single ''Fireball''! What might be the reason? I suppose it is that our customers do not really associate us with this kind of merchandise. It isn't quite our ''thing.'' Even so, we had scores of people coming in to play the machine, and quite a few actually stayed to buy something else. So it wasn't a complete failure. But it does seem to be good policy not to confuse your customers about your line of merchandise.

different pieces of merchandise. More often than not, these omnibus ads have a theme, sometimes connected to a special occasion. For instance, I show you here a Father's Day omnibus ad and an automobile omnibus ad. In the in-between weeks, we may run "special sale" ads. These are usually catalog items, for which a price is established, on which we may be slightly overstocked, or for which we have some other reason to put them on sale. The important thing as far as you are concerned is to have something called "Special" every so often. It really brings the customers into the store.

In that connection, of course, it's also important that the Sale be strictly limited. Each of these "Special Sale" ads gives a date deadline and we are adamant about it. We don't sell anything at a special price after the date has passed. We feel that this is important in order to maintain our direct mail and catalog business and to maintain the credibility of our offers.

Naturally, if we have something special, perhaps something brand new that is not even yet in the catalog, we may run a special store ad on that also, even though it is not a "sale" item. Have a look at our Casio CQ-1 ad for instance. Oh yes, Macy's and the Emporium, our two large department stores, were not too happy about this ad. But it was true, they did actually charge $.10 more.

We do one other thing for our store customers that I want to tell you about. And this, again, I very much recommend to you.

Because of the store and because of our being headquartered in San Francisco, we do have a disproportionate number of our customers right close to home in the San Francisco Bay Area. Excepting the Christmas season only — we don't want anything to conflict with our catalog — we mail a special promotion to our Bay Area customers every month. This promotion follows essentially the same format, month after month. We do this for easy recognition and also to make production a little easier. It is a postcard that is printed on both sides. There is every month a "Special Sale" for our established customers, and a little "Bonus" — either a "Freebie" or an established item that we sell at a token price with any purchase over a given amount.

It is a technique that you should follow in your mail-order business. It will put your store on the local map, it will keep the local customers faithful and it will make money.

free
Visit us at our store
It will be our pleasure to give you a free Henniscales (nifty postage scales) as our present with any purchase over $25.00.
This offer good through May 15, 1976 only. You must bring this card to get the free bonus of Henniscales.
henniker's
779 Bush St., Box 7584, San Francisco, CA 94120
BULK RATE
U.S. POSTAGE
PAID
PERMIT #10894
SAN FRANCISCO
TO:

April Special Sale
to our Bay Area customers only. Acrylic Clock with exquisite battery movement (alkali battery included). Nationally advertised at $59.95, this month and for this special sale only, just
$39.95
Offer limited to supplies available and through May 15, 1976 only.
Come and visit our downtown San Francisco store in April. You will love our new merchandise, and we have a special Sale just for you! Yes, we would like to renew friendship and shake hands with you during the month of April at our downtown San Francisco store. Many of our customers think of Henniker's only as a mail order house. But we have a really nice and fully stocked store in downtown San Francisco. If you have not been by to see us lately, do come during this month. We have a very special offer for our Bay Area store customers only—our Acrylic Pendulum Clock which is listed in our catalog at $59.95. But during April, it's yours for just $39.95—one-third off nationally advertised price. It is a magnificent accessory for the modern home or the contemporary office, as practical as it is handsome. The clock is 20 inches high and keeps accurate time for one year on just one battery. It is our own exclusive import. We are located at 779 Bush Street, between Mason and Powell, and we are open daily (except Sunday) from 10:00 to 6:00. So, please do come and visit us. There is a "catch": we must ask you to bring this card for the special discount on the Acrylic Pendulum Clock and for the special bonus that we describe on the reverse side of this card.
henniker's
779 Bush Street, (between Mason & Powell)
San Francisco, CA 94120 (Ph. 433-7540)
Please turn this card for special premium during this month.

Another example of how we cultivate and ''pamper'' our hometown customers. We have a monthly ''special'' just for them and send them this kind of postcard. There is always a ''special offer'' limited in time, and a little freebie for all who take advantage of this offer. It really works and further helps in cementing the relationship with our store area customers and keeping our retail store profitable.

There is no need to run through the arithmetic once more, but let me just say that, at Henniker's, our store sales, because of this special emphasis we are giving the retail store, are now about 10% of our total sales. Not all of it is a bed of roses. There are many difficulties in this business, but the store is a key part of what we are doing and a very important contributor to our profits.

Go back a few pages and see how we arrived at store profits and you can apply these figures to your own situation. It is very helpful. There is no reason at all why you should not be as successful with your store as we are with ours.

One final word about stores: you will find your retail store business so attractive and so profitable that you will soon consider opening several additional stores.

At Haverhill's, we finally had four retail stores — three in the San Francisco Bay Area and one in Beverly Hills. All of them did well. At Henniker's, we are now seriously considering putting a second store either into the East Bay (Berkeley/Oakland) or on the Peninsula — Palo Alto or San Jose.

But before you think about opening a second store or additional stores, keep the following points in mind:

- In contrast to your first store, where you had to compromise on location, all subsequent stores should be in prime shopping locations — shopping centers are very good.
- Unless you are in a very large city (New York, Chicago, Los Angeles), do not put your second store in the same city. You will partly have the same clientele and it will take business away from your main store.
- Do, however, put your second store within, say, 50 miles of your main office. This will enable you to give it periodic supervision and make the logistics of merchandise delivery, etc. workable. Typically, it would mean that your main store and office would be, as planned, in a downtown location. Your second store would be typically in a suburban shopping center.
- Your expenses for the second store will be proportionately much larger than for your main store. Because in your main store, you could get by with one salesperson and when she took a break or when things became very busy, someone

from the office crew could help out. Also, all "overhead services" were borne by the main office operation. In a second store, you have to provide for adequate staffing, which means having at least two people on duty at all times.

- Before you proceed, take a sharp pencil and figure realistically all of your expenses — including the amortization of improvements that you have to provide. Then make a reasonable assumption as to what your sales may be. You will not get as much fallout from advertising for your second store, of course, as you will for your first store, because the address won't be routinely mentioned in your mail-order advertising. So you will have to rely mostly on local advertising and on walk-in trade. You should be prepared to run at break-even or even at a slight loss in your first year. If you can project profits for your second year, go ahead!
- Do not, except under the most unusual circumstances, consider a location in another city, for your second store. Certainly do not think of it during the time span of five or six years that we are talking about in this book. Supervision, supply of merchandise, investment of management time and other services that such a store would require would be out of proportion with anything you could possibly accomplish.

I don't know if I have been able to make a complete storekeeper out of you in this one chapter. I just want to impress upon you that a retail store in a mail-order business is almost a necessity. More than a necessity, you will find it to be a very substantial source of profit if properly organized and if properly run.

Our next chapter deals with two rather unrelated but, I think, very important topics: how to control your inventory and what to do about the wholesale and premium businesses. I think you'll get some new and important ideas, so please read on.

Chapter 7

HOW TO CONTROL INVENTORY

WHAT TO DO ABOUT THE WHOLESALE AND PREMIUM BUSINESSES

There are a couple of other things I think we should talk about that don't quite fit into any of the other chapters so I have put them together in this one. In a way they could be classified under "Odds and Ends" but they are deserving of your attention.

INVENTORY AND SALES

Quite obviously, you will have to carry inventory to fill the orders received from your customers. There will be a few items, mostly because of their weight or because they are customized or because they are very expensive, that will be drop shipped by the manufacturer. But, in any normally run mail-order business, they will play only a very small over-all role. You will fill your customers' orders from stock. In order to do this properly and to avoid the problems of backorder situations you will have to carry adequate inventory. And if your merchandise line consists of several hundred items, inventory can very easily become a major proposition.

The inventory problem will get aggravated as you discontinue merchandise items — do no longer advertise them in space or no longer carry them in your catalog. You can quickly acquire a load of "white elephants" that are a drag on your financial liquidity.

While we are on this topic: how much inventory should you carry in relation to yearly sales? This, as many other things, is difficult to generalize. It depends on a number of factors, such as sources of supply (leadtime), profit margin, number of items carried, seasonality, and some more. In the kind of business I run and which I visualize for you, I think in terms of not less than 6-times turnover per year.

What does that mean? It means that if you have sales of, say, $500,000 per year and if your profit margin is, let's say, 55%, these sales will represent an inventory value of $225,000. And if your inventory is one-sixth of that, or about $37,500, you have a turnover of 6-times. Any time your turnover is less than that, you are likely to have an inventory problem, and it behooves you to pinpoint that problem and to remedy it. If turnover is more than 6-times you are likely to be all right. The higher your turnover of inventory, the better of course — provided that you can still fill your orders without any undue delay.

But even within a given business, things are never quite that cut-and-dried. Because when you look at that over-all turnover factor, you cannot locate possible trouble spots — inventory that is languishing and not moving at all. The reason for that is that some of your merchandise, just a few items — likely making up a large percentage of your total sales — have a very fast turnover, perhaps even as high as 20 to 30 times a year or more. These fast movers tend to mask the sluggards, of course.

You must get rid of merchandise that doesn't move. You cannot afford to keep it gathering more dust. And that is not just advisable, but a survival necessity if you deal in perishables (food) or items subject to fashion (clothing).

There are a number of ways to get rid of merchandise. Let's talk about the most important.

Sales

We have already talked about the "mini-sales" that we have in our store about once or twice a month, usually on five or six related items. Their purpose is solely to generate store traffic. They have nothing to do with what we are talking about now. What we are talking about now is how to liquidate obsolete or excess merchandise. Once a year, usually in early September and about a month before our Christmas catalog mailing, we have our great Clearance Sale. In its way, it has become a minor merchandising event in San

Francisco. Our customers write us and phone us to find out when the Sale will take place. We have heard of people (I don't think there are too many of them) who have changed their vacations so as to not miss the Sale.

We usually have the Sale in our warehouse. Our store could not handle the throng of people. Also, the warehouse, apart from being able to hold the merchandise, provides the no-nonense, pipe-rack, down-to-the-essentials atmosphere that a successful Sale should have. There are no amenities, little help, everybody picks up what he needs and lines up at the check-out counter. But everything is well displayed, usually one item unpacked, the rest in boxes — and clearly marked, both with its catalog price and the Sale price. The Sale price is usually 30% to 40% off list, in some cases 50% or even more. It depends on how heavily we are stocked in a given item and what our own profit margin is. We never price anything below cost. We put everything on Sale that we shall not be carrying over into the new catalog, all odds and ends, samples, one-of-a-kinds, damaged and returned merchandise. We try to move it all.

We start our Sale on a Saturday and reserve that date exclusively for our San Francisco Bay Area customers, and not the general public. We think it is important to prefer our established customers and to show them — by giving them that preference — how important they are to us. Have a look at the invitational post-card that we send them. They *really* have to bring it to be admitted, although we do not make an undue fuss, of course, if somebody should forget it. An almost unbelievable 10% to 15% of the customers that we contact show up for the Sale. Most of them come on Saturday.

The Sale lasts a week. The week preceding the Sale, we run three ads in the *San Francisco Chronicle/Examiner* telling the general public about the Sale. I show you the reproduction of our Sale ad. Note that, as far as the general public is concerned, the Sale starts on Sunday, and Sunday is usually as wild as Saturday. The rest of the week is a little tamer.

We usually dispose of about 70% to 80% of the merchandise that we have put up for Sale and we help things along by "slashing" an extra 10% off on the last day. Then we let some local retailers in and let them pick out what they want and give them a discount off

779 Bush Street,
Box 7584, San Francisco, CA 94120 **henniker's**

yes, you can now do most of your Christmas shopping at remarkable savings. Because we are putting on sale all of our merchandise that we shall not continue in our 1978 catalog. These are beautiful things, featured in our 1977 catalog.

Why do we discontinue them? Because we are committed to replace at least one-half of all merchandise every year So there are many wonderful things that we cannot take along into the new catalog. And then there are "singles", samples, one-of-a-kind's—all brand new and up-to-date merchandise. Everything is marked down, minimum of 33⅓%—most of it 40%, 50% or even more. And everything put up for sale must go! Because our storage space is very limited and we have to make room for our 1978 merchandise.

This sale, on Saturday, September 10, is just for you, our mailing list preferred customers. Sale will continue through Friday, September 16, for the public at large. Pickings are going to be best on Saturday, September 10th. So come on that day and come early. Be sure to bring this card for identification and admittance.

SALE WILL BE AT OUR DOWNTOWN WAREHOUSE
771 Bush Street (next to our store)
between Mason & Powell
Sale Hours: 10:00 AM to 5:00 PM

All Sales are final—No mail or phone orders for this sale.
Ample parking available (minimal charge).

● **THIS IS A PRIVATE SALE. BE SURE TO BRING THIS CARD FOR ADMITTANCE!**

This is the kind of invitation to our Yearly Sale that we send to all of our San Francisco Bay Area customers. The first day Saturday, is reserved just for them. The card is required for admittance. An astonishing percentage of our local customers show up for the Sale — as many as 10 to 15%

Hurry, last days, today thru Friday!
SALE
Come to our Annual
Clearance Sale
and do your Christmas shopping at savings of up to 50% or more. All merchandise not continued in our 1978 catalog must go. Also, many samples, one-of-a-kind — brand new and up-to-date merchandise. Sale days:
Sunday — September 11 through
Friday, September 16
daily from 10 to 5.
henniker's
Sale will be held at 771 Bush St.
(next to our store) between Mason & Powell
No mail or phone orders for this sale, please
All sales are final
Ample Parking
(minimal charge)

We advertise our Yearly Sale in our hometown paper, THE SAN FRANCISCO CHRONICLE-EXAMINER. We run at least three ads, before and during the Sale. For the general public, the Sale starts on Sunday, one day after the day reserved for our established customers. We usually sell between 70 to 80% of all Sale merchandise and dispose of the balance in some other way.

list of 50% to 60%. In my old Haverhill's days, when I dealt with more heroic quantities of merchandise and dollars than I do now, I used to pick out the merchandise that I felt we ought to keep and then called in three "liquidators" who would bid against each other for anything that was left. The high bid would usually be about 20% of sales price or 40% to 50% below cost. But I thought it was worthwhile to get rid of the stuff even at a loss — we are talking only about the last remnant, a fraction of our total inventory — to transform deadwood into at least some money and make a new start.

If you have a store or, better yet, an accessible warehouse, you should *definitely* have a yearly Sale for the customers in your area. You will not just attain your immediate objective to liquidate merchandise, but you will also get your customers more involved with you. That is, of course, what you want.

I have experimented with Sale by mail — including package inserts informing about items available on a discount basis. I don't find it too successful and I have abandoned it. The reasons were primarily these:

- A Sale, in order to be successful and serve its purpose, has to be on a no-return, no-refund basis. It is not easily possible or even advisable to sell merchandise by mail on that basis. And if you should allow returns, you have partly defeated the purpose of the Sale. If merchandise comes back, you have to determine whether the customer bought at full price or at Sale. That is quite a bit of trouble and it is hardly worth it.
- There is the problem of being out of stock of the Sale item that the mail-order customer might want. Naturally, it has to be on a first-come/first-served basis. That makes people unhappy, they often wish to cancel the whole order if you cannot supply one item. Bookkeeping and labor is involved for the items no longer in stock. Again, it isn't worth the trouble.

We do make one "exception" if you wish to call it that. Our catalogs usually carry a few items at steep discounts, displayed as "extra specials." These are items that are "staple merchandise," are now moving slowly and with which we are substantially overstocked. Our customers have seen these items, for years perhaps, in our catalogs and recognize a good value when they see it. And I think that it helps the catalog to sprinkle a few such "price nuggets" throughout.

Gift-of-the-Month Club

While Sales are the most feasible way to move excess or obsolete merchandise, it is not the only way. At Haverhill's, we developed the concept of *Gift-of-the-Month Club.*

It is a concept that was very successful, but you have to have at least the size of Haverhill's (over $10 million sales per year) to make it really feasible. You are not going to be there for a while, so this concept is not immediately applicable to you. It is just something to put in your idea file for later use.

We recruited members for the Club by three means: 1. By space advertising, mostly in *Time* Magazine; 2. By package inserts to our own customers; and 3. By circularizing our own and outside lists by mail.

I don't have the exact numbers on hand, but I believe that we had about 5,000 members before I stopped recruiting. The club operated roughly on the same principle as book clubs, including the so-called "negative option." Members got a gift to join and, in joining, purchased an initial selection. Their "obligation" was to purchase a minimum of three selections per year. Most fulfilled that obligation, and many did better than that. But, of course, it is an "obligation" that is impossible to enforce, and only feeble attempts should be made in that direction.

The point of telling you all this in this context is that I found it to be a feasible way to move merchandise. In fact (and not surprisingly), it turned out, of course, that we actually had to make special purchases for "surprises" for club members. In other words, our excess inventory soon turned out not to be sufficient for the purpose. But to repeat: this is a technique that you won't be able to use successfully until you have attained a pretty good size. At that stage of Haverhill's development, we had a mailing list of approximately 800,000 names.

Surprise Packages

There is, however, a way to dispose of merchandise at a lower level of activity. That is something that you might try in your first

add some pizzazz to your life...

Join me as a member of Haverhill's Surprise of the Month Club and I'll send you this practical and handsome Money Clip/ Credit Card Wallet with my compliments. Your obligation as a Club member is to accept three "surprise gifts" during the first year of membership.

My name is Gerardo Joffe. I'm president of Haverhill's. And at Haverhill's we think a lot about how to add pizzazz to the lives of our customers and friends

After a lot of cogitating we have come up with what we think is a perfect solution—**the Haverhill's Surprise Gift of the Month Club.** Here is how it works Right off the bat we are going to send you one of our practical Money Clip Credit Card Wallets This exceedingly handsome wallet is finished in the most supple kid skin It lists in our catalog at $9 95 (although some of our competitors sell very similar ones for $20 or more). It is our gift to you . . . just for joining the Club and for fulfilling the membership obligation

HOW ARE WE GOING TO MAKE YOUR LIFE MORE ZIPPY? Every month we are going to send you a surprise gift What kind of surprise can you expect? Well, one month's surprise might be a fine Watch, next month's might be an exquisite Danish Teak Toast and Jam Set, or there might be a Stainless Steel Salad Bowl, a set of good Steak Knives, an Optical Instrument and many, many more things Whatever it is—it's going to be a surprise a top-notch quality item, the kind of thing you will be delighted to have (or give as a gift to a favored friend) But it will also be the kind of thing that you might not be likely to buy for yourself or even find if you were to look for it

Some of the things we are going to send you will be listed in our Catalog but most will have been especially created for Club members And here—beyond the thrill and surprise of getting a "mystery" gift every month—is where the real hard-buck advantage of membership in the Club comes in Because here is our promise to you The list price of any "surprise" that you are going to receive is going to be **at least 50%** higher than what you will be billed for. An item for which you will be charged $10 will list for **at least $15** in our Catalog or, if it isn't a Catalog item, that is what you could expect to pay

HOW DO YOU ENROLL—HOW DO YOU PAY FOR MERCHANDISE? This must be the easiest club in the world to join. Just jot down which of the four great introductory gifts you want as your first surprise . . . at the special Club membership price Then, every month, we'll drop you a note telling you what your next surprise is going to be and what it's going to cost Chances are you'll be delighted with our suggestion But if you aren't, you can notify us on a form that we'll provide and that'll be that.

By the way it is just as easy to quit the Club as to join it. Your only obligation is to accept and pay for three surprise gifts during the first year of your membership. After that, if you don't continue to be delighted, you may simply send us a note asking us to cancel your membership and it will be done immediately. And, of course, if any of the surprise gifts should fail to please you, you may return them for prompt cancellation of all charges

LIVE A LITTLE—BECOME A MEMBER TODAY!
Enjoyment is the sum of many little things. Membership in **Haverhill's Surprise Gift of the Month Club** will add a real dash of romance to your life. You don't take any risk, because, except for your introductory purchase, you'll never have to pay beforehand and you're always the only judge If at any time you don't think that membership in the Club gives you what you had hoped for, simply tell us and that is that

But do let us hear from you today Let us send you the welcome-to-the-Club gift, that super-handsome wallet. Pick your first month's surprise from our selection, at the special membership price.

Welcome to the Club!

1 LITTLE BLOW HARD
Italian fan Moves astonishing amount of air Plastic body Blades can't hurt baby or pet Hang or stand up 7" tall 6" blades, 110V Reg $12 95
Members price $8.

2 DIGITAL COMPUTER WATCH
is a new concept in showing time Fine Swiss movement and gold finished case Shows days, hours and minutes in separate windows Reg $16 95
Members price $11.

3 SATELLITE WEATHER STATION
brass and lucite sphere 3½" German quality baro, thermo and hygrometer Stand or suspend like satellite in orbit Reg $32 95
Members price $21.50.

4 TRAVELERS COMPANION
is a fine AM battery radio/alarm and a valet for jewelry One hour doze shut-off Built-in alarm wakes you next morning 6"x 4"x 2" Reg $29 95
Members price $19.00.

Yes, I wish to become a member of **Haverhill's Surprise Gift of the Month Club**, in accordance with the conditions explained in this ad. As my introductory gift I am going to receive a kid leather money clip/credit card wallet As my first selection I choose [1] [2] [3] [4] (Circle your choice)
I enclose my check for the special member's price indicated, plus $1 for post. & insur. (Calif resid. add tax.)

☐ Please add handsome chrome initials (__________) to my wallet. I am adding $3 to my remittance

Name ____________________
Address ____________________
____________________ Zip ________

584 Washington
San Francisco
94111

haverhill's

266-1

We founded a "Surprise of the Month Club" at Haverhill's, when we had about 800,000 customers. It was a successful way to dispose of overstocked merchandise. The Club worked on the same basis as a book club, including the "negative option" principle. This is a great way to dispose of merchandise and to create customer loyalty. You cannot use this technique successfully if you do not have a mailing list of, say, at least 500,000 current customers.

years of operation — either in addition to a Sale or instead of a Sale. It is the offering of "surprise packages."

Quite a few mail-order houses offer such "surprise packages" in their catalogs. They usually come at different price levels and promise merchandise value substantially in excess (a minimum percentage is often given) of the amount charged. And, of course, the customer has the right to return the "surprise" if he is not pleased. But, if you play the game straight, if you provide good merchandise at really good prices, you will have very few returns. One thing about mail-order buyers: they love to get things in the mail (of course!), and they do love to get surprises. If you make it your job to see that they get full value and that they will not be disappointed, you should be able to move quite a bit of merchandise by this method.

We never did follow this route at Haverhill's, I suppose, because we never failed to get rid of all of our excess merchandise by the other methods we have talked about. We have now started doing it at Henniker's, and first results are just about as good as we had expected. Have a look at our "Trust Me" letter. It has a nice person-to-person touch. Since you don't ever really get to see most of your customers, you want to "personalize" your correspondence and all your dealings with them as much as possible. And a warm personal letter like this one and a picture of the person who makes him/herself responsible does help to establish an additional bond.

The point of this whole story is that you must watch your inventory carefully. You must watch for proper turnover of the entire inventory and of specific items. It is very important, because you can tie up a whole lot of money in useless inventory. Your balance sheet and your profit and loss might look good, but if your inventory figures hide soft spots, it is up to you to locate them and to eliminate them. And these methods are the way to do it.

There may be other ways to dispose of excess merchandise successfully and at a small profit, rather than at a loss. These three have proven to be the most practical for me and for other mail-order operators. The yearly Sale is perhaps the most important, certainly in my own experience.

WHOLESALE AND PREMIUM BUSINESS

The other "odd and end" I want to talk about in this chapter is that of selling merchandise in quantity — in ways other than retail.

Trust me!

henniker's
779 Bush St., Box 7584
San Francisco, CA 94120

My name is Anne Finnegan and I am Henniker's Warehouse and Shipping Manager. Even in these enlightened times it is a rather unusual job for a woman. But my boss trusts me. You can trust me too!

My biggest warehouse problem is shelf space. Our Merchandise Manager, Priscilla Joffe, has one bright idea after another about new things to add to our line, but it's up to me to find room for it all. Since I have only so much shelf space, something has to give. The only way to solve my problem is to dispose, even at a loss, of some of the perfectly fine merchandise that we have to phase out in order to make room for the new.

And here is where I had my "bright idea". I have made up a number of "surprise packages", each containing various items of our merchandise--all things that are featured either in our current catalog or in catalogs immediately before it. The merchandise is factory fresh, of course. There are optical goods, travel items, gourmet ware, automotive gadgets, jewelry, decorative accessories -- just about the full range of what we handle. Each package typically contains three items or more.

I have two sizes of surprise packages: "The Big Surprise" which costs $12.50 and which contains merchandise with catalog value of at least $20 (but probably more); and "The Enormous Surprise", which costs $25.00 and contains merchandise with catalog value of at least $45.00 (but probably more).

I think that I can assure you that you will be very pleased with my surprises -- either the "big" one or the "enormous" one. You will find items that you would have liked to order for yourself or as a gift -- but perhaps didn't feel quite like paying the full price for. You'll be getting very nice things at very much of a bargain price.

continued on reverse

Our "Trust Me" promotion, featuring our warehouse manager, Anne Finnegan, and offering the "Big Surprise" and the "Enormous Surprise" turned out to be an inspired merchandising gambit. It moves lots of goods. Our customers seem to love it. The "secret" of success in this method lies, of course, in really giving honest value — and having the customer be pleasantly surprised, rather than terribly disappointed.

you get? Simple: just return it to my
you will get full refund or credit
ake only two "conditions":

u are not 100% pleased with your
urn the entire surprise package --
f it;

se package, you may not order another
onths.

?

hat about guarantees on the surprise
Here's the answer: everything you
arantee as anything else you buy from
us at regular prices.

Fill out and detach the order form and let me send you one of my surprise packages. You will be very pleased. Trust me!

Cordially yours,

Anne Finnegan

Anne Finnegan

PS: Would you like to send a surprise package to a friend? Tell me your friend's preferences and I'll try to put something together and will include a nice gift card for you. I won't let you down. I'll make you look very good.

Mail to: Anne Finnegan, Warehouse Manager
Henniker's, 779 Bush St., Box 7584
San Francisco, CA 94120

ok, anne...

I trust you, although I am "hedging" my bet by your guarantee and ground rules. Send me:

○ "Big Surprise Packages" @ $12.50 each

○ "Enormous Surprise Packages" @ $25.00 each

☐ My check for this amount plus $1.50 per package for postage and insurance, (plus sales tax for California delivery) is enclosed.

☐ Charge my BA/MC account number________________ exp.______

My name is________________________________
I live at__________________________________
In____________________ State__________ Zip__________

Please send "Surprise" to addressee shown on attached note

This field may be divided into two sections, namely *wholesale* and *premium.* Let's talk about them separately.

The *wholesale business,* as I define it, is to sell merchandise to others, usually other retailers, other mail-order houses or to people who sell merchandise door-to-door or by some other means. Naturally, you can do this only with merchandise on which you have some kind of "exclusive," that you import or manufacture yourself and on which you, therefore, have a greater than usual profit margin. You need that extra margin, because, naturally, those who buy from you need to make a profit also. Forty percent discount from the established retail price is usually about the maximum you can charge a wholesale buyer (or a "re-seller," if you prefer). If your original retail profit margin was, say, 60%, you will have a 33-1/3% profit margin after granting the 40% discount. That would be acceptable.

I used to go after this business by advertising in trade media, exhibiting in gift shows and by direct mail solicitations. Inevitably, quite a bit of business came in, and still does (unsolicited). But I do not do it anymore, and I discourage most of the unsolicited business that we receive. The reason is that it is a business of "onesies and twosies," there are many returns, claims for malfunction and for breakage, and a rather heavy bad debt problem. In short, I have come to the conclusion that it simply isn't worth the bother. My advice to you is to stay away from this kind of business, and for the same reasons. I think you would find that any possible profits would be eaten up by bad debts.

We have been reasonably successful in a rather specialized form of wholesale selling. We would take a product in which we had a good profit margin, for instance our Swiss Army Style Knife. We would address a direct mail campaign to selected retailers whose names and labels we would get from special list compilers, who are concentrated in New York City. In the case of the Swiss Army Style Knife, for instance, we would address hardware stores, tobacconists and drug stores. We would offer twelve knives on a "guaranteed sales" basis — no money up front. This means that the customer would get the merchandise simply on his signature. The package would include a very nice point-of-sale display unit that we had designed. He could pay for the merchandise within 30 days or return the balance with payment for those that had been sold.

swiss army style knife

Yes, it's true . . . you should be able
to make minimum of at least
$50 NET EVERY WEEK – week after week
(and without any work or investment
or risking a single penny!) . . .

Dear Dealer:

Our **Swiss Army Knife** is the kind of gadget that every man wants and needs. It is almost a universal "pocket tool kit." **It is the real old classic,** 3½ inches long, red baked-on enamel, and it contains **eleven stainless blades and tools – from knife and corkscrew, manicurer,** scissors, saw . . . to fish scaler and hook disgorger. As our advertising says, ". . . anything you cannot fix with it may well be beyond repair."

Swiss Army Style Knife is manufactured exclusively for us and to our own stringent specifications. Please do not confuse this quality unit with inferior imitations. The unit is distinctly and handsomely boxed. Your customers have seen our advertising on **Swiss Army Style Knife** in such national media as **The New Yorker, The New York Times Magazine, Wall Street Journal, The National Observer, Christian Science Monitor** and many more.

Similar knives have been on the market for years, at prices up to $39.95. There never has been a quality knife like this for just $9.95. Since we brought **Swiss Army Style Knife** on the market it has become one of our great sales successes.

We would like for you to share in this success. Please allow us to send you:

- Our handsome point of sale display unit
- One dozen **Swiss Army Style Knives** which you will place in the display unit
- One-half dozen belt-looped vinyl carry cases for **Swiss Army Style Knife**
- Slick proof of ad 2 x 67 lines for your local paper (just like the one shown on back of this mailer).

You don't have to send us any money now. We would like to ship this to you on a **30-days guaranteed sale basis.** That means: Set this up in your store, close to the cash register where people can see it. Watch your **Swiss Army Style Knives** move. With any traffic at all you should sell your first dozen in a week. But, if for any reason at all, you should not have sold your first dozen **Swiss Army Knives** within 30 days, simply return the display unit and the **Swiss Army Knives** that you have left, and **you pay only for those that you have sold.**

Swiss Army Style Knife has an absolutely protected retail price of $9.95. The optional belt-looped carry case retails for $2.95. Your basic discount is 40%. If you run an ad in your local paper, we shall give you an extra 5% advertising allowance. That means that you net over $4.25 per unit. Since we are confident that you will sell at least one dozen **Swiss Army Style Knives** per week, this will give you over $50 extra profit per week. And this does not even consider profit on carry-cases – our experience is that at least two customers in three want that nifty belt-looped pouch.

Give this terrific profit-building program a try – **without any risk at all.** Detach the bottom part of this letter, fill it out and **return it to us today.** We will send you a complete **Swiss Army Style Knife** package immediately. You will be glad you did – and remember: **send no money, take no chance – the risk is on us.**

Sincerely yours,

Gerardo Joffe
President

This is the kind of specialized wholesale business in which we are reasonably successful. This is the campaign for the Swiss Army Style Knife and the point-of-sale display units that we make available to participating merchants. We conduct similar campaigns with other merchandise.

We did quite well with this program. But here, too, we found that we had bad debt problems and much correspondence, billings and adjustments over comparatively small potatoes. While these programs — there were quite a few of them in the course of the years — were very much more successful than selling assorted merchandise to retailers, we still found it to be a rather unattractive business and let it fizzle out.

All in all, I am not enchanted with the wholesale part of the mail-order business. I think you would have the same experience. You will get many requests from those who will want to sell your merchandise. My advice is not to get too involved, unless the circumstances are exceptional. But every once in a while a wholesale customer approaches you and wants to buy $400 or $500 worth of merchandise for which he wishes to pay on the spot. Naturally, we do go ahead and fill such an order. This is an "exceptional" circumstance.

The *premium business,* however, is a different kettle of fish altogether. In case you are not familiar with the term "premium," let me see if I can define what it is. It is a rather encompassing term that takes in all kinds of purposes in which merchandise is either given away, used as "self-liquidators" (those that use it for that purpose just want to get part or all of their money back, not make a profit), executive gifts, employee incentives, and scores of other uses.

The beauty of the premium business as far as you and I are concerned is that you are almost always dealing with large and substantial firms. You will usually get orders for a nice round quantity of the same item, which you can ship in bulk to one address, or which you may be asked to drop ship to a gift list. In that case (in addition to regular postage) you would be expected and justified to add a "drop ship charge" that more than compensates you for your out-of-pocket expense for labor and packing materials. And, best of all, you are now dealing with substantial revenues, and you don't have to spend one sleepless night worrying about getting paid.

I love the premium business and only regret that I don't do as much with it as I should and could. When I had a little more time to give to it, I used to have a booth at the yearly Chicago and New York Premium Shows. They are good business getters. My suggestion

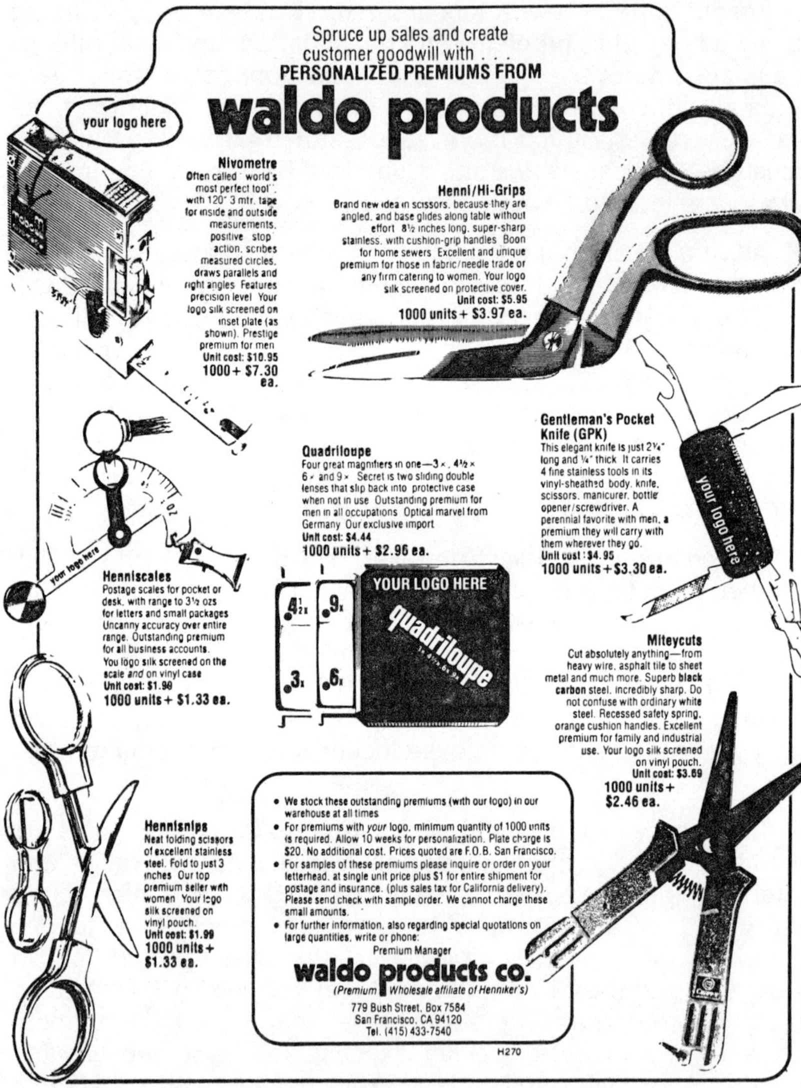

If you form a premium/wholesale division it is not a bad idea to give it a separate name. We call ours "Waldo Products (Premium/Wholesale Affiliate of Henniker's)." This ad features "personalized" items which are especially attractive in the premium field. This kind of ad runs in THE WALL STREET JOURNAL and other business media.

is that, as soon as you feel that you can afford it — and provided that your merchandise line is sufficiently unique and competitive to lend itself to it — you go after the premium business. You can do that initially by taking a booth at either of the two premium shows. If you have no geographical preference, the New York Show might be better for you, but the Chicago Show isn't too far behind.

In the last few years, building Henniker's from a cold start to its present position, I had to neglect the premium business and I really regret that. Something had to give and it turned out to be the premium business. Try to do better than that, because there is real pay dirt there. It takes some digging to be successful, but it should be well worth your while and will provide you with an unexpected source of profit.

Even though I haven't been as active in the premium business in the last few years as I should have been and would like to have been, we still do a steady premium business. All of it comes in "over the transom" or, if you prefer, unsolicited. We get orders from many large companies from all over the country, who buy in quantity, either for their internal use or for bona fide premium purposes, and we get many inquiries about premium sales. In order to save time and to provide uniformity, we reply to such inquiries with a form letter of which I show you copy. In fact, there are two versions, namely one for "promotional" and one for "real" merchandise.

Since we haven't been soliciting premium business lately, we get most of our unsolicited business through satisfied customers. These people may be executives in charge of such programs for their companies or they are in a position to suggest to others what should be done. Treat all of your customers right! You should anyway, of course. But you can never tell which of these anonymous people may be the one who will steer an unexpected $5,000 premium order your way on which you are going to make an unbudgeted "bottom line profit" of $1,500 or $2,000. And after you have opened envelopes all day containing checks for $15 or $20, to find one for $3,000 or $5,000 is a great source of joy.

To summarize:

- Forget about the wholesale business. It is more trouble that it is worth.

henniker's
779 Bush St., Box 7584, San Francisco, CA 94120
Tel. (415) 433-7540

Thank you for your inquiry about our wholesale discounts on the item indicated above.

The following discounts apply to all merchandise (except "promotional items", i.e. items selling for less than $2). For those items we do not import directly, refer to Group B below:

Group A:	25 minimum to 48 units	list less 20%
	49 to 144 units	list less 25%
	144 units, plus	list less 33-1/3% (maximum discount)

For those items that we do not import directly, the following discount schedule applies:

Group B:	25 minimum to 48 units	list less 15%
	49 to 144 units	list less 20%
	144 units, plus	list less 25% (maximum discount)

All prices are FOB San Francisco.

The item you selected pertains to Group_____.

The above discounts are essentially for premium accounts. If you want this merchandise for bonafide resale purposes, we might be able to make different arrangements from case to case. If this is indeed your situation, please let us know.

Please excuse this form letter. We get many inquiries of this kind and this is the fastest way to serve our customers.

We hope we may be of service to you. Please call us if we may be of any further assistance.

Sincerely yours,

Chris Simpson
Chris Simpson
Customer Service

GB-4

You will get many inquiries from those who wish to buy in quantity. Reply by form letter! We have two such forms, for "regular" merchandise (above) and for "promos" (below). We divide "regular" merchandise into two categories — "A" and "B" — the former being merchandise that we import ourselves (and have larger profit spans), and the latter being merchandise that we buy in the United States.

henniker's
779 Bush St., Box 7584, San Francisco, CA 94120
Tel (415) 433-7540

Item:
Retail Price:

Thank you for inquiring about quantity purchases of the above "promotional" item(s).

As you can well imagine, this is essentially a profitless item for us, because its main (and perhaps only) purpose is to make friends and customers for our company. Even so, in sufficient quantities, modest discounts are possible.

Discount schedule would be as follows:

100 to 500 units	Less 20%
501 to 1000 units	Less 25%
1000 units +	Less 30% (maximum discount)

Quantity discounts are the same for all promotional items.

If you wish a sample of any promotional item not yet in your possessionm please send us the amount indicated above plus $.50 for postage and handling.

We have many inquiries regarding personalization. The following apply:

1. Personalization is impractical unless quantity is minimum 1000
2. Personalization takes time -- count on minimum of 8 weeks.
3. Some items, because of the material of which they are made, cannot practically be personalized. Others can be personalized conveniently only on the cover or pouch.
4. For the item above, the following applies:

I hope this is the information you need and that I shall be hearing from you.

Sincerely yours,

Chris Simpson
Chris Simpson
Customer Services

CS - 69

- Make a real effort to develop the premium business. It is a good source of additional revenue and an easy and pleasant way to make extra dollars.

After this excursion into "odds and ends" we are now getting back on the main track. In the next chapter, we are going to talk about the rather important topic of data processing. As you will see, it is difficult — you might say impossible, to run a successful mail-order business without it.

Chapter 8

HOW TO PUT DATA PROCESSING TO BEST USE

Once you are in the mail-order business, you will be deeply enmeshed in data processing.

Even if you have never had any experience with data processing before, you will soon become very familiar with it. It will be your main tool.

I often wonder how, in the old days, such large companies as Sears, Ward's and others got along without data processing. The volume of work and the number of clerks that they would have had to employ must have been staggering.

Data processing, if you use it properly and if you make it your servant, rather than your master, will make your life fairly simple.

You will be able to get a great deal of work done, keep good controls and keep track of all of your orders and of all of your customers. And, considering what you are accomplishing, it is all really done with very little work on your part.

Most of it will be done for you by the "Almighty Computer."

In working with data processing and with computers, you must keep in mind that the information you get out will never be any better than the information that you put in. If you put in poor data, you will get poor information. Or, as the truism has it, "garbage in, garbage out."

Data processing will do two principal jobs for you, which we shall talk about in some detail. They are:

1. Order processing.
2. Master file maintenance.

ORDER PROCESSING

Regardless of what kind of data processing system you will be using, or which processing firm you employ, even at the very earliest stages of your mail-order life, all orders should be processed by computer. We shall see in a minute why this is important and why it is not as formidable as it may sound at first.

HOW YOU WILL GET YOUR ORDERS

Let's look at the typical mail-order coupon and let's see what information is provided that will be captured by the computer.

First of all, there is the name and address of the purchaser which will be directly copied by the "entry" operator, by keypunch or some equivalent method.

Then there is the merchandise order. In this case we shall assume that the customer orders two items, namely two of our Emoskop Vestpocket Optical Systems. We don't have to earmark the merchandise on the coupon, because all orders for this one item will be put into a single batch, the keypunch operator will punch one "header card," and all following orders will automatically be punched with the code for this particular piece of merchandise.

Unless it is especially brought to her attention, the keypunch operator will assume that the customer ordered only one unit. If, as in this case, the customer orders more than one unit, the mail clerk will circle the quantity and thus bring it to the keypunch operator's attention.

Another important piece of information that we mark (by circling it) is the Source Code. In this case, it's YN0910, which means that this ad appeared in *The New Yorker* Magazine of September 10. Each publication has its "publication code," which in the case of *The New Yorker,* happens to be YN. "0910" signifies September 10, and thus clearly defines the publication from which the coupon was clipped and the date on which it appeared.

There are also two additional pieces of information which we either put on the coupon, or which are understood by their absence. These are the *Payment Code* and the *Tax Code.*

For control purposes it is important for us to know how the customer paid, namely either by check (or equivalent), by BankAmericard, by MasterCharge, or whether he is being invoiced.

Mail to: **Henniker's** (YN0910)
779 Bush St., Box 7584, San Francisco, CA 94120
Yes, send me (2) **Emoskops** @ $24.95 ea.
☐ My check, plus $1 for post. and handling (and tax for Calif. deliv. only) is enclosed).
☒ Charge my BA, MC acct. (B2)
#4234-698-72316 exp. 6/78
or for fastest service call TOLL FREE (800) 648-5311
[IN NEVADA (800) 992-5710] IN SF BAY AREA CALL 433-7540
My name is JOE ROGERS
I live at 114 PRESIDIO LANE
City SANTA BARBARA State CA. Zip 93107

henniker's

DUMMY ORDER

DATE: 12/13/77

SEND TO: NAME FRANK A. CARLATTI
ADDRESS 355 ELM ST., APT. 14
CITY NEWARK STATE DE ZIP 19713

ITEM(S) 1 # 21055 MILIT. RADIO 19.95

NO LABEL

PHONE (302) 525-1187
BA/MC # 516 3219 864 32 EXP. 8/79

SOURCE: WE 1128 ORDER WRITTEN BY: C.S.

Two original entry media: on top, a typical mail-order coupon, such as you will receive in the mail. Since the quantity ordered is more than "1," it is circled for the attention of the keypunch operator. Source code YN0910 is also circled. In this case it stands for THE NEW YORKER, September 10 issue. Code "B2" shows that it is a BankAmericard transaction and that California Sales Tax (non-BART) applies. The bottom is a "dummy order" taken over the telephone. It will be hand processed, and the computer is therefore instructed to print "no label."

Each of these modes of payment has a code — cash being "A," BankAmericard "B," MasterCharge "C," and invoiced "D."

Most customers of course prepay by check and then we don't put any payment code on the coupon at all. The keypuncher understands that if no payment code appears she must punch "A."

Then there is a Tax Code. All merchandise that we ship outside of California is not subject to sales tax. All merchandise that we ship within California has to pay California sales tax. We have two different kinds of sales tax, namely one for the so-called BART counties (those served by the Bay Area Rapid Transit System) and one for all other California counties.

If no tax applies, the tax code is "1." If the "regular" California sales tax applies, it is "2," and if BART tax applies, it is "3."

Our data processing program has now been modified to compute the proper tax automatically. That is derived from the zip code of the address, so our entry clerk no longer has to enter it manually. This new method also gives us a statement for our sales tax payments to the state of California and all information needed in case of a sales tax audit.

In the coupon shown, the Code "B-2" is written in by the order clerk. This means that this customer paid by BankAmericard and that "regular" California sales tax applies.

These coupons, duly annotated as necessary, are our main input medium, and almost everything else follows from them.

We also have a "dummy" order form which we use either for telephone orders or when people write us a letter, telling us what they want or if, for some reason, a coupon is not available. I show you such a "dummy" form properly filled in.

You will notice that the dummy order, as shown, has "No Label" stamped across its face. This is an interesting concept that you should try to apply. We use that either for rush orders or for any special cases in which we want to short-cut the regular data processing procedure. In other words, we use it when we want to command the computer to go through all other steps, but not to print a label. In these cases, we hand-process the label, and get this order on the road immediately, without waiting several days for the computer to produce a label.

By the way, we use this "No Label" system also for our toll-free telephone service. These orders are processed immediately, because we do promise our customers that they get "fastest service by toll-free phone." Naturally, we want to keep our word. It adds a little to our work load, but we think it is worthwhile.

The "No Label" concept also applies to the store sales tickets, of course, and "No Label" is prominently printed across the face. I show you one of the tickets. We want our data processing system to record all store transactions. We need this for cash and inventory control and also to get the customer on our master file. But since the customer has already taken the merchandise home, we want to make very sure that no label is printed.

It would be awful if this were not done consistently and in a foolproof manner. Because each customer would then pick up the merchandise in the store, and if a label were printed, we would ship it again — a fast way to the poorhouse.

All store sales, by the way, have a conventional source code, namely YY0000. This source code is already preprinted on the sales ticket, and so is the tax code, because naturally, all sales that we make in San Francisco have to pay that BART sales tax.

WHAT YOU SHOULD GET FROM YOUR COMPUTER SERVICE

Depending on your volume of work, you will wish to deliver your input once or twice a week to your computer house. We deliver twice a week — Wednesday and Friday. The purpose of doing it twice a week is just to get the input processed quickly. Each work cycle and each recording cycle is one calendar week.

Having received input material on Wednesday and Friday, the computer house is able to process all of our work over the weekend. This gives complete results for the preceding week on Monday afternoon or on Tuesday morning following.

Here is what we usually get:

1. A complete Set of Labels.

These labels are computer-printed on a continuous form. They are in order of merchandise, with single units in each category being batched first and with multiple units following. The labels are in zip code order within each product category.

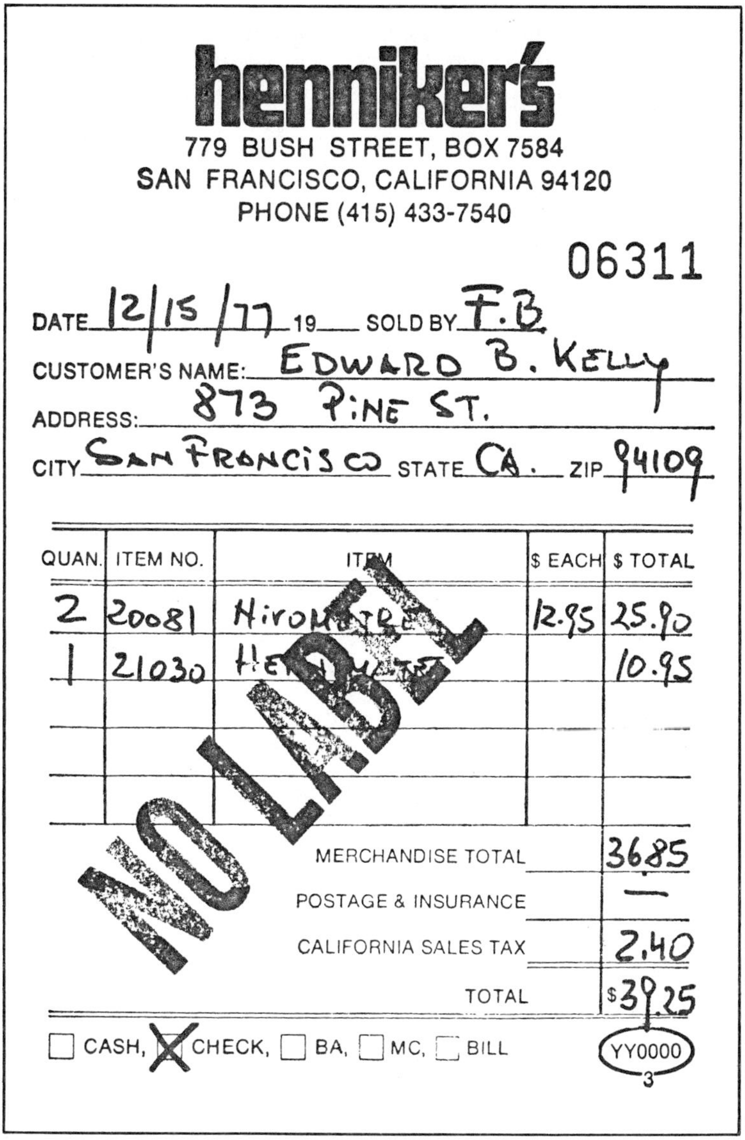

hennikers
779 BUSH STREET, BOX 7584
SAN FRANCISCO, CALIFORNIA 94120
PHONE (415) 433-7540

06311

DATE 12/15/77 19__ SOLD BY F.B
CUSTOMER'S NAME: EDWARD B. KELLY
ADDRESS: 873 PINE ST.
CITY SAN FRANCISCO STATE CA. ZIP 94109

QUAN.	ITEM NO.	ITEM	$ EACH	$ TOTAL
2	20081	Hiro[illegible]	12.95	25.90
1	21030	He[illegible]		10.95

MERCHANDISE TOTAL	36.85
POSTAGE & INSURANCE	—
CALIFORNIA SALES TAX	2.40
TOTAL	$39.25

NO LABEL

☐ CASH, ☒ CHECK, ☐ BA, ☐ MC, ☐ BILL

YY0000
3

Filled-in sales ticket also serves as original entry medium. It, too, is overprinted with the "No Label" designation. If this were not done, a customer could pick his purchase up in the store and might get a duplicate through the mail.

This is convenient, because it makes it easy to locate a customer. This sorting is mandatory for these items that we ship by "bulk mail." In those cases, the postal service has rather stringent rules of zip sorting, bundling, etc., but they do not concern us right now.

Some points about labels: in addition to the name and address, the label also carries the item to be shipped (spelled backward), the number of units to be shipped (nothing is printed in that space if there is only one unit), the item number (each item has a special computer control number), the order number (which is a sequential number) and the cycle date.

There are also multiple labels for those customers who order different categories of merchandise at one time — these are usually catalog orders. These multiple labels are computer printed in their entirety on a continuous strip, with the bottom of the strip being essentially a packing list. This tells the packer exactly what the order contains and when she is through packing, she cuts this part of the label off and puts it inside the package as a control for the customer.

2. Weekly Sales Listing by Item and Customer.

This record, of which I show you part of a sample page, lists all sales made in the same sequence as the labels themselves, only printed out in line format. There is one difference, however. It is that in this report *all orders* are shown — not just those for which labels have been printed, but also those that are "No Labels." As you can see, these are marked by the letter "N," which simply means that we ourselves have processed the label, rather than having had the computer print it.

This is an important point and an important record. Because it gives us control over what merchandise we have sold in a given week. Also, we can quickly address ourselves to a customer's inquiry about a specific piece of merchandise in the given week. It has quite a few other uses.

3. Weekly Sales Report by Item.

This report shows in a similar form how many units we have sold in each merchandise category and what the source of these sales were, etc.

hennikers
779 BUSH ST., BOX 7584, SAN FRANCISCO, CA. 94120

DR J BRINKLEY SPINSINNEH
1220 CENTRAL AVE *12*
GREAT FALLS MT 59405

59405BRINK122 G5 0 1216/00042*430713

hennikers
779 BUSH ST., BOX 7584, SAN FRANCISCO, CA. 94120

*BARCO INTERNATION SPINSINNEH
660 SOUTH MYERS STR *12*
LOS ANGELES CA 90023

90023BARCO660 G5 0 1216/00042*430718

hennikers
779 BUSH ST., BOX 7584, SAN FRANCISCO, CA. 94120
BULK RATE
US POSTAGE PAID
HENNIKERS

MR B JELLY REZINAGRO
171 HARRBEL ST
PITTSFIELD MA 01201

01201JELLY171 G5 0 1216/00331*430726

hennikers
779 BUSH ST. BOX 7584, SAN FRANCISCO, CA. 94120
BULK RATE
US POSTAGE PAID
HENNIKERS

MR M MODAN REZINAGRO
82 DAWES
PITTSFIELD MA 01201

01201MODAN82D G5 0 1216/00331*430728

String of computer produced labels. In addition to name and address, the customer's "matchcode" is printed out, date of order, item number and order number. Name of item to be shipped is printed out (spelled backward) and so is quantity, greater than "1." For certain merchandise, the bulk mail indicia is computer printed directly on the label.

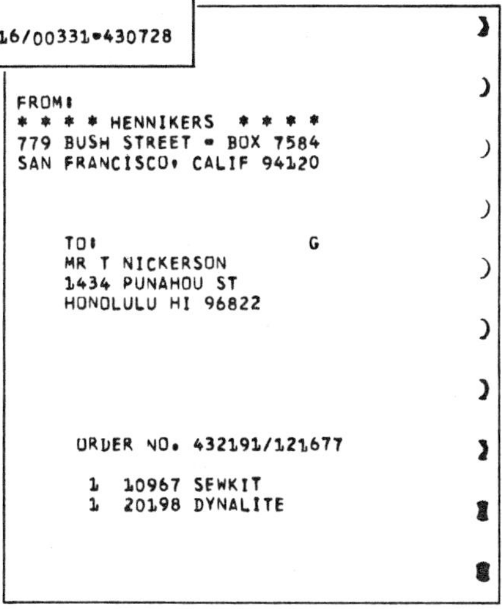

FROM:
* * * * HENNIKERS * * * *
779 BUSH STREET - BOX 7584
SAN FRANCISCO, CALIF 94120

TO: G
MR T NICKERSON
1434 PUNAHOU ST
HONOLULU HI 96822

ORDER NO. 432191/121677

1 10967 SEWKIT
1 20198 DYNALITE

Multiple labels are entirely computer printed. The bottom portion gets torn off and serves as packing slip.

There is a lot of information and a lot of meat in here. The most important thing for us is, of course, to see quickly which medium produced what results for any given merchandise category.

A summary line totals the entire activity of the week. It gives the financial information required to reconcile the actual bank deposit made during the week and what the deposit should have been. It also gives sales tax summary information from which quarterly sales tax reports are directly produced.

4. Sales Report by Source.

This is the report with which we work most closely, and which is of most immediate usefulness to us. In a later chapter, we shall talk about record keeping. It is from this report that we derive most of our statistical data, primarily how many sales and how much profit (and possible loss) each ad or each promotion has produced. Most of the decisions that you will have to make in the mail-order business are based on information of this kind.

This report is also very helpful in that it immediately pinpoints errors. Have a look at the sample page. From our advertising schedule, we know exactly what merchandise was sold with each source code. For instance: ad WE0920 sold the Supermirror. If we would find any other item listed under this source heading, we would know that some error must have occurred. There would be two possibilities: 1. That the merchandise is correct, but the keypuncher read the wrong source code; or 2. That our operator put the coupon in the wrong item batch.

In the first case, not too much damage would be done. The customer would get the merchandise he ordered, and we simply would have a statistical error. In the second case, however, it would be troublesome, because the customer who had ordered Item A would be receiving Item B. In either case, however, it is flagged to our attention. We can go back into the batch immediately, look at the original source document, and quickly discover any error. If, as often happens, it is a batching error, the shipping department can be alerted and the label in question can be changed to the right merchandise.

As you can readily see, the last three reports are essentially a resorting of the same information, presented in each case for one most important application. This is the marvelous thing about

RUN DATE 10-28-77 CYCLE F8 HENNIKERS 1 WEEK SALES REPORT PAGE 0007

TITLE		N A M E	STREET ADDRESS	C I T Y	STATE	MATCH KEY		ITEM NAME	QNTY	MPT	LBL	BATCH	ORDER
MR	M	JENSEN	PO BOX 3190	SAN LEANDRO	CA	94578	JENSE319	MAPMEASURE	01	A3		102877	410067
MR&MRS	R	HOOKER	60 CORTE ORTEGA APT 14	GREENBRAE	CA	94904	HOOKE601	MAPMEASURE	01	A2		102877	410068
MRS	C	WILSON	~~65 PATTERSON AVE~~	GREENWICH	CT	06830	WILSO65P	MAPMEASURE	02	A1		102877	410069
MR	R	CASTLE	TUCKERTON RD-HOUNDSTOOTH	MEDFORD	NJ	08055	CASTLTUC	MAPMEASURE	03	B1		102877	410070
MR	G	HEISEL	177 UNIVERSITY AVE	ROCHESTER	NY	14605	HEISE177	MAPMEASURE	03	C1	N	102877	410071
MR	J	RYAN	KRAFT ~~COURT-KRAFT INC~~	GLENVIEW	IL	60025	RYANXKRA	MAPMEASURE	03	A1		102877	410072
MR	B	CHRISTENSEN	9933 PINEAIRE DR	SUN CITY	AZ	85351	CHRIS993	MAPMEASURE	03	A1		102877	410073
MS	J	SUDBOROUGH	R 3 BOX 66B	SANTA FE	NM	87501	SUDBO366	MAPMEASURE	03	A1		102877	410074
MS	K	STETSON	192 ~~BELMONT AVENUE~~	SPRINGFIELD	MA	01108	STETS192	GPK	01	A1		102877	410075
*		MARAN MARKET CO	1441 BROADWAY	NEW YORK	NY	10018	MARAN144	GPK	01	A1		102877	410076
MR	R	BENDER	2203 GREENERY LANE	SILVER SPRING	MD	20906	BENDE220	GPK	01	A1		102877	410077
MR	M	FOX JR	5 E ~~REDWOOD~~ ST	BALTIMORE	MD	21202	FOX J5ER	GPK	01	A1		102877	410078
MR	L	KOLE	9027 JACKWOOD	HOUSTON	TX	77036	KOLEX902	GPK	01	A1		102877	410079
MR	J	BAXT	BOX 55389	HOUSTON	TX	77055	BAXTX553	GPK	01	C1	N	102877	410080
MR	K	WOODWARD	P O ~~BOX 178~~	ABILENE	TX	79604	WOODW178	GPK	01	A1		102877	410081
MR	A	WARD	270 BELMONT AV	LONG BEACH	CA	90803	WARDX270	GPK	01	A2		102877	410082
MR	N	LIVSON	C/O IHD TOLEMAN HALL	UC BERKELEY	CA	94720	LIVSOCOI	GPK	01	C3		102877	410083
MR	R	BISHOP	~~140 BEAR FLAG RD~~	SONOMA	CA	95476	BISHO140	GPK	01	A2		102877	410084
MR	R	ADOLPH		SEAL ROCK	OR	97376	ADOLP	GPK	01	B1	N	102877	410085
MR	E	LORRAINE	2103 SW 110										
MR	G	THOMAS	~~R-2 BOX 103~~										
*		HY-GRADE SHOE F	186 LIN										
MR		COFF											

PAGE9 HENNIKERS WEEKLY SALES REPORT FOR WEEK ENDING 12/02/77 CYCLE NUMBER G3

ITEM NO. 10579 BUTTERFLY PRICE 9.95 P & H 1.00

SOURCE	NO. SOLD					
CA0178	1	9.95	TOTAL	CA	1	9.95
MP0178	1	9.95	TOTAL	MP	1	9.95
PI0000	2	19.90	TOTAL	PI	2	19.90
TOTALS	4	39.80				

ITEM NO. 10587 GPK PRICE 6.95 P & H 1.00

SOURCE	NO. SOLD					
CA0178	14	97.30	TOTAL	CA	14	97.30
TY0000	1	6.95	TOTAL	TY	1	6.95
WE000		382.2				

Weekly Sales Listing by Item and Customer sorts weekly orders primarily by item and secondarily by zip code. Note the "N" ("No Label") designation for those orders that have been hand processed.

Weekly Sales Report by Item shows the source of every sale in every merchandise category.

PAGE 55 SUMMARY OF HENNIKERS WEEKLY SALES REPORT FOR WEEK ENDING 1/21/77 CYCLE NUMRER F7

ITEMS SOLD	CASH SALES	BANKAMERI CARD	MASTER CHARGE	BILL SALES	OTHER UNITS	NON BART CAL TAX	BART CA TAX	TOTAL CAL TAX	PRE TAX ITEM SALES	TOTAL SAIFS TAX	TOTAL ITEM SALES
3853	2740	596	484	33	3053	558	242				
	29025.65	8791.40	8010.54	471.19		405.74	190.70	596.44	46298.78	596.44	46895.22

The Weekly Sales Summary is just that: it gives basic information about the week's activity — both in items sold and in dollars. There is also complete sales tax information and the means to reconcile payments actually received and deposited during the week. A sidelight: note that over one-third of all sales are by BA and MC. So you can see how important this service is. A good proportion of these sales comes through the toll-free phone service.

PAGE 20
HENNIKERS WEEKLY SALES REPORT FOR WEEK ENDING 1/21/77
CYCLE NUMBER F7

SOURCE CODE	WE0907		
10934	FLOTECA	1	9.95
	TOTAL	1	9.95
SOURCE CODE	WE0908		
70052	GARNET/P	1	29.95
70060	GARNET/S	1	29.95
	TOTAL	2	59.90
SOURCE CODE	WE0913		
10199	SASK	3	29.85
21006	KNIFE&CASE	1	12.90
	TOTAL	4	42.75
SOURCE CODE	WE0920		
21618	SUPERMIROR	11	142.45
	TOTAL		142.45

The Weekly Sales Report by Source is a re-sorting of previous information. This is a very useful report. Promotions are sorted alphabetically and by date, and one quick scan shows us what all of the promotions — there are scores running at one time — have produced during the reported week.

computers. They truly excel in sorting things very quickly, in whatever sequence, order or category you prefer for your special purpose. We are so used to this now that it doesn't call our attention any more, but it is really helpful and a marvelous aid for business.

5. Label and Inventory Control Report.

From information provided from coupons and other input media, the computer gathers all data on sales for the week.

This information is summarized in a so-called "Label Report," of which I show you part of a sample page. It is a straightforward report that lists every item by number and computer name, in those categories in which sales have been made for the week. It shows us how many labels were printed for each category of merchandise. It shows how much merchandise in each category was sold as "No Label," and it gives us the total of both.

This report gives management and warehouse personnel a quick overview of how much merchandise in each category will be needed and how much will have to be packed for the current week. Also, by referring to the "Total" line we get a quick overview on how many packages altogether have to be shipped for the week, how much postage will be needed, if our box and packing material inventory is adequate and whether we may need additional packing personnel or perhaps schedule overtime.

One reason all of this is important information is that we have one inflexible rule, which I suggest you follow from the very beginning of your own mail-order business: all merchandise must be shipped within a week of receipt of order. If for any reason it cannot be — which should be very rare — the customer should be notified and told what is going to happen. We shall have more to say about this when we talk about Customer Services in the next chapter.

6. Perpetual Inventory Report.

The information from the Label Report is "re-massaged," amplified and additional information added to give us a "Perpetual Inventory Report."

This is a *13-Week Moving Report.* It means that this report carries a 13-week (1/4 year) merchandise movement history on

HENNIKERS WEEKLY LABEL REPORT   CYCLF NO. B2   12/10/76

ITEM		BONUS LBL ITEMS	NO-LABEL ITEMS	TOTAL ITEMS
40113	35XLENS	0	2	2
40238	Z-CHAIR	4	3	7
40246	SUPERSTICK	1	0	1
40279	BLACKCOMBO	1	3	4
40311	ELECTMASS	0	1	1
40337	OPTIC 600	1	1	2
40345	SHOWERHEAD	1	1	2
40352	EXERGYM	1	0	1
50013	MDSE50	0	93	93
50021	SLIMHIP832	0	1	1
50047	MULTIBAND	0	2	2
50088	STATMASTER			
50120	DEFENDER			
50138	BICEN			
50179	CUISINART			
50245	DIPLOMAT			
50344	LENS&TRIPD			
50427	BINO7X21			
50435	SHIPSCLOCK			

Label and Inventory Control Report gives management and warehouse personnel a quick overview of activity for the week, merchandise, packing material and personnel needed. It is also an important control form, since merchandise shipped must correspond to merchandise summarized in this report.

The Perpetual Inventory Report gives a 13-week moving summary on the activity of each "A" (current) item. It shows sales, merchandise receipts and other pertinent information on all "A" (current) items, inventory status in quantity and dollars, and open orders (if any).

HENNIKERS INVENTORY REPORT   12-09-77

70813 PCARN   4.0 A   ON HAND   254 $ 1,016

	09-16	09-23	09-30	10-07	10-14	10-21	10-28	11-04	11-11	11-18	11-25	12-02	12-09
SALES	0	0	0	0	0	0	0	0	0	0	0	0	0
RECEIVED	0	0	0	0	0	0	0	0	0	0	0	0	0
RETURNED	0	0	0	0	0	2	0	0	0	0	1	0	0
RESHIPPED	0	0	0	0	1	0	0	0	0	0	0	0	0
ADJUSTMENT	0	0	0	0	0	0	0	0	0	0	252	0	0

70821 SCARN   4.0 A   ON HAND   237 $ 948

	09-16	09-23	09-30	10-07	10-14	10-21	10-28	11-04	11-11	11-18	11-25	12-02	12-09
SALES	0	0	0	0	1	0	0	0	0	0	0	0	0
RECEIVED	0	0	0	0	0	0	0	0	0	0	0	0	0
RETURNED	0	0	0	0	0	0	0	0	0	0	0	0	0
RESHIPPED	0	0	0	0	1	1	0	0	0	0	0	0	0
ADJUSTMENT	0	0	0	0	0	0	0	0	0	0	240	0	0

92049 INSURANCE   .5 A   ON HAND   903 $ 451

	09-16	09-23	09-30	10-07	10-14	10-21	10-28	11-04	11-11	11-18	11-25	12-02	12-09
SALES	7	45	15	6	3	4	6	6	0	0	1	2	4
RECEIVED	0	0	0	0	0	0	0	0	0	0	0	0	0
RETURNED	0	0	2	0	0	0	0	1	0	0	0	0	0
RESHIPPED	0	0	0	0	0	0	0	0	1	0	0	0	0
ADJUSTMENT	0	0	0	0	45-	0	0	0	0	0	0	0	0

TOTAL A $ 106,187

every item. In each weekly report, the oldest week is "knocked off" and a new week, namely the current week, added.

The report is ordered by item of merchandise. The first thing we see is what the current inventory on hand is. Under that, we have Sales by Week — which is, of course, information that has been provided in previous weeks. It also shows merchandise received from manufacturers, merchandise returned by customers, merchandise replaced to customers (because of non-arrival, breakage, etc.) and "adjustments."

Our computer service has all sales information, of course. We have to provide all other information separately. Here is what we give them every week:

- All purchase orders opened during the week
- All merchandise received during the week and under what purchase order
- All merchandise returned from customers
- All merchandise re-shipped
- Adjustments

What are "adjustments"? In every 13-week period we take actual physical inventory on each of the items that we carry — perhaps 20 or 30 items every week — until, in a 13-week period, we have inventoried everything at least once. The "adjustment" figure is simply the difference between the merchandise that should be on hand according to the perpetual inventory record and that which actually is on hand.

Usually we find that there are only small differences, the kind of thing that one would expect in a business moving that volume of merchandise. Sometimes we find that there are large discrepancies and those, of course, must be investigated immediately. Usually, when we look into it, it turns out that these mistakes are harmless — somebody forgot to list a wholesale order or something of that nature. In some cases we find that merchandise we should have received was actually not received or was short-shipped. In such cases we can approach the manufacturer for clarification and for appropriate adjustment. In some cases, however, it is a danger signal. It could mean that you have "leakage," which is a fancy term for sloppiness or for employee dishonesty. Both, of course, are serious.

The report also provides information on open purchase orders. Since we know ahead of time what promotions we shall be running, we have an approximate idea on what sales to expect in each merchandise category. Thus, we can tell at a glance whether our inventory, together with open purchase orders, is adequate. We also know what our order points are, which depends on how long, approximately, it takes us to get the specific merchandise. If it is domestic merchandise, the order point may be very small, because merchandise may be ordered on the phone and is usually immediately available. If it is imported merchandise, and much of ours is, then we might need 90 or even 180 days to fill our requirements.

Running out of merchandise is one of the most common and one of the most unpleasant and most destructive things in the mail-order business. It happens to all of us from time to time. If it happens frequently, it is a sign of sloppy and unprofessional operation. But this report gives us all the information we need in order to avoid these pitfalls, or at least to reduce them to a minimum.

The Perpetual Inventory Report has a summary page which is the up-to-date inventory, with dollar values extended. It gives a quick overview of the status of inventory (without the historical detail of the main report). The final total line gives us our inventory position in dollars at all items.

You will notice that all merchandise that we have shown on this sample summary page carries the code "A." We summarize our inventory under three categories: "A," "B," and "C." "A" is merchandise that is current, listed in our catalog or currently being advertised in media or by direct mail. "B" is merchandise that is being phased out and that, for one reason or another, we do not plan to feature in our next catalog. "C" is merchandise that we consider obsolete.

In the last chapter, we talked about the yearly Sale in our San Francisco store. All "B" and "C" merchandise is available for the Sale, and this summary is helpful for planning. But it also gives us a general overview of the up-to-dateness of the inventory. As a rule of thumb, the "B" and "C" groups together should not be more than 15% in dollar value of the total inventory (and "C" should not be more than 40% of that). If these ratios are exceeded, we feel that we have an inventory problem and that we must take more rigorous measures to move the merchandise that is being phased out or which is already obsolete.

7. 13-Week Sales Report.

This is the most important report for our day-to-day work, especially for our customer service department.

The first part of this report is exactly the same as (2) "Weekly Sales Listing by Item and Customer," except that, instead of being primarily sorted by item, the information is sorted primarily in zip-code order. That part of the report covers only the current week.

Immediately following this 1-week report are *all transactions of the preceding 12 weeks, also in zip-code order.*

Let me tell you why this is such an important report.

First of all, we can immediately correct the entries of the current week, which is separate from the rest of the report for that very reason. We turn it over to an employee, who goes over it line by line to look for misspellings of names or addresses, wrong zip codes, etc. She corrects information as best she can determine it.

She then sends the corrected information back to the data processing service where the corrections to the master file record are immediately made.

Thus, it is possible that a customer has his name or address misspelled on his first order. But if our employee has done her work properly, any mistakes should be corrected. Any follow-up mail that we direct to this customer should have name and address right.

After we have taken the current week off, we are left with the entire sales record, in zip code sequence of the immediately preceding 12 weeks. This record stays for one week with our Customer Service Department. It is extremely useful, as we shall see immediately, when we talk about Customer Services.

Just as we did with the preceding report, the "Perpetual Inventory Report," we discard this report every week. Every twelfth week we keep the report. It is bound and preserved and presents a permanent history of all customer transactions. This allows us to go back and look up a sale that took place, say, a year or so ago, in the unlikely case that it should become necessary.

There are, in addition, certain minor or subsidiary reports that we get every week and that I should mention to you for the sake of completeness.

HENNIKERS INVENTORY REPORT

70334	ELEPHPEND	1.0	A	ON HAND	46	$	46			
70342	SHARKTOOTH	1.0	A	ON HAND	83	$	83	OPEN ORDERS	#3339	36
70359	CRVDCLELPH	56.0	A	ON HAND	8	$	448			
70367	CHINPEND	8.5	A	ON HAND	14	$	119			
70375	HDCVDOXPND	2.0	A	ON HAND	36	$	72	OPEN ORDERS	#3451	36
70383	CLOSJDENCK	11.0	A	ON HAND	13	$	143	OPEN ORDERS	#3376	16
70391	CLOISBRACL	3.0	A	ON HAND	57	$	171			
70425	JADE/SCREW	3.0	A	ON HAND	70	$	210			
70433	RDBLCRLBCL	1.0	A	ON HAND	36	$	36	OPEN ORDERS	#3421	12
70441	MTHPRLBRCL	1.0	A	ON HAND	9	$	9	OPEN ORDERS	#3353	15
70458	PRIDOTNCKL	17.0	A	ON HAND	17	$	289			
70466	INTLGLDPND	9.0	A	ON HAND	17	$	153			
70474	ADDTLINITL	2.0	A	ON HAND	23	$	46	OPEN ORDERS	#3356	26
70482	RDAGTELVPD	3.0	A	ON HAND	69	$	207			
70490	HDCVDONXHG	3.0	A	ON HAND	24	$	72	OPEN ORDERS	#3339	12
70508	CORALNECKL	5.0	A	ON HAND	35	$	175			
70516	SANDCLOCK	10.0	A	ON HAND	3-	$	30-	OPEN ORDERS	#3323	48
70524	RDAGTESTDS	5.0	A	ON HAND	66	$	330			
70532	ANTQSLVCHN	5.0	A	ON HAND	24	$	120			
70540										
70557										
70565										
70573										

The Inventory Summary lists totals of all items in stock, and open orders. Note item 70516, showing a ''negative inventory.'' It means that we are temporarily back-ordered in this item.

The 13-Week Sales Report is our most important day-to-day tool, especially in customer service. All orders placed within the last three months are sorted by zip code. Any complaints for non-receipt, any adjustment can be promptly handled because the customer's order can be located immediately while he is still on the phone. All necessary information is available.

RUN DATE 12-09-77 CYCLE G4 HENNIKERS 13 WEEKS SALES REPORT PAGE 0256

TITLE		NAME	STREET ADDRESS	CITY	STATE		MATCH KEY	ITEM NAME	QNTY	MPT	LBL	BATCH	ORDER
MR	K	TEMPLIN	850-C BERKSHIRE DR	READING	PA	19601	TEMPL850	ORGANIZER	01	A1		111877	418505
MS	D	WENRICH	842 CHURCH ST	READING	PA	19601	WENRI842	LGHTNRINGS	01	A1	N	112577	423993
MS	D	WENRICH	842 CHURCH ST	READING	PA	19601	WENRI842	STLTQWEDS	01	A1	N	112577	423993
MR	J	WOODSON	120 WINDOVER	LANCASTER	PA	19601	WOODS120	AUTOCOMPTH	02	A1		111877	419449
MR	M	DITZLER	316 S 5TH ST	READING	PA	19602	DITZL316	ISIS	01	A1		120277	426817
MR	M	DITZLER	316 S 5TH ST	READING	PA	19602	DITZL316	GARNFT/S	01	A1		102177	408579
MR	M	FRAZER	339 S 18TH ST APT #2	READING	PA	19602	FRAZE339	SASK	01	C1		111877	419188
MR	S	BASS	BOX 659	READING	PA	19603	BASSX659	ORGANIZER	01	A1		111877	418507
MR	G	KIEFER	216 N 6TH PO BOX 1312	READING	PA	19603	KIEFE216	HENNISNIPS	03	A1		102177	407715
MR	I	COHEN	1505 LORRAINE RD	READING	PA	19604	COHEN150	ORGANIZER	01	A1		111877	418508
MS	M	DGRAY	836 NORTH 9TH ST	READING	PA	19604	DGRAY836	HENNISNIPS	01	A1		093077	403962
DR	S	ROWAN	1825 LORRAINE RD	READING	PA	19604	ROWAN182	CALLUSAWAY	01	A1		111177	416844
DR	S	ROWAN	1825 LORRAINE RD	READING	PA	19604	ROWAN182	RECHARFLAS	02	A1		111177	416844
MR	J	KEARNEY	120 PROSPECT ST	READING	PA	19606	KEARN120	HENNISCOPE	01	A1		111177	416408
MR	W	WILLIAMS	104 S 25TH ST	READING	PA	19606	WILLI104	ORGANIZER	01	A1		111877	418509
MR	J	FREEHATER	BOX 404 RD #1	READING	PA	19607	FREEH404	ORGANIZER	01	A1		111877	418510
MR	D	STEWART	110 ASHLEY ROAD	SINKING SPRINGS	PA	19608	STEWA110	FMBOOSTER	01	A1		110477	413960
MR	C	CONSTEIN	2705 CRAIG AVE	READING	PA	19609	CONST270	VERTCOMP	01	B1		111177	416040
MS	K	WEIKEL	2311 PENN AVE	WEST LAWN	PA	19609	WEIKE231	RUMTOPF	01	A1		111177	416845
MR	H	FRY	1156 OLD MILL ROAD	WYOMISSING	PA	19610	FRYXX115	LABISQUERA	01	A1		093077	404376
MR	J	KNOX	1646 DAUPHIN AVE	WYOMISSING	PA	19610	KNOXX164	HCHRONTWO	01 R	A1		092377	403723
MR	J	KNOX	1646 DAUPHIN AVE	WYOMISSING	PA	19610	KNOXX164	HENNISCOPE	01 R	A1		092377	403723
MRS	M	LAWRENCE	FAIRVIEW AVE	WYOMISSING	PA	19610	LAWRE104	LOGGER	01	B1	N	111877	420302
MR	W	[illegible]	...FIELD AVE	WYOMISSING	PA	19610	ROTHE166	LABISQUERA	[illegible]	C1		102877	410364
				WYOMISSING	[illegible]	[illegible]	ZIEME55C	[illegible]				100777	405220

8. Gold Star Customer Report, Catalog Purchasers Listing

We have a special "Gold Star" stamp that we apply to large orders — in our business, everything over $100. We get a weekly print-out of those customers and write a special "Thank You" letter to everyone of them. It is a pre-typed letter, and the customer's name is dropped in by the same typewriter. It is really indistinguishable from a personally typed letter. We usually accompany this "Thank You" letter with a small present.

Naturally, those "big buyers" are your most important customers. It pays to pamper them, to show them your appreciation and to segregate them on your master file for special handling in the future.

While I don't show you a special print-out of it, let me just tell you that we also have the capability to identify and print out all those customers who *have purchased through the catalog.* Regardless of how you acquired your customer in the first place — by space advertising or by direct mail — the fact that he responded to a catalog offer makes him "special." Mail-order operators are agreed that catalog buyers are the most valuable, the most faithful, and the most likely to make repeat purchases. Having these catalog buyers separately available enables us to pull them out for special promotions. Also, if you can separate the catalog buyers you will be able to get a premium for them in your list rental business. It is an easy thing to set up, if you think of it in the very beginning. So, be sure to tell your data processing people that you want that capability!

9. Duplication Record.

This record lists all customers, and their purchases, who have made more than one purchase in a given week or in the current and preceding week. The reason that we have this printed out is that it is really rather unusual for any customer to order merchandise in two consecutive weeks. Naturally, we are not talking about a customer buying several things at the same time. We are now concerned with those who, it appears, have made more than one transaction in one week or in two subsequent weeks.

This is usually a short report and we scan it quickly. The reasons that it deserves our attention are the following:

- There is a possibility of entry errors, which means that by some fluke an order was entered twice and that the cus-

hennikers
779 Bush St. Box 7584. San Francisco, CA 94120
Tel. (415) 433-7540

December 20, 1977

Dear Mr. Dawson:

It doesn't really make much difference to us whether a customer buys $1 worth of merchandise or $500 worth. Everyone gets the same good treatment and we do our very best for them.

But naturally, special recognition is due those who do make an especially large purchase such as you did with us recently. It was brought to my attention and I want to thank you for it personally and express the hope that your order arrived in fine shape, that you are satisfied with it -- both with the merchandise and with our service.

We hope we may serve you again soon for your personal or gift needs.

Thank you for your confidence.

Sincerely yours,

Gerardo Joffe
President

Mr. James Dawson
113 Clearwater Drive
Portland, OR 93702

CS-40

A good customer must be treasured and the Gold Star Customer Report makes it a little easier to do that. The names and addresses of these special customers are generated by computer every week, and we write this fill-in letter. We could, of course, generate the entire letter, including name and address, by computer, but we feel that it would lose the important personal touch. You should ''pamper'' your good customers — those who make large purchases or repeat purchases. You will find that they account for a disproportionate share of total sales and profits.

tomer, having ordered and paid only once, would receive a double shipment.

- It is a pattern in which fraud or experienced bad check artists would operate. These people know that it takes two or three weeks before a bad check bounces back. They also know that they will be on the "alert" list once the check has bounced and that no more merchandise will be shipped to them. Therefore, they usually hit quickly and make three or four "purchases" in a two or three week period.
- We might find a wonderful customer who deserves "Gold Star" status. We could not have found him by our Gold Star Report because that records only dollar values of individual orders. Naturally, we feel as positive about a customer who makes several smaller purchases in a row as about one who makes one major purchase and then perhaps nothing for a while.

All in all, we feel this to be a helpful report, especially for catching bad check artists. This used to be a very small problem in this business, but it is beginning to assume some importance and deserves vigilance.

The "Almighty Computer" data processing plays two important roles in the mail-order business. We have just now discussed the first role, namely that of order processing and providing statistical information for controls, source information, etc.

The other important function that data processing has in the mail-order business is that of *list maintenance.*

I don't think that it is an exaggeration to say that the most important asset that any mail-order business has is its list of customers. You can make several assumptions, but my rule of thumb is that every bona fide customer that you have on your list is worth at least $3 to $5. That, by the way, is an asset that does not appear on your balance sheet, but it is still the most important asset you have.

HOW MUCH IS EACH CUSTOMER WORTH?

While this is not entirely related to data processing, I might just pause here a minute and tell you how I arrive at this value per customer — about $3 to $5.

You may simply figure that, if you follow the suggestions that I have given you so far, you will circularize your customers on an average of ten times per year — with direct mail pieces and with catalogs. This, assuming a rational mix of different kinds of mail pieces and catalogs, will cost you about $2 per customer per year.

Depending on the kind of mail pieces and the mix between catalogs and mail pieces, and using the very roughest rule of thumb, you may assume that you will sell $600 worth of merchandise for every 1,000 pieces mailed to your list. Or, you may call it sales of $.60 per unit mailed. This sales figure may be somewhat higher for catalogs and somewhat lower for direct mail. Thus, the sales volume per 1,000 pieces mailed depends to some extent on the mix between catalogs and direct mail pieces. Or you can say it depends on whether you publish one, two or more catalogs per year. Your solo direct mail pieces will usually be for relatively high margin merchandise — you may assume 65%. Averaging this with your catalogs, which will bring you approximately 55% gross margin, you may assume that all mail you send out — catalogs and direct mail pieces — will average 60% gross profit. Or to word it differently, you will sell each customer approximately $6 of merchandise per year with 10 mailings. You will have 60% gross profit on that, which is $3.60. If you deduct from that the $2 expense that you had in mailing these ten pieces to this customer, you will be left with a net profit of $1.60 — call it $1.50 per customer per year.

That doesn't sound like a whole lot of money. But by the time you have a mailing list of 100,000 customers, and I expect you to have that in 2 or 3 years, you obviously will have a fairly formidable business. It does add up!

Now if you give each customer a "life" of 3 years — and that is being quite conservative, you can safely say that each customer on your list is worth three times $1.50, or approximately $4.50.

As I just said, you may assign each customer on your list a somewhat higher or lower value. It depends pretty much on your experience regarding the "active life" of each customer, the kind of business you have, and how actively you solicit each customer on your list. But although your accountant won't believe it, and although you can't put it on your financial statement, it is a pretty safe bet to say that every customer that you have is actually worth at least $3 — probably more.

So it goes without saying that here is an asset that you must protect very carefully. It is an asset composed of very many individual "pieces." In the case of your small business, it may be just 50,000 or 100,000 "pieces." In a large mail-order business, it may be millions. But whatever the number, each of these "pieces" is a real person and a customer of yours. It is your absolute duty as a successful mail-order operator to keep these customers satisfied with your merchandise and with your service. And it is also your duty to get the names and addresses of your customers right in the first place, to correct them if you didn't, and to keep track of your customers as they move. That means that you must maintain your master file with the greatest care.

HOW TO MAINTAIN YOUR CUSTOMER MASTER FILE

Americans are funny people. They move around a lot, they get married and do all other kinds of crazy things. And that means that they change their names, they change their addresses and even their zip codes. So you have to work at keeping your list up-to-date. The computer is your trusty friend to help you with that.

The first important tool in helping you to keep your list clean is the "current week" portion of the 13-week report that we just mentioned. You will remember that it is separate from the other twelve weeks. You take this current week, dealing only with the transactions that you had during the week that just passed and carefully go over the report line by line. This is not quite as forbidding as it sounds. Suppose you are now at the stage at which you have sales of $10,000 per week, and an average sale of, say, $10. You will have to look at approximately 1,000 names. You (or a smart employee) can do it in one hour.

What you look for are obvious misspellings of names, obvious misspellings of city and street addresses, and, worst of all, those that have slipped into the wrong zip code. Those are easy to find because the list is sorted in zip code order. If an address has a wrong zip code, a California address may appear within Arkansas, Chicago within Miami Beach. These mistakes stick out like that proverbial sore thumb and are quickly spotted.

In addition to the scanning of each week's input, we subject the whole list to visual inspection once a year. This is the kind of work that is best not done in the office, but by some outside person who is conscientious, methodical and patient. We shall talk in a minute about computer programs that clean the list and you will see that I consider them indispensable. But such cleaning should be *in addition to, not instead of* cleaning the list by inspection. Because, however smart the sophisticated computer program may be, the computer cannot make on-the-spot decisions based on judgment that only human beings (not necessarily all of them) can make. We find that the yearly visual scan will produce at least 2% to 3% of misspellings and similar errors and, perhaps 1% to 2% of duplications throughout the list. This is one of our very important "cleaning tools."

Each customer is provided with a *"Match Code."* It is printed on the mailing label and contains the zip code, the first 5 letters of his last name, and the first 3 digits of his house number. Turn back and have a look at our standard mailing label. The bottom line contains the customer's match code and you can readily see how it is determined. If we find any mistake at all (or if the customer notifies us of a mistake or of a change), we simply put that customer's match code on the correction form, together with just the corrected portions of his name/address that were incorrect or that have been changed. Sometimes, of course, the entire name and address have to be changed.

Each of our employees who has any contact with the public — in person, by phone, or by mail — keeps one of the correction forms on his desk at all times. This enables him to correct immediately any misspellings, errors, changes, etc. that come to his attention. These forms are gathered before each update so that the corrections can be entered.

Another source for list correction is the "Address Correction Requested" endorsement on a piece of mail that we send out. Please turn back to the examples of direct mail pieces and note that endorsement. It is not the most inexpensive thing in the world to do (as of this writing the postal service charges us $.25 for each correction), and we therefore cannot afford to apply this endorsement indiscriminately. We plan our mailings in such a way that we pass each name through an address correction endorsement mailing once every three months approximately. Then, if that customer has moved, the postman will bring it back with the correct new address. We would like to clean the list more often, but passing

henniker's DELETION AND CHANGE RECORD DATE: 9/22/77

MATCHCODE	DELETE	TITLE	INITIAL	LAST NAME	STREET	CITY	STATE	ZIP
345Ø2SMiTH324								30312
94123FOXXX1BA	X							
75328ARDEN247		Ms.		ARLENBERG				
65247BULLi36A					38 ARLINGTON			
82316CANDE477					479 CULVERT			
75318CUNNi225							TX	
66329WALDO3BR	X							
94121HAGOP356		DR.				SAN FRANCISCO		
75116CURTI42C								
53141RANDO2Ø6				RANDOLPH				
4ØØ32SAMPS333	X							

Each of our employees who has any contact with the public has a correction/update form on his desk. Each customer is identified by his ''matchcode,'' which is the first information we enter. We then enter only that part of the customer's name or address that has to be altered — either because there was an initial error or because the customer actually made a change. Once every five weeks, at every masterfile update, we turn these sheets over to our data processing service.

each name through the correction process every three months is sufficient and keeps the list quite clean.

One little "trick of the trade" is to put the endorsement "Postman — if addressee has moved, please deliver to current occupant" on all mail, catalogs, etc. that does not carry the address correction requested endorsement. The reason is obvious: if your customer has moved, you may as well go to the successor. Since he lives in the same house or apartment in which your customer used to live, chances are that he is a person of similar tastes and background. And while the expectation that he will buy anything from you is certainly much less than it would be with your own customer, it is preferable that he get the catalog or mail piece, rather than its going into the postal trash bin.

A further way to correct addresses — the least expensive, but unfortunately also the least effective, is "self-correction" by the customer. On every mail piece that we send out and every catalog, we ask the customer to make a correction, if his name or address are not exactly right or if anything at all is misspelled. We also appeal to his sense of cooperation and his wish to preserve resources. We ask him to return duplicate labels to us so that we may eliminate those duplicates from our master file.

Naturally, this cannot be too efficient, because if this customer has really moved and we do not have an "Address Correction Requested" endorsement, the piece will not arrive and the customer will have no chance to reply. If it is just a slight misspelling, he may correct it, but he will usually do it only if he places an order. Since, on the average, not more than 4% or 5% of your customers will respond to any given offer, you can see that it is not the most efficient way to correct your list. Still, since it is essentially free, there is no harm in doing it. Also, misspellings of names and addresses are a source of irritation to most people. In showing your customer that you sincerely wish to correct any errors you soothe some of that irritation.

In any case, any corrections, any changes, etc., are made in this same manner and on the same form.

There is a final "scientific" way of cleaning your list, and after your list reaches a certain size — say 100,000 to 200,000 names, it will probably become your most important list cleaning tool. Or I should say, perhaps, your most important tool *after* you have made visual inspection and correction of each week's data input and the yearly name-by-name inspection. This "scientific" way is list cleaning, unduplicating by computer.

Specialized firms have developed specific, very sophisticated programs that examine all names on the list and compare them with others for possibility of duplication (or worse). Naturally, simple duplications — those in which the match codes coincide — will already have been eliminated by your own computer service. But those "tricky" duplications such as Mr. Miller's name being spelled Muller, Moller or Milner on a repeat order, his house number being listed three different ways, or errors in the zip code, cannot ordinarily be caught by your own processing program. These firms, at about a rate of $2 to $3 per thousand names tested, will catch all those "suspects" and print them out for you. You can then decide which of the two (or more) names you wish to eliminate or even if you wish to eliminate any at all. Because, naturally, you have the privilege of overriding the "judgment" of the computer and you may decide that Mr. Miller and Mr. Milner are indeed two different people.

You will find that, even in a well-maintained list — one that gets careful visual inspection before input and systematic at least once-a-year eyeballing, a minimum of 1% real duplicates will remain that can only be caught by computer. Assume once again that you mail to your list ten times a year and that the cost of your doing that is $2 per year per customer. You can readily see that a 1% duplication rate would cost you $20 per 1,000 names per year and that, therefore, paying $2 or $3 per 1,000 names to get those "dupes" out is very good business. And this does not take into account the intangible factors of annoyance to the customer and the impression of lack of control that multiple mailings to the same customer will cause.

While we're on this topic, I should tell you about something that will play an important and ever-increasing role in your direct mail and especially in your catalog business. It is the merge/purge procedure.

Briefly here is what it involves: you are sending a catalog mailing to your list and at the same time you will wish to send catalogs to test groups of perhaps quite a few outside lists. People who are mail-order buyers are very likely to be on quite a number of lists, and that likelihood is enhanced if the demographics of those outside lists and the kind of merchandise being sold resembles yours. So there is a good chance that a fair number of your customers will appear on one or more of those outside lists.

These same specialized computer firms have very "smart" programs that will *merge* all of the lists used in the mailing and will *purge* all internal duplications (those within the list) and all mutual duplications (those in one or several other lists). The identity of the remaining names will be preserved so that you will still know which list produced what. Also, you will get a print-out of those of your customers who appear on your list and on one or more other lists. Obviously, those dedicated mail-order buyers are of great value and might warrant some special handling.

There is little question that you cannot launch a major mailing — say one involving one million names or more, involving ten lists or more — without a merge/purge program.

Why is it so important that you keep your list "clean"? There are two related reasons: we have already seen that it is fairly expensive to mail to your customers. Even in the best-organized and most cost-conscious mail-order business, you will probably keep on mailing to any customer for at least a year (usually longer) after his last purchase, before you discontinue mailing to him.

As we have seen, you will most likely spend about $2 in just one year in mailing to just one customer. But, instead of being a potential source of profit, a "phantom customer" is a sure-fire source of loss to you. Keep in mind that, even if you do not make any mistakes at all, anywhere between 5% to 10% of all people in the United States make a move every year. So you can readily see that your list will quickly become outdated, obsolete and filled with "dead" names ("phantom customers") if you do not constantly work on cleaning it.

You can and will make money in mail order if you follow the suggestions that I have given you so far. But everything I have told you will come to naught, if you do not keep your list "clean." We have talked about it before, but think about it again in a somewhat different way: it will cost you an average of $200 to mail 1,000 direct mail pieces or catalogs. Let's say you expect to sell $600 of merchandise with these 1,000 pieces of mail. And let's assume that you have an overall gross margin of 60%. Then you will have a gross profit of (.60 x $600) = $360, and a contribution to profit of that, less your mailing costs of $200. This comes to $160 net contribution per 1,000 pieces.

What would happen if 25% of your list is not "clean" (and that can come about quickly if you don't watch it)? Well, it simply means that you will be reaching only 75% of your customers and will be selling only 75% of the $600 that you would have sold otherwise — or just $450. Your cost of mailing these 1,000 pieces is still the same — $200. And your gross margin is also the same, 60%. So these $450 in sales will give you a gross profit of $450 x .60 = $270. Deduct the mailing cost of $200, and this leaves you a net contribution of just $70. Think of it: $160 contribution per 1,000 pieces mailed reduced to just $70! A 25% error rate in your list reduces your profit by almost 60%! And you are lucky at that. Because if your response is smaller, your gross margin smaller, or your error factor even greater than 25%, profits can very quickly be reduced to the vanishing point and turn to losses. I have seen it in my own and in other people's business. Yes, it takes *constant attention and vigilance to keep your list as clean as humanly possible.*

The second reason that you want to keep your list clean is that of list rentals, about which we shall talk immediately. But briefly, other firms — mail-order houses, publishers, fund raisers, politicians, and many others will rent the use of your list. Whether they will continue to do so depends on how well the list works for them. If you handicap yourself by having your list loaded down with 20% to 25% of bad names, your list renter will have very poor results with your list and will not come back for more.

LIST RENTAL — IMPORTANT SOURCE OF PROFIT

This is as good a time as any to talk about list rentals. It can be one of the most important sources of profit in any mail-order business. Stories circulate about mail-order houses that are in business supposedly only to create a good list that they can successfully rent to others. Their merchandising activities are incidental. This may or may not be true and depends on how one looks at it. What *is* probably true in many, or perhaps most, mail-order houses, is that income from list rentals is the difference between good profits and small profits or between small profits and losses. You will find it to be the case in your business. List rentals will be one of the most important sources of profit for you. There is little or no overhead or expense associated with it and very little work. And it goes right down to that famous bottom line.

Let me show you how and why. First of all, at Henniker's we have a list rental agent, whom we pay 10% of all list rental income. This is not a common practice in the mail order industry, but it is a practice that I can very heartily recommend to you. Because, naturally, since he is *your* agent, he has every incentive to go out, beat the bushes and actively promote the use of your list. In other words, he will not be just a passive order taker, but he will hustle for business. And if he is any good at all, he will pay for his commissions many times over.

In all of these list rental deals, a list broker is involved. The broker will be engaged by the firm that wishes to rent lists. He performs valuable services in selecting them for his client's use. The broker gets 20% of the rental proceeds.

The out-of-pocket cost that you have in producing rental names is quite small. We figure a cost of approximately $2 to $2.50 per 1,000 names produced on standard labels (or perhaps a little more if it's on self-adhesive labels). Quite a few requests will be for names on magnetic tape, rather than on labels. The mailer will take all the separate tapes — his own and those that he rents from others — and will join them in a "merge/purge" procedure. We have talked about that. The cost of providing magnetic tape is just about the same as for labels.

If your data processing house is on the ball (and you want to make very sure that they are), they have programs by which you can select names by sex, by state, by zip code, by recency and/or frequency of purchase, and by many other criteria. Any such selection increases the cost per 1,000 labels slightly, usually $5 per thousand. Since virtually no added cost is involved for you, these "special selections" mean substantial added revenue to you.

Another selection that is usually available is the so-called "hot line." That is generally defined as your last 3-months buyers. It also brings an additional premium, and it is usually the list segment prospective renters will try first. You want to make really sure that your processing house can provide the "hot line" selection as well.

You should "update" your master file every five weeks. During those five weeks you will cumulate all corrections and deletions.

Your data processing system will cumulate all customers during the five-week period. The deletions and corrections are then entered on the master file. All those who made purchases during the period are checked against the master file. If they are found to be already on the file — if they are established customers — their status, their purchasing history, will be updated. If they are not found on the master file, they are entered as new customers.

Your program should be designed so that the following will happen immediately after the update:

1. You will get a set of labels of all new customers, that is all customers who have made their first purchase since the last update. You can then send them immediately a catalog and perhaps a "welcome to the fold" letter from the president.
2. You will get an updated "Recency/Frequency" Matrix.

The Recency/Frequency Matrix is one of your valuable tools for the analysis of your customers' purchasing performance. It is also of great help in your list rental business, because your prospective renters know what they are getting and they can carve out whatever section of the list they wish to rent.

Each line of the Matrix corresponds to a 10-week span (a separate schedule relates recency cycles to calendar weeks). The headings of the frequency columns are somewhat misleading. "0" means a purchase of less than $10. "1" means a purchase of over $10, or two subsequent purchases of under $10 each. The following columns tabulate additional purchases. It is important that you be able to segregate those customers that make only a minimal purchase (column "0"). There are two reasons for that:

1. You want to keep a keen eye on this group. Some of them just purchase your "promos" and have apparently no intention of ever making a "real" purchase. You may carry these customers for as long as a year. If they do not "upgrade" their status by then, you can no longer afford to carry them, should spend no more money on them and should consign them to the "Lost Sheep" group. That means that you will no longer send them catalogs or regular mailings, except for occasional "revival specials." Those are offers that they (hopefully) cannot refuse and may bring them back into the fold. Also, of course, unless

henniker's

RECENCY / FREQUENCY MATRIX 01/03/78

RECENCY	FREQUENCY 0	1	2	3	OVER 3	TOTAL
00-09	1,654	1,343	67	8	7	3,079
10-19	1,208	1,557	42	6	2	2,815
20-29	2,369	1,834	45	4	8	4,260
30-39	3,577	3,188	96	15	3	6,879
40-49	6,462	4,237	93	11	4	10,807
50-59	5,620	4,148	365	70	49	10,252
60-69	8,437	4,823	59	16	11	13,346
70-79	7,708	5,503	292	23	3	13,529
80-89	6,714	6,053	501	63	13	13,344
90-99	1,523	10,391	692	95	44	12,745
A0-A9	876	15,545	1,340	191	37	17,989
B0-B9	1,871	10,901	3,873	495	95	17,235
C0-C9	3,792	13,258	1,455	256	78	18,839
D0-D9	3,414	12,030	2,149	425	149	18,167
E0-E9	5,082	8,762	1,363	339	128	15,674
F0-F9	2,766	9,263	1,887	438	185	14,539
G0-G9	7,694	7,081	1,426	319	131	16,651
H0-H9	0	0	0	0	0	0
UNKNOWN	0	0	0	0	0	0
TOTAL	70,767	119,917	15,745	2,774	947	210,150

This is a recency/frequency matrix. It is an important tool for our own mailing purposes and for list rental. Each line encompasses ten weekly cycles (except the last line, which is six cycles). The labelling of the frequency columns is somewhat misleading because the headings express not only the number of transactions, but in some measure also the amount of purchase.

specifically requested, you will not make available to any rental clients any names that have been designated as "Lost Sheep."

2. Your list rental customers will occasionally request that you eliminate all those who have made purchases of less than $10. The "0" classification makes this possible. You would lose many rental customers if you did not have this capacity.

This Recency/Frequency Matrix is, of course, rather "elementary" and provides only the most important selection criteria. As your list grows, you will certainly wish to make several refinements. You might wish to show your customers' purchases by merchandise category, by dollar amount per purchase, or during any given period, or even any customer's entire purchase history.

Naturally, although not shown on this Matrix, you and your list rental clients will have other selection options, for instance:

- Title Selection
- Sex Selection
- State Selection
- Zip Code Selection

And, if you program your list as I suggested to you earlier, you will also be able to select:

- Gold Star Customers (big ticket purchasers)
- Catalog Purchasers

Here is one final selection idea that we originated at Henniker's and which I find to be outstandingly useful. It is the ability to select customers by last *two digits* of zip code.

Most lists can give you an "nth" selection. That means that you can select, say, every 10th (or any other number) name throughout the list for any test that you or your list rental customers may wish to conduct. Let's assume that you have 100,000 names on your list. If your "n" is 10, you might select customer numbers 10, 20, 30, . . . 99,980, 99,990, 100,000 for this test. Suppose your test was successful and you or your client now want to run the remaining 90% of your list. If you had a list update since the first test, this is not possible because your customers are no longer in the same position, you might repeat customers that you have tested before and leave out those that you have not. So you might be forced to run the entire list and would have to repeat those that you have already tested. This would be a waste of money and would not make your list rental client happy.

This can be avoided if you program for "last two digits of zip code." Suppose you want to run an n = 8 test. You could, for instance, run all zip codes ending in 02, 10, 18, 26 . . . 82, 90, 98. Then if your test is successful, you can then run all other zip codes, and you will have no duplication, even though you might have had one or several updates since the test.

This was somewhat of an excursion into technicalities and I hope you enjoyed it. I know you will profit from it. But now, let's go back to the nitty-gritty of list rental.

On the average, you may assume that (at today's prices) a list like the one you are going to have, will rent for approximately $35 per 1,000 names (disregarding for the moment any "selection"). Since the broker and the agent get 30% off the top and since your expense for producing rental names will be approximately $2.50 per 1,000, it is clear that you will net, and by that I mean money right into your pocket, approximately $20 to $22 per 1,000 names rented. This, I assure you, "ain't hay" at all.

Take Henniker's list. As of this writing, it is approximately 200,000 active names, which we "turn over" about 10 to 12 times a year. That means that, through the efforts of our agent, and because our list has been carefully built and is productive for most purposes for which it is used, we will rent somewhere in the neighborhood of two million names per year. At $20 to $22 *net contribution* to us, this amounts to about $40,000 per year. When I ran Haverhill's, our list contained approximately 750,000 names. The turnover was about the same. It doesn't take too sharp a pencil to realize that, with so much money at stake, your successful list rental business may well be a decisive factor in your mail-order business success.

Even if you are still quite small, list rental will be an important source of profit for you. Let me just give you a few "last words" about this part of your business:

- Your list will not be readily rentable, unless it contains at least 25,000 active names. Try to get to this level as quickly as possible. "Promotional" merchandise will help.

- Keep your list as clean as you can. Your list *must* be productive to your renter. If it is not, you will not get repeat rentals and your list business will not get off the ground.
- Provide adequate selection criteria for your prospective list rental customers. As a minimum, you should have selection by title, by sex, by state, by zip code, by elimination of "low ticket" customers, and, by recency/frequency.
- Don't be too selective to whom you rent. Don't worry about competition — you can't keep people from learning about other offers anyway. The only exception might be in the case of a "head-on collision," which means the same offer by another firm at just about the same time you are planning to mail. This does not happen too often. But do not allow your list to be used for anything that you consider immoral, illegal, pornographic, or in very bad taste. Your customers will find out that you have provided their names for such a purpose and they will bitterly resent it. If your agent is any good, he will not even submit such offers for your approval. But if he does, tell him what your policies are, and that will be that.
- Be scrupulously honest: tell your agent exactly how your names were recruited, who are inquirers and who are buyers. Do not exaggerate average sale. Your agent needs to know exactly what he is selling or he cannot be effective. Most important, be very careful to resist the temptation to pad your list with names that you may have acquired by any means other than in the ordinary course of your business. And whatever else you do or don't do, *under no circumstances "pirate" names that do not belong to you,* that you may have rented (for one-time use) from other firms. They *will* find you out. Word of your activities will spread and you will be "dead" in this business.

SUMMARIZING DATA PROCESSING

I am sure that by now you agree with me how important data processing is in your growing mail-order business:

- It is absolutely essential and inevitable for the processing of your orders on a day-to-day basis, to keep proper records and to get the statistical information you need.

- It is indispensable to keep a "clean" master file, which will reflect an up-to-date and accurate record of your customers. This record will be the basis for your own periodic direct mailings and the underpinnings of your list rental business. Your list rental business will be a major source of income for you.
- Your customer list, your master file, is your single most important business asset. It does not appear on your balance sheet, but without it you are out of business. As one of my colleagues somewhat whimsically put it: "If there was a fire, I'd grab my list first." You *must* have good data processing systems to keep your list current and clean and to preserve and enhance this valuable asset.

As your business grows, data processing will in all likelihood play many other roles for you, especially in the areas of accounting, statistics, control, etc. But for the first years of your business life, you should concentrate on these two aspects. You will find the computer to be your very best friend, and not the ogre that many people make it out to be.

There is perhaps one final clarification required before we close this chapter. The systems that I have described to you are definitely not the "ultimate in sophistication." There are astonishing things that can be done with data processing systems, but I believe that much of that does not have practical application to a beginning and a growing mail-order business. Once you are beyond the first five years, you may consider different methods of inputting information, for instance by having your own computer terminal and having on-line access to a large computer. You could couple this with immediate visual access to information on a CRT-screen (like a fancy TV picture tube) right in your office, a computer steered printer in your office and other refinements. But, please, do not get enamored with all those marvels, because they are not economically justified for a small and growing company. The systems that I have described to you, or some variant of them, are about what you need in the first three to five years. Let the computer be your servant, and not your master and avoid its being a large source of fixed expense.

We shall now have a complete change of pace and talk about customer service. As you will see, it is perhaps more important in the mail-order business to build your customers' confidence and to keep it than in any other business. Because your customer cannot look you in the eye, he has to deal with you at a distance. And that takes confidence on his part. Therefore, please read the next chapter carefully. This is a very important subject in which many otherwise successful mail-order firms fall down. I think I can give you policies and techniques to run a very successful customer service.

Chapter 9

HOW TO RUN A SUCCESSFUL CUSTOMER SERVICE DEPARTMENT

We shall now talk about what you may well think of as a most unglamorous aspect of the mail-order business. It may be a little tedious, and it may be work that you won't see immediately paid back in hard cash. Yet, it is one of the most important aspects of your mail-order business. We are talking about *customer services.*

People who go into the mail-order business are usually "turned on" by the marketing, merchandising, promotional and (why not?) profit potential of the business. The "backroom" aspects of the business, such as packing, shipping, handling of returned merchandise and, most of all, customer services, are a "necessary evil" at best. More likely they consider it a pain in the neck. There is a tendency to sweep this kind of work under the rug or to delegate it to secondary personnel.

I am not too much different in that respect. I do enjoy working with people and dealing with my customers. It can, however, appear as somewhat unrewarding to "handle problems." I have long ago come to realize, however, and so must you, that it is perhaps the most important aspect of your business. It can really make you or break you. Also, it does not have to be a "wasteful" part of your business at all. If you conduct it well, it can be a creative activity. You can learn to get enjoyment out of it by conducting customer service properly. You will get a much better feel for your business. You will be able to avoid mistakes (that gave rise to customer service complaints in the first place) and this will reduce over-all work load. You will make many actual friends in correspondence, on the telephone and even in person.

THE CUSTOMER IS ALWAYS RIGHT

The most important thing to keep in mind in customer services is really quite simple. It is the old saw that *the customer is always right.* You will often be convinced that the customer is not right at all, and technically you will be correct. But as far as the customer is concerned, lean over backward in any case to give him what he wants. Do that even if he is actually not really entitled to what he is asking for, even if he is "unreasonable," and even if you would be legally or morally justified not to accede to his wishes.

There are, of course, exceptions. For instance: a demand made on you may not only be totally unreasonable and unjustifiable, but could also cause you more damage and expense than you feel you can afford. Such cases are rare. Satisfying a customer's request may in certain cases be a tacit admission of wrongdoing in the first place that may leave you open to possible legal action. We are all entitled to make mistakes, even to admit mistakes that we haven't made. But it may sometimes be wise not to accede to such a request, especially if the customer had invoked consumer protection agencies, the Federal Trade Commission, etc. These cases are fortunately quite rare and it takes some judgment to discern them. Generally if you are guided by the motto that the customer is always right, you can't go too wrong.

Another maxim that you should always keep in mind in customer service is to handle every complaint, every inquiry, every customer action within 24 hours. I really mean that: *within 24 hours.* At Henniker's, we literally handle over 90% of all customer actions on the same day on which we receive them. We usually conclude them with one single action on our part. The few remaining cases need some research or have some other complications. In those few cases, however, we immediately send the customer a postcard, assuring him that we are aware of the problem and that we are taking action on it.

Another point of importance is not to keep any files on customer services at all. This may strike you as peculiar at first. But if you were to keep files, it would drive you out of your office because in just a few months you would have more customer files than you could possibly accommodate. All letters that customers write and that do not need response are thrown away after we have handled them. If we have reason to reply to the customer, his letter

QUICK NOTE

henniker's 779 Bush St., Box 7584, San Francisco, CA 94120

We hope you will forgive us for the informality of our reply to your inquiry. We have put it right on the bottom or on the back of your letter. This may not be very elegant, but many of our customers have told us that they find it efficient. It gives us the chance to respond quickly and to the point and we know that you prefer that to a longwinded "formal" reply that takes forever in coming and causes further delay.

Best regards,

Chris Simpson

Chris Simpson,
Customer Services

CS-39

---

henniker's 779 Bush St., Box 7584, San Francisco, CA 94120

Dear Customer:

This is just a short note to let you know that we have received your inquiry.

We are giving this our immediate attention Although chances are that your concern will be fully resolved before that time please do allow three weeks before you assume that anything at all might be amiss. If, against all expectations, there should still be some loose ends at that time do write me again, including this postcard and any short explanation that might be in order. But I am very confident that will not be required.

I know you will excuse this rather "impersonal" communication, but I thought you would rather have a sign of life from me right away, rather than wait for an elaborate letter several weeks from now. But please be sure that I am taking care of your problem

It is a pleasure to be of service to you.

Sincerely yours,

Chris Simpson
Chris Simpson
Customer Services C.S. -82

You can handle many customer inquiries by writing a short, but responsive, reply right on the customer's letter. Clip this "Quick Note" to it. Customers really don't want "formality"· they want quick and responsive handling of their problems.

Make it an absolute rule to handle all customer correspondence within 24 hours of receipt. In the few cases that you cannot fully resolve things right away, be sure to acknowledge that you are aware of the problem and that you are working on it. A postcard like this will do the job. Be sure to hand sign all correspondence, even form letters.

is returned to him, right with our reply. In quite a few cases, in order to move things along, we jot our reply right on the customer's letter and clip a little explanatory note to it. We have done some research on it and the outcome is not too surprising. People don't mind a little informality — in fact, they seem to prefer it, because it appears that an honest-to-goodness human being has involved himself in the case. What does drive people up the wall is to get no reply at all, to get some stupid or non-responsive reply by a computer or to have a person reply who obviously doesn't understand what the problem is all about.

The only copies of correspondence that we keep are of those rare cases which, for some exceptional reason, are not concluded on the first round of correspondence, or which we feel should be kept because they might have some legal significance. There are not too many of those. And, naturally, they too get thrown out as soon as the matter with which they are concerned is laid to rest.

Customer service problems fall essentially into the following categories:

- Non-receipt of merchandise.
- Guarantee, warranty and quality correspondence.
- Returned merchandise, refunds, credits.
- Miscellaneous.

NON-RECEIPT OF MERCHANDISE

This is, by far, the most frequent customer service action and accounts for perhaps as much as 70% of all correspondence. It is in the best interest of your business that you handle anything concerning non-receipt as professionally as possible.

Naturally, the starting point for such professional action is to have good systems to begin with — systems that assure that orders received are promptly and properly filled.

You would be doing yourself a great disservice, and would threaten the destruction of your business, if you were to engage in the practice of advertising merchandise that you did not have in stock, or that you will not have in stock in sufficient quantity to satisfy expected demand. Not only is it destructive to your business, in that you will lose customer goodwill and confidence, but you will soon be in conflict with Federal Trade Commission guidelines and applicable state laws regarding mail-order businesses. And make no mistake about it: customers are very demanding (rightly so) and very savvy. If you make it a practice not to deliver merchandise on time — either because of poor planning or because you intentionally advertise what you don't have in stock, your customers will not only call you (and call you very nasty names) but they will contact consumer protection agencies, the Attorney General of your state and the Better Business Bureau. And all these agencies will write you and call you — and you had better respond to *them* or you will *really* be in trouble. They will drive you to distraction and you will not be able to conduct your business. You will be too busy defending yourself against claims by customers who have not received their merchandise.

What To Do If You Do Run Out of Stock

But even with the best laid plans, things sometimes do go wrong. Even at Henniker's we do have this problem occasionally. We have a built-in problem in that we work primarily with imported merchandise, and for promotional purposes deal with large quantities of low-priced goods. And believe me, the lady who bought those $1.99 *Hennisnips* or who sent her dollar for the *Organizer* can be just as unhappy and vociferous about non-receipt as that other customer who bought the $225 *Cuisinart* or the $699 *Fireball Pinball Machine.*

The Federal Trade Commission is now very demanding in its regulations regarding your handling of orders that you cannot ship promptly. Be sure to read the Regulations carefully and make sure to follow them. These rules are really minimum standards. If you run a reasonably tight ship you should have no problem with them. In fact, you should do much better. I take some pride in the fact that Henniker's has for years been doing what the guidelines demand, and more.

If, for any reason at all, we cannot ship an item within one week of receipt — and somebody will have to give me a pretty good explanation of why the item is not in stock and why it should take so long to get it — we immediately send the customer a postcard.

In some cases, if something goes horribly wrong and if we have an ad scheduled in a major publication, say *Parade* or *The National Enquirer* that we cannot possibly scratch (they have a lead

Merchandise:
Expected Shipping Date:

A VERY SLIGHT DELAY

Will you please forgive us for a very slight delay in the shipment of your order?

We thank you for your order for the merchandise we show on top of this card. You picked one of the most popular pups in our litter. There is a back order situation on this item right now and, unfortunately, there will be a short delay. We have put the expected shipping date on top of the card also. Our manufacturer has faithfully promised a shipment to arrive just before that date. The minute we receive it your order will go out super-pronto.

We are usually very good about filling orders, manage to dispatch all mail orders within an average of four working days and all telephone orders usually the same day we receive them. This doesn't help you or us with your present order; we just want you to know that to be back ordered on anything is very much the exception with us. Sometimes, however, with advertising commitments being made months in advance and especially with imported merchandise, these things are unavoidable—no matter how hard we try.

Please be assured that your order will be shipped on or about the date that we show above. We regret the slight delay and thank you for your courtesy and forbearance. Please allow us to serve you again soon. I am quite confident that on the next round we shall be able to shoot merchandise right out to you.

Sincerely yours,

Chris Simpson

Chris Simpson,
Customer Services

779 Bush St., Box 7584,
San Francisco, CA 94120 **hennikers**

C.S.-61

So sorry, not available
until late February
HENNICADDY

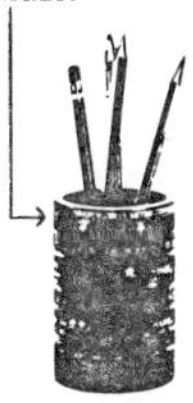

hennikers
779 Bush Street, Box 7584, San Francisco, CA 94120

Dear Customer:

We thank you for your request but unfortunately we shall be unable to comply with it immediately. The reason is that a mistake was made in scheduling the ad for this item in The New York Times -- what we meant to schedule was our Organizer. The Organizer, equally practical and lovable, is of course immediately available from sotck (because we had planned for it) and a $2 Gift Certificate is included. The Metric Caddy will be available in Late February, 1978.

This is one of life's little mishaps that is regrettable but cannot really be helped. We can-do any of the following:

☐1. Send you the Organizer immediately.
☐2. Have you wait until late February, 1978 and send you the Metric Caddy.
☐3. Refund your $1 postage contribution.

Assuming that you will be equally happy with the Organizer, we shall wait ten days and then send it to you instead of the Metric Caddy. Thus, if you agree with this solution, you need do nothing: we shall automatically send the Organizer. If you prefer either of solutions (2) or (3), please mark the appropriate box and return this postcard to us in your envelope, addressing it to:

Hennicaddy, 773 Bush St., Box 7584, San Francisco, CA 94120

To repeat, you need not do anything if you will accept the Organizer with our compliments instead of the Metric Caddy. If you choose either of the other solutions, we shall of course comply with your wish immediately. In the meantime, please do accept our apology for this error.

Thank you for your forbearance.

Sincerely yours,

Chris Simpson

Chris Simpson, Customer Services

ORGANIZER →
We'll send you this unless
we hear from you right away.

C.S.-109

Two examples of postcards that we send to our customers in case of late delivery. Late delivery and non-receipt are the most frequent (and most destructive) problems in the mail-order business. You will save yourself much grief if you hold them to a minimum, but do notify your customer promptly if they do occur. The upper postcard is "general"; the lower one deals with a special minor disaster. We printed a separate postcard for this event, because, unfortunately, thousands of customers were involved.

time of over 6 weeks), we may find ourselves with backorders of 3,000 or 4,000 units at one swoop. This is a dreadful situation. It has not happened often, but it *has* happened. And it has to be handled.

We usually spare no expense and import even relatively heavy merchandise by air freight so as to break a backorder log jam. Even then, a waiting time will be involved and we immediately notify the customer by postcard.

Key points to hold non-receipt trouble to the minimum are:

- Don't advertise what you don't have or don't have in sufficient quantity. Plan ahead!
- If you run out of merchandise, spare no reasonable expense to bring the merchandise in by air. Do it even if you drastically reduce your profit on the promotion. Ship it out by first class mail or other fast means.
- If, despite best laid plans, backorders in any item should develop, notify all customers promptly, tell them when to expect delivery, and offer them their money back, if that is what they prefer.

Form Letters Will Serve for most Purposes

Most customer service work is done by form letters. Customers really don't seem to mind that. They realize that their case is not unique and they would very much rather have a quick answer by an intelligent form letter, than having to wait two or three weeks for a personally typed reply to a routine inquiry. We have conducted many tests on this and found this to be the case. Think of it yourself — isn't that how you would feel about it too? The deadly sin is to send the wrong form letter or any reply that is not fully responsive to the customer's inquiry or the customer's needs.

The most frequently used letter for non-receipt of merchandise is the one which, among ourselves, we somewhat inelegantly call the "10-day stall letter."

We look the customer's order up in our "13-Week Sales Report" and locate the order quickly, since everything is arranged in zip-code order. We can then give the customer all the pertinent information about his order right in the body of the form letter. In

henniker's
779 Bush St., Box 7584, San Francisco, CA 94120

Item:
Date Order Received:
Date Order Mailed:
Order #:

Dear Customer:

We have your letter giving us the bad news that you have not yet received the merchandise that you ordered from us.

We checked it out immediately and found to our relief that we did indeed receive your order, that we processed and shipped it promptly. Please have a look at the right-hand upper corner of this letter. You will find the date on which we received your order, the date on which we shipped it and the order number.

The mails are often not as fast as one would hope. Please be patient and wait ten days after the receipt of this letter. If you have not received the merchandise by then we must presume it lost. In that case, please notify us on the back of this letter and we shall then immediately send you a replacement. But, PLEASE, do wait these additional ten days.

We regret having unwittingly caused you inconvenience, but assure you that we shall give you complete satisfaction.

Sincerely yours

Chris Simpson
Customer Service

henniker's
779 Bush St Box 7584 San Francisco, CA 94120

Item:
Order#:
Date Order Received:
Today's date:

Dear Customer:

We have your letter that you have not received the merchandise shown above.

Our records show that we shipped it promptly after receipt of your order.

Since so much time has elapsed, we must assume that it got lost in the mail. To try to trace this shipment and to get countless forms filled out would delay you further and cause you further annoyance. Naturally, we want to avoid that by all means.

We are responsible to our customers for safe arrival of all orders. A replacement will therefore be shipped to you within the next three days. Since merchandise goes by parcel post (which is slower than first class) please allow a little extra time for arrival.

We hope that you allow us to serve you again in the near future. Once more, we regret any annoyance that this mishap may have caused you.

Sincerely yours,

Chris Simpson
Customer Services

Two customer service form letters. We call the upper our "10-day stall letter." This is not a very elegant term perhaps, but it does take care of the majority of inquiries about non-receipt.

The lower letter is an acknowledgement that something is really wrong — too much time has elapsed. Don't speculate what the trouble may be, worry about that later! The customer is right, reship the merchandise that he paid for and has not received!

the majority of non-receipt cases, simply not enough time has elapsed for the customer to have received his order. Almost always, the customer has received the order by the time he gets this letter, or certainly within the ten-day period. That ends the matter and everybody is satisfied.

Naturally, it is clear that something is really wrong if too much time has elapsed — we usually allow a maximum of four weeks — and the customer has still not received the merchandise. No purpose is ever served in questioning the customer's word about non-receipt of merchandise. As a practical matter, everything that is sent by UPS is insured, and we can quickly get a receipt. Anything we send by mail is insured if its value is over $40. We have a receipt for that, too.

It is really quite rare that a customer will actually lie about non-receipt of merchandise. What does happen sometimes is that another member of the family or of the office staff has received the merchandise and has not informed the person who has ordered it. These cases are usually straightened out quickly.

What if four or five weeks have elapsed and your customer has not yet received merchandise that you know you have shipped? The thing to do is to reship it — pronto! In such a case we immediately send an appropriate form letter. That settles it quickly and in a friendly spirit.

If you will review the last two letters and all other customer correspondence that I shall show you, you will notice that we always express regret for having caused the customer annoyance. It is not just a gesture; I really feel that way about it, and I think to assure the customer of that feeling and of that concern is only common courtesy. The person with whom you deal has a grievance; he has paid you his money and he wants complete satisfaction. If you have not been able to give him this satisfaction on the first round, and even if it were somebody else's fault (let's say it's a post office strike, an act of God, a loss, a theft, or whatnot) he looks to *you* for redress. No purpose is served in trying to pinpoint "fault." It is up to *you* to express regret for any annoyance that has been caused — whoever may be *really* at "fault."

What do we do with an order that we simply cannot locate? The customer writes us that he has not received a certain piece of merchandise. We look it up in our 13-Week Sales Record and find no evidence of it. In that case, we have a pretty fast and easy rule: if it is merchandise for under $15, we reship it even if we cannot locate the order. If it is merchandise for more than $15 and if we cannot locate it, we send the customer a letter for clarification. We do not ask for photocopies of checks, etc. We simply ask the customer to look up whether his check has cleared, what the endoresement number is, etc. Sure, for a determined deceiver, there is a possibility of doing us some damage by what you may offhand think of as "loose business methods." But the number of those who want to deceive you and want to play games with you is really quite small. Most people who go to the trouble of writing you have a legitimate grievance. If you cannot find the order, or if things don't exactly mesh on your end, make up your mind that it's probably a flaw in *your* handling and in *your* systems, rather than a customer trying to deceive you.

Remember, the customer is always right (and usually is).

Another frequent cause of customer correspondence is the case in which the customer ordered, say, three units, and received only one. We know that this is a very easy error to make. If you will look once more at a standard coupon, you will see that we carefully circle any quantity larger than "1". Sometimes our operator may be inattentive and may not make that circle; sometimes the keypunch operator makes a mistake and punches "1", instead of "3"; or sometimes our packer has a bad day, and although the label says "3", she packs only "1".

In all of these cases, we immediately reship merchandise; it would just not occur to us to engage in correspondence or question the customer about how much he paid, etc. He knows what he ordered and he knows what he got. The customer is right!

We reship the missing merchandise immediately and include a little note expressing apology.

By the way, this is another thing that you should keep in mind: don't ever send any "naked" communication to your customer. You should always include a "personal" note, a letter or sales offer — always a little something extra, either to create goodwill, to make an extra sale or both.

Suppose you send a customer a refund check. Naturally, the most important thing for him is to get that check. But it will mean a

If there is anything out of the ordinary, anything "special," be sure to let your customer know what you are doing. Here are three package enclosures: 1. for late delivery; 2. for replacement of a shipment that went astray; and 3. for "make good" of an order that was short-shipped.

henniker's
779 Bush St., Box 7584, San Francisco, CA 94120

WE ARE LATE!

We take great pride in processing all orders within 48 hours of receipt and in having them out of our warehouse and on their way within five days thereafter. Our batting average is pretty good.

Sometimes, unfortunately, things don't quite work out as we planned. Delivery problems do occur, especially with merchandise that has proved popular beyond our expectations and with imported merchandise. Your choice just happened to be one of these cases.

We regret any inconvenience this delay may have caused you. We thank you for your understanding and patience and assure you that this is not our normal way to fulfill orders.

Please try us again and give us a chance to prove it to you.

Sincerely yours,

Chris Simpson
Chris Simpson
Customer Services

---

henniker's
779 Bush St., Box 7584, San Francisco, CA 94120

THIS IS A REPLACEMENT

Dear Customer:

It looks as though your original order went astray. Naturally, we are responsible for safe arrival. We are repeating your order and it is included in this package.

It is a pleasure to be of service to you. We regret any annoyance that this mishap may have caused you.

Please allow us to serve you again in the very near future.

Cordially yours,

Chris Simpson
Chris Simpson
Customer Services

CS-26

---

henniker's
779 Bush St., Box 7584, San Francisco, CA 94120

THIS IS A MAKE-GOOD

Dear Customer:

Looks as though somebody didn't count quite right when we shipped your original order or that our computer wasn't quite able to get your wishes through its electronic brain.

For whatever reason, we "short-changed" you and we ask you please to accept our apologies for that. We are making up the deficiency and it is included in this package.

It is a pleasure to be of service to you. We regret any annoyance that this mishap may have caused you.

Please allow us to serve you again in the very near future.

Cordially yours,

Chris Simpson
Chris Simpson
Customer Services

CS-27

whole lot more to him (and a lot more to you in the long run) if you include a letter expressing your regret that his purchase wasn't to his entire liking. It is important that you tell him of your hope that you might serve him again in the near future. Since he is now in a good mood, has a check in his hand and knows that you are an honest person, be sure to include a mini-catalog or any special merchandise offer that might appeal to him right away. You will be surprised how much quick turn-around you will get on that.

If the customer gets a replacement because he has never received his first shipment, we send him a little note with that. It just makes all the difference to the customer to have a kind word, in addition to having his merchandise replaced. It doesn't cause much work, but it shows thoughtfulness and it pays good dividends in customer goodwill.

How do we handle the customer who is complaining (justifiably so) about a backorder, about which we have already notified him by postcard. We must assume that he has not received the postcard or has not read it (although we try to put the picture of the item ordered on the postcard so that the customer can readily recognize and relate to it). In that case, we send him a form letter that essentially repeats what we told him in the postcard, namely that the item is out of stock and when it will be shipped.

As a final note about backorders, have a look at the note that we include with all packages in which we ship backordered merchandise. It expresses regret and concern and the assurance that late delivery is not our usual way of handling orders. Of course, in all of these cases, the customer has been notified of the delay. Therefore, chances are that he is not too mad at you. Arrival of the merchandise, although somewhat delayed, and your expression of regret should re-establish goodwill.

There are, of course, other possible complexities in non-receipt of merchandise. We are running a pretty large operation at Henniker's, and we have quite a few other form letters to take care of specialized cases. But those I have shown you in the preceding pages are the most usual and those that will cover about 80% to 90% of all non-receipts that will happen in your business. Until you get up to a fairly large volume, you should be able to handle all the remaining backorder situations by individually typed letters. If you handle things right and if you are sure not to advertise things that you cannot deliver (and if, in the rare case in which you can't deliver, you notify your customer promptly) your entire non-receipt problem will not be burdensome, your correspondence, headache and aggravation will be manageably small.

You may perhaps think that I have dwelt overlong on the matter of backorders, non-receipt and non-delivery. But I really don't think so. The degree to which this aspect of your business is under control is a measure of your professionalism and thus of your eventual success. Sloppiness of order handling, unpunctual delivery, non-delivery, not responding to customer inquiries, giving the impression of indifference or worse are the "bad things" that are often associated with the mail-order business in the public mind. It is up to you to dispel these thoughts quickly as far as your business is concerned. You can only do it by planning, by having proper systems and by quick follow-up.

Once you are into this business, you will realize that this is indeed the case. You will never get off the ground if you don't do it right and you will have a dreadful time fending off, not just your outraged customers, but all kinds of private and public consumer protection agencies.

So, give this part of your business your best shot. It deserves it!

WARRANTY AND GUARANTEE PROBLEMS

In contrast to what we have just discussed, namely non-receipt, your warranty, guarantee and similar problems will form a very small part of your customer service actions.

Our Guarantee is quite clear-cut and is stated, at least in an abbreviated version, in every space ad that we run, and in its complete version in our catalog and in every mail piece. Go back once more to the chapters on space advertising, direct mail and catalog. We spell our Guarantee out in detail. It is really quite simple. We take everything back within two weeks of receipt if the customer is not completely satisfied. Everything that the customer keeps is guaranteed "for parts and workmanship" for one year.

Let me first talk about the two-week return privilege. As far as we are concerned, it is mostly a matter of limiting our legal liability and of not subjecting ourselves to demands that may be totally unreasonable and which, even with all of our goodwill toward our customers, we should not be expected to bear.

For instance, hard as it may be to believe, we have had a fair number of cases in which an executor liquidated the estate of a deceased and found merchandise that the deceased might have purchased from us several years ago. The executors tried to return this merchandise. We don't really think that our obligation to a customer reaches beyond the grave and we usually decline the return of such merchandise. If we had put no time limit on it, we might be legally and morally obligated to take it back.

Then there is the occasional case in which the customer may perhaps be a little on the shorts and attempts to return for refund something after a year or so, that has given him pretty good service (and shows it). Naturally, we sympathize with these customers, but we don't really think we should take such merchandise back. We are in the merchandising business, but we are not a pawn shop or a bank. Again, if we had not established a time limit, we might be legally and morally obligated to take it back.

These are, admittedly, very rare cases. In the more usual case in which a customer attempts to return something, say, after a couple of months (instead of the 2-week period), the merchandise is immediately accepted and the customer gets his refund. Naturally, a good case could be made that somebody should make up his mind whether or not he wanted a piece of merchandise after he had kept it for two weeks. But, again, except in the most unusual cases, *the customer is right* and we do what he wants. It avoids hassle, correspondence, and creates goodwill. From a quite practical point of view, it is usually less expensive to do what the customer wants, rather than engage in several rounds of increasingly acrimonious correspondence.

All of this is, of course, especially true for relatively inexpensive merchandise in which it is simply not worthwhile to antagonize anybody, no matter how "wrong" he may be. Send the man his check and make him happy! He will not forget your being a square dealer and he will come back for more. And, who knows, next time the purchase might "stick."

Before I close this topic, I want to share with you a delightful Snoopy cartoon that illustrates very well the kinds of problems that

If you should ever get a letter like this from Snoopy (or anybody else), try to grin and bear it and remember that the customer is always right. Try to work something out (perhaps along the lines of the next illustration).

henniker's
779 Bush St Box 7584 San Francisco CA 94120

Item:
Order #:
Date Order Received:
Todays Date:

Dear Customer:

We acknowledge return of the merchandise shown above. You request that we refund for this return.

Much to our regret, we cannot comply with your request for the following reason(s):

☐ Our refund period is two weeks from receipt. Your order was placed on date shown above.

☐ Merchandise is damaged, and not in resaleable condition

☐ ______________________________

In order to preserve your good will, we attach a credit certificate for the full amount of your purchase. It is valid for one year and you may apply it during that time.

We regret that we could not fulfill your wishes entirely, but expect that you are satisfied with this solution. We hope you will allow us to serve you again in the very near future.

Sincerely yours, Chris Simpson, Customer Services

CS-25

SPEEDY CREDIT VOUCHER

henniker's
Customer Service
779 Bush St., Box 7584, San Francisco, CA 94120

Date ______

The amount noted on this voucher is the adjustment owed you for your recent transaction with us. It is not a check, so please do not deposit it. Please use it for credit with your next order. We use these vouchers to make small adjustments safely and speedily.
Our next Catalog or merchandise offer will be sent to you shortly so you can make your selection.

$ ______
Not valid for more than $10

NAME ______________
ADDRESS ______________
____

____
AUTHORIZED SIGNATURE

Note: Do not send copy of this voucher. We must have original.

SPEEDY CREDIT VOUCHER
SPEEDY CREDIT VOUCHER

C.S.-4I DO NOT DEPOSIT—NOT A BANK CHECK

There will be that very rare case (something like Snoopy's case) in which the request made on you is so unreasonable that you cannot really be expected to honor a demand for refund. Usually, the customer knows that. But even in those cases, don't let the customer go away empty-handed. Tell him why a refund is not in order and give him full credit for the merchandise. He will be satisfied.

you can run into in customer services. I must confess that I wiped away a manly tear when I saw that because, really, I have been on the receiving end of quite a few of such letters. But if the customer service man in the tennis racket factory is worth his salt, he'll probably write back: "Dear Snoopy: You are the customer and you are right. Let's see if we can work something out . . . . "

Special Warranty Cases

There are cases, of course, in which you will be dealing with relatively expensive merchandise that the customer has had for a considerable time, and which is so battered and used that it cannot be disposed of, even in a sale. What do we do in these cases? One thing is certain: we would never let the customer go away empty-handed, however "unreasonable" his request may be. The least we will do for him is to write him a letter in which we tell him why we are unable to give him a cash refund or bankcard credit. We then send him at the same time a merchandise certificate, a "Speedy Credit Voucher." I show you samples of both of these forms. 99% of all cases handled in this manner are resolved quickly and amicably. In his heart, the customer really knows that he has made a somewhat unreasonable request and he feels that we have treated him very nicely. A minor technical point about the form. It states that it is "Not valid for more than $10." This is simply a protection. We can, if we want to, eliminate this clause and have someone in authority initial it.

The majority of merchandise that we sell is "static"; i.e., things that don't move, that have no motors that can go too fast or too slow, in other words, merchandise that nothing very much can go wrong with. Of the merchandise that we handle, only clocks, watches and electronic equipment may have a tendency to give trouble.

If you handle "potential trouble" merchandise like that, you must have a well thought-through plan for handling warranties. That is especially true, of course, for merchandise that is produced abroad and that has no local representation, i.e. for which you are the first-line importer.

Watches, because of the large quantities we handle, are the most bothersome problem.

We have solved that problem to our satisfaction by engaging a wholesale watch repair service in New York. We have a contract with this service, by which they take care of all watches under our warranty for a fixed amount. They bill us once a month.

We include a warranty slip with every watch and urge the customer not to send it to us, but directly to the service. Have a look at the form. It states clearly that *we* are responsible and that we want the customer to send the watch to the repair service only for *his* convenience. The important thing is to make sure that the customer understands that *you* are ultimately responsible because he paid his money to *you* and you are, therefore, the one he may look to for redress if things should really go wrong. And, of course, you must really believe that and feel that way about it.

Clocks are less of a problem, but since they are somewhat heavy, there is usually reluctance on the part of the customer to ship the clock back to us. Considerable packing, trouble and extra expense, postage and so forth are involved. Frankly, we are not too happy to see a clock returned either. We have no in-house facilities to fix clocks ourselves (except to exchange the clockwork), so we would have to take it to our local clock service. How do we solve this problem? We simply tell the customer to take any defective clock that is still under warranty to a local clock shop, to send us the bill and we shall pay it. It makes for goodwill, saves the customer aggravation, and saves us some money, too. Usually, the bill from the clock shop is less than the round-trip freight would have been.

Shavers are the next largest customer service problem, but only because we sell such a large quantity of the Monaco Shaver, which we introduced in the United States. Fortunately, the shaver is incredibly sturdily built, and nothing is likely to go wrong. If a customer drops the shaver, he usually just breaks the plastic shell and we simply send him a new one, telling him how to install it himself. It is very rare that anything at all goes wrong with the mechanism itself within the first few years. If anything should go wrong within the first year, we simply send the customer a new shaver.

We have a special wrinkle with the shavers in that we offer the customer "a lifetime shaver plan." Please have a look at the back cover of our shaver guarantee. For the rest of his life, the customer can buy a new shaver at half-price, by trading in his old shaver. We throw the old shaver away and give him a new one. Since our gross margin on the shaver is about 60%, we do just a little better than breaking even. But we have created loyalty and faith with this action. Just a few months ago, I received a warranty card and a request to buy a shaver at half-price from a customer who had bought his original one from me when I first started at Haverhill's, way back in 1966. I was very touched, and although I am no longer technically connected with Haverhill's, I honored his warranty immediately.

Electronic equipment, quite frankly, can be the most bothersome. If you are dealing with a supplier located in the United States, you don't have much of a problem; you simply send defective equipment back to him. We try to avoid buying electronic equipment in the United States, because profit margins are very slim. We import most of our electronic equipment directly from Japan, from Hong Kong, or from Taiwan, which gives us acceptable profit margins. On the other hand, we are reasonably stuck with returned merchandise because there is nobody immediately to turn to. Fortunately, we deal with reliable suppliers, the quality is pretty good. Also, except for electronic clocks in which there are moving parts, nothing much can go wrong with solid state equipment. We don't have too many warranty problems. Even so, there is a small pile of radios, sound equipment, electronic clocks, etc., that we don't know quite what to do with. And, sorry to say, most of it is pretty expensive stuff.

But, considering the large amount of goods that we move, it is not a real worry to us.

Perhaps a word about directly imported merchandise is in order here. There is a problem that really did not exist at all only a few years ago, but it is a potential problem now and you must be aware of it. It is the problem of *product liability.* You are responsible for damage caused and incurred by everything you sell. Federal courts hold now that you are responsible even if the merchandise was used improperly, against instructions, even if it has been tampered with or modified. If it is merchandise that you have purchased in the United States (unless you yourself acted carelessly or knew the merchandise to be defective or dangerous), you are generally able to pass any liability on to the manufacturer. But, since the courts cannot reach a foreign manufacturer, you are ultimately responsible — just as though *you were* the manufacturer — for merchandise that you imported directly. So you want to be

henniker's
779 Bush St., Box 7584
San Francisco, CA 94120

DATE: ____________

WATCH SERVICE GUARANTEE

Your watch is guaranteed for any defects in parts and workmanship for one year from date stamped above. Your watch has been carefully tested and adjusted by electronic instruments before leaving the factory and manually tested once more before leaving our warehouse. If, however, anything should go wrong with your watch during the guarantee period, **do not return it to us**, but send it to our repair service:

Genova Watch Service
Suite 605, 37 W. 39th Street
New York, NY 10018
(tel. 212-563-1756)

(over)

GUARANTEE

The number of this shaver, the name of the purchaser, and the date of purchase, are registered with us.

1. We guarantee the MONACO for one year to be free of defects in material and workmanship. We shall immediately replace a defective shaver. The shaving head is not included in this guarantee. Replacement shaving heads are available at $5.95.
2. MONACO LIFETIME PLAN! At any time after 1 year, you may return the MONACO (for whatever reason) and trade it in for a brand new model at $14.50*. Please return this guarantee when requesting a trade-in.
3. This guarantee is void if any of the following has occurred:
   a. The shaver has been opened or any of the 3 aluminum caps removed.
   b. The shaver has been dropped or intentionally damaged.

*which includes $1.00 postage/insurance.

henniker's

779 Bush St., Box 7584, San Francisco, CA 94120

Guarantees are important in the mail-order business. You cannot tell your customer often enough that you stand behind your merchandise. We sell many watches and to have the customer deal directly with our repair service is a comfort to him and saves us much work. The back of the guarantee spells out that we are absolutely responsible and that we direct him to the service only for the sake of his convenience.

The Monaco shaver guarantee adds the interesting wrinkle of the Lifetime Guarantee Plan. It turned out to be a powerful concept. See if you can do something similar!

extra careful that the merchandise that you import is safe and not likely to cause damage. And, of course, whether you import directly or not, you want to be sure that you carry adequate coverage for product liability in your insurance package.

Let me comment on the phrase "Guaranteed for Parts and Workmanship." This may sound a little like an old-time "hedge phrase" and, perhaps, in a way it is. We used to say that things were "Guaranteed for All Causes," but — believe it or not, we had people who had dropped equipment out of an 8th floor window or who had run over it in an automobile. And there was at least one case in which a customer intentionally had destroyed a piece of equipment with a hammer. All these people felt that "All Causes" included such contingencies and that we should honor our Guarantee. We did, but decided that we didn't like that and changed the wording.

What do we do now? In all likelihood, despite the "hedge," we would still replace the watch that fell out of the 8th floor window, but we would probably decline with regrets to make good for the man who destroyed his radio with a sledgehammer.

RETURNS AND REFUNDS

This is an area in which you should really have no trouble at all, once you make up your mind about two things:

1. Returns and refunds are part of the mail-order business. They are like the dirty dishes in a fine restaurant. They are not the fun part of the business, but they have to be handled, and they have to be handled professionally.
2. Your customer is entitled to get his money back when he returns merchandise. And he is entitled to get it quickly.

After all these years, I still am not really crazy about signing those weekly refund checks. But I grit my teeth and I do it because I know it is part of the job. That is the way you have to look at it. It is something that has to be done, and there is absolutely no purpose served in moaning and hedging.

It is just a matter of technique. We have an employee who logs in all returned merchandise. This employee turns over this form once a week to Customer Services, and Customer Services, as

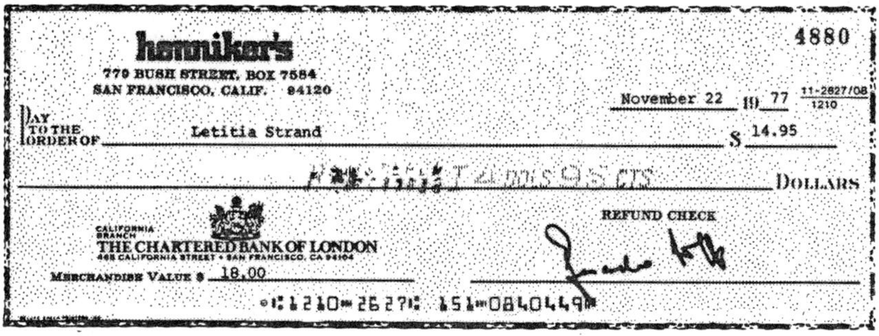

hènniker's
779 BUSH STREET, BOX 7584
SAN FRANCISCO, CALIF. 94120
4880
November 22 19 77
11-2627/08
1210
PAY TO THE ORDER OF Letitia Strand
$ 14.95
DOLLARS
CALIFORNIA BRANCH
THE CHARTERED BANK OF LONDON
465 CALIFORNIA STREET • SAN FRANCISCO, CA 94104
MERCHANDISE VALUE $ 18.00
REFUND CHECK

You are well advised to have an entirely separate check series for refunds, clearly marked "Refund Check." It conveys to your customer that refunds are a natural part of your doing business and that you have made provision for that. Our refund checks also carry a "Merchandise Value." It encourages the customer not to cash the check, but to order something else instead. We find a good number of conversions and I think so will you.

hènniker's

779 Bush St. Box 7584 San Francisco. CA 94120

*Please read for important bonus information!

Dear Customer:

We try really very hard to please each one of our customers, and when merchandise is returned we are always a little sad. Not that we love to make refund -- we don't pretend that we are really happy about that part, who would be? But what does nag us is that we didn't make our customer happy. So all we can hope for is that you will give us another chance and that we'll be able to please you next time.

Your refund check is enclosed. This is for the full amount of your purchase, excepting only postage and insurance. In the lower left-hand corner of your check you will find a dollar amount preceded by the letters MV (merchandise value). This is about 20% more than the cash value of your check. If you want to hold on to the check (you can always change your mind if you prefer) you may use it in that amount for purchase of merchandise at any time.

Thank you for your confidence. We hope to be able to serve you again very soon.

Sincerely yours,

Chris Simpson

Chris Simpson, Customer Services

Even something as welcome as a refund check should not go out "naked." Accompany it by a cover letter such as the one shown, and some promotional material! You have treated the customer in a friendly and professional manner. You will be pleasantly surprised by how often he will turn right around and use this refund check for another purchase.

routinely as anything else, writes the refund checks, always within a week of receipt of returned merchandise.

We accompany each refund check by a short letter. It is an interesting concept. What we do is to encourage the customer *not to cash his check,* but to use it for merchandise. Then at the bottom of the check there is the "merchandise value," which is larger than the face value of the check, by approximately 20%. I regret that I have no precise statistical information available as to what percentage of customers take advantage of this option, but it is a fair share. It does not take much explaining why it is an advantage to us to have the customer take this option. A refund is a total loss and it does not necessarily preserve the customer. If we can induce him to make another purchase we have kept him as a customer. And, of course, we have at last partially recovered the total loss that an out-and-out refund would have been.

Another, somewhat more subtle, advantage of this system is that it provides us with a considerable amount of "cash float." Even those customers who ultimately cash the refund check, are likely to hold on to it for quite some time before they make up their minds whether to cash the check, or whether to use it for merchandise. This provides us with "hidden working capital" that would otherwise not be available.

One piece of statistical information might be of interest in this connection. I find that, year in, year out, our return/refund ratio is approximately 2% to 3% of total sales. I consider that normal. A certain amount of return/refund is unavoidable. Regardless of the quality of the merchandise, there will always be an irreducible number of people who will not be happy. So don't worry about making refunds. It's simply part of doing business.

When your refunds exceed, say, 5% of sales, you do have a problem. Analyze what merchandise is being returned, and you will probably find that certain items of merchandise account for the bulk of your returns. Look into that merchandise carefully. See if you can improve anything. In quite a few cases, you will have to realize that the problem is intrinsic and that you might well be better off eliminating this product altogether.

Often, however, a simple step can solve the problem. For instance, we had one item — a great profit producer, *La Bisquera* (a clay cooking utensil) — which had a very high return ratio. It was a real problem. We looked into it and found that the principal reason for returns was the chipping of the clay in transit. We made a basic improvement in the packing and cut the return ratio to about one-quarter of what it was before. We were thus able to save this part of our business and to make it very profitable.

Not only is a return a lost sale, but it does, of course, cost you money just to handle it. What is more, even if you handle the refund in the most professional manner, you have inevitably left a customer dissatisfied. Also, you may assume that for every piece of merchandise that is being returned, at least one other customer may keep it because he does not consider it worth his while to return it. That will, of course, be especially true with inexpensive merchandise. But the customer who has kept the merchandise that he didn't like, is not very likely to be a prospect for future sales. You have not made him happy. And you are in the business of making people happy, so that they will continue to purchase from you.

To summarize on returns and refunds:

- Refunds are a normal part of the mail-order business. Handle them professionally.
- Make refunds promptly — do not take more than a week.
- Watch your percentage of return/refunds, and analyze trouble spots, especially if refunds exceed, say, 5% of sales.

MISCELLANEOUS CUSTOMER CORRESPONDENCE

Most of this "miscellaneous correspondence" has to do with customers wanting to tell you about changes of address; customers not understanding how a specific piece of merchandise works; customers giving you the benefit (and I really mean *benefit*) of their opinions, either brickbats or bouquets.

Read all of it very carefully and reply to all those that call for an answer.

You may also wish to look at that form in which we ask customers about packing and delivery. We just don't want to make any conjectures. We do want to find out what impression people get when they receive our merchandise, what condition the package arrives in, and how long it takes to get from here to there.

DID HAVERHILL'S SERVICE STRIKE YOU
LIKE THAT OF A TORTOISE..
OR THAT OF A HARE?

We try to ship orders within 48 hours of receipt (in the rare instance that we cannot ship right away, we promptly notify our customers). Then we ship merchandise by fastest means -- this means by air or truck to Chicago and then distributed by UPS, or it may be UPS all the way, or it may be parcel post. But after a package leaves our warehouse we have no more control over it and naturally, we are very interested in what happens to it. Will you help us by answering a few questions?

- The order # on my package was____________________
- The date on the package showed shipment on____________________
- I received the package on____________________
- The condition of the package was____________________
- I have these comments on the merchandise and on the packaging____________________
- I have these comments on your service____________________
- My name____________________
- Address____________________
- ____________________Zip__________

Thank you very much. Will you just put this post card in the mailbox? It is prepaid. No postage is required.

Sincerely yours,

Ken Phillips

Ken Phillips
Customer Services

OFFICE USE ONLY

DATE SHIPPED__________

☐ UPS CH.		
☐ UPS NY	☐ UPS OR.	☐ BULK
☐ UPS ATL.	☐ PP	☐ FGT.
☐ UPS BLU.	☐ PPINS	☐ AIR
☐ UPS CA.	☐ PP SP.	☐ TRUCK

Sprinkle this kind of questionnaire, in the form of a prepaid postcard, at random into your packages. Your response will be very high. The principal purpose is to learn whether you have any deficiencies in your service or in your merchandise, to learn what your customer likes and dislikes about them, and how different carriers and mail services perform on their routes. With this information you should be able to improve service and product. Also, your customers will be pleased to know that you take interest in them and that you are concerned about their views.

Never fear, your customers will let you know.

Precisely because "Miscellaneous Correspondence" cannot be put into form letters, this is an area in which a good customer service person can earn his or her spurs. In an operation such as ours, for instance, there are at least 10 or 20 letters a day which do not fall into any of the "standard" categories, but that need to be answered. I still think a skillful customer service person can create a lot of goodwill — or lose it.

One thing to keep in mind in the mail-order business is that the person who communicates with you, whether he praises or condemns, is a person who is interested in communicating with you. The mail-order business is one of interacting. Therefore, even those who may act a little "nasty" are people who should be cherished, because they really want to get and stay involved with you if given half a chance. I have countless examples of customers who sounded off in their letters and who appeared to be the most intractable "trouble makers." With fair and courteous treatment, proper apology for any wrong that we might have done, or perhaps even a small present, these people can usually be turned into very good customers and boosters.

I cannot close this whole area on customer services without asking you to look at something that I am really quite proud of.

We have a radio station in San Francisco (KCBS), which has, as so many radio stations in the United States, a customer service program — ours is called "File 74." Complaints dealing with mail-order firms (and the heroic measures by which the moderator of the program rescues consumers and gets them their due) are the main staple of those broadcasts. We monitor the program quite regularly and are happy to notice that we are never mentioned.

Imagine my pleasure and surprise when at Christmas a few years ago the program moderator mentioned Haverhill's (of which I was president at the time) telling his listeners that we were *the only mail-order firm that he knew of that took care of customer problems before they even arose.* I have never met the conductor of the program, nor have I ever advertised with the station. Naturally, I was pleased — I knew we had been running our Customer Services right. And that's the way *you* must run *your* Customer Service Department. It is *the only way* to do it. It is the only way to keep out of trouble, and it is the only way to build a business in mail order.

A CBS Owned Station
Represented by CBS Radio Spot Sales

KCBS NEWSRADIO 74
NEWS

FILE 74 - The Merry Christmas (#10, week of 12/18/72; 2:00)

Theme Cart: Sound
Voice: Hello. This is Fred Wilcox with File 74..and a bouquet of Christmas wishes to all those who have helped us so much in the past year! A Merry Christmas to John Porter, Hershel Elkins and their staffs in San Francisco and Los Angeles offices of the Attorney General. There are the various state boards and the office of the Postal Inspection Service -- often run with small budgets, but never too busy to dig out background material for File 74. A Merry Christmas to them..and may they get more money and tougher laws to work with. And, of course, there are those agencies which seem to hear only complaints all year long: Medicare, Blue Cross, Blue Shield. Hampered by big backlogs and public misunderstanding, their attitude toward File 74 has always been, "How can we help?". A Merry Christmas to them. And, I think a note at this season is due, to the San Francisco mail order firm of Haverhill's -- the only business of its kind that I know, which seems always to resolve its consumer problems in favor of the customer right or wrong....and quickly.

When I heard this broadcast, I knew that we were doing things right! This is an "action line" program and, naturally, it made me feel very good to get such an opinion from such a critical source. Try to conduct **your** customer service in such a way that people will say about you, too, that you ". . . always resolve consumer problems in favor of the customer, right or wrong — and quickly."

Perhaps, before closing this chapter we should have a quick look at reading material. Interestingly, there is quite a lot of literature on customer service, and some of it is quite good. Like so many other things, you really have to learn by doing, but you can help yourself along by reading some technical books.

Here are a few that I find helpful:

Assuring Customer Satisfaction
by Rodney L. Cron
Van Nostrand Reinhold Co., Publ.

This is a rather thorough treatment of the subject, possibly more than you may wish to tackle the first time out.

How to Handle Claims and Returns
by J. R. Kissel and A. Kissel Grun
McGraw-Hill Book Co., Publ.

A concise volume, with many practical applications, forms and sample letters. Useful in your business, but perhaps most suited to the needs of the small manufacturer.

Keep Your Customers (And Keep Them Happy)
by Stanley J. Fenvessy
Dow Jones-Irwin, Publ.

Here you have a really down-to-earth book, which may well be your first introduction to the subject. Its subtitle is *How to Turn Complaints into Compliments,* and, naturally, that is what you want to do.

The foregoing is certainly not meant to be an exhaustive "bibliography," but it is a start. Business is a little like making love: you have to learn by doing, you can't learn it from a book. But it might help your technique and your performance if you read a few good books written by experts.

Take heart: you are pretty close to getting your "diploma." There are only two more chapters to come. The last is the pay-off chapter: how to sell your business for a million dollars or more — how to make the big score! But before we come to that, there is one more hurdle, one more lesson. It is how to keep records. The successful mail-order business is very orderly and systematic. You will go nowhere if you do not record your results properly. So, please, although it is all downhill from now on, do read the next chapter carefully.

Chapter 10

HOW TO KEEP GOOD RECORDS

The mail-order business is one of numbers. In order to be successful you will have to keep close track of everything you are doing. You will have to keep good records so that you will know at all times exactly where you are standing.

The main purpose of record keeping is to be able to bore in on those items of merchandise and those media that are successful for you, and to increase your advertising budget in those; and to cut out (or improve, if you can) those media and that merchandise that do not cut the mustard.

When your business is very small and when you work only with very few media and very few items, you probably can keep most of the important information in your head. But it is to your advantage that you set up good control records right from the very beginning. Let me show you how we do things at Henniker's. I think these are examples that you can follow to your benefit.

BASIC ENTRY RECORDS

Space Advertising Insertion Record is a basic entry form which we keep separately for each publication. In the heading of this form, we list the name of the publication, the circulation and the "Net Cost Per Line" (which is the cost after all discounts). In our case, since we have a house agency, it means less 15% advertising commission. Since we pay our bills on time, i.e. ten days after they are presented, it means an additional 2% off.

The next item is the *Dollar Cost per Thousand for a 7 x 10" Space* (this is the size of a standard magazine page). In this particular publication it takes 560 lines to make up such an area*; thus, we arrive at the cost by multiplying 560 x $1.35 and — since circulation is 200,000 — dividing by 200. This is an important piece of information for us, because it makes it possible to compare apples with apples and to know how much, from one medium to another, it costs us to reach a given number of readers with a standard advertising space.

As to the columns in this form, they are really quite self-explanatory. The "Ran Last" column is of importance so that we won't inadvertently repeat an ad that had run quite recently. Also it allows us to tell the publication when the ad had run before, so that they can pick up art from that issue. Cost, of course, is the lineage of the ad multiplied by cost per line.

The next column (GM$) is our gross margin for this particular item of merchandise. For the knife listed in the first line, the gross margin is $9.00. This means that we have to sell thirty units to break even, which is stated in the column that follows.

The next column is the number of units sold, which we fill in when we believe that the ad has run its course, usually three months. Dividing that by the break-even of 30 units and subtracting 1 (which represents our investment), we get a factor of .60. This means that we have recovered our investment of $270 and have made a profit of $162, 60% on our investment.

You may recall that I gave you a "go/no go" factor of 50% return on investment. Here is an item that we certainly would be repeating because we exceeded our minimum requirement by 20%: we made 60% return on our investment — instead of 50%.

The next line shows a brooch which, with 160 lines, has a space cost of $216. We have a gross margin of $8 per unit on this item and therefore a break-even of 27 units. Unfortunately, we only sold 19, which gives us a factor of 19/27 minus 1 or -.30. Here is an item that falls short by 30% of even paying its cost back. Unless we see a pretty clear way of how to improve this ad or the offer dramatically, we should certainly drop that. Offhand, it would seem kind of difficult to put this into the winner's column, let alone to bring it to

---

* I hope you remember that one "line" is 1/14 inch. Thus, with column width of 1-7/8 inch, we have 4 columns x 10 inches = 560 lines.

hennikers	PUBLICATIONS ADVERTISING RECORD				
	PUBLICATION: Daily Star	CIRCULATION: 200 M	NET COST/LINE $ 1.35	7"x10"/M $ 3.78	

Publication	+.	O	+	#!	—
Date	1/3	1/10	1/17	1/24	1/31
Item	Knife	Brooch	Telescope	Watch	Loupe
Size	200 l.	160 l.	182 l.	240 l.	140 l
Cost	$ 270	$ 216	$ 246	$ 324	$ 189
GM $	9	8	12	23	4
BE $	30	27	21	14	47
50% Contr.	45	41	31	21	71
100% Contr.	60	54	41	28	94

Period Ended	This Pd.	To Date	This Pd.	To Date	This Pd.	To Date
1st week	13	13	6	6	10	10
2nd "	12	25	2	8	8	18
3rd "	13	38	3	11	4	22
4th "	5	43	—	11	—	22
5th "	3	46	1	12	4	26
6th "	1	47	2	14	—	26
7th "	—	47	—	14	—	26
8th "	—	47	1	15	2	28
9th "	1	48	3	18	2	30
10th "			—	18	1	31
11th "			—	18	1	

Publication Advertising Record is kept up-to-date, week by week until the response to the promotion has run its course. Response needed to reach break-even, and for 50% and 100% return on investment are shown. Marks on top of each column are in-house symbols representing the results obtained in each promotion.

hennikers

SPACE ADVERTISING INSERTION RECORD

PUBLICATION: Daily Star CIRCULATION: 200 M NET COST/LINE $ 1.35 7"x10"/M$ 3.78

DATE	ITEM	AD#	SIZE	RAN LAST	COST	GMS	BE#	#SOLD	FACTOR	REMARKS
1/3	Knife	284	200 lines	11/8	270	9	30	48	.60	
10	Brooch	316	160 "	new	216	8	27	19	(.30)	
17	Telescope	192	182 "	10/4	246	12	21	32	.56	
24	Watch	155	240 "	10/18	324	23	14	51	2.62	!!
31	Loupe	82	140 "	9/13	189	4	47	45	(.05)	?
2/7	Fastener	314	160 "	new	216	6	36	52	.44	
14	Heater	182	120 "	12/13	162	10	16	23	.42	

Space Advertising Insertion Record is a running record of insertions placed in any medium and gives a quick review of results obtained.

the 50% return on investment that we have stipulated as the minimum acceptable.

As you will see in a moment, we keep much more elaborate records and statistics on performance of media and items. This is just a "quick and dirty" record for the moment, which serves to get a fast overview of how items have performed before we re-schedule them or decide to drop them.

Publications Advertising Record is the next record we keep. It repeats to some degree the information from the *Space Advertising Insertion Record,* but on this report we put down the *history* of what actually happens and how many of each item we sell with each ad or each promotion every week. We have already discussed what the information in the upper right-hand corner means. That is identical with what we had on the previous report. Also, in the top portion of each column, we repeat the information that we previously had. Now, in addition to the break-even information, we also put down how much we would have to sell to make 50% profit contribution, and how much in order to make 100% profit contribution. "100% profit contribution" means to double our investment in the promotion.

We enter this information every week from our "Sales Report by Source," which we talked about in the chapter on data processing. You may wish to turn back to the example of that Report to see how this relates. We are programmed to have this information presented in alphabetical source code order. You should insist on the same. It will make the weekly manual recording and cumulation of sales a very quick job.

You see that we provide 13 lines for each item. This corresponds to 13 weeks. It is the exceptional item that sells beyond that time and if it does, you may in all likelihood disregard it because it will be just a stray sale. You can readily see that the bulk of sales is done in the very first few weeks — faster if it is a daily publication and a little more slowly if it is a weekly or monthly publication.

These two preceding records assist us in re-scheduling advertising on a week-to-week basis. We can make quick and good decisions with that — push the winners and cut out or improve the losers.

After an ad has run its course, however, (after about 13 weeks) we go into a deep analysis of the performance of each medium and of the performance of each item. These two reports are important analytical tools. I shall take a little time to tell you about them.

PERMANENT ANALYTICAL RECORDS

Media Effectiveness Report is the first of two such Records. Again, in the upper corner, you have the information with which you are already familiar. Also, you will readily understand the information in columns [1] through [6]. Column [7] represents 95% of all items sold from this particular ad. The 5% that we subtract is a conservative allowance for returns.

We then multiply Column [7] (Net Number of Items Sold) by Column [5] (Gross Margin per Unit) and subtract from that Column [4] (Cost of Ad). This gives us the Gross Profit which is entered in Column [8].

Dividing Column [8] by Column [4] gives us our *Profit Factor.* It is recorded in Column [9].

Column [11] is the running total of Column [10] (Cumulative Gross Profit). Column [10] is the same as Column [8] and therefore not really necessary. Column [12] is the running total of Column [4] (Cumulative Cost).

Dividing [11] by [12] gives us [13] *Cumulative Profit Factor* for this particular medium. This is, of course, what this Report is all about and what we really want to know. We find that with all ads run in the *Daily Star* we had a profit factor of .76. This means that we recovered our investment of $1623 and made a profit of $1240 or 76% on the total dollar amount invested. This is a fine performance (remember 50% return is what we are shooting for). Naturally, this is a medium in which we shall continue and in which we shall try to increase our schedule. We shall further try to improve performance by pushing those items and those categories of merchandise that seem to perform well in this medium and eliminating those that perform poorly. All of this information is available in this Report.

The next example is *The Daily Bugle,* which features a some what grimmer set of figures. We find that column [13], our Cumulative Profit Factor, is -.18. We invested $3,419 and recovered $2,820, i.e. we lost $599. This means that we failed by 18% to recover our

henniker's

MEDIA EFFECTIVENESS RECORD

MEDIA: Daily Star
CIRCULATION: 200m
NET COST/LINE $ 1.35
7"x10"/M $ 3.78

(1) DATE	(2) ITEM	(3) LINES	(4) COST $	(5) GM $	(6) BE #	(7) .95 x NO. SOLD	(8) G.P.	(9) FACTOR (8)/(4)	(10) (9)x(4)	(11) Σ(10)	(12) Σ(4)	(13) (11)/(12)	(14) RE-MARKS
1/3	Knife	200	270	9	30	48	162	.60	162	162	270	.60	
10	Brooch	160	216	8	27	19	(64)	(.30)	(64)	98	486	.20	
17	Telescope	182	246	12	21	32	138	.56	138	236	732	.32	
24	Watch	240	324	23	14	51	849	2.62	849	1085	1056	1.03	!!
31	Loupe	140	189	4	47	45	(9)	(.05)	(9)	1076	1245	.86	?
2/7	Fastener	160	216	6	36	52	96	.44	96	1172	1461	.80	
14	Heater	120	162	10	16	23	68	.42	68	1240	1623	.76	

henniker's

MEDIA EFFECTIVENESS RECORD

MEDIA: Daily Bugle
CIRCULATION: 380m
NET COST/LINE $ 2.78
7"x10"/M $ 4.16

(1) DATE	(2) ITEM	(3) LINES	(4) COST $	(5) GM $	(6) BE #	(7) .95 x NO. SOLD	(8) G.P.	(9) FACTOR (8)/(4)	(10) (9)x(4)	(11) Σ(10)	(12) Σ(4)	(13) (11)/(12)	(14) RE-MARKS
1/5	Wand	130	361	4	90	95	19	.05	19	19	361	.05	
12	Brooch	160	445	8	56	38	(141)	(.32)	(141)	(122)	806	(.16)	
19	Knife	200	556	9	62	58	(34)	(.06)	(34)	(156)	1362	(.11)	
26	Roller	180	500	10	50	50	–	0	–	(156)	1862	(.08)	
2/2	Stapler	140	389	6	65	39	(155)	(.40)	(155)	(311)	2251	(.14)	
9	Book	420	1168	8	146	110	(288)	(.25)	(288)	(599)	3419	(.18)	

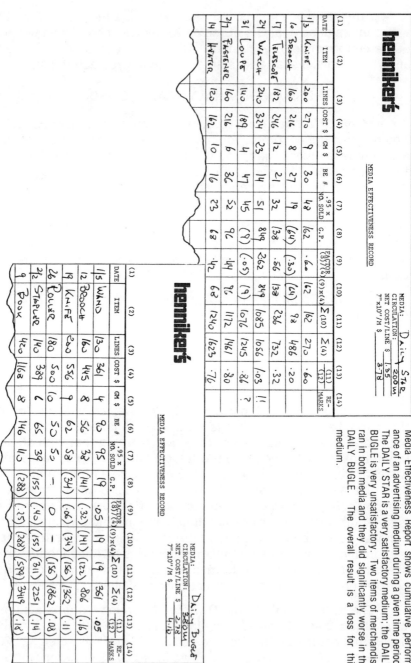

Media Effectiveness Report shows cumulative performance of an advertising medium during a given time period. The DAILY STAR is a very satisfactory medium; the DAILY BUGLE is very unsatisfactory. Two items of merchandise ran in both media and they did significantly worse in the DAILY BUGLE. The overall result is a loss for this medium.

investment in this medium. This is so bad, so far from what we wish to achieve, that we are going to drop this medium immediately like the proverbial hot potato.

Item Effectiveness Record is the next Record that I want to talk to you about. It is essentially the same as the *Media Effectiveness Record,* with one important difference: in the *Media Effectiveness Record,* we listed *all items* that we had run in a single medium, in order to determine how the medium performs for us on an over-all basis. In the *Item Effectiveness Record*, we sort information by any one item and track its performance in all different media in which it has run. It shows us how "good" this particular item is.

The numbering of the columns is somewhat different from that of the previous Record (since we don't list the Gross Margin which is the same for all items), but the principle is the same. Column [12] gives us our *Cumulative Profit Factor* for this particular item. We find that our knife achieves a cumulative profit factor of 1.47. This is an exceptional item, a spectacular profit performer — remember that a factor of .50 is what we strive for. So this item returns $1.47 on every dollar invested — almost 3 times our minimum expectation! We shall try to spread this item through all possible media, hopefully including those with very large circulation. Obviously this is a winner and we will ride it for all it is worth. We have to get in there with the mostest before the competition catches on.

Our next item is the brooch. It has a *Cumulative Profit Factor* of -.20, which means a loss of 20% on our media investment. It is an item that we shall have to discontinue because we are pretty consistently losing money on it. Although it made a little money in some media, it is a loser over-all. Thus, we shall phase it out, not reorder it, take it out of the catalog and put the balance of our inventory on sale in our store.

You will be well advised to develop a system of record keeping similar to the one I have just shown you. We only talked about recording space ads. Naturally the same principle applies to keeping records of your direct mail and of your catalogs.

HOW TO TRACK RESULTS OF DIRECT MAIL

The principle of how to track the results of your direct mail is of course pretty much the same as for space advertising. You just

henniker's

ITEM EFFECTIVENESS RECORD

ITEM: KNIFE

GROSS MARGIN $ 9

(1) DATE	(2) MEDIUM	(3) LINES	(4) COST $	(5) BE #	(6) .95 x NO. SOLD	(7) G.P. $	(8) FACTOR (7)÷(4)	(9) (8)x(4)	(10) Σ(9)	(11) Σ(4)	(12) (10)/(11)	(13) REMARKS
1/3	STAR	200	270	30	48	162	.60	162	162	270	.60	
8	OBSERVER	"	340	38	134	866	2.55	866	1028	610	1.69	
19	BUGLE	"	556	62	58	(34)	(.06)	(34)	994	1166	.85	
22	JOURNAL	"	360	40	154	1026	2.85	1026	2020	1526	1.32	
2/3	HOLMES WEEKLY	"	800	89	294	1846	2.31	1846	3866	2326	1.66	
8	CAVALCADE	"	760	84	158	662	.87	662	4528	3086	1.47	

Item Effectiveness Report is similar in concept to the Media Effectiveness Report, but analyzes the performance of one piece of merchandise in different media. This knife is an excellent performer, yielding a profit factor of 1.47, almost 3 times our minimal goal of $.50 return per dollar invested.

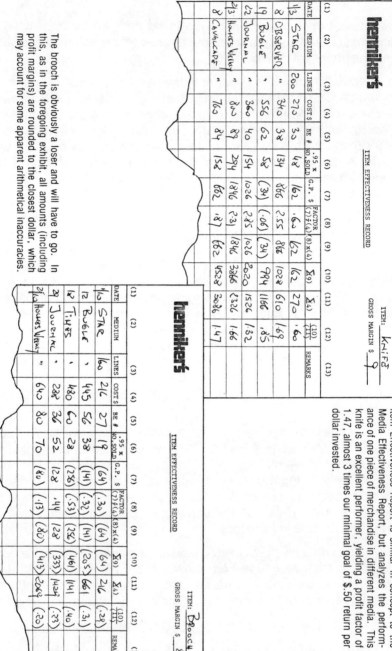

henniker's

ITEM EFFECTIVENESS RECORD

ITEM: BROOCH

GROSS MARGIN $ 8

(1) DATE	(2) MEDIUM	(3) LINES	(4) COST $	(5) BE #	(6) .95 x NO. SOLD	(7) G.P. $	(8) FACTOR (7)÷(4)	(9) (8)x(4)	(10) Σ(9)	(11) Σ(4)	(12) (10)/(11)	(13) REMARKS
1/10	STAR	160	216	27	19	(64)	(.30)	(64)	(64)	216	(.29)	
12	BUGLE	"	445	56	38	(141)	(.32)	(141)	(205)	661	(.31)	
18	TIMES	"	480	60	28	(256)	(.53)	(256)	(461)	1141	(.40)	
29	JOURNAL	"	288	36	52	128	.44	128	(333)	1429	(.23)	
2/10	HOLMES WEEKLY	"	640	80	70	(80)	(.13)	(80)	(413)	2069	(.20)	

The brooch is obviously a loser and will have to go. In this, as in the foregoing exhibit, all amounts (including profit margins) are rounded to the closest dollar, which may account for some apparent arithmetical inaccuracies.

have to adapt your forms to the different medium. But the objective does not change: you want to determine what the return on the investment (or, heaven forbid, the loss on investment) of every promotion is. More precisely, you want to determine what the result of every segment of your promotion is, or of every variant, in case you do not just test lists but also different approaches. That will let you determine what to continue, what to drop, what to change, or what to attempt to improve.

Let's look at the special form that we have designed to track our direct mail results.

It is really quite straightforward. We list the promotion, the sales price, our gross margin (the difference between cost and sales price), and the total cost per thousand pieces in the mail. We also list the cost to outside lists, which we have arrived at by the methods of marginal analysis that we have talked about.

We also determine, by simple arithmetic, what the break-even is for the house list and for outside lists, and how many units per thousand we have to sell, either to reach our minimum goals of $50 per thousand contribution (an acceptable mailing) or $100 per thousand contribution (a good mailing).

Each line in this schedule represents one segment of the mailing, with the top line being that segment of the house list that this promotion is being mailed to. The columns show the number of pieces mailed in thousands, the date of mailing, the key imprint on the label (if it is different from the code that is entered in the data processing system to identify the segment) and the number of units that have to be sold to break even on this segment. We spell this out. We find that it is important to keep it in mind at all times, because one thing is to make money and to know how much you are making; another even more important thing is to know what you have to do in order not to lose any. And, of course, you need to reach at least the break-even point to accomplish that.

There are thirteen columns for thirteen weeks, and we enter the results by week and cumulatively until the mailing has run its course — usually before the end of the 13-week period.

The "net" refers to the dollars contributed or lost in this segment of the mailing. In the house line, we find that we have sold 1,014 units. Since we have mailed 38.5 m pieces, this corresponds

henniker's DIRECT MAIL CONTROL FORM

Promotion: Table Ware
Sales Price: $14.95
Margin: $9.00 (incl. returns & bonus)
Cost of Mailing/m (house): $120
Cost of Mailing/m (out): $150 (marginal costing)
BE/m (house): 13.3
BE/m (out): 16.6
Drop Date(s): 12/23
Remarks:

Response per m needed for contribution per m of:
(House): $50: 18.9 $100: 24.4
(Out): $50: 21.1 $100: 26.7

List	# m	Date	Key	Code	BE	1/8	1/15	1/22	1/29	2/5	2/12	2/19	2/26	3/5	3/12	3/19	3/26	4/2	Net	Remarks
House	385	12/23	0073	—	512	82	466	286	80	36	24	17	3	9	6	3	-	2	$4506	!!
						82	548	834	914	950	974	991	994	1003	1009	1012	1012	1014	$12/m	
Ill. Cheese	5	12/23	0074	—	83	-	22	13	10	8	2	6	-	3	4	3	3	1	$(75)	
						-	22	35	45	53	55	61	61	64	68	71	74	75	$(15)/m	repeat?
Hogan's	5	"	0075	—	83	-	31	20	15	14	7	2	-	3	-	2	1	1	$114	
						-	31	51	66	80	87	89	89	92	92	94	95	96	$23/m	+10,000
Sunshine	5	"	0076	—	83	12	18	3	7	5	4	4	6	3	-	2	-	-	$(174)	
						12	30	33	40	45	49	53	59	62	62	64	64	64	$(34)/m	Out!
Blackstone	5	"	0077	—	83	26	18	20	10	8	6	4	5	3	-	-	1	-	$159	
						26	44	64	74	82	88	92	97	100	100	100	101	101	$32/m	+10,000
U.S. Trail	5	"	0078	—	83	-	23	3	10	4	3	6	-	2	1	2	—	—	$(219)	
						-	23	31	41	45	48	54	54	56	57	59	59	59	$(44)/m	Out!

A simple form to track down direct-mail results. In this promotion, the house list is performing very well. Two of the five outside lists are performing well and will be expanded to 10,000 pieces on the next round. The one list is a small loser, but we shall retest it. Two of the lists do not perform at all and will not be continued.

to 26.3 pieces per thousand. Gross margin per unit is $9.00, so this is equivalent to $236 gross margin per thousand. Our cost of mailing is $120 per thousand, so this gives us a contribution of $116 per thousand pieces mailed.

This is very good — frankly, we think it is somewhat exceptional. There are not too many successes like this around. Remember, we decided that a mailing that would give us a contribution of $100 per thousand was a "good" mailing — one that should by all means be rolled out to other lists. This mailing substantially exceeds these goals, so naturally, you are going to do just that.*

Before having access to the results of this mailing, we routinely tested, together with our house list, five outside lists of 5,000 names each. With the help of our broker, we had carefully selected these lists so that they would be targeted as closely as possible to the offer itself and to demographics similar to those of our house list.

Let's look at the results: our break-even with outside lists is $150/9 = 16.6 units sold per thousand, or 83 units for every 5,000 tested. All of these, except *Sunshine Mailer* and *U.S. Trails* will be retested with 10,000 names each, on the next round. Yes, we'll even retest *Illinois Cheese* which pulled only 75 units, i.e., about 10% less than break-even. The reason for that, without going too deeply into the mathematics of it, is that this "deficiency" may well be due to statistical variation.

HOW TO KEEP TRACK OF CATALOG PERFORMANCE

We are agreed that your catalog is your most important promotional tool and it might therefore be deserving of the closest analytical scrutiny. But catalog analysis is also more complex than analysis of space advertising or direct mail results. Because you have not just the overall analysis of dollar results to your own list and to outside lists, but you also have to analyze the many components of your catalog, the different pieces of merchandise — usually 200 or more. You need to do that in order to "fine tune" your

---

* In these, as in other examples in which specific sources, media, other companies' mailing lists and specific merchandise are illustrated by numeric examples, names are changed in order to protect privacy. In certain of these examples, results have been simplified or adjusted to illustrate a point.

henniker's

GROSS CATALOG ANALYSIS

Date: 9/28 List: House Quantity: 140M Code: CA0177

Date: 9/23 List: Mo. Trading Quantity: 5M Code: CA0277

	THIS WEEK			CUMULATIVE			THIS WEEK			CUMULATIVE		
W/E	#	$	Average	#	$	Average	#	$	Average	#	$	Average
10/7	150	4873	32.5	150	4873	32.5	3	83	27.7	3	83	27.7
14	699	20271	29.0	849	25144	29.6	6	145	24.2	9	228	25.3
21	399	12449	31.3	1248	37593	30.1	5	140	28.0	14	368	26.3
28	386	11040	28.6	1634	48633	29.8	8	278	34.8	22	646	29.4
11/4	363	12705	35.0	1997	61338	30.7	8	198	24.8	30	844	28.1
11	266	7820	29.4	2263	69158	30.6	4	112	28.0	34	956	28.1
18	246	7700	31.3	2509	76858	30.6	3	92	30.7	37	1048	28.3
25	271	8910	32.9	2780	85768	30.9	4	133	33.3	41	1181	28.8
12/2	439	13390	30.5	3219	99158	30.8	4	82	20.6	45	1263	28.0
9	306	8711	28.5	3525	107869	30.6	2	58	29.0	47	1321	28.1
16	190	5408	28.5	3715	113277	30.5	1	30	30.0	48	1351	28.1
23	70	2156	35.1	3785	115433	30.5	–	–	–	48	1351	28.1
30	18	567	31.5	3803	116000	30.5	1	29	29.0	49	1380	28.2

Projected Sales: $127,000
Gross Profit (58%): $73,660
Cost (@ $.25): $35,000
Total Contribution: $38,660
Contribution p. Catalog: $ .276

Projected Sales: $1518
Gross Profit (58%): $880
Cost (@ $.26 – marginal): $1300
Total Contribution: $(420)
Loss per Catalog: $(.084)

Two steps are involved in catalog analysis. This is Gross Catalog Analysis, cumulating sales experience for each list. This is for our Christmas Catalog. We know by experience that we shall sell an additional 10% from each list after the holidays.

catalog, to be able to decide what merchandise to continue and what to withdraw from the catalog.

We need a little more space to tabulate catalog results, because our purpose is not entirely served by just recording "number of units sold," as we did in space and direct mail. Even in the summary report, which is abstracted from the detailed computer printout, we need to know the *number of sales made,* the *total dollar sales,* and *average sale per customer.* Sure, the total dollar sales (at the average gross margin) are ultimately the most important and decisive, but it is important for us to understand the purchasing habits of our house list customers and of outside customers. We need to know whether they purchase in large numbers, but in smaller dollar amounts, or vice versa. Observation of these results gives us valuable clues in regard to merchandise strategy and list management.

Let's just look at two of these tabulations, namely the performance of our house list for the Christmas catalog mailing, and that of one outside list that we tested with 5,000 names.

We mailed 140,000 catalogs to the house list (we cut out all those who had not made a purchase in 14 months, all "Lost Sheep"). We made 3,803 sales, for a total of $116,000, i.e., an average sale of $30.50. These results are as of December 30. Experience shows that there will be an additional 10% trickling in over the next two months or so. Thus, we can project total sales of, say, 4,200 orders and ultimate dollar volume of $127,000.

Divide this into the 140,000 catalogs mailed out and you get sales of just over $.90 per catalog. This is not quite the magic figure of $1.00 per catalog that we had been shooting for, but we consider it quite good. We had a large proportion of high-margin jewelry in this catalog and many orders for this attractive merchandise. This gave us an exceptionally high overall margin of 58%. Work out the arithmetic yourself (go back to the chapter on catalogs if you need to). But with a cost per catalog in the mail of just over $.25, you can see that we make just about $.27 contribution (profit, if you prefer) per catalog. That is quite good. Naturally, it is Christmas, and it ought to be good. If you can't make it at Christmas, you just can't make it at all, and major changes are in order.

The outside list that I show you, *Missouri Trading Post,* looks much less promising. Until December 30, we have altogether sold only $1,518 (projected), just over $.30 per thousand, producing a gross margin of just over $.17 and a *loss* of about $.084 per catalog. You might say that we acquired 54 customers, and that is correct, but they cost us about $8.00 each. Even if the result had been better and sales had been such that we could have acquired customers at a cost of, say, $1.00 each, my advice would have been to discontinue mailing to this list. You may remember that we decided that each customer is worth $3 to $5. That is quite true, but there *is* a difference between what something is worth and what you should pay for it. We have learned techniques in this book how to acquire customers without any cost at all, even at a profit. So, my advice is again: stay away from trying to buy customers. You don't have enough money to do it, and you shouldn't do it even if you had that much money. And in line with this decision, let's drop this list. It's a shame, too, because *Missouri Trading Post* has almost a million customers. It certainly would have been nice if it had worked for us.

We now have talked about what you might call "gross analysis" or "list analysis" of catalogs. In closing, let me just quickly show you how to keep records of the performance of the individual pieces of merchandise. It is from such records that your decisions on which items of merchandise to keep in the catalog and which to discontinue will be based. Have a look at our *Catalog Summary by Rank.*

I won't take you through the entire arithmetic, but what we do is essentially quite simple: we take the entire cost of the catalog — everything that goes into it, including photography, typesetting, all preparatory work and, of course, printing, postage, fulfillment, etc. We divide this total by the number of pages, which gives us the cost per page. Then we determine (without attempting to go into undue precision) what fraction of a page every given item occupies. This is quite easy if we have a modular catalog (look back to it if you have forgotten what that is). It takes a little "eyeballing" if you have a non-modular catalog.

Now let's look at the form. It shows part of the tabulation of one of our previous catalogs. The first four columns are quite clear. Column [5] is simply the number of items sold through the life of the catalog. If the catalog had not yet run its full course, we would apply a factor to "Sales to Date" in order to arrive at what experience teaches us will be the final sales figure.

henniker's

CATALOG SUMMARY BY RANK:

(1) Rank	(2) Item #	(3) Item	(4) Page	(5) # Sold	(6) $ Unit Sales	(7) $ Total Sales	(8) $ Unit Margin	(9) $ Gross Margin	(10) Space Factor	(11) $ Space Cost	(12) $ Contribution	(13) $ Contribution/ $ Invested	(14) Index	(15) Remarks
41	30734	INTERCOM	13	19	25	487	17	323	.17	136	187	1.38	1.16	
42	30776	STOPWATCH	I	9	25	225	17	153	.08	64	87	1.36	1.15	
43	20974	INCLINO	I	21	13	273	9	189	.10	80	109	1.36	1.15	
44	10538	CALLAWAY	20	60	10	600	5	300	.16	128	172	1.34	1.14	
45	50690	LEATHBAG	1	26	32	836	17	442	.24	192	250	1.30	1.12	
46	10975	CAMPTOOL	17	46	10	465	8	368	.20	160	208	1.30	1.12	
47	21162	RELOGER	20	33	17	561	11	363	.20	160	203	1.27	1.11	
48	20438	JUMBOVAC	3	25	17	433	13	327	.18	144	183	1.27	1.11	
49	10058	BEDCLAMP	11	24	17	408	12	288	.16	128	160	1.25	1.10	
50	30585	MAGNIFY	6	54	7	378	6	324	.18	144	180	1.25	1.10	
51	50021	BRASSMENA	16	50	12/13	637	9/10	484	.27	216	268	1.24	1.09	
52	50187	SLIMHIP	6	4	90	405	60	240	.14	112	128	1.14	1.04	
53	21055	COFFEEMAC	8	6	165	990	65	390	.23	184	2[illegible]	1.12	1.03	
		MULTIRADIO	23	24			12	288	.17	13[illegible]			1.03	

Catalog Summary by Rank is the analysis of every item in the catalog. Its cost of publication, its contribution to profit, and its "index." It is the indispensable tool for planning which merchancise to continue and which to discontinue in the next catalog.

Column [6] is the *Unit Sales Price*, rounded to the nearest $.50, and Column [7] (*Total Sales*) is the product of Columns [6] and [7].

Column [8] is the *Gross Margin per Unit.* By multiplying it by Column [5] we get Column [9] (*Total Gross Margin*).

Column [10] is the *Space Factor,* which is the fraction of a page the item occupies. In case of this particular catalog, we find that each page costs us $800. Thus, with a space factor of, say, .23, we have a *Space Cost* of $184. This is shown in Column [11].

Column [12] is the *Contribution,* namely Column [6] less Column [8].

Column [13] is what really counts — again, we have to compare apples with apples — and it gives us the *Contribution per Dollar Invested.* It is how much contribution (or how much "profit," if you prefer) we make on this item for every dollar invested. We arrive at that by dividing Column [12] by Column [11]. This puts all items on a comparable basis.

We then rank these items from No. 1 (the best) down to the last and worst. When we approach the bottom of the list, we have items which not only do not make any contribution, but which actually will be losers — they don't even pay for the space they occupy.

We then apply one final parameter which is the *Index* listed in Column [14]. This is a system that is common in Europe — it was pioneered by Heinrich Heine GMBH in Karlsruhe — and we adapted it to our purposes. We take the *Total Contribution* (the sum total of Column [12]) and divide by the *Total Cost* (the sum total of Column [11]). This gives us the *Average Contribution per Dollar Invested.* We call that *Index 1.* In this particular catalog the average contribution per dollar invested was $1.06, which therefore is *Index 1* by definition.

The Index of each particular item is arrived at as follows:

$$\text{Index Item} = \frac{[13] + 1}{(\textit{Index 1} + 1)}$$

All this sounds a little complicated. But, once you understand it, it is very quickly done on any electronic desk or pocket calculator. The really important thing is to understand it because quite weighty decisions will hinge on it.

We then apply the following criteria on what to keep and what to throw out of our next catalog:

1. At least one-third of all items must be taken out to make room for new ones. To rephrase it: there must be a one-third minimum merchandise turnover from catalog to catalog. That is simply a matter of policy. It keeps us on our toes and keeps each catalog fresh. Possibly, proven items that have been discontinued temporarily may be used again in a later catalog.
2. All items that do not have a minimum index of .5 must be replaced.

Naturally, if more than a third of our items happen to fail the index .5 test, more than one-third of the items will have to go. But if this happens, the merchandise manager and several other people will have to listen to some very harsh words. Something would have to be definitely wrong in merchandise selection, pricing or catalog make-up.

Of course, an even more fundamental test of the catalog as a whole is the *absolute value of Index 1,* the average contribution per dollar invested in the catalog. In this example it was $1.06. This is really quite excellent and, frankly, a little better than we usually do. It means that we had over 100% return on our catalog investment. Go back to the tabulation in the catalog chapter. On an investment of $.33 per catalog, we made a contribution of $.13+. This is equivalent to a contribution of .13/.33 = $.40 per dollar invested, i.e. an *Index 1* of .40. That is okay for a beginning operation. For a mature mail-order house, an *Index 1* of .40 would be just about the lowest acceptable minimum. If you don't attain this, you are in trouble. Something is wrong with the cost of your catalog, with your merchandise, or both. You should shoot for a minimum *Index 1* of .50 — and try to do better.

One final word about the preceding. When we talk about continually eliminating merchandise, we do not go *entirely* by formula and by rote. Sometimes there are special reasons why something should be continued even if it does not quite meet the acceptance or continuation tests. For instance, you may have a very heavy inventory in an item, and you decide to continue it. You decide to do it because you think you might make out better that way than by liquidating the merchandise at less than cost. Perhaps you will change its price, the approach, or the space allotted to the item in the next catalog. Or you may have commitments with manufacturers which make it almost mandatory for you to continue this item in your catalog. Or you are making money with it in direct mail or space advertising and therefore may feel obligated to back it up by continuing it in the catalog. Such cases, however, will be very much the exceptions. In almost all cases you are probably well advised to throw out that which does not meet your profit criteria.

Naturally, the opposite is also occasionally true. You may have an item that does meet all of your criteria for profit and for index ranking and you may still have to decide to let it go. It could be, for instance, that you see competitive factors on the horizon that you do not wish to tangle with. That was very true with us in the case of electronic calculators and electronic watches, for instance. They were a terrific bonanza, but we decided to kiss them goodbye when the market began to be flooded and prices started collapsing. Or you may find that an item gives rise to too many customer complaints, or you may know that the manufacturer will discontinue it.

What we have just discussed is the most important part of record-keeping in the mail-order business, namely the tracking of results from promotions in all media. Your most important business decisions will be based on that. You can make up such records only if you have good and reliable data to draw on. These will have to be provided by good data processing systems and good input media. We now know how to do all this, and how to do it right. But while the records that we have just discussed are indeed the most important, they certainly are not the only ones. Once you have reached a certain size, you have to keep track of many things — inventories, personnel, accounts receivable, store performance, and much more — and all are based on keeping good records and interpreting the information properly.

To Wind Up About Record Keeping

Just to summarize:

- Mail order is a business of numbers. You must know at all times exactly what you are doing, which items are profitable, which are not.

- You have to have common denominators, ways of comparing one medium and one item with another. You accomplish that by reducing ads to "Unit Space" and reducing investment in all media to "Unit Dollar."
- Keeping records is work and not always fun. But you will not get a true handle on your business and you will not be able to make good promotional and merchandising decisions if you don't have a very close control on where your profits come from and which your losers are.

———— • ————

You may now heave one great big sigh of relief, because the "work part" of this book is over. You have learned how to merchandise, you have learned how to make great ads, write direct mail and make fine catalogs. In these last chapters you have learned some of the very special tricks of the trade, which are different in the mail-order business from any other. I really think that, if you follow the advice that I have given you, if you use your native wit, some midnight oil and elbow grease, you will now be in position to build a very fine business.

But wait until you come to the next chapter. That is where the payoff is. That is what your business is going to be all about and that's what you bought this book for.

In the next chapter I shall show you how to cash in on all the effort you have expended. I shall show you how to position your mail-order business so as to sell it for *at least one million dollars.* I shall show you *How to Make the Big Score!*

Chapter 11

HOW TO MAKE THE BIG SCORE

I have now told you about everything I know about the mail-order business. If you have followed my advice and my suggestions, you should be pretty much of an expert.

You have learned how to pick that niche in this wide field that is best suited to your own talents and interests. You have learned how to select merchandise, how to write space advertising, how to make catalogs, and how to design direct mail pieces that sizzle and sell. And you have learned those special angles that are unique to the mail-order business, and which you need to have a handle on. You should be able to make an excellent living at it, to have the satisfaction of seeing it grow and become nationally well-known. But to live well, important and desirable though it is, is not what you bought this book for. This last chapter deals with what this book is *really* about. I shall show you how to make the "big score," how to parlay your mail-order business into at least $1 million — right into your pocket.

Please remember that the whole purpose, the whole thesis of this book is not just to teach you how to create a mail-order business and how to run it. Sure, you need to know that and you need to do it before you can take the last step. But this is only the means to the end that you and I have planned for all along. The *real* purpose of this book is to teach you how to become a millionaire. The way to accomplish it is to build a smoothly running and profitable mail-order business, to bring it along to a point at which it will be desirable as an acquisition to a major corporation, and then to sell it for at least $1 million.

I started Haverhill's in 1966 and I sold it to Time Inc. in 1971 for 18,000 shares of Time Inc. stock. The stock at that time had a market value of $56.50*, so this amounted to just over $1 million. Not bad, if you consider that I started this business from a standing start, just five years earlier and with virtually no capital (certainly less capital than I have recommended that you should have). I also made a very nice living for myself and for my family in those five years. I had lots of fun, learned many things, did much foreign traveling and felt very fulfilled and creative.

There is no reason why you should not do as well as or perhaps better than I did. When I started Haverhill's, I really didn't have much going for myself. I was over 40 years old, had three children and absolutely no background in the mail-order field. You may remember that I was really a mining engineer by profession. I had no previous marketing experience of any kind, had taken no courses in this subject, had no friends or mentors in the industry that could give me any help, and had not read any book on the subject. I latched onto it, literally by accident. I launched myself into this business without really knowing what I was doing. I learned as I went along and I succeeded. Chances are that you are younger than I was at the time. This may sound a little immodest, but you do also have the great advantage of this book, my personal guidance in how to go about building such a business step by step. *You* know what you are going to do and you have a clear goal to shoot for.

Your path will be quite clear if you keep firmly in mind what you are trying to accomplish. It should not be primarily to make a very good living; your ultimate and unswerving purpose should be to build a mail-order business with a record of ever-increasing earnings, a business that you will eventually be able to sell for at least one million dollars.

From the time that you start your business until you eventually sell it, you must be as careful with expenditures as you can. You must above all resist the temptation of greatly increasing your personal standard of living by pulling excessive monies out of this business. You should in fact try to live just as simply as you can. You need to do that in order to preserve and increase your working capital, but most importantly, in order to create an ever-increasing record of earnings. It is difficult to produce such a good record of earnings if, as your business prospers, you begin to divert ever

---

* The stock has since split 2 to 1. As I am writing this, it is quoted at 38½. My 36,000 shares are worth $1.4 million.

larger amounts out of it for your own use. Try to "rough it" — just a little. I mean, just try to do without the yachts, condominiums, Italian sports cars, for a few years longer. If things go right, and if you follow my advice, it should take you about five years until you have a salable company. A salable company is one that has sales between $1 million and $2 million and that has pre-tax earnings of not less than $100,000. After you have built that company and have sold it, you can live it up with a vengeance, you can go the yachts and condominiums route, if your tastes run in that direction.

WHY LARGE CORPORATIONS LIKE MAIL-ORDER BUSINESSES

The mail-order business is *the ideal business* to sell to a large corporation. This is one of the reasons why I stayed in it and why I went all the way with it once I had stumbled onto it. My goal was right along to do exactly what I wound up doing. By their very nature, mail-order businesses are national rather than local or regional in scope. They can readily be expanded to very large size, by timely infusion of additional capital, by additional management, by access to national media or to national markets, or by any combination of these.

Large national corporations have no interest at all in local or regional businesses. They are interested only in national businesses which they can expand by bringing their own capital, their own management talent and their own access to markets and media to bear. They will inevitably gravitate toward successful mail-order businesses.

There is another factor at work here. It is the glamor, the "sex appeal" of this business. This glamor is not based on any superficialities. It is based on hard-nosed recognition by the most knowledgeable marketing people that *mail-order is the marketing wave of the present and of the future.* We are only in the beginning of this true marketing revolution. If you get in on it now, you will be almost literally on the ground floor. It is the recognition of its enormous potential that has impelled so many of our largest publishers, entertainment conglomerates, marketing and consumer goods corporations, to get into this business. Very few large corporations attempt to start such businesses from scratch. They don't have the time or the know-how. No, they are constantly on the lookout for mail-order businesses with sound growth and earnings records and they are willing to pay very handsomely to acquire such businesses and the expertise that goes with them.

Also, keep something else in mind: by the very nature of the mail-order business, you will create multi-millions of advertising impressions. The name of your firm, even if still on the modest level of about $1 to $2 million of annual sales, will have large public recognition and will almost literally have become a household word. Those in charge of acquisitions in major corporations will know about you and about your business. They will have formed a positive impression about your business and will be predisposed toward acquiring it.

Virtually every large corporation in the United States — and I am not just talking about "conglomerates" whose very existence is based on buying other companies — has its "acquisitions" department (often disguised under other names, such as "Corporate Development Department"). These people are constantly on the lookout for good businesses to acquire so that they may diversify, enter promising new fields of activity, have their eggs in more than just one or a few baskets, and increase their stockholders' earnings.

I AM REALLY JUST A PIKER — OTHERS HAVE DONE SO MUCH BETTER!

As I have told you repeatedly in this book, my purpose is to teach you how to start a successful mail-order business, how to run it and to nurture it to growth, and how to sell it — perhaps after five years or so, for at least one million dollars.

As you know, I have done just that. And that, I believe, enables me to teach you how to do it, step by step.

Before selling Haverhill's to Time Inc., I was seriously negotiating with at least three other companies who had eagerly approached me to buy my firm. I am not talking now about the many half-hearted "feelers" and semi-serious offers. I am only talking about those really serious negotiations which, in at least two cases, resulted in preliminaries to merger. In both cases we couldn't quite get together at the last minute.

Two of the prospective suitors were in the entertainment business — the first was one of our three national networks, the second was one of the large movie/entertainment conglomerates.

I also had very serious merger discussions with one of the country's most prominent manufacturers/distributors of packaged food products, a large corporation that already had about five or six large mail-order houses in its stable.

But I couldn't really blame you too much if you took all of this with a mighty grain of salt and if you believed that what happened to me was perhaps somewhat of a "fluke" and that it cannot readily be repeated. But, the exact opposite is the case! There are scores, hundreds of people who have done pretty much the same thing that I have done. I am not trying to teach you something that is very rare or unique in this business. I am teaching you something that is standard procedure.

In fact, among my fellow mail-order executives, I am known as somewhat of a piker for letting my business go for "just a million dollars." I have to accept my share of good-natured ribbing when I meet with some of my colleagues — those who held out a little longer or had a little more "nerve" and who sold their businesses for $3 million, $5 million, $10 million or even more. And most of them hadn't been in business much longer than I. But, all of them, without exception, had the same idea — some had it from the very beginning, and to others it came a few years after they had started to build a mail-order business: to create a record of growth in sales and earnings and then to sell this business for a great deal of money — at least *one million dollars but hopefully more,* to a large publicly-held company. That is what I am trying to teach you, and that is what this book is about.

But, in order to give you a "flavor" of what I am talking about, here are just a few capsule case histories. I have picked them, almost at random, from my files. As to the accuracy of the data: in most cases, the information is based on public records; in some it is based on personal communication or on "industry consensus." There may be some slight errors in detail, but I assure you that they are not significant.

- *Boris Leavitt* and his associates, sold *Hanover House* (including its Lana Lobell and Lakeland Nurseries divisions) to the Horn & Hardart Company in 1972. Leavitt had founded his firm in the 40's. When he sold the business, it had sales of approximately $17 million per year and pre-tax profits of about $1.2 million. He received about *$7 million* for the company.

- *Leonard P. Carlson* and his associates sold *Sunset House* to Broadway-Hale Stores Inc. in 1969. The company had been in existence for just twelve (12) years. The last full year before the merger for which data are available (1967) sales of Sunset House were $24.9 million and pre-tax earnings were $440,000. The company was sold for securities with a market value at the time of approximately *$14 million.*
- *Peter Alport* and his associates sold *Norm Thompson* to the Parker Pen Company in 1973. He had been in business for about 20 years. In the year immediately preceding the merger, sales were $2.9 million and pre-tax profits $180,000. Parker Pen paid *$1.8 million* in cash.
- *James Wooters* founded *National Needlecraft* in 1947. He sold it to CBS in 1969 and, as of this writing, still continues as president of this division. This is somewhat of a record. When he sold the company, it had sales of approximately $6 million and pre-tax profits of about $1 million. He sold the company for approximately *$8 million* in cash.
- *Luther Breck* was principal owner of a family firm called *Breck's* which, until he took charge, was primarily in the seed business. He steered the firm into general mail-order merchandise and, by 1965, had attained sales of approximately $10 to $12 million per year, with pre-tax profits of about $1.5 million. At that time, the business was sold to MacDonald's (the trading stamps, not the hamburger people). Hard figures are not available, but it is understood that he received approximately *$10 million.*
- *Margaret Rudkin* started tinkering around in her kitchen in 1937 and gradually went into mail-ordering her breads and similar products. She sold *Pepperidge Farm* to Campbell Soup Company in 1961 for approximately *$28 million.*
- *Sidney Fink* and *Ralph Fried* started Lee Wards in 1945. The firm specialized in patterns and embroidery kits. They sold it to General Mills in 1969, having attained sales of $14.5 million and pre-tax profits of about $1.5 million per year. The purchase price was *$11.8 million.*

- *William F. Nieni, Sr.* and his son *William F. Nieni, Jr.* sold *Eddie Bauer* to General Mills in 1971. The business had been started in 1920 and specialized in outdoor clothing and equipment. The firm did not really get going and hit its stride until 1968 when the Nienis bought out the original owners. In the year preceding the merger with General Mills, sales were somewhat in excess of $9 million and pre-tax profit approximately $800,000. The sale/merger was a stock transaction worth *$10.5 million.*

- *Rudolph and Nancy Talbot* started *The Talbots, Inc.* in 1948. Talbots manufactures clothing, mostly of the casual and leisure variety and sells primarily by mail. In 1972, sales were approximately $7.5 million and pre-tax profits approximately $700,000. They sold the business to General Mills in 1973, in a stock transaction valued at *$6 million.*

- *Dr. S. Cowan* founded *Veratex* in 1951, manufacturing certain medical and dental specialties and supplies and selling them mostly by mail. In 1965 sales were just over $2 million and pre-tax profits approximately $230,000. He sold the business to W. R. Grace and Company in 1965 in a stock transaction valued at *$2.5 million.*

- *John Figi* went into the mail-order business in cheeses and gourmet foods in 1942. He didn't really get going on a national scale until the mid-1960's. In 1967, sales were over $7 million and pre-tax profits about 1.2 million. He merged *Figi's* with W. R. Grace & Company and received stock worth *$6.3 million.*

- *Joy and Murray Hall* founded *Ambassador Leather Goods* in 1962 in Niagara Falls, New York. Their business was based on an "organizer" wallet that Joy Hall had developed. Other small leather (and later, vinyl) goods were added. About 1967, the Halls had to leave upstate New York for health reasons and they started all over again in Tempe, Arizona. In 1972, sales, all by mail order, were about $11 million and pre-tax profit approximately $1.5 million. In the year following, they sold the business to Dryden Associates for approximately *$7 million.*

Please keep in mind that the foregoing is just a sample. I could go on and on. And I mentioned only fairly substantial transactions, firms that you are in all likelihood familiar with — you may even be their customer.

But, there are countless others, on this level or on a smaller scale — people who had founded a mail-order business and after just a few years sold it for a few hundred thousand dollars, for a million or for a whole lot more.

Aren't you amazed that people, people just like you and me — could have created this kind of wealth in just a few years? Hardly any of them were "geniuses," just men and women who kept their eye on their goal and kept plugging along. Most of them were in their late twenties or early thirties when they got started and wound up being millionaires, often many times over, when they were 35 or 40 years old. You see, it *can* be done. And there is no reason why you cannot do just as well.

HOW TO ATTRACT "CORPORATE SUITORS"

How do you get major corporations to come look for you as a possible acquisition? Easy! Remember, large companies have their "bird dogs" out all the time. A going and growing mail-order business is a prime acquisition target, and that is why so many of these bird dogs are looking for companies just like yours. You are constantly exposed. Your ads are constantly in front of the public. As soon as these bird dogs have reason to believe that your company is of the right size and right profitability, they will come and seek you out. "Right size" means sales of $1 to $2 million per year and commensurate profits; "right profitability" means pre-tax profits of at least $100,000 per year.

But, there is no reason that you should just stand by passively and wait for things to happen and for "suitors" to come calling on you. There are some things that you can do yourself to make things happen when you think you are ready.

First of all, you can make yourself personally known in your community and in your industry. You can, for instance, avail yourself for interviews with the financial editor of your local newspaper, who is always on the lookout for a success story. Who knows, your story may be picked up by a national syndicate or a national magazine. Another good opportunity is to wangle an invitation to a TV talk show which may give you instant national publicity. The combination of getting personally known, in addition to the large exposure that your business already has in national media, can be extremely helpful.

You can take even more positive steps. Here is a "ploy" that I used successfully at Haverhill's in order to get personally acquainted with the "vice president in charge of corporate development" of companies that I thought would be a real "fit." I went to my attorney for assistance and I asked him to write a letter to the man I had in mind. He did not give him the name of my firm, but he described it in some detail, gave basic financial and marketing information and inquired whether there might be any interest. He acted as a "finder," as his own agent. That is what he actually was, because he stood to earn a fee if the merger/sale was consummated. In this case, it happened that it was not, but it is a worthwhile approach. Many deals are made through professional "finders." It does not make too much difference whether the finder found you or whether you found the finder. There might be some slight psychological disadvantage in the latter case, but you can handle that.

As a practical matter, however, at the level of sales and success that we are talking about now, principals and professional finders will mostly come to *you.* In fact, since most of the inquirers that finders may suggest may not at all be entirely suitable, you may have some problem in fending them off. Also, you want to be somewhat careful in revealing too much information, especially that of confidential and proprietary nature, to those who come to call. For obvious reasons, at any step of your negotiations, you do not want to reveal more than you really have to. While "finders" do play a very important role at this stage of the game, you are well advised to be somewhat wary of them. Many are simply fishing for information and have really no potential acquisitor in mind, much less have been commissioned by anybody to look specifically at you. You may form part of their "inventory of potential deals." Other finders do, of course, have the mandate of a large firm to look for companies in specific areas, for instance in the mail-order business. In some cases, the finder really doesn't find anybody. Somebody in charge of such things in the potential acquiring company has his eye on you and has studied your operation from afar. He likes what he has seen and now he wants to know more. By using an outsider he has less commitment and can withdraw more gracefully and without too much involvement if he begins not to like things. It is a very legitimate approach. You come out as well dealing with a finder, because you won't have to pay him anything. In all of these cases, all commissions will be paid by the acquiring company for which he acts essentially as an agent.

At an early stage of serious negotiations, however, you, yourself, should begin to deal directly, rather than through an intermediary. You should see that you are personally put in touch with the high level officer, your opposite number, of the major company that is interested in you.

WHAT POTENTIAL MERGER PARTNERS ARE LOOKING FOR

Before we go much further, I think you should consider what a potential merger partner would be looking for. And, of course, what he will be looking for is what you should shoot for. It is what you should be prepared to present to make your mail-order business attractive to him.

He will be looking for attractive operating results, for substantial sales, for steady growth in sales and profits, and the ability to project such steady growth into the future.

Let me show, abbreviated and somewhat stylized, what I would expect your first five years of operations to look like, as reflected on your financial statements. Only slightly modified and simplified, these statements approximately reflect the growth of Haverhill's from its standing start, from the beginning of year one to its sale to Time Inc. at the end of year five. These results were obtained, not by fluke or by magic, but by systematically applying the methods and principles that I have discussed with you in this book. And you should have an easier time producing such results, because I had to feel my way — step by step, and you have the advantage of my guidance and of this book.

So, let me give you these "stylized" figures and then we shall discuss them.

The first thing to remember, the guiding principle always to keep in mind, is that advertising ("promotional input") is *not an expense* of your business, but it is rather the *input* which makes your business go and grow and which produces sales and profits.

Perhaps it is not simplifying too much to say that the growth of your mail-order business is a function of the amount of promotional input that you can successfully apply, and of being able to *handle* (in every respect) the resulting sales. Therefore, we put *promotional input* right in the top line of our financial statements, defining the *input we can apply and handle* in any year.

We start from a minimum base of $150,000 of promotional input in the first year and project growth to successfully applied and handled promotional input of $700,000 in the fifth year. This is about the year in which I expect you to sell your company.

With this input, I project your sales to be on the order of $390,000 for the first year, increasing by orderly progression to $1.82 million in the fifth year.

Mail-Order Business
Pro-Forma Profit & Loss for First Five Years
($000)

	Year 1	Year 2	Year 3	Year 4	Year 5
Promotional Input	$150	$250	$375	$ 525	$ 700
Gross Sales	$390	$650	$975	$1365	$1820
Net Sales	$351	$585	$878	$1229	$1638
Less: Cost of Goods	(140)	(234)	(351)	(492)	(655)
Gross Margin	$211	$351	$527	$ 737	$ 983
Less: Selling Expense	(20)	(33)	(49)	(68)	(91)
Gross Profit	$191	$318	$478	$ 669	$ 892
Less: Promotional Input	(150)	(250)	(375)	(525)	(700)
Trading Profit	$ 41	$ 68	$103	$ 144	$ 192
Add: List Rental Income	$ 39*	$ 65	$ 98	$ 137	$ 182
Income before G&A Expense	$ 80	$133	$201	$ 281	$ 374
Less: G&A Expense	(71)*	(105)	(147)	(168)	(191)
Profit before Taxes	$ 9	$ 28	$ 54	$ 113	$ 183

As you can see, your first year of operation, in which you have a promotional input of $150 m, will be essentially a break-even year. You should make a small profit of about $9 m. Naturally, at this modest level of operation, any small change can increase or decrease profit substantially. In the fifth year we project a pre-tax profit of $183 m, based on promotional input of $700 m.

* In this schematic pro-forma treatment, both List Rental income and G&A Expenses are over-stated for the first year — by approximately the same margin. Profit for the year, therefore, should not appreciably change.

Naturally, I must emphasize again, that these are formalized and somewhat idealized statements, but they are essentially what you should strive for. They are quite close to what I attained at Haverhill's. I am now in my third year at Henniker's and I am somewhat ahead of these projections.

Just to show you that these are valid goals and relationships, I am going to reveal to you here (slightly simplified) a recent *quarterly* (not yearly) statement of Henniker's during its third year of operation. You will see that we are quite a bit ahead of target. But that is not the main purpose of showing you this quarterly statement. The main purpose is to talk with you about the very important area of *operating ratios.*

Henniker's
Specimen Quarterly Operating Statement
Third Year of Operation
($000)

Promotional Input	$205
Gross Sales	550
Net Sales	509
Less: Cost of Goods	(197)
Gross Margin	312
Less: Selling, Expense	(19)
Gross Profit	293
Less: Promotional Input	(205)
Trading Profit	88
Add: List Rental Income	2
Income before G&A	90
Less: G&A Expense	(53)
Profit before Taxes	$37

Naturally, what I, as a businessman, look for and what I will expect you to look for, is the firm's "bottom line" (perhaps we should call it the "line before the bottom line" because we are dealing with *profits before taxes*). In this particular quarter, this profit is $37 m. This is quite all right as quarterly profit for the third year of operation of a mail-order business.

HOW TO WORK WITH FINANCIAL RATIOS IN THE MAIL-ORDER BUSINESS

But this peek at the bottom line, important though it is, is not really what we want to use as an analytical tool. We do that with ratios and I shall have quite a bit to say about that. Before we look at the ratios, let's also have a look at our promotional input. That is $205 m for the quarter. That is better, by a good margin, than we had targeted for this stage of our business life. Therefore, if — and that is the important "if," — if we have employed this input efficiently, we should be doing all right.

The two most important ratios that you want to look at are:

- Gross Sales/Promotional Input, and
- Gross Margin/Net Sales

The first ratio simply means how many dollars of gross sales you have produced for each dollar of promotional input; the second shows you what the gross profit percentage is. Naturally, it is the *interplay* of these two ratios that is important. In other words, you may produce higher volume of sales per dollar of promotional input, but make relatively little profit per unit sale. Or, your business may be such that things are just the other way around. The net result may be the same. As for the kind of businesses that I run, and the business that I am planning for you, here are some rough guidelines:

- Gross Sales/Promotional Input should be better than 2.5. Shoot for 2.6!
- Gross Margin/Net Sales should be better than .60. Shoot for .63!

Now let me show you all the ratios that I work with, that you should be looking at and that a sophisticated potential purchaser would be looking at. We shall apply these ratios to the abbreviated quarterly statement that we have just looked at. We shall decide how well we have done, what areas need improvement and in which areas can we be pretty satisfied. In looking at these ratios (and I am aware that I am getting slightly repetitive) always keep in mind that *promotional input* is what everything else is ultimately related to. It is what makes your business go — all ratios really just show you how well you have done with this input in its various aspects.

Here is the complete list of ratios that I work with and the values that I plan to attain:

Henniker's Target Operating Ratios

1.	Gross Sales/Promotional Input	GS/PI	2.60
2.	Net Sales/Gross Sales	NS/GS	.90
3.	Gross Margin/Net Sales	GM/NS	.63
4.	Selling Expense/Gross Sales	SE/GS	.05
5.	Profit Ratio	PR	.34
6.	Other Income/Promotional Input	OI/PI	.05
7.	Profit before Expense/ Promotional Input	PE/PI	.39
8.	G&A Expense/Promotional Input	GA/PI	.13 + $25m per quarter (or plus $100m per year)
9.	Profit before Taxes	P	.26 PI – $25m per quarter (or less $100m per year)

Let's look at these ratios one by one:

1. Gross Sales/Promotional Input: This, as I told you, is one of your two most important ratios. It simply tells you how many dollars of gross sales each dollar of promotional input generates. If this ratio falls below, say, 2.3, you may be getting into trouble, unless you have inordinately high profit margins. But it is really not too easy for you to manipulate profit margins. You certainly cannot arbitrarily increase your prices (and thus your unit profit margins) if your sales volume declines. Your customers won't have it. Therefore, this is the ratio that you really want to keep your eye on all the time. Any promotion, any medium, any item that does not produce (at least in Henniker's case) a minimum of $2.50 to $2.60 in sales for each dollar in promotional input, except in some unusually high margin items, must promptly be discontinued, unless we can find a way to make improvement.

2. Net Sales/Gross Sales: The difference between gross and net sales is composed of these items: *Returns and Allowances, Sales Tax,* and *Postage Income.* You have no influence on Sales Tax, of course. Under present laws, you must collect sales tax for sales to any address in your own state (only), so you are just holding the money for your state government until you transmit it.

Postage Income is, of course, real income. You must make quite sure that it at least meets or, hopefully, exceeds actual postage expense. If it does not, you must adjust the postage charges you assess your customers.

The other component on which you have any real influence is Returns and Allowances. In a well-run mail-order operation, net returns (that is returns of merchandise that result in refund or credit, rather than in exchange or replacement) should not exceed 3.5% of gross sales. If you run over 5% you may well be in trouble. If any single item or product line gives you more than 5% returns, you must analyze it carefully. Determine whether you can either improve the product, the package (if breakage is a problem), the instructions or anything else. Or, you may consider discontinuing this item or this line altogether. It may be a drain on your profit, despite good front end sales and it may annoy many of your customers. Because, naturally, for every customer who returns an item, isn't there very likely one (or more) out there who is unhappy with his purchase, but who just doesn't want to go through the hassle of returning it? And, you are in the business of making people happy, and not unhappy. Never forget that — *they* won't!

There is another point about returns that is not reflected in the ratios and not immediately in the financial statement. Each returned item is just about ten times as much trouble and expense in handling than the same item being processed and shipped for sale. So it does behoove you to watch this ratio, and especially its most important aspect: Returns and Allowances.

3. Gross Margin/Net Sales: This is the other most important ratio, because it is really the interplay between it and the Gross Sales/Promotional Input ratio that primarily determines your gross profit. In this business you cannot afford to work with low-margin items — 50% to 60% gross margin is about the minimum feasible. This means that any item that you sell for $10 (usually $9.95) should not cost you more than $4 or maximum $5, delivered to your warehouse. In fact, since selling expense is usually the same (or not too much different) for a fairly high-priced item as for a low-priced one, you might have to attain a somewhat higher profit margin for low-priced items. On the other hand, you may be able to shave the margin somewhat when you deal with expensive gear. In those cases, often branded items, where price comparison and price shopping is possible, you may be able to compensate for the lower margin by high dollar volume. But, always keep the interplay of the two ratios and also the associated selling expense, in mind. At Henniker's, just as it was at Haverhill's, .63 (63%) is our goal, and we usually attain it.

4. Selling Expense/Gross Sales: We group packing materials, list maintenance and data processing, credit card discounts, and the expense of our toll-free telephone line as "Selling Expense." Postage expense is also included under this heading, but it is offset by postage income (which is one of the items we use to determine net sales from gross sales). And, as I've already told you, if you run things right, your postage expense (what you actually pay for mailing and UPS charges) should be less than your postage income. Thus, a postage expense item offset by postage income, should be a *negative* amount, and thus reduce total selling expense.

There are other items that you could perhaps include under selling expense, such as packing wages, mail handling and data processing wages, etc., etc. It would be justified, but we don't try to slice it quite that fine. We try to keep selling expense to 5% (.05) or less, of gross sales. This is what this ratio means. We usually attain this or do better, which means we have a somewhat lower ratio.

5. Profit Ratio: This is the important "way station" before we come to our "bottom line." It isn't really a ratio of its own, but rather a function of the preceding relations. It is the *Gross Margin less Selling Expense, divided by Promotional Input, less 1* or

$$\text{Profit Ratio (PR)} = \frac{\text{GM-SE}}{\text{PI}} - 1$$

Or, we can also express it in terms of the ratios that we have talked about so far; designating the ratios by their numbers, we have:

$$\text{Profit Ratio (PR)} = [1] \times ([2] \times [3] - [4]) - 1$$

This may sound a little technical or "theoretical" to you, but please look at it carefully. This, except profit itself, is the most important composite "ratio" of your business. You will do well if you keep this ratio up and you simply cannot be successful if you do not. You should attain a "Profit Ratio" of at least .30. By the goals for the preceding ratios that we have set for ourselves, we get a profit ratio of .34. We usually manage to do a little better than that but you should get at least .30. If you do not, you will have to go to work on the effectiveness of your promotions, on your gross margin or on your selling expense.

6. Other Income/Promotional Input: In the mail-order business there is really only one kind of "other income" of any consequence, and that is *list rental income.* By the time you are in your third year of business you should have about 100,000 to 200,000 names on your customer list — your "master file." If you have a good list rental agent, you should be able to "turn" your list ten to twelve times per year. This means that you should rent that many times the number of names you have on your master file in the course of a year. At about $40 per thousand, rental of, say, 1.5 million names per year is an important source of income for you. There is no actual relationship between this income and promotional input, except perhaps that promotional input reflects the size of your business at any point. But, since we relate everything else to promotional input, we have been setting ourselves a, perhaps somewhat arbitrary, goal of .05. In other words, for every $1000 of promotional input (which we expect to produce $2600 in gross sales) we expect and plan to take in $50 in "other income," and that means essentially list rental income.

7. Profit before General and Administrative Expense/Promotional Input: Just as the Profit Ratio [5], this is not a true "ratio" but a function of the preceding. It is quite simply the sum of [5] and [6]. Since we had fixed .34 as our goal for [5] and .05 as our goal for [6] this ratio should be .39 or better for Henniker's. It should be a minimum of, say, .33 for any mail-order business. If it is less, you may have a little problem paying for your overhead and making a profit.

8. General and Administrative Expense Factor (Overhead Factor): We consider overhead or more properly "General and Administrative Expenses" (for short, "G & A") all remaining expenses that are not selling expenses and not promotional input. The most important of these expenses are salaries and wages (and associated payroll taxes and employee benefits), office supplies and expenses, rent, telephone and telegraph and utilities. The reason I prefer to call these expenses "G & A" rather than "overhead" is that "overhead" has a connotation of being something fixed and being rather unrelated to the volume of business. Some people even call it fixed expense. But everyone who has ever run a business knows that that is not so. There are certain expenses that are essentially fixed, but others are very much related to gross sales.

I have found in my mail-order experience that, beyond about $1 million of gross sales per year, G & A should be $25 m per quarter (or $100 m per year) plus 5% (.05) of gross sales. But since

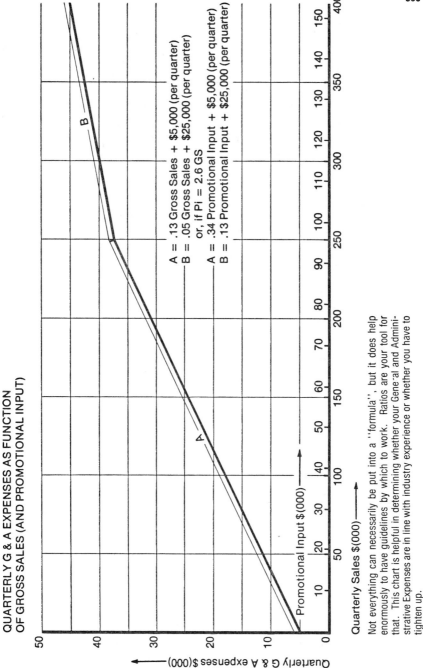

QUARTERLY G & A EXPENSES AS FUNCTION
OF GROSS SALES (AND PROMOTIONAL INPUT)

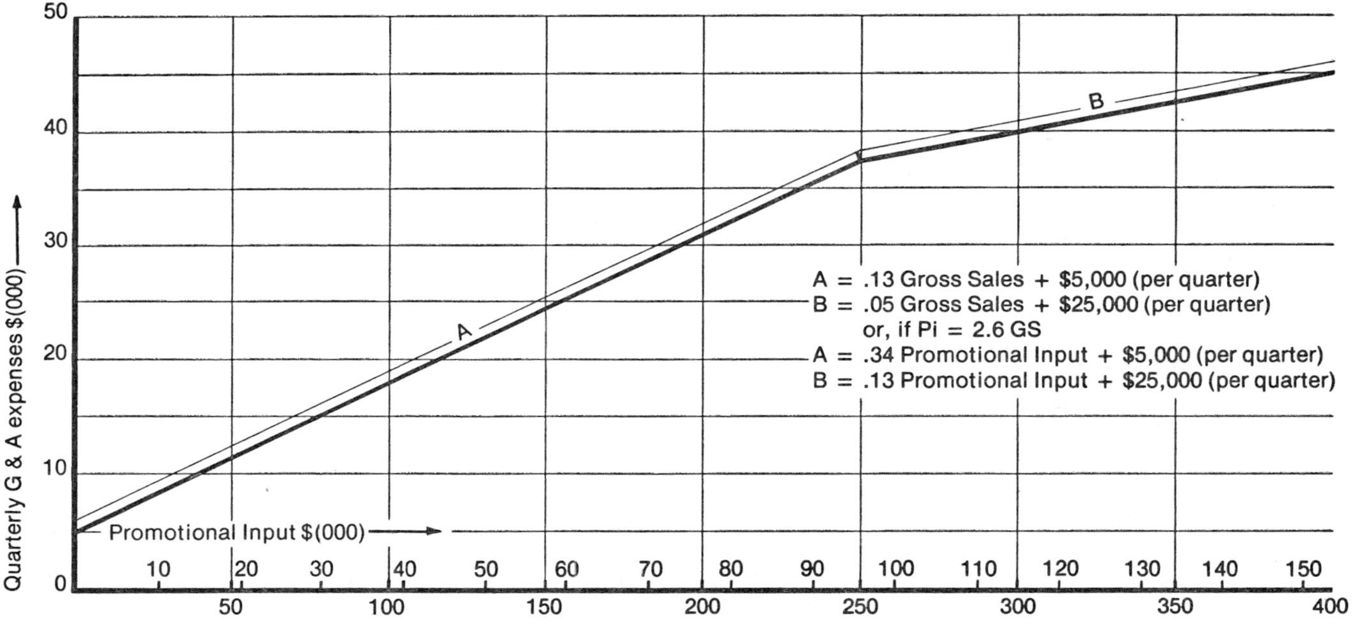

Not everything can necessarily be put into a ''formula'', but it does help enormously to have guidelines by which to work. Ratios are your tool for that. This chart is helpful in determining whether your Gene-al and Administrative Expenses are in line with industry experience or whether you have to tighten up.

we have targeted Gross Sales/Promotional Input (please refer to our ratio [1]) as 2.6, we can also relate this directly to promotional input. We can say that at or beyond this level of sales, G & A should be .13 of promotional input (which is 2.6 x .05) plus $25 m per quarter, or .13 plus $100 m per year.

Naturally, you want to keep both the factor and the fixed component as low as possible. It is my personal experience that below $1 million gross sales per year ($250 m per quarter) the fixed component of G & A expenses seems to be less weighty than the variable component. The experience relationship and what you should strive for through about the third year of your business would be about .34 of promotional input plus $5 m per quarter, or .34 of promotional input plus $20 m per year, respectively.

9. Profit before Taxes: This is the famous "bottom line" (or, as we said, the "line before the bottom line"). But this bottom line is the result, or the "function" if you prefer, of all the foregoing ratios. All that you have done right or wrong (or that has gone right or wrong by itself) will be reflected in those preceding ratios.

These ratios, and that of course is their purpose, let you quickly pinpoint where trouble (if any) lies, how and why your profit goals were or were not attained, and what you might have done right or wrong. Are you selling enough merchandise related to your promotional input? Are your net sales an acceptable ratio of gross sales — i.e., essentially are your returns in line? Is your profit margin on your merchandise adequate? Are your selling expenses appropriate for your level of sales? Are you getting the list rental income that you should? Are your G & A expenses not any higher than they should be? The ratios will tell you all, will give you constant control and will pinpoint possible trouble spots, as they all come down to and make up the *profit before taxes,* the bottom line which becomes:

Profit before Taxes = [P] = PI x ([7] - [8]) - $25 m (quarterly)
or
Profit before Taxes = [P] = PI x ([7] - [8]) - $100 m (yearly)

Even though you may not think of yourself as much of a numbers man, I urge you to read, re-read and truly try to understand all of the foregoing. You must have financial controls over your business, you must understand the relationships between cause and effect and you must familiarize yourself with these ratios. It is obviously of importance that you know what you are shooting for and how you perform against your own goals and against industry standards.

Factors Applied to Actual Experience

Let's go back for a minute to that quarterly statement of Henniker's a few pages back and let's see how we were performing if we apply these ratios that we have just discussed.

Ratios Applied to Henniker's Quarterly Statement

		\$(000) (Actual)	Ratio (Actual)	Ratio (Should Be)
1. Gross Sales/Promotional Input	GS/PI	550/205	2.68	2.60
2. Net Sales/Gross Sales	NS/GS	509/550	.93	.90
3. Gross Margin/Net Sales	GM/NS	312/509	.61	.63
4. Selling Expense/Gross Sales	SE/GS	19/550	.03	.05
5. Profit Ratio	PR	$\frac{312-19}{205}-1$	.43	.34
6. Other Income/Promotional Input	OI/PI	2/105	.02	.05
7. Profit before G&A Expense/ Promotional Input	PG/PI	90/205	.44	.39
8. General & Administrative Expense	GA	$\frac{53-25}{205}\times PI + \$25m$	.14 PI + \$25m	.13 PI + \$25m
9. Profit before Taxes corresponding to:	P	\$205m(.44−.14)−\$25m \$37.2m		\$205m(.39−.13)−\$25m \$28.3m

First of all, our bottom line, our Profit before Taxes for the quarter is \$37.2 m instead of targeted \$28.3 m. This is about 41% above planned, so that this is very good. I must hasten to add that this result is not necessarily typical. It was an exceptionally good quarter; we usually do not exceed our budget by quite that margin.

The principal contributor to the successful performance is our GS/PI ratio, which is an exceptionally high 2.68, instead of the targeted 2.60. Our NS/GS ratio is .93 instead of .90, so that, too, is quite favorable and helps the over-all result. Our profit margin, GM/NS does, however, not quite come up to snuff — it is just .61 instead of the targeted .63. Our selling expense ratio, SE/GS, is just over .03, instead of the allowed .05, so that also is favorable. All of these factors combine to give us the all-important "profit ratio," which becomes a gratifying .43, instead of .34 budgeted. In plain English, this means that for every dollar invested in promotion, we succeeded in bringing down \$.43 as "profit," before list rental income and G & A Expenses.

We are doing a very poor job on list rental in this quarter — only .02 instead of .05, so this is something that definitely needs working on. In fact, I was so concerned about this unsatisfactory result that I fired my rental agent. It was clear that he was coasting. We got a new man, a real hustler, and this ratio is right back up where it ought to be.

Our G & A factor is .14, instead of .13. This is just a shade more than it should be. G & A Expenses might need a little tightening or fine tuning. They get easily out of hand and need constant watching. But in this case they are reasonably close. All of this comes together to give us profit before taxes of .30 PI - $25 m equal to $37.2 m instead of .26 PI - 25 m, which would have been the projected (and acceptable) profit of $28.3 m for this quarter, at this level of promotional investment.

If you hate numbers and analyses of this kind, you might have been somewhat turned off by the preceding, but all of it is really very important. You have to be the planner, scheduler and controller of your business and you have to understand the facts that make it successful.

YOU CAN DO AS WELL AS I HAVE DONE — AND MIGHT BE DOING BETTER

But let's get on to more entertaining things. Let's look back once more a few pages, at the pro-forma financial statement that I expect you to turn in during your first five years of operation. I do wish to repeat that this is a rather schematic schedule (which is based on the ratios we have just discussed). But it is close to what I did at Haverhill's in just over five years and very much resembles what I am doing now at Henniker's in my third year. In fact, as you have seen from the quarterly statement that we have analyzed together, I am actually a little ahead of my targets. That is, perhaps, as it should be — after all, this is the second time around for me, and I should be able to avoid a few mistakes and make a few short-cuts.

Do you think that obtaining such results marks one as a person of exceptional ability or great luck and that the proverbial "average mortal" could not attain such results? Not so! Luck plays no role, or certainly not a significant one. I am doing exactly the same thing now, with virtually identical results, for the second time.

The picture that I paint, the developments and results that I describe are nothing very unusual. They can be attained by anybody who is willing to work hard and to use his wits to build his business. My success in the mail-order business is nothing very much out of the ordinary. While I am very happy to have done and to be doing as well as I am, I am really fairly small potatoes in this game; in fact, I am not really in the big leagues having sold Haverhill's for "just a million dollars." Go back a few pages and read once more the thumbnail sketches of the men and women who *really* cleaned up, selling their mail-order business for $2 million, $5 million, $10 million or more.

Without being a genius, you should be able to do as well as I or perhaps even as well as some of my colleagues. You should, by following my advice, be able to build a mail-order business that should have sales of close to $2 million per year and pre-tax earnings of close to $200,000 within about five years. I have told you about living pretty frugally, and not to invade your capital and impair your earnings record by paying yourself a fat salary. But, naturally, by the time you are in your fourth or fifth year, by the time you have pre-tax earnings of $150 m to $200 m per year, you are going to treat yourself fairly well. I assure you that you and your family will not suffer. And, of course, there are other interesting "perks" in this kind of business. There is lots of entertaining, lots of travel — domestic and foreign, to trade fairs and to visit suppliers. That is not a bad life at all.

It's entirely possible that, by the time you have built your business to the level which I have described, you are so taken with it that you will wish to go on with it, make a wonderful life for yourself and for your family, or perhaps groom one of your children to take over from you. If that is your wish, more power to you! You will be very successful. My personal inclination is to build something and then to sell it. I have more fun in the creating than in the running, so the thrust of this book is toward the building and then selling of such a business. But this does not exclude that you can adapt all of the advice that I have given you and continue to run the mail-order business that you have created, instead of selling it. The ultimate purpose of this book, however, is to show you *how to sell the business that you have created.* That is what I did with Haverhill's, that is what I am going to do with Henniker's, and that is what I really advise *you* to do.

By the end of your fifth year of operation, having pre-tax earnings of, say, $180 m, *you should be able to sell this business for not less than $1 million.*

WHY BIG CORPORATIONS WANT TO PAY A LOT OF MONEY FOR YOUR MAIL-ORDER BUSINESS

You may begin to wonder why anybody, especially the hard-nosed people who run our major corporations, would want to pay $1,000,000 for a business that is earning $180,000 before taxes per year. This, assuming roughly a 50% corporate tax rate, boils down to about $90 m after-tax earnings per year. Why would anybody want to pay $1,000,000 for that?

If you haven't been into this sort of thing before, here is where you have a great and pleasant surprise coming.

The companies that are likely to merge with you, or the only ones you should be really interested in, are large publicly held and publicly traded companies. One of the important "facts of financial life" is the *"multiple"* at which their stock sells on the Stock Exchange. This multiple (also called p/e ratio — price/earnings ratio) varies, of course, from company to company, from industry group to industry group and perhaps with the stock market as a whole. But, under usual market conditions, it would not be unreasonable to assume that the stock of the company with which you would merge, would sell at a multiple of, say, 10 to 15 times their own earnings. In other words, if you were approached by a company that has $10 million in after-tax earnings and that is capitalized by 5 million shares, then a share would be earning $2.00 per year. And chances are that each of these shares would trade on the New York Stock Exchange, or perhaps on the American Stock Exchange at 10 to 15 times those earnings, which means anywhere between $20 and $30 per share. Thus, an acquiring company can afford to pay you just about the same multiple on *your* earnings, let's say 12½ times your $90,000 present yearly after-tax profit, without in any way diluting the per-share profit of their present stockholders. And 12½ times $90,000 would be over $1,000,000!

Naturally, in acquiring your business they certainly do not plan on keeping it at its present level of sales and earnings. They plan on contributing their know-how, their management talent, their capital, their own marketing network and perhaps even their own access to media to increase your present earnings from, say, $90,000 after taxes to perhaps twice or three times that within a year or two. By doing that, they increase the earnings of each one of their present shares. That, to increase their own earnings per share, is the principal reason why large corporations make acquisitions.

That is what the whole game is about, and that is what they try to accomplish. As a national mail-order firm, you have great expansion possibilities and that is the reason they want you. They are getting a bargain by buying you at a "multiple" less than their own. The merger-acquisition boys have a nice word for it. They call it "synergism." It means that by putting their own shoulder behind your wheel, they can make your business worth more than it is now. You and I might call it making two and two turn out to be five, seven or perhaps seventeen.

In my own case, for instance, in the year 1971, in which I merged Haverhill's with Time Inc., each share of Time Inc. stock earned $2.92 at the time of the merger; the market value of each Time Inc. share was $56.50. That was a multiple (or price/earnings ratio) of over 19. That is quite a bit better than one usually sees today, between 10 to 15 is more like it as I am writing this. Sure, it was a very good deal for me to sell Haverhill's to Time Inc. But the point is that it was a real bargain for Time Inc. to buy Haverhill's and its earnings for just 18,000 shares of their stock, which represented just over $50,000 of their earnings. Of course, they rightly expected to expand this business greatly within the next few years following, mostly because of the immediate access that they could give Haverhill's to the vast circulation of their publications. And that is just what happened.

It is important that you clearly understand the significance of the "multiple" (the price/earnings ratio) and why it gives you great leverage in selling your business at many times your present yearly earnings. You also must be clear that the larger the multiple of the acquiring company is, the more "generous" they can be in terms of their own stock, and the more "generous" you should insist for them to be in merging with you. And it is also important that you understand why you, as a national mail-order business, are such an attractive acquisition for them.

I know I am somewhat repetitious, but since it is pretty much what this book is about, it is important that you have it clearly in mind:

A national mail-order business that is well managed, reasonably mature, has national recognition and acceptance, has sales of at least $1 million, pre-tax profits of at least $100 m, has shown a record of increasing earnings, and shows the prospect of increasing these earnings substantially, perhaps by the magic of "synergism," is an absolutely irresistible acquisition to many major companies, on very favorable terms for the seller.

Again, I don't want you to think that I am fantasizing or exaggerating, or that my experience with Haverhill's, my being able to sell it to a large and sophisticated company, was a fluke. Please turn back once more and look at the small and partial list of mail-order firms, some of which had not been in business much longer than Haverhill's, that have merged with major corporations. Not a single one of these sold for just one million dollars. But, please, don't judge me too harshly for selling perhaps too quickly and for just $1 million! Keep in mind that I was over 50 years old at the time. I decided it was time to cash in a few chips. You are probably younger, and there is no reason why you should not hang on a few years longer, build your earnings to, say, $300 or $500 m per year, and really *hold out for the very big pay-off.* I am talking about $5 million, $10 million or perhaps even more. I am quite serious.

Let's go back to some of the mechanics of the acquisition of a mail-order business by a large corporation.

NEVER MIND CASH — SHOOT FOR A TAX-FREE STOCK EXCHANGE!

One thing that may occur to you is why I am talking about the other company's stock all the time, when what you are thinking about is "real money." Why should you sell your fine business for some engraved stock certificates instead of for real folding money.

It is a good question. There are two answers.

First: the acquiring company can afford to be much more "generous" (or at least they feel they can, which amounts to the same thing) in dealing with their stock, rather than with cash. That is especially true if the stock commands a high multiple.

Second: in taking another company's stock, rather than cash, you have one very great advantage. If your attorney is even moderately skilled, he will be able to set it up as a "tax-free exchange." This means that you come suddenly into very large capital and have to pay no taxes at all, until such time that you eventually decide to sell the shares that you received in exchange. You may not wish to do that for a long time, if at all. And if and when you sell those shares, or any portions thereof, you only pay the much lower capital gains tax, instead of the higher income tax.

Back to my own example: I started Haverhill's in 1967 on very little capital. In 1971 I had over $1 million in Time Inc. stock. I didn't pay a penny in taxes and I haven't paid any yet.

Naturally, there is some danger. And that is that you might become connected with a company whose stock will decline, or perhaps even disastrously fall. Frankly, chances for this happening over the long term are dim. A large American company is not likely to collapse and stock prices have been generally up over the last few decades. Naturally, these could be famous last words, and if you had the terrible misfortune of having merged with the Pennsylvania Railroad or something like that, you would look pretty silly, to put it kindly. But these are truly quite exceptional cases, and while you want to get good advice as to the soundness of the acquiring company, you should not ordinarily have to worry about any such unusual occurrence.

In general, however, it is a very good risk to take. You can stick with that stock for a long time, and then perhaps sell it little by little so as to diversify your holdings. In all likelihood, in making your sale to and merger with a large corporation, you will be asked to stay on as president of this subsidiary for a number of years. In fact, most companies would insist on your staying. They might feel, quite rightly, that you are the mainspring of that business, and that it would not function well without you until you train a staff of their people to run it. This puts you into another excellent bargaining position. You will be able to negotiate a very sizeable salary, and, if you play your cards right, you should also negotiate for participation in profits. In my own case, I negotiated with Time Inc. for a salary of $40,000 per year (which was pretty good in those days) and the participation of 15% on pre-tax profits during the term of my contract. That was not bad at all, coming on top of that $1 million in Time Inc. stock.

WHAT HAPPENED TO HAVERHILL'S?

People ask me sometime: How come the romance with Time Inc. terminated after a few years. This is really a different story and perhaps another book should be written about that.

Let's just simplify it and put into a nutshell. As I look at it, there were primarily three reasons:

1. The goals that I had set for Haverhill's and those that Time Inc. had set and what we expected from each other were not entirely compatible.
2. Although I tried very hard and being quite aware of the potential problem, I did not turn out to be a very good "company man" — I guess that having been in business so long for myself made me sort of "independent," and perhaps not too easy to deal with. I must admit that.
3. Time Inc. ultimately was not as interested in this business as they thought they would be. They decided that they wanted to concentrate all of their resources into publishing and in forest/paper products, and they eventually did just that. Quite a few divisions were terminated and chopped off.

Obviously this is not too pertinent to what this book is about, but since the question may arise, I think I should answer it. At least this is my version of it. It is entirely possible that a different viewpoint might emerge if the same story were told by a representative of Time Inc.

Essentially, however, as long as we were together, Haverhill's was a profitable venture for Time Inc. But, for the reasons stated, an amicable divorce was eventually arranged. The company was moved from San Francisco to Chicago. I stayed in San Francisco. Time Inc. took less and less interest in it and there was nobody really left to run it. Like the proverbial old soldier, it eventually faded away.

I AM BUILDING MY SECOND FORTUNE I CAN HELP YOU WITH YOUR FIRST

I am now in my third year of the building of Henniker's. You have seen what we are doing, I have held nothing back. I have even given you a financial summary, which is usually pretty confidential in a privately held company. I am well on my way to building Henniker's just exactly as I built Haverhill's. I firmly expect to sell it within the next two or three years for at least $1 million. But perhaps I'll hold on a little longer this time and do a little better than I did the first time around with Time Inc.

This is really the essence of my story, and I hope that I have been able to convey it. It is to build a business in the mail-order field and to sell it to a large company. I have done it once and I am going to do it again. I have shown you in detail how I have done it, and I have given you a listing of people, just like you and me, who have done a whole lot better. I wonder sometimes why I continue to work at this, because I don't really "need it" — certainly not from a financial point of view. Perhaps doing these things satisfies an inner need, the desire to be "creative," to continue to be successful, and to keep active and busy. Who knows, it may even be that I am trying to continue to prove something to myself.

I won't bore you with the many things people can do with a great deal of money. My own tastes don't run particularly to luxury. It may be that I am more interested in success than in the fruits of it. But I do have more comforts than perhaps 99% of all people: a nice home, kids in private schools, large trust funds established for each of my children, pretty fancy vacations and everything I want that money can buy. The most rewarding aspect perhaps is complete freedom from financial worries, which is something that overhangs most people. It certainly bothered me constantly until I had my financial safety assured. Chances are that you are younger than I am. If you follow my advice and go to work, you might be able to make that million dollars before you are 40 years old. Then you will be able to enjoy many things that I did not enjoy or did not enjoy until later. Because I really did not get started quite soon enough.

I have told you all I know about this business and how to build it and how to sell it. I think that if you have the right outlook, the right attitude, reasonable smarts, a little money that you are willing to invest, and the willingness to work like the dickens for a few years, you can, with the help of this book, and, of course, improvising as you go along, become very rich. Never lose sight of what this book is about. It is to build a successful mail-order business, to bring it to financial maturity, and then to sell it, at a high multiple of its earnings, to a large publicly held corporation, preferably in a tax-free exchange.

There are many rich people in this country and many self-made men. There are perhaps many ways to build a fortune. I simply cannot think of a single one in which your chances for planned success are as great and in which you can build with as much expectations of success toward your goal as in the mail-order business. There are no guarantees and no "sure things." There are no "magic formulas." But this is about as good a shot as I can think of. And, with hard work and just a little bit of luck you should be able to do as well or perhaps much better than I have done. You bought this book. You took the first step. There is a lot of meat in this book. Read it once more and then work toward your own success. You can do it. Good luck to you!

THE END

Sidney Fischer designed this book. He also created the cover and supervised production.

Type used in this book is Helios Condensed. It belongs to the sans serif family of type faces, and is not customarily used to set a whole book. We used this type because it is somewhat of a "trademark" of Henniker's ads, mail pieces and catalogs. Type was set by **Bonnie Brown** on a CompuWriter II Phototypesetter. **Leslie Gold** did production and paste-up.

Copy was prepared by **Carolyn Hagopian. Marina Curtis** proofread and corrected final copy.

Thanks to all.

This book was printed by
BookCrafters in Fredericksburg, Virginia, U.S.A.